STOP

This is the back of the book!
Start from the other side.

NATIVE MANGA readers read manga from *right to left*.

1
2
1
3
2
3
5
4
4
6
5
7
8
6

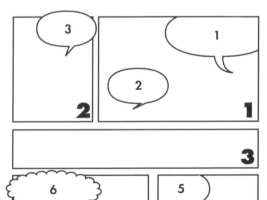

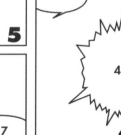

*If you run into our **Native Manga** logo on any of our books... you'll know that this manga is published in it's true original native Japanese right to left reading format, as it was intended. Turn to the other side of the book and start reading from right to left, top to bottom.*

Follow the diagram to see how its done.
Surf's Up!

NATIVE MANGA
READ RIGHT TO LEFT

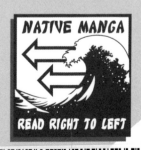

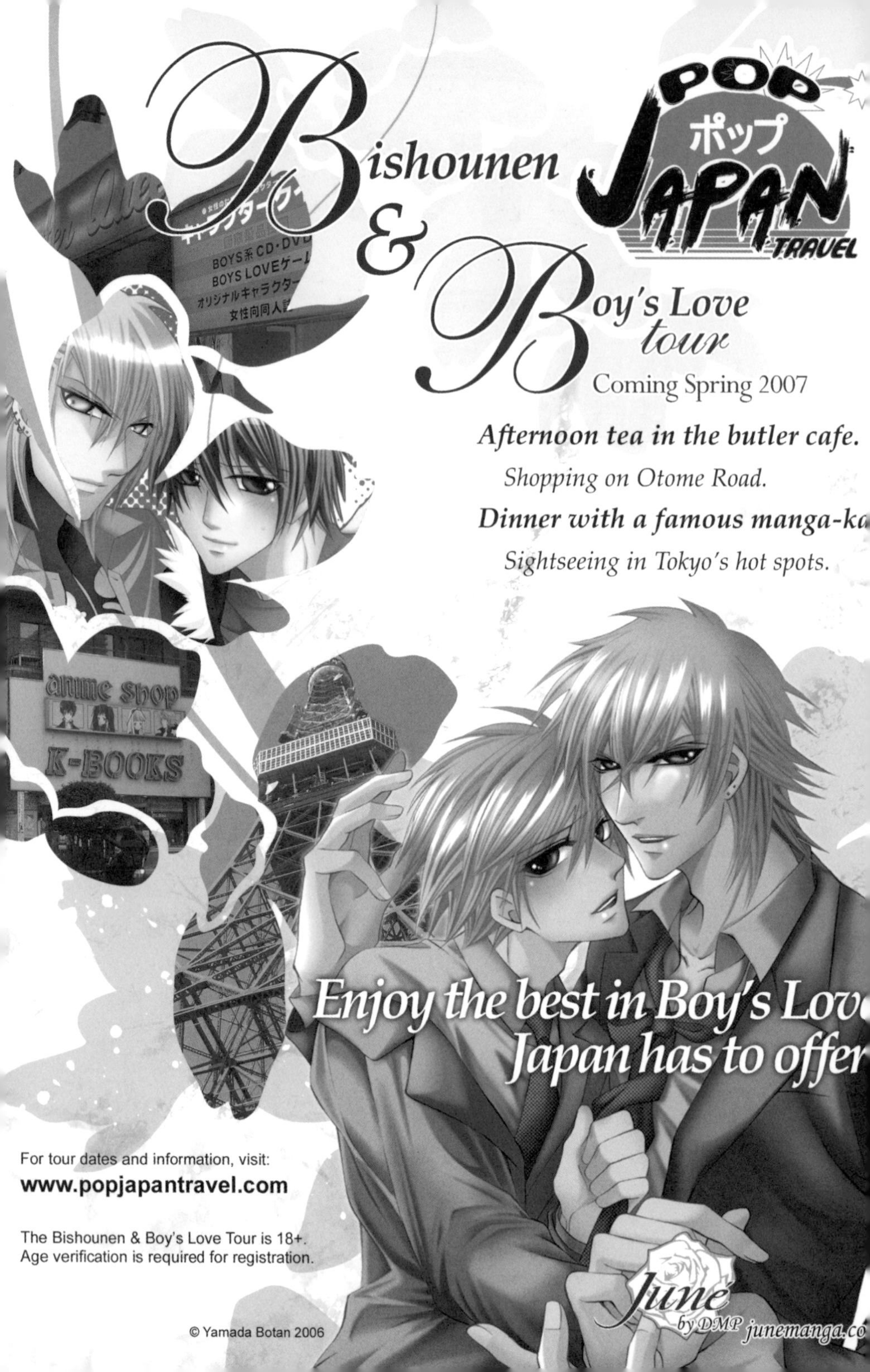
Bishounen & Boy's Love tour
Coming Spring 2007
POP ポップ JAPAN TRAVEL
Afternoon tea in the butler cafe.
Shopping on Otome Road.
Dinner with a famous manga-ka
Sightseeing in Tokyo's hot spots.
BOYS系CD・DVD
女性向同人誌
anime shop
K-BOOKS
Enjoy the best in Boy's Love
Japan has to offer
For tour dates and information, visit:
www.popjapantravel.com
The Bishounen & Boy's Love Tour is 18+.
Age verification is required for registration.
June by DMP junemanga.co
© Yamada Botan 2006

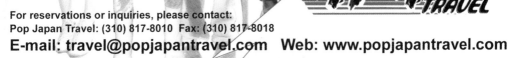

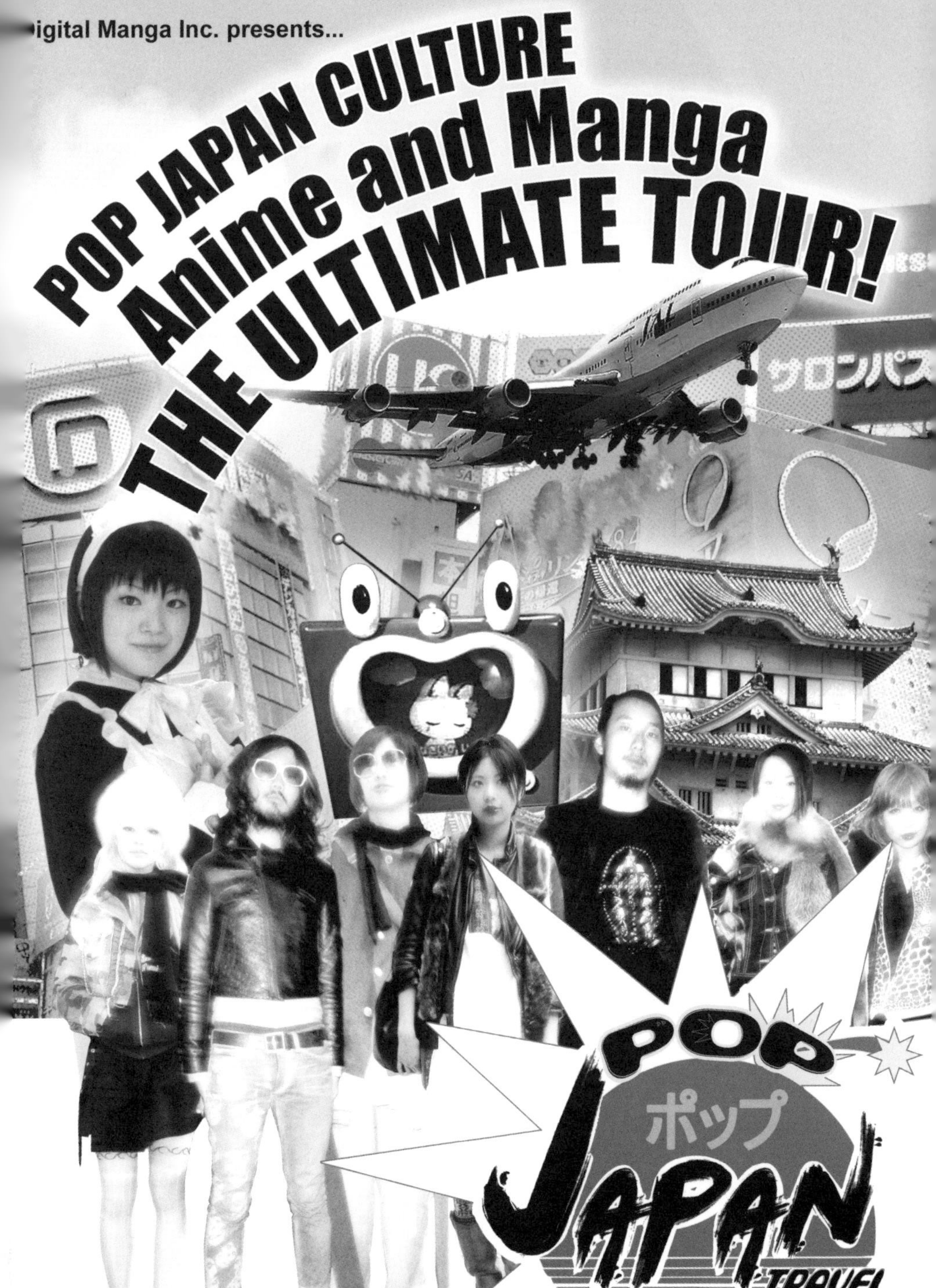
Digital Manga Inc. presents...
POP JAPAN CULTURE
Anime and Manga
THE ULTIMATE TOUR!
POP
ポップ
JAPAN
TRAVEL

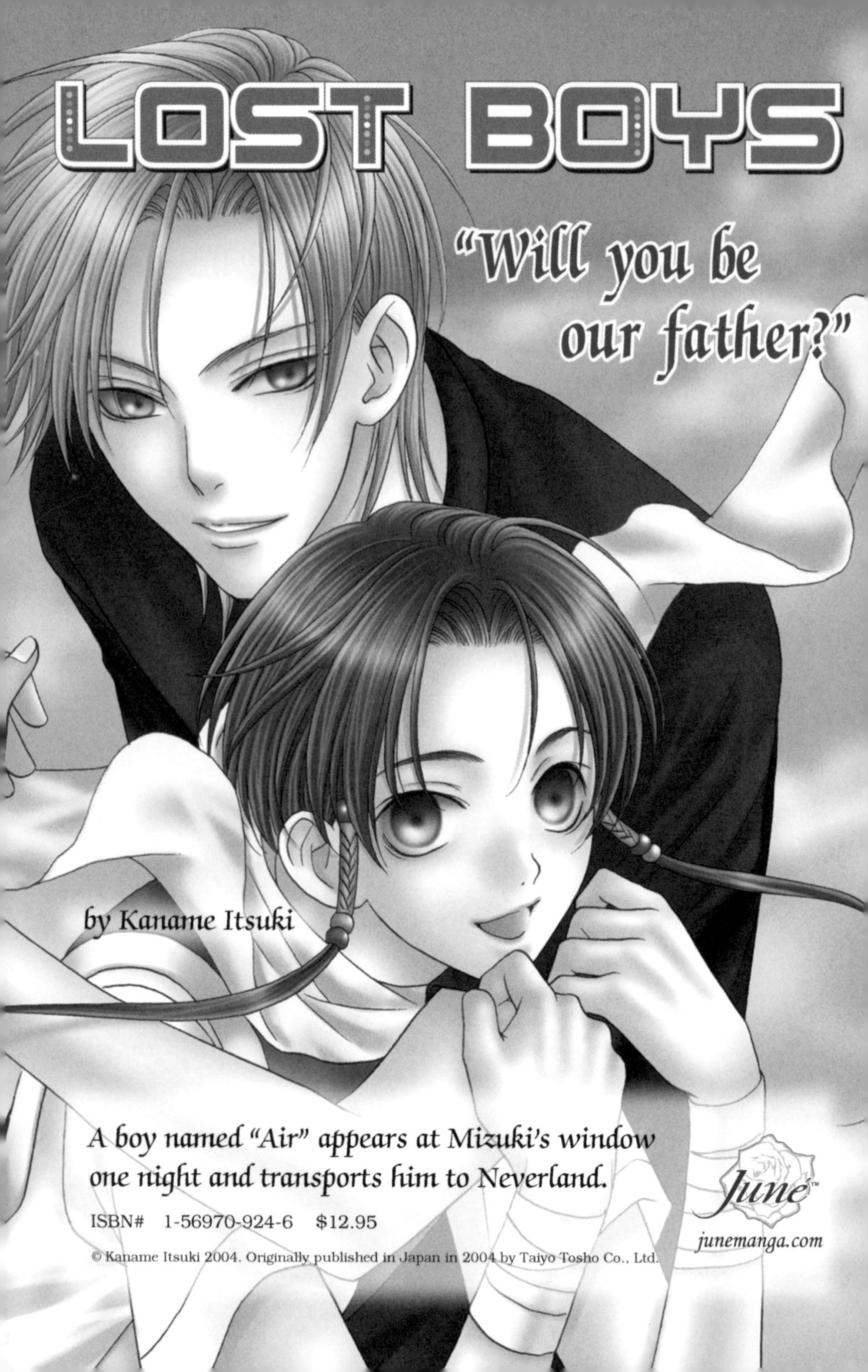
LOST BOYS
"Will you be our father?"
by Kaname Itsuki
A boy named "Air" appears at Mizuki's window one night and transports him to Neverland.
ISBN# 1-56970-924-6 $12.95
© Kaname Itsuki 2004. Originally published in Japan in 2004 by Taiyo Tosho Co., Ltd.
June™
junemanga.com

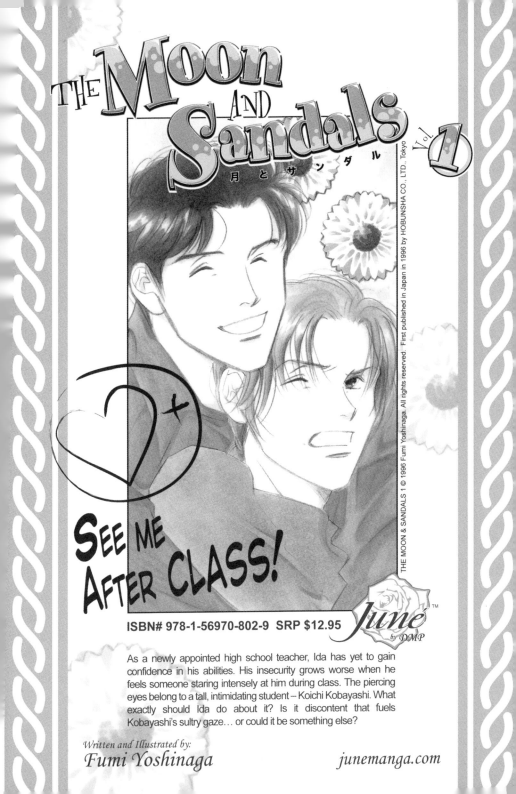

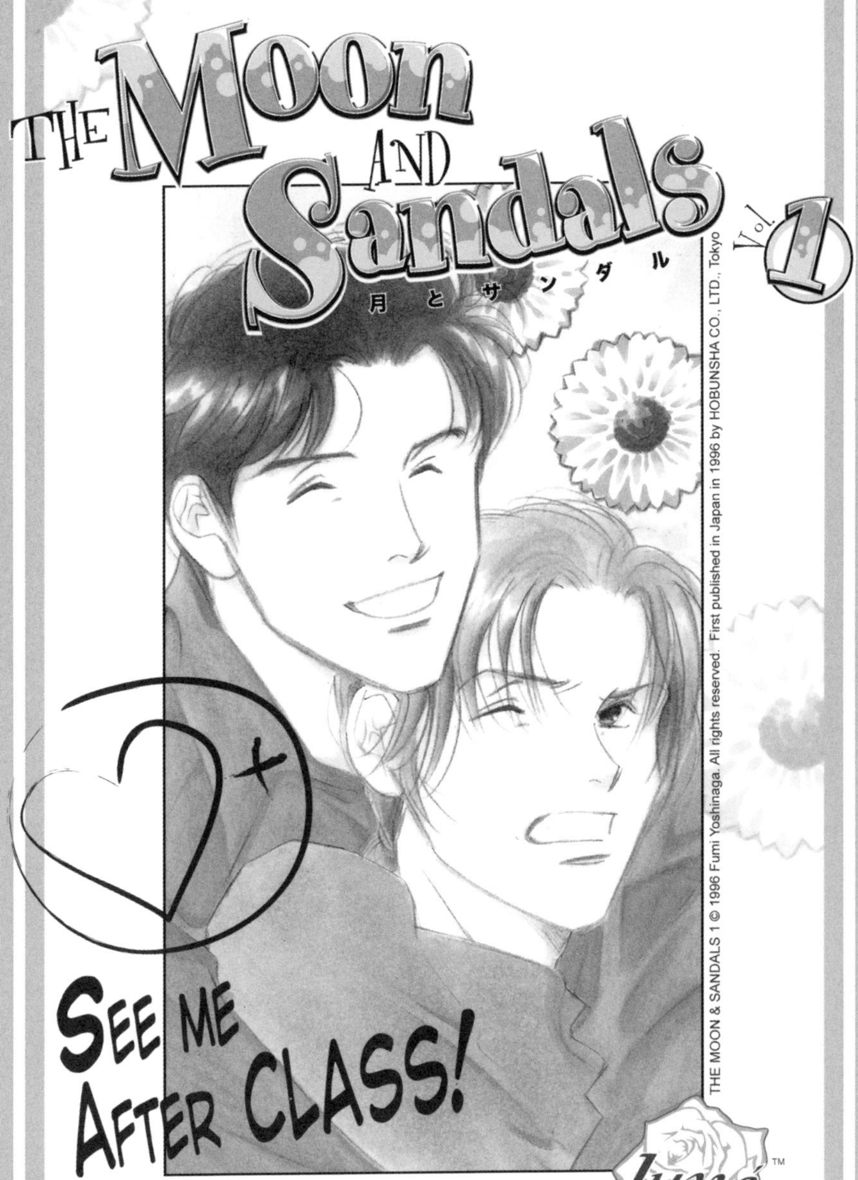
THE Moon AND Sandals
月とサンダル
Vol. 1
SEE ME AFTER CLASS!

ISBN# 978-1-56970-802-9 SRP $12.95

June™ by DMP

As a newly appointed high school teacher, Ida has yet to gain confidence in his abilities. His insecurity grows worse when he feels someone staring intensely at him during class. The piercing eyes belong to a tall, intimidating student – Koichi Kobayashi. What exactly should Ida do about it? Is it discontent that fuels Kobayashi's sultry gaze… or could it be something else?

Written and Illustrated by:
Fumi Yoshinaga

junemanga.com

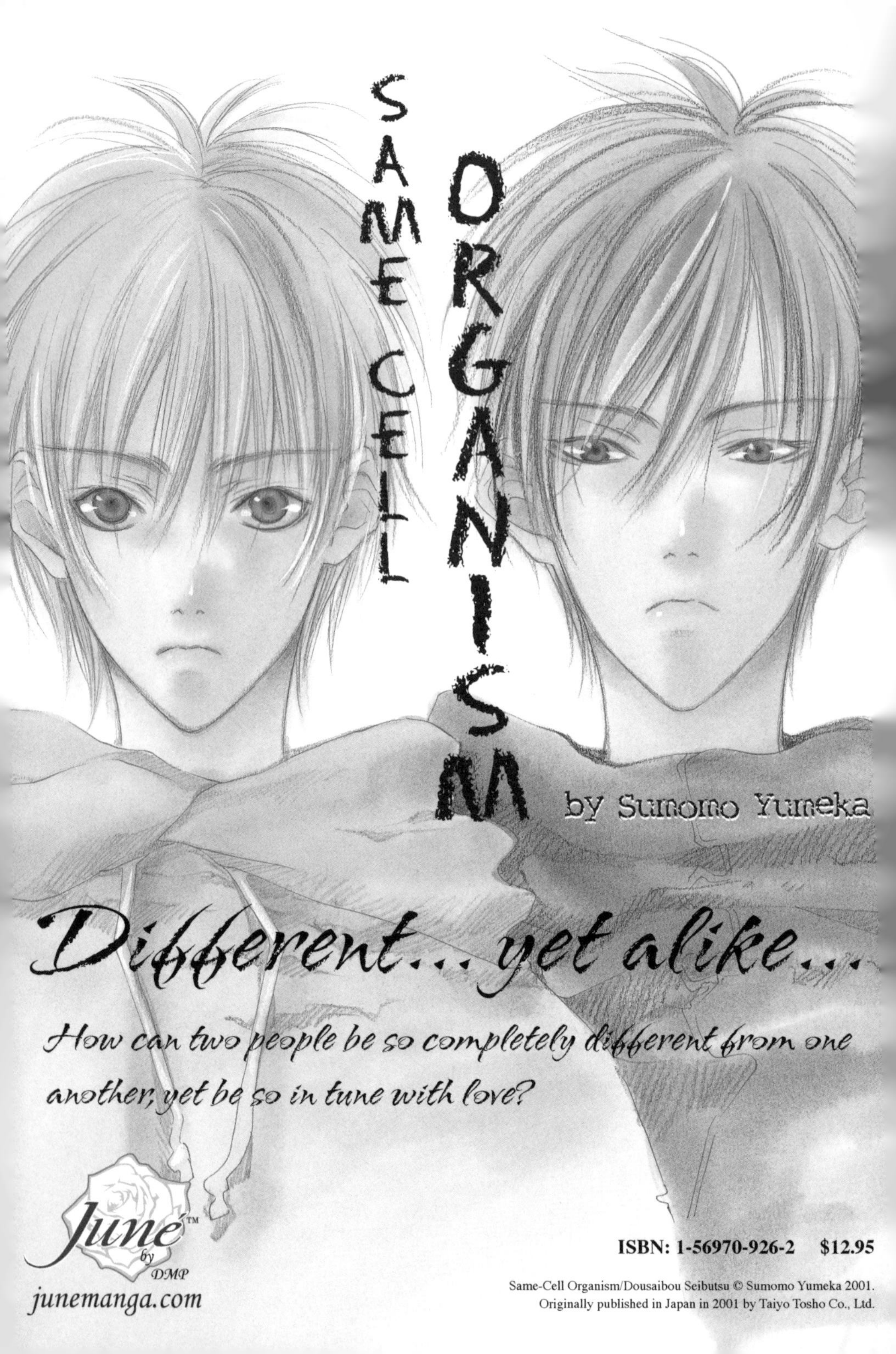

SAME CELL
ORGANISM
by Sumomo Yumeka
Different... yet alike...
How can two people be so completely different from one another, yet be so in tune with love?
June™ by DMP
junemanga.com
ISBN: 1-56970-926-2 $12.95
Same-Cell Organism/Dousaibou Seibutsu © Sumomo Yumeka 2001.
Originally published in Japan in 2001 by Taiyo Tosho Co., Ltd.

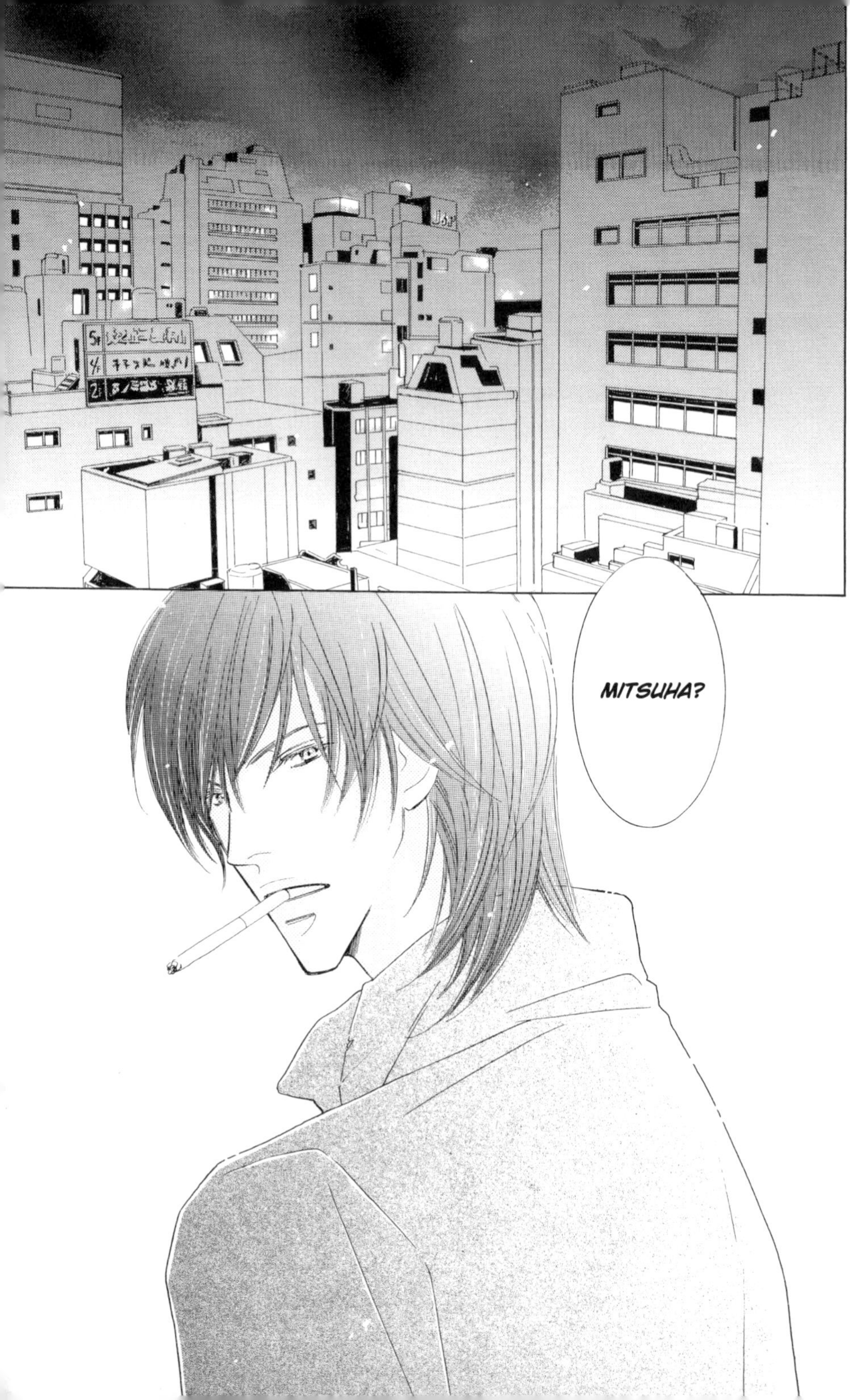
MITSUHA?

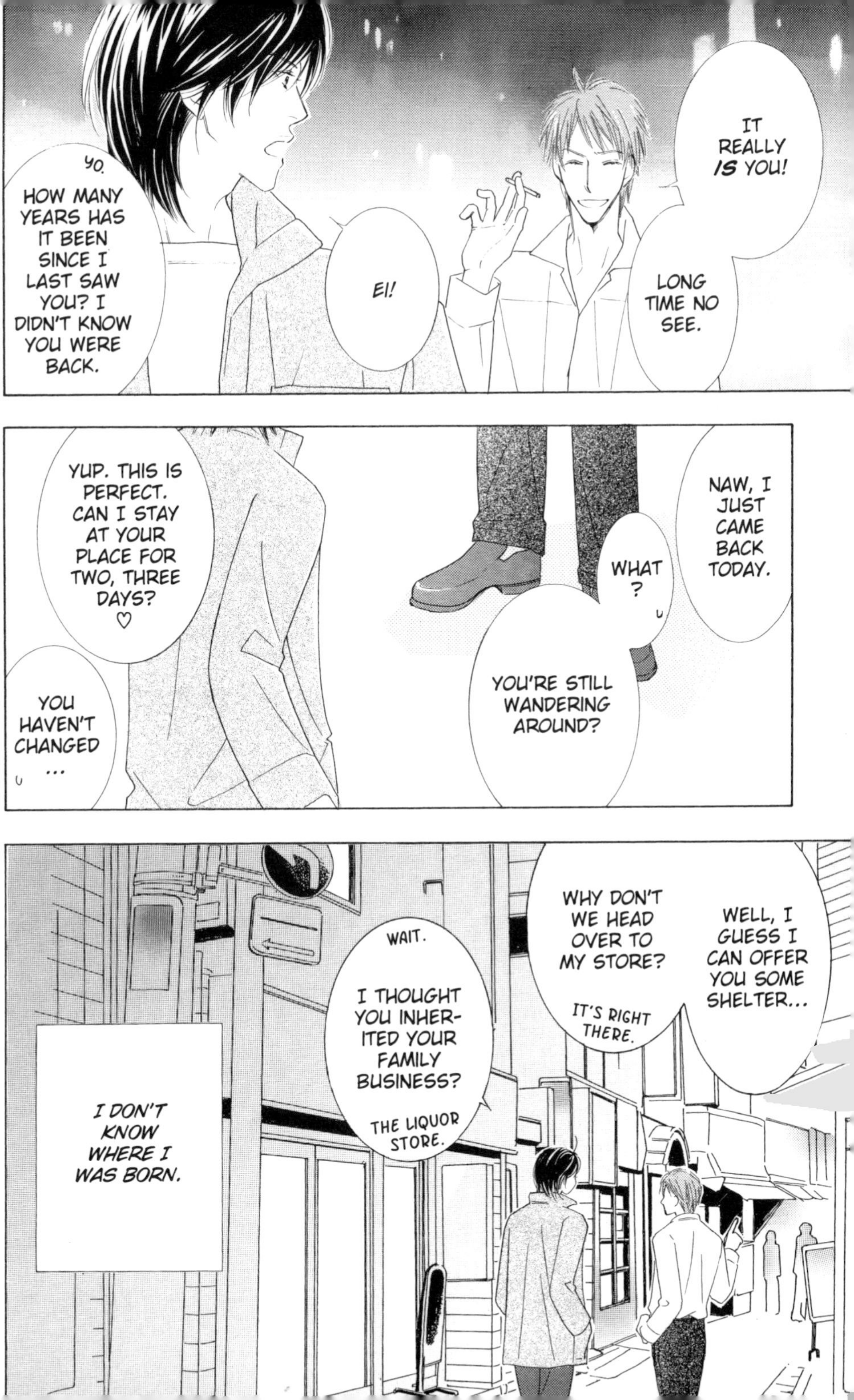
IT REALLY *IS* YOU!
LONG TIME NO SEE.
EI!
YO. HOW MANY YEARS HAS IT BEEN SINCE I LAST SAW YOU? I DIDN'T KNOW YOU WERE BACK.
NAW, I JUST CAME BACK TODAY.
WHAT?
YOU'RE STILL WANDERING AROUND?
YUP. THIS IS PERFECT. CAN I STAY AT YOUR PLACE FOR TWO, THREE DAYS? ♡
YOU HAVEN'T CHANGED...
WELL, I GUESS I CAN OFFER YOU SOME SHELTER...
WHY DON'T WE HEAD OVER TO MY STORE? IT'S RIGHT THERE.
WAIT. I THOUGHT YOU INHERITED YOUR FAMILY BUSINESS? THE LIQUOR STORE.
I DON'T KNOW WHERE I WAS BORN.

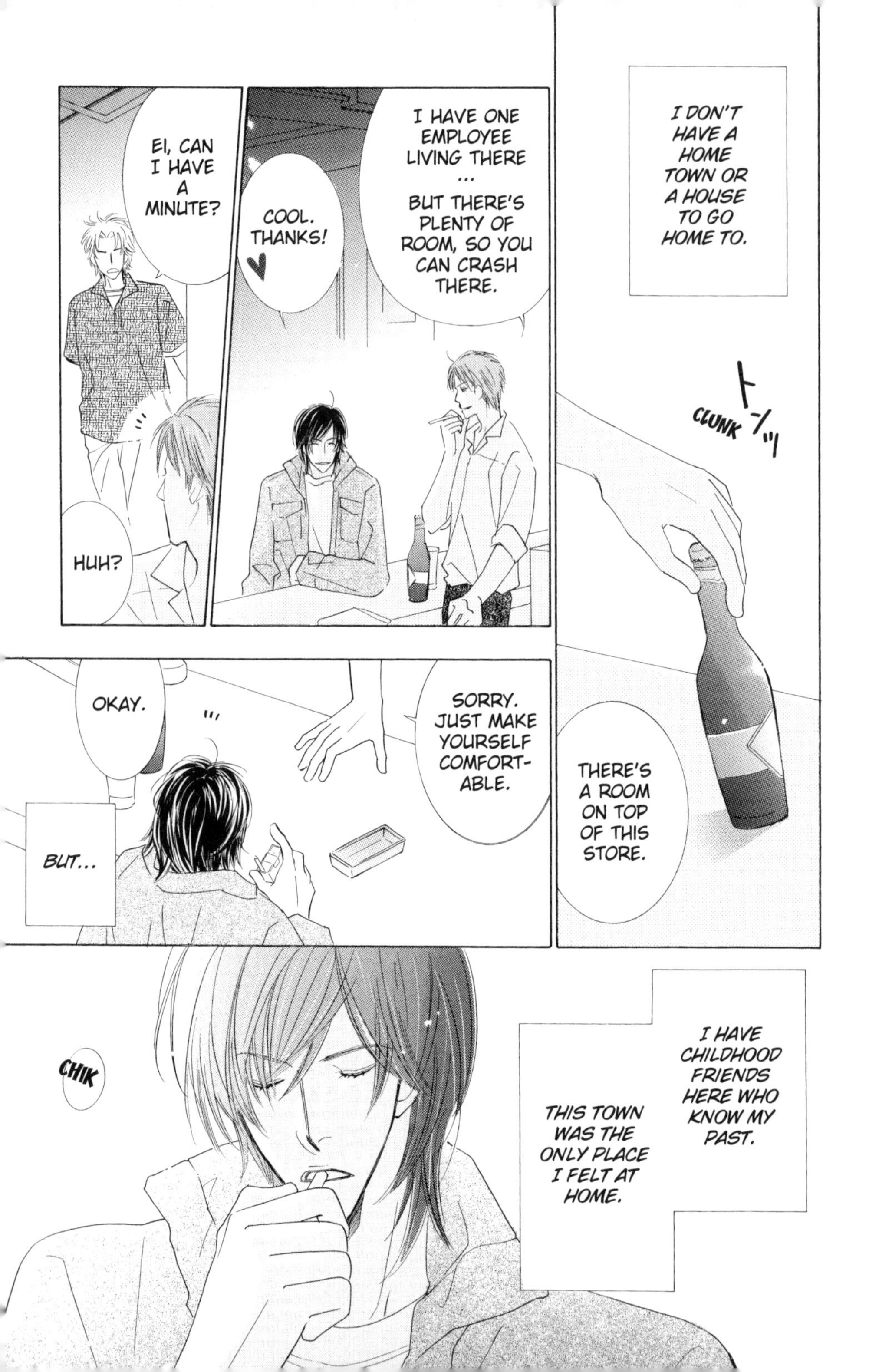
I DON'T HAVE A HOME TOWN OR A HOUSE TO GO HOME TO.
CLUNK
THERE'S A ROOM ON TOP OF THIS STORE.
I HAVE ONE EMPLOYEE LIVING THERE ... BUT THERE'S PLENTY OF ROOM, SO YOU CAN CRASH THERE.
COOL. THANKS!
EI, CAN I HAVE A MINUTE?
HUH?
SORRY. JUST MAKE YOURSELF COMFORT-ABLE.
OKAY.
BUT...
I HAVE CHILDHOOD FRIENDS HERE WHO KNOW MY PAST.
THIS TOWN WAS THE ONLY PLACE I FELT AT HOME.
CHIK

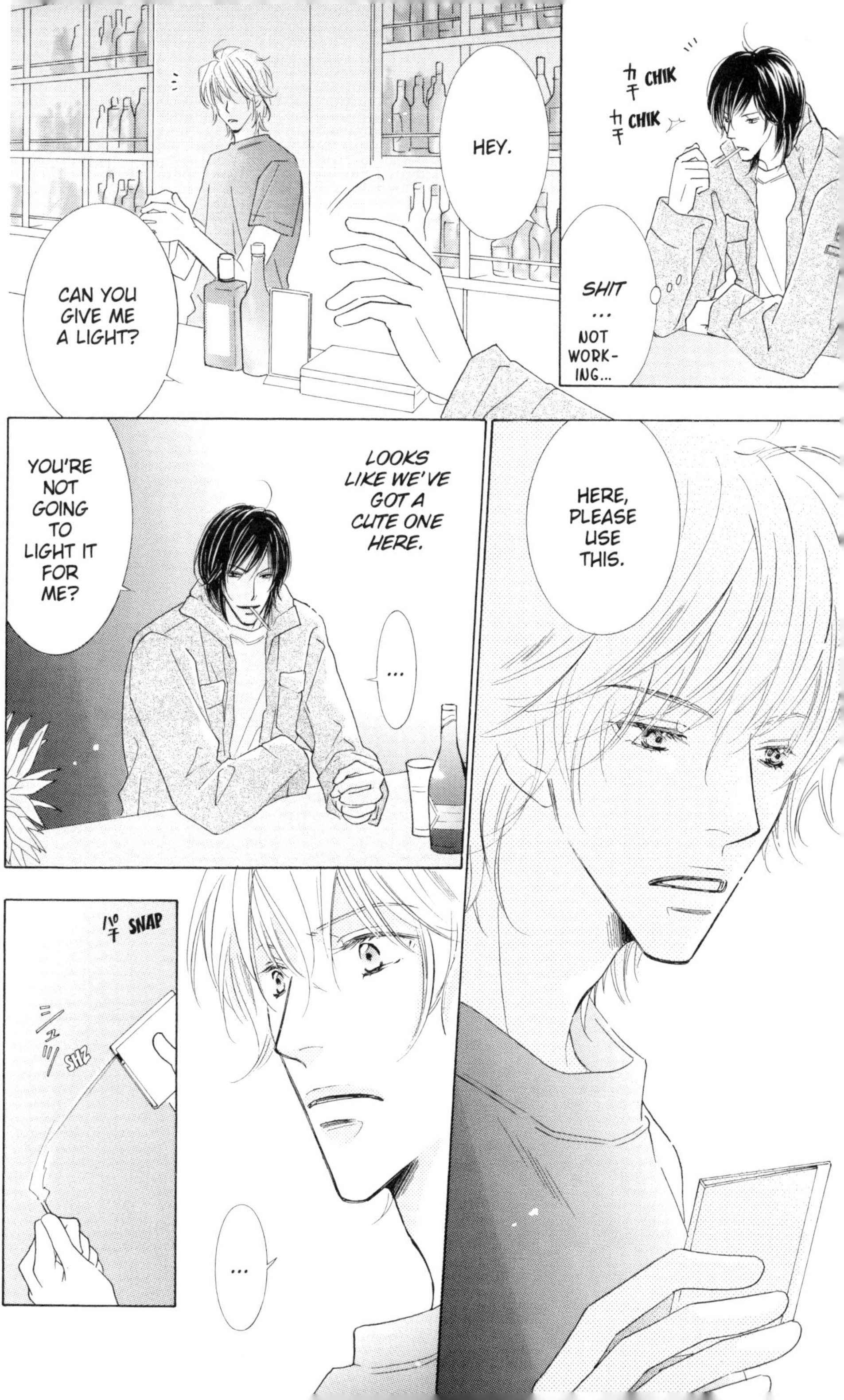
カチ CHIK
カチ CHIK
SHIT ... NOT WORKING...
HEY.
CAN YOU GIVE ME A LIGHT?
HERE, PLEASE USE THIS.
LOOKS LIKE WE'VE GOT A CUTE ONE HERE.
...
YOU'RE NOT GOING TO LIGHT IT FOR ME?
...
パチ SNAP
シュッ SHZ

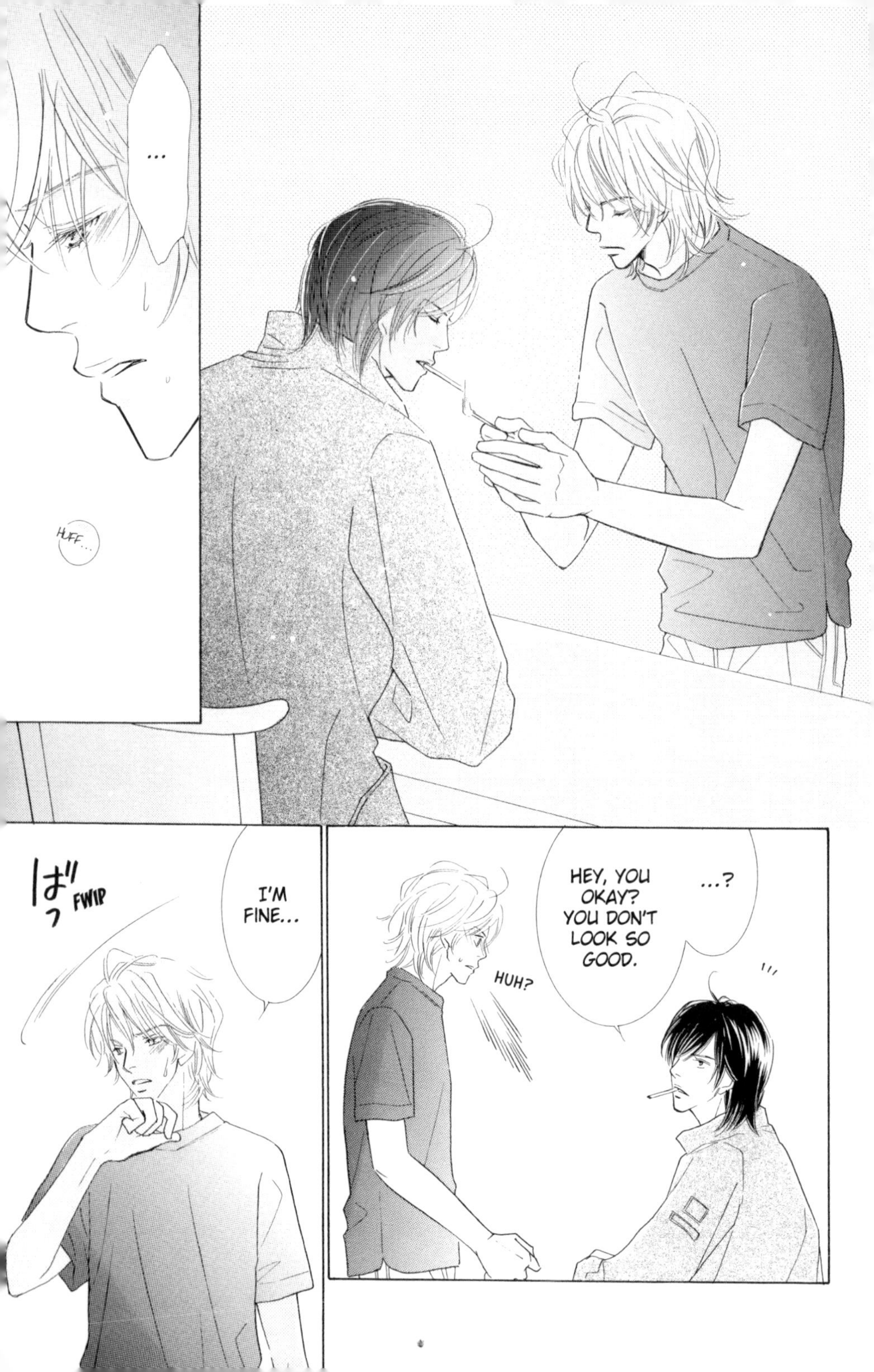
...
HUFF...
...?
HEY, YOU OKAY? YOU DON'T LOOK SO GOOD.
HUH?
I'M FINE...
ばっ FWIP

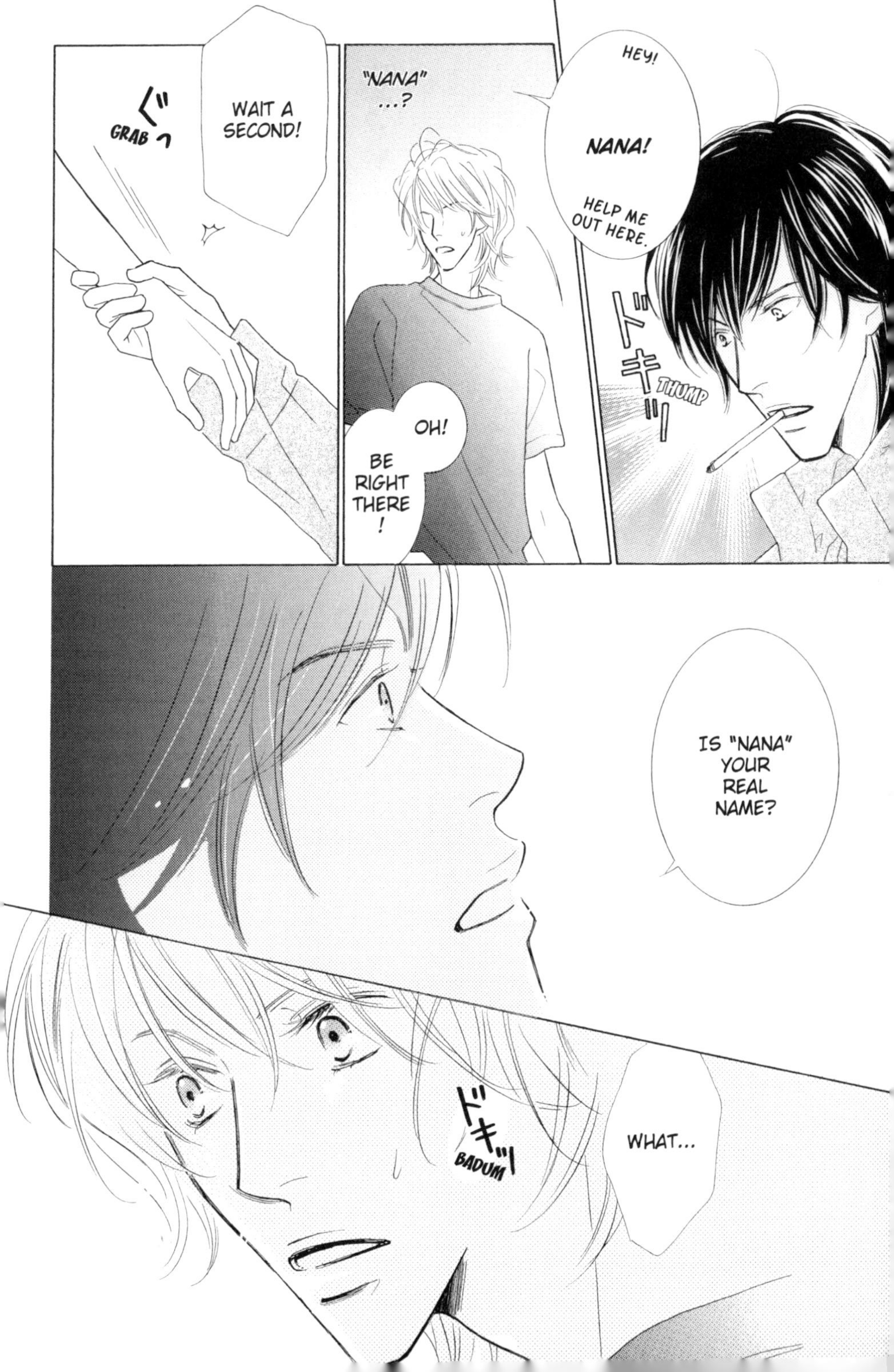
HEY!
NANA!
HELP ME OUT HERE.
ドキッ
THUMP
"NANA" ...?
OH!
BE RIGHT THERE!
WAIT A SECOND!
ぐっ
GRAB
IS "NANA" YOUR REAL NAME?
ドキッ
BADUM
WHAT...

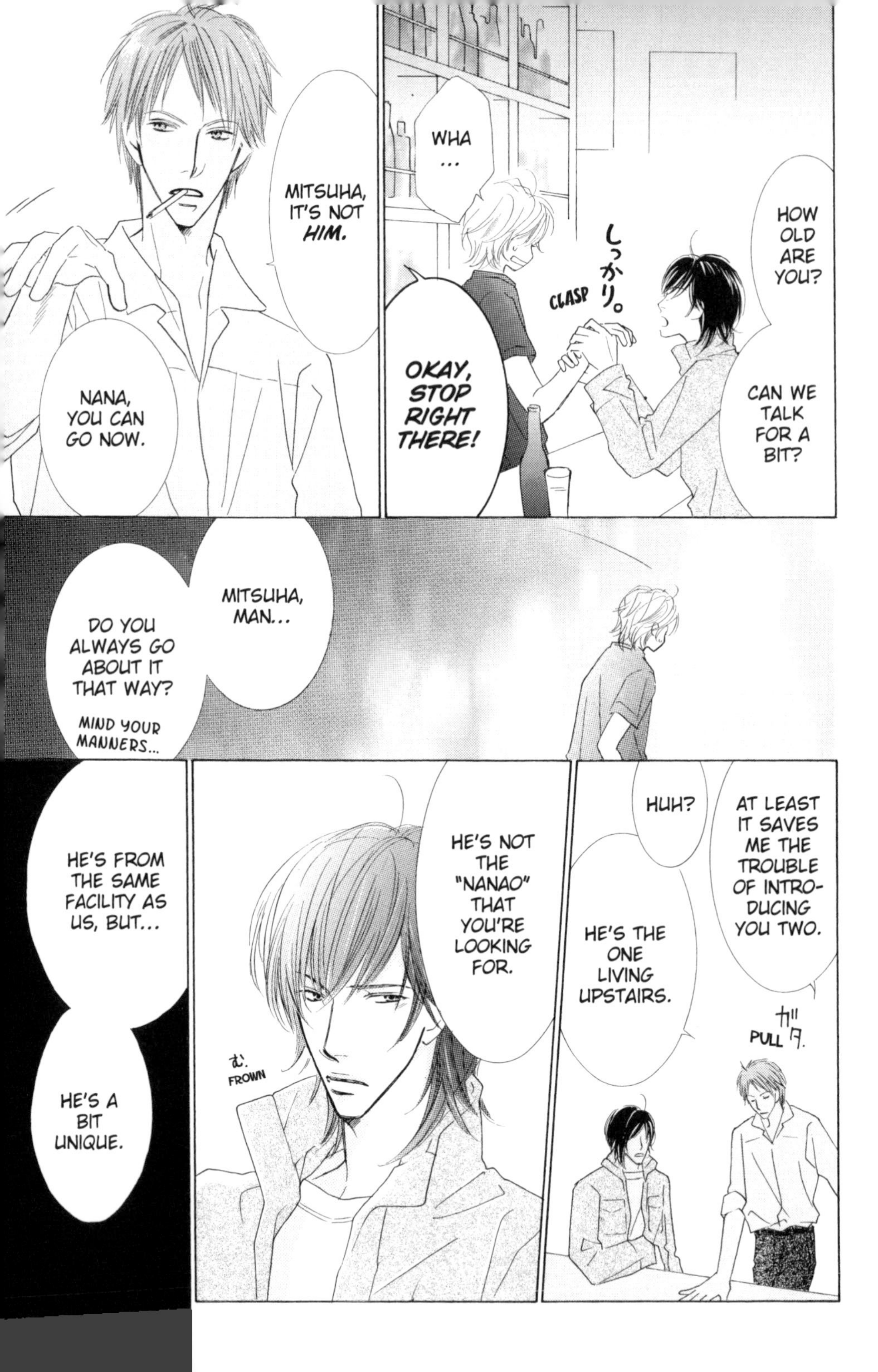
HOW OLD ARE YOU?
CAN WE TALK FOR A BIT?
WHA ...
しっかり。
CLASP
OKAY, STOP RIGHT THERE!
MITSUHA, IT'S NOT *HIM.*
NANA, YOU CAN GO NOW.
MITSUHA, MAN...
DO YOU ALWAYS GO ABOUT IT THAT WAY?
MIND YOUR MANNERS...
AT LEAST IT SAVES ME THE TROUBLE OF INTRO-DUCING YOU TWO.
HUH?
HE'S THE ONE LIVING UPSTAIRS.
ガタ
PULL
HE'S NOT THE "NANAO" THAT YOU'RE LOOKING FOR.
む.
FROWN
HE'S FROM THE SAME FACILITY AS US, BUT...
HE'S A BIT UNIQUE.

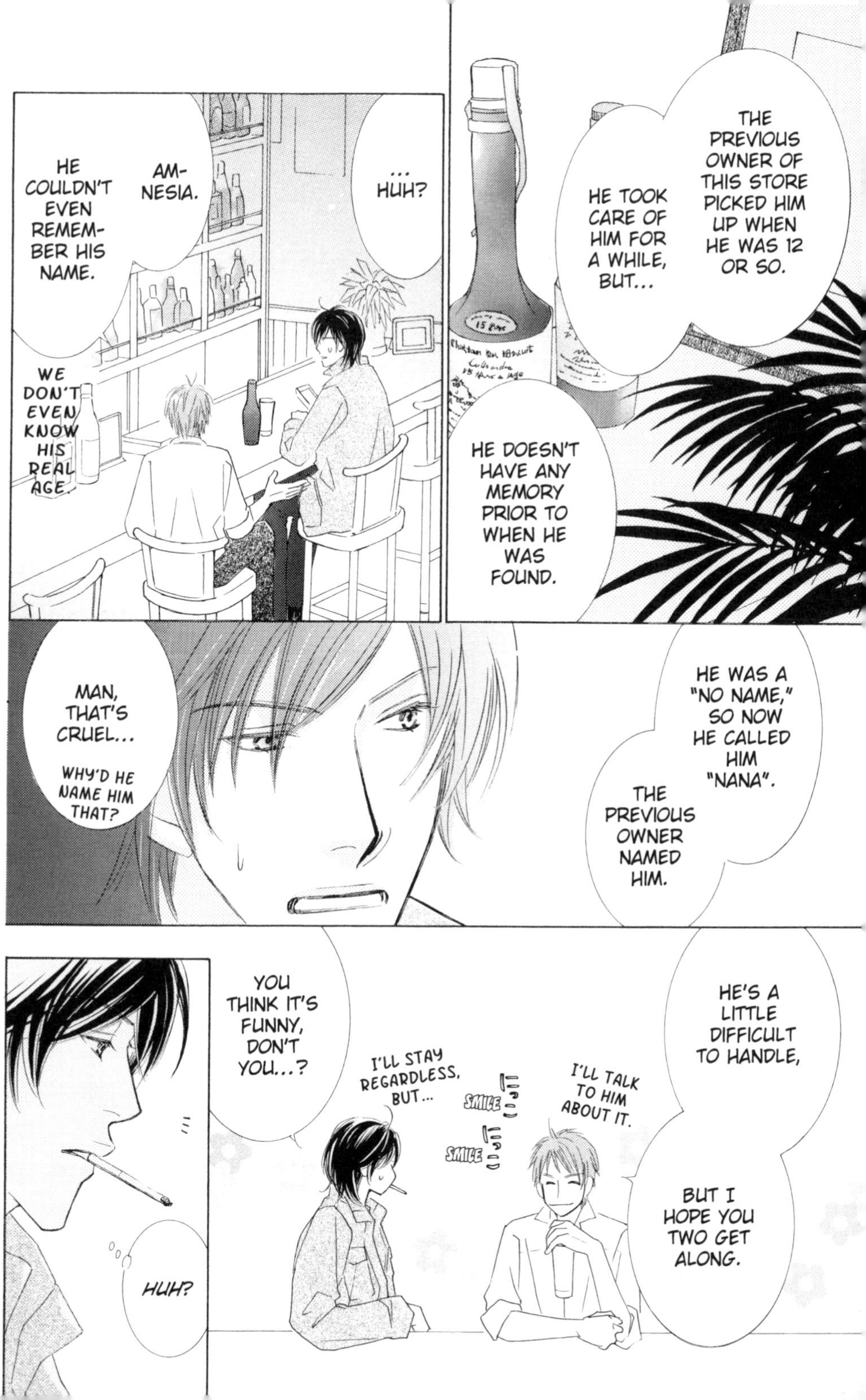
THE PREVIOUS OWNER OF THIS STORE PICKED HIM UP WHEN HE WAS 12 OR SO.
HE TOOK CARE OF HIM FOR A WHILE, BUT...
HE DOESN'T HAVE ANY MEMORY PRIOR TO WHEN HE WAS FOUND.
...HUH?
AM-NESIA.
HE COULDN'T EVEN REMEMBER HIS NAME.
WE DON'T EVEN KNOW HIS REAL AGE.
HE WAS A "NO NAME," SO NOW HE CALLED HIM "NANA".
THE PREVIOUS OWNER NAMED HIM.
MAN, THAT'S CRUEL...
WHY'D HE NAME HIM THAT?
HE'S A LITTLE DIFFICULT TO HANDLE,
I'LL TALK TO HIM ABOUT IT.
BUT I HOPE YOU TWO GET ALONG.
SMILE
SMILE
I'LL STAY REGARDLESS, BUT...
YOU THINK IT'S FUNNY, DON'T YOU...?
HUH?

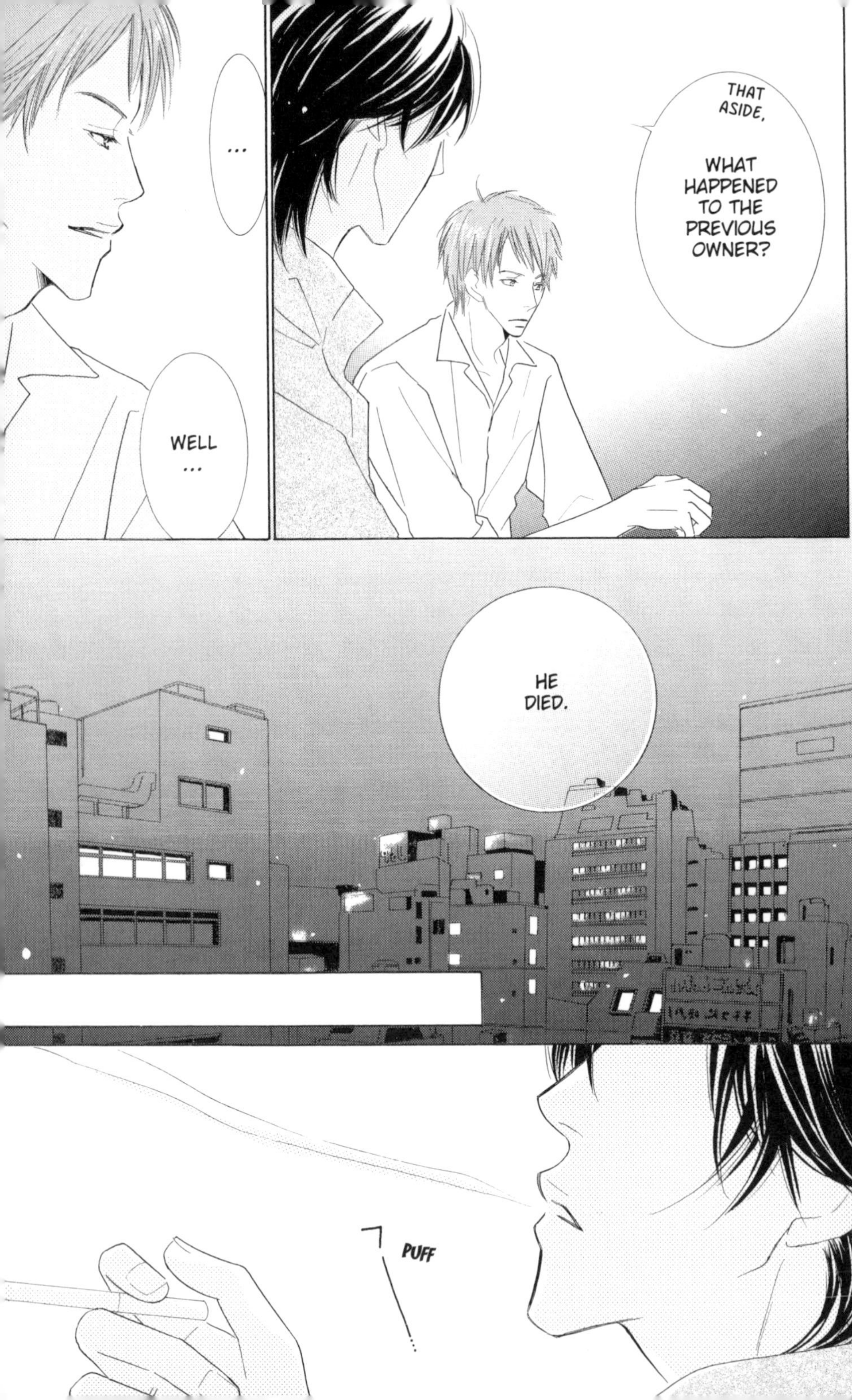
THAT ASIDE,
WHAT HAPPENED TO THE PREVIOUS OWNER?
...
WELL ...
HE DIED.
PUFF
...

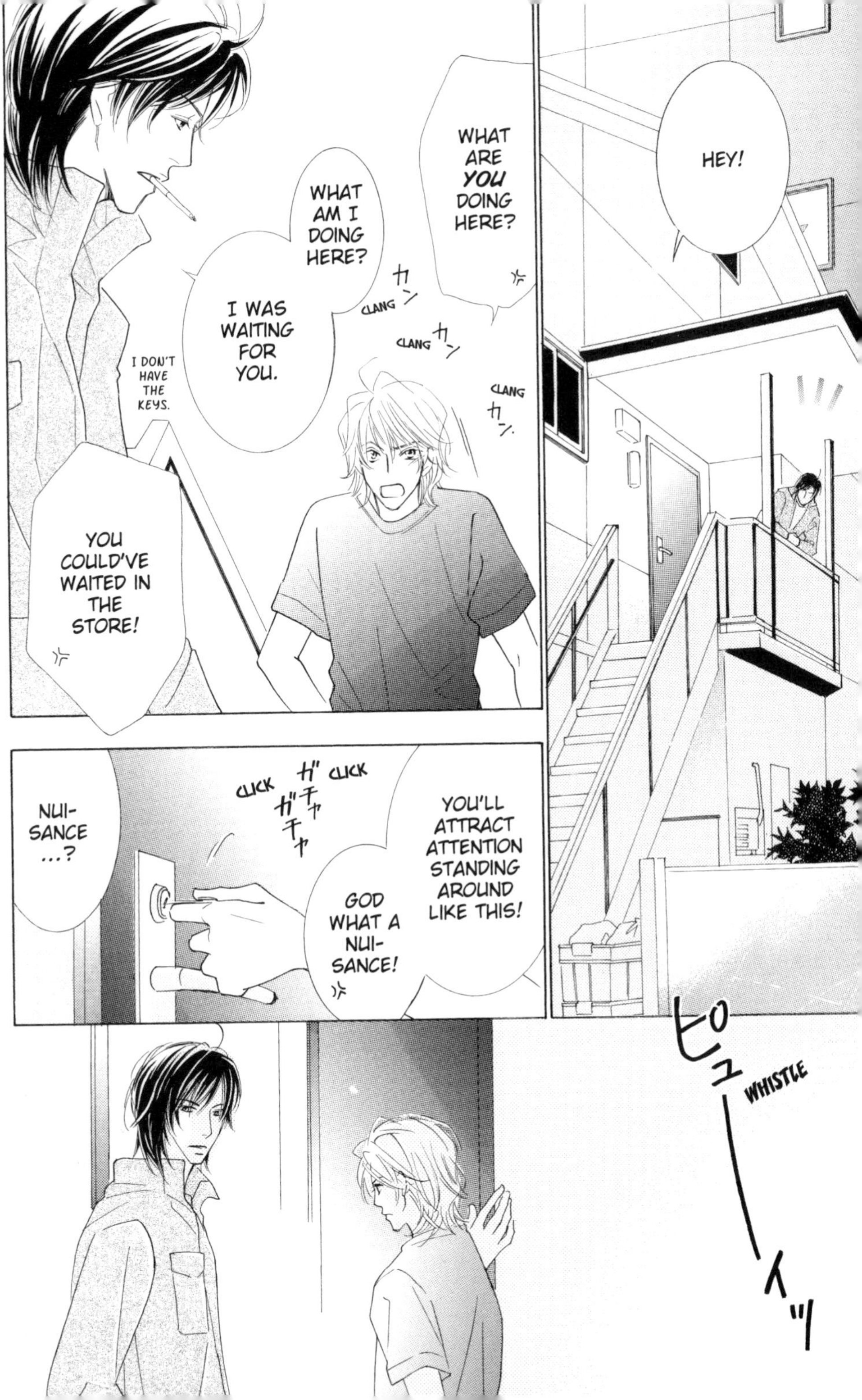
HEY!
WHAT ARE YOU DOING HERE?
カン CLANG
カン CLANG
カン CLANG
WHAT AM I DOING HERE?
I WAS WAITING FOR YOU.
I DON'T HAVE THE KEYS.
YOU COULD'VE WAITED IN THE STORE!
ガチャ CLICK
ガチャ CLICK
YOU'LL ATTRACT ATTENTION STANDING AROUND LIKE THIS!
GOD WHAT A NUI-SANCE!
NUI-SANCE ...?
ピューイッ WHISTLE

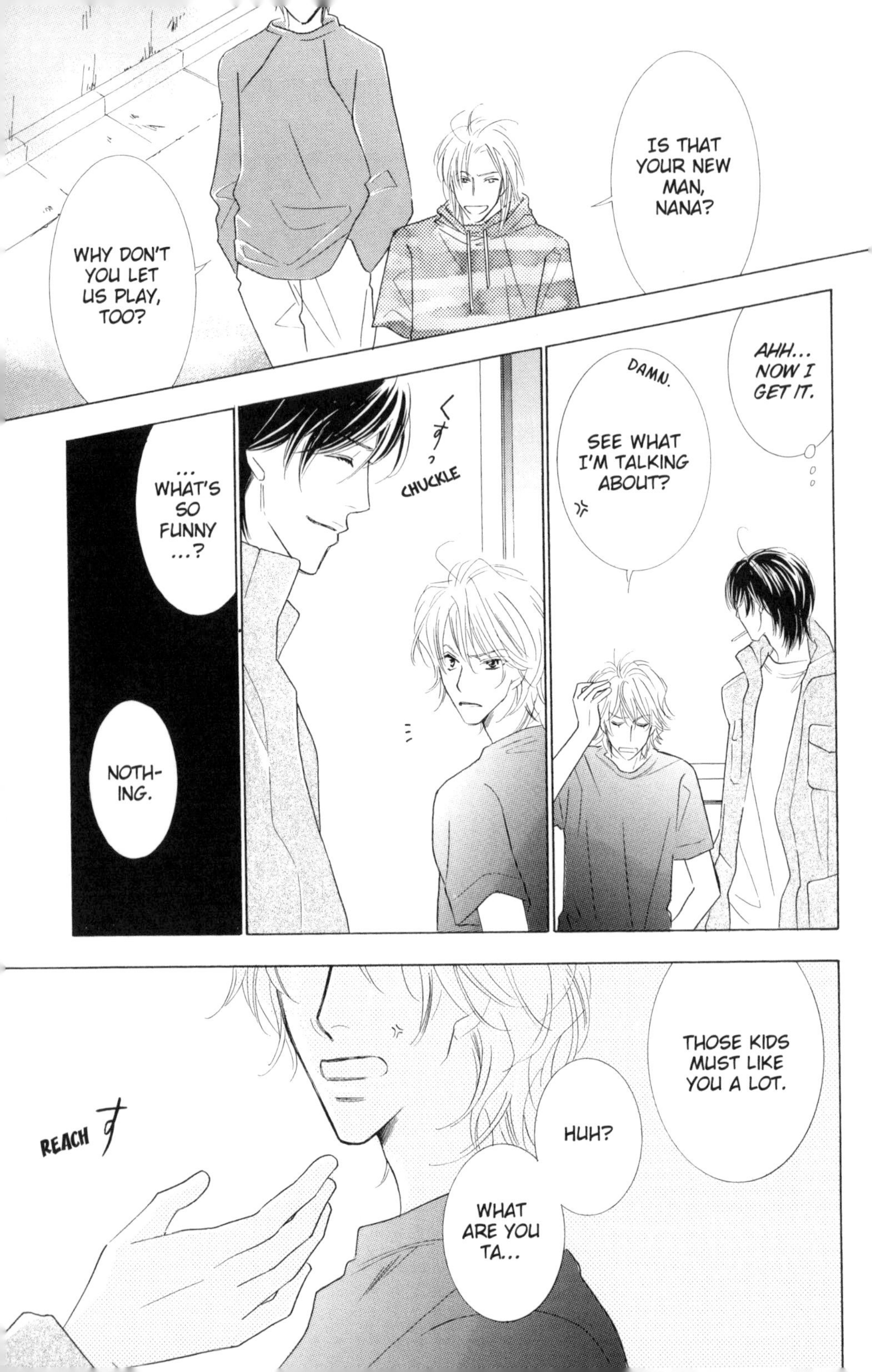
IS THAT YOUR NEW MAN, NANA?
WHY DON'T YOU LET US PLAY, TOO?
AHH... NOW I GET IT.
DAMN.
SEE WHAT I'M TALKING ABOUT?
くすっ
CHUCKLE
... WHAT'S SO FUNNY ...?
NOTH-ING.
THOSE KIDS MUST LIKE YOU A LOT.
HUH?
WHAT ARE YOU TA...
REACH す

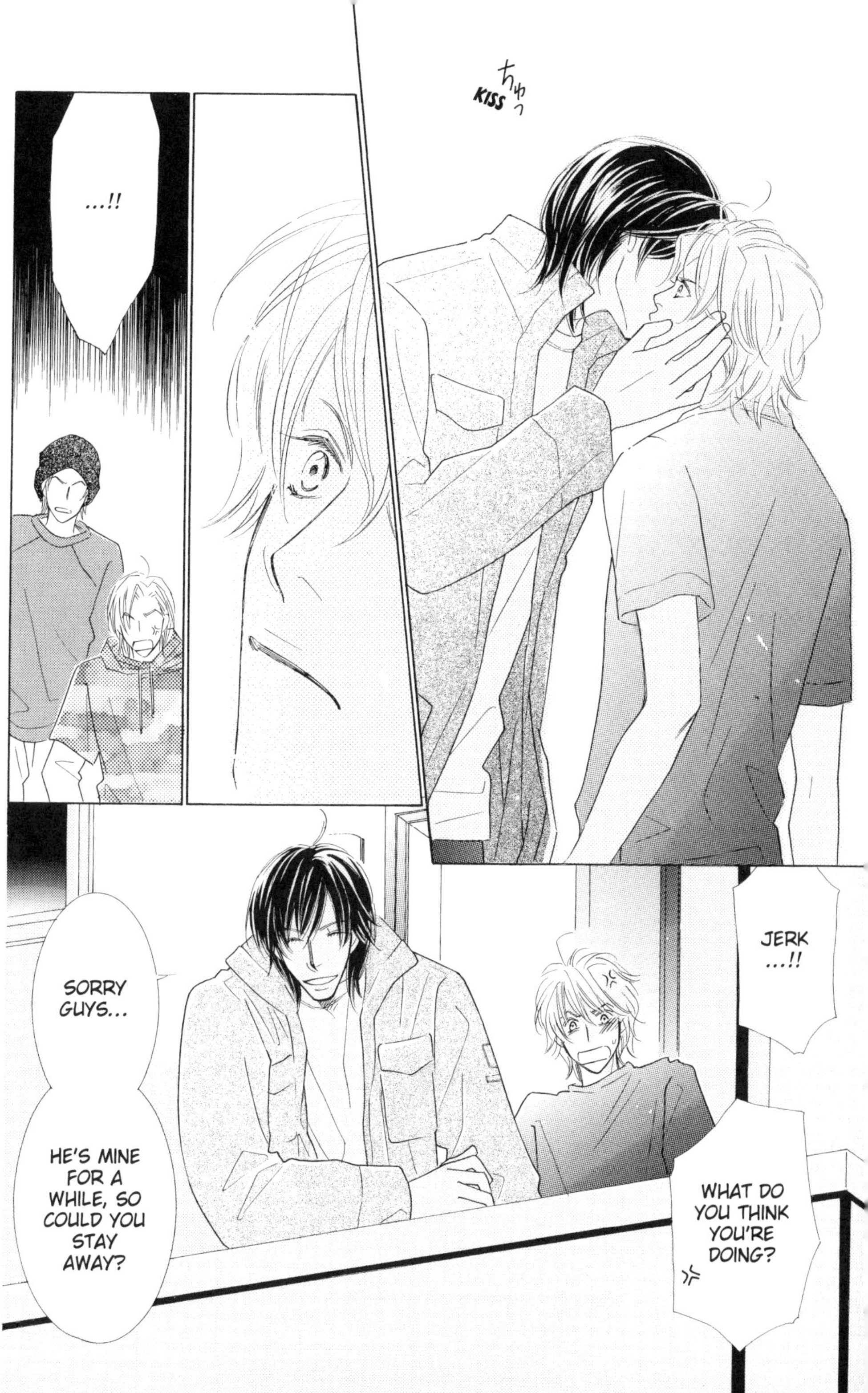
ちゅっ
KISS
...!!
JERK ...!!
WHAT DO YOU THINK YOU'RE DOING?
SORRY GUYS...
HE'S MINE FOR A WHILE, SO COULD YOU STAY AWAY?

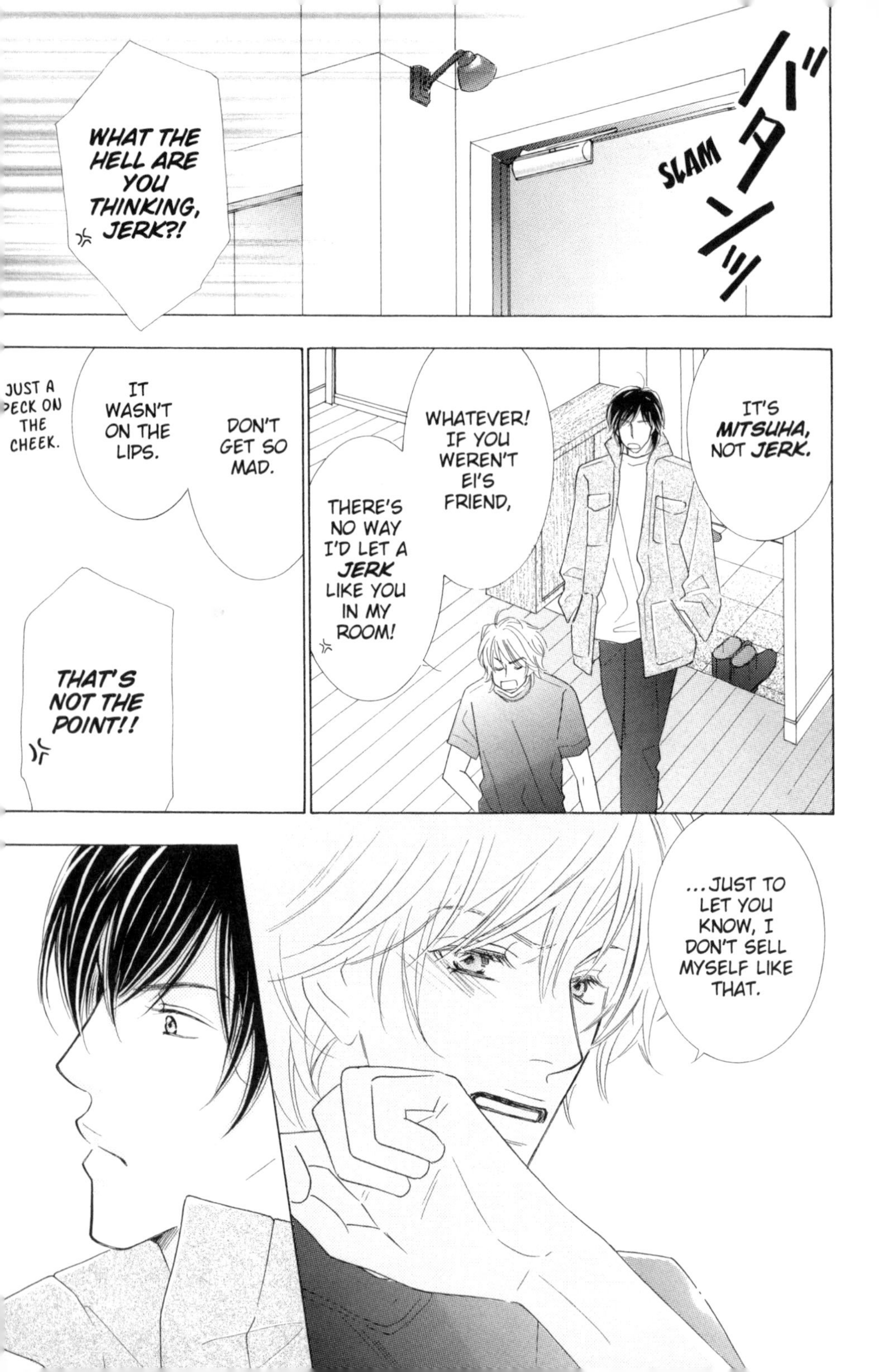
バタンッ
SLAM
WHAT THE HELL ARE YOU THINKING, JERK?!
IT'S MITSUHA, NOT JERK.
WHATEVER! IF YOU WEREN'T EI'S FRIEND,
THERE'S NO WAY I'D LET A JERK LIKE YOU IN MY ROOM!
DON'T GET SO MAD.
IT WASN'T ON THE LIPS.
JUST A PECK ON THE CHEEK.
THAT'S NOT THE POINT!!
...JUST TO LET YOU KNOW, I DON'T SELL MYSELF LIKE THAT.

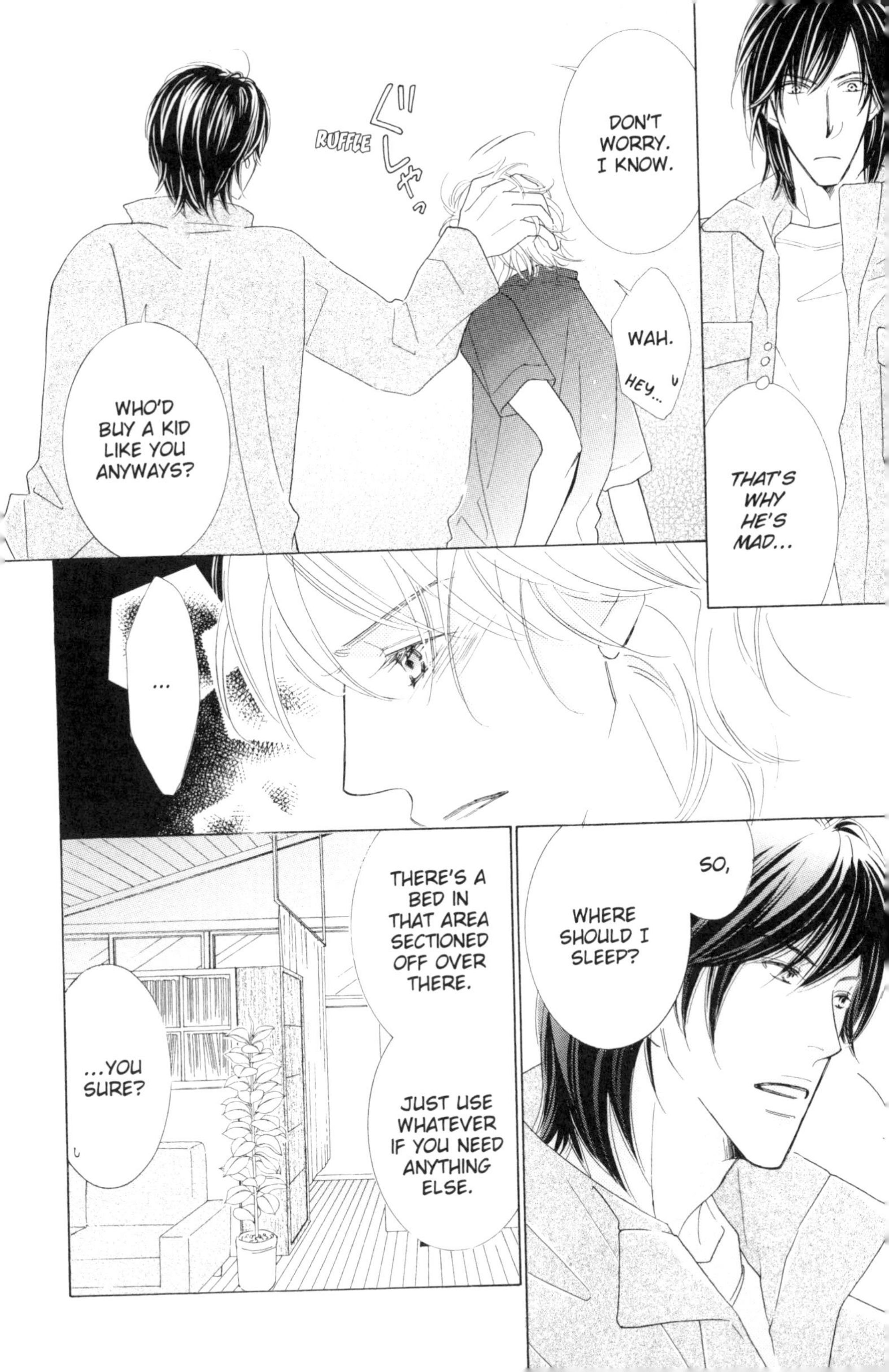
THAT'S WHY HE'S MAD...
DON'T WORRY. I KNOW.
ぐしゃっ
RUFFLE
WAH.
HEY...
WHO'D BUY A KID LIKE YOU ANYWAYS?
...
SO,
WHERE SHOULD I SLEEP?
THERE'S A BED IN THAT AREA SECTIONED OFF OVER THERE.
JUST USE WHATEVER IF YOU NEED ANYTHING ELSE.
...YOU SURE?

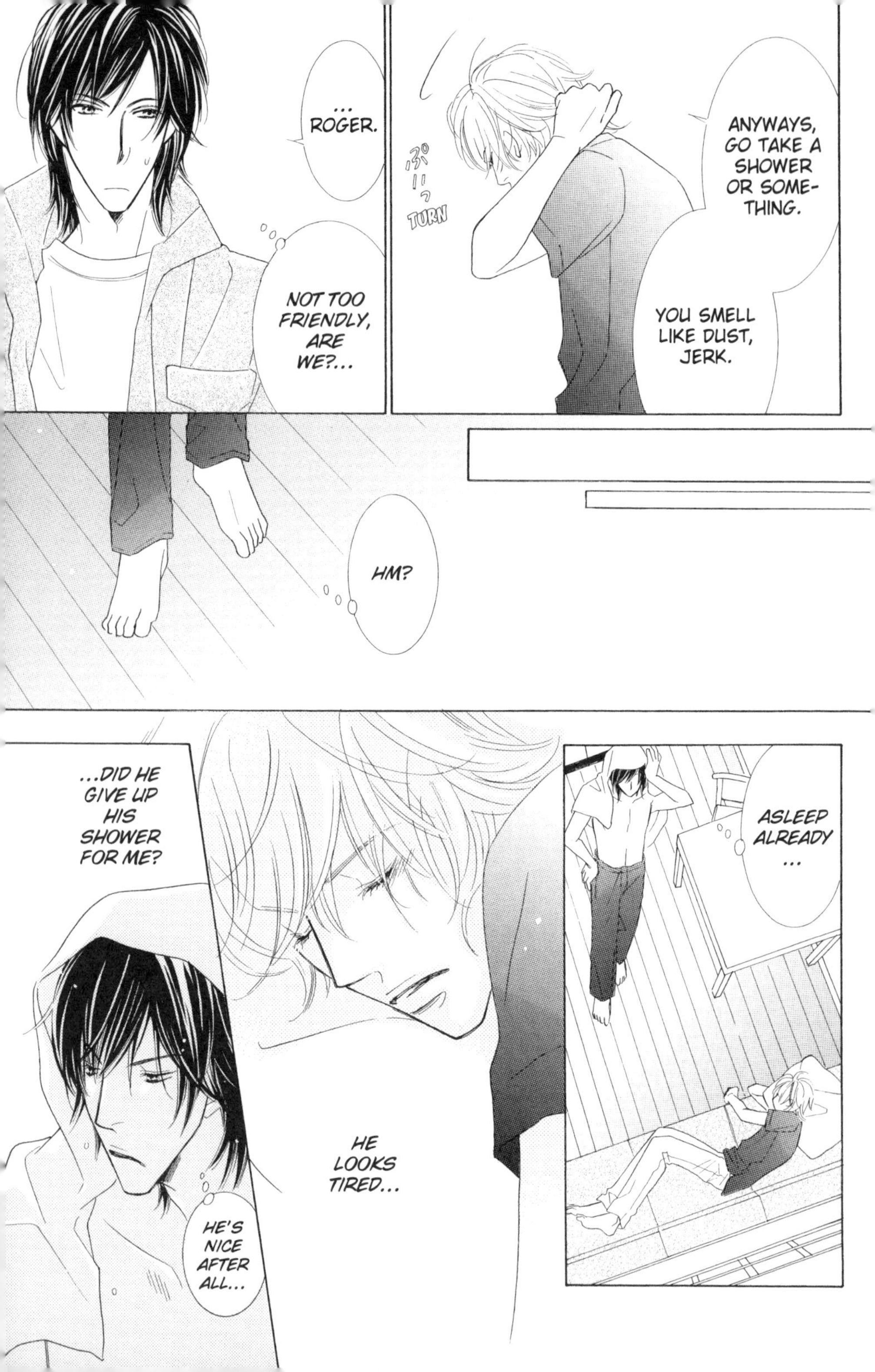
ANYWAYS, GO TAKE A SHOWER OR SOMETHING.
TURN
YOU SMELL LIKE DUST, JERK.
... ROGER.
NOT TOO FRIENDLY, ARE WE?...
HM?
ASLEEP ALREADY ...
...DID HE GIVE UP HIS SHOWER FOR ME?
HE LOOKS TIRED...
HE'S NICE AFTER ALL...

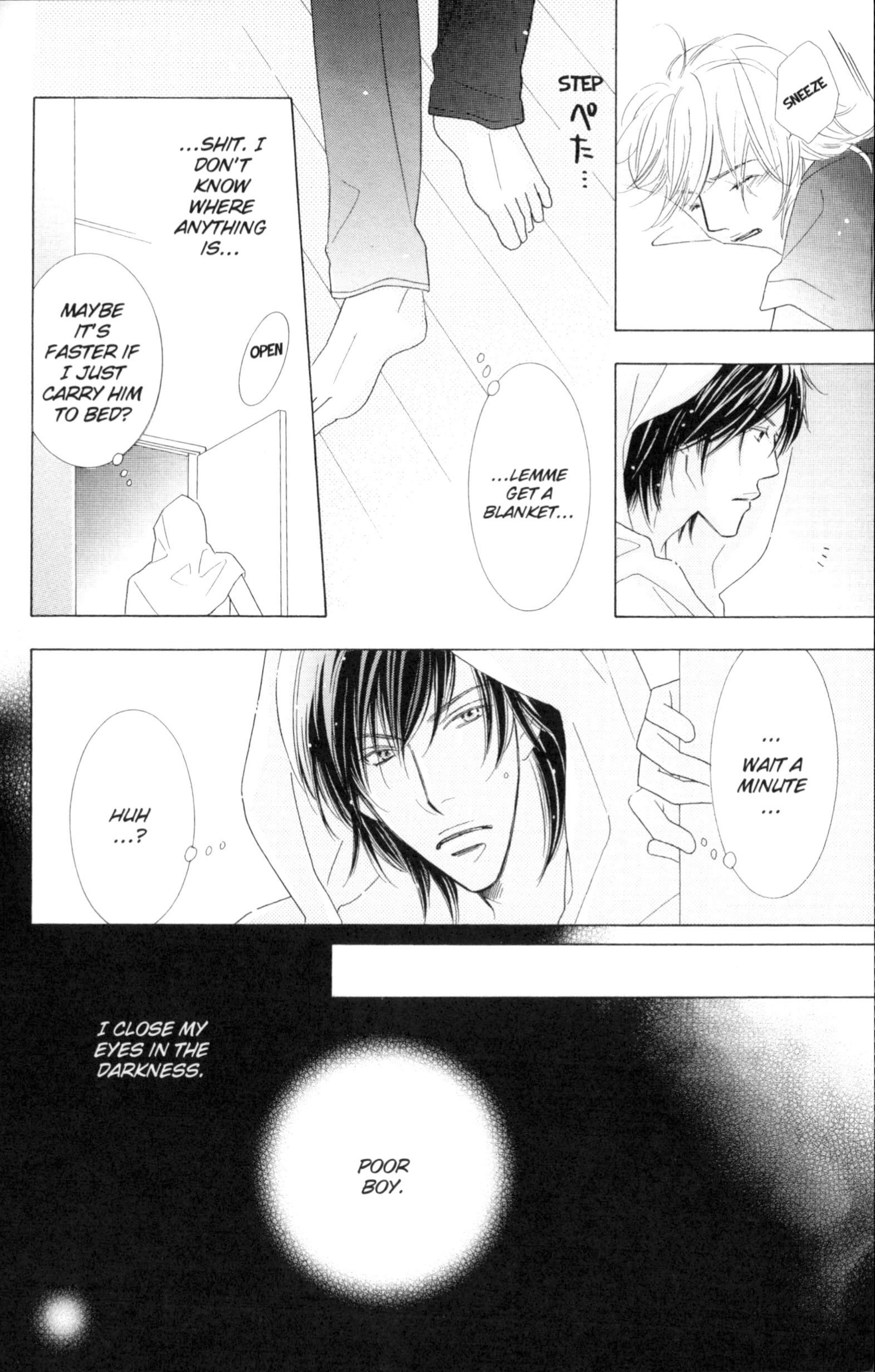
SNEEZE
STEP
ぺた…
...LEMME GET A BLANKET...
OPEN
...SHIT. I DON'T KNOW WHERE ANYTHING IS...
MAYBE IT'S FASTER IF I JUST CARRY HIM TO BED?
... WAIT A MINUTE ...
HUH ...?
I CLOSE MY EYES IN THE DARKNESS.
POOR BOY.

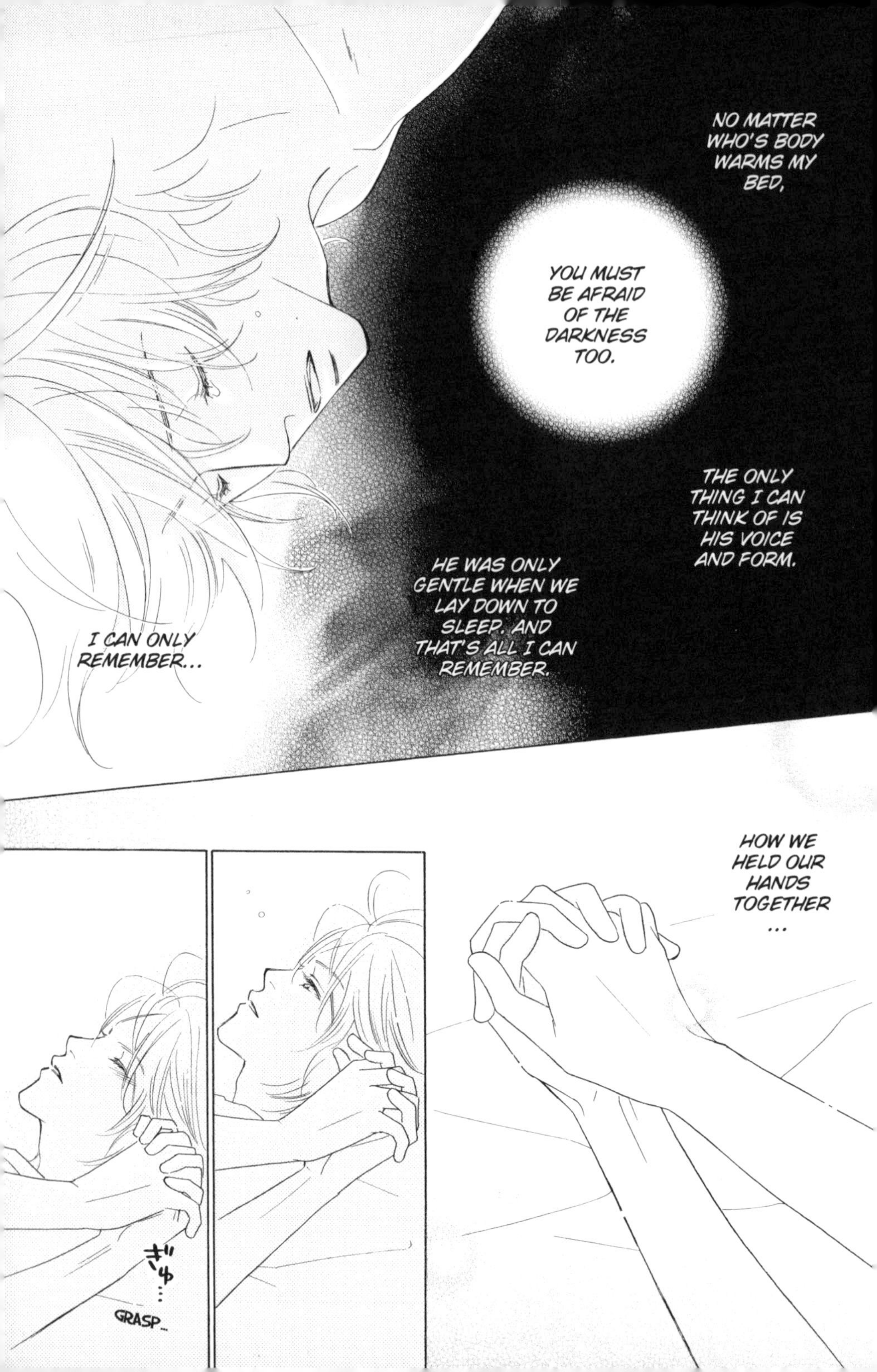
NO MATTER WHO'S BODY WARMS MY BED,
YOU MUST BE AFRAID OF THE DARKNESS TOO.
THE ONLY THING I CAN THINK OF IS HIS VOICE AND FORM.
HE WAS ONLY GENTLE WHEN WE LAY DOWN TO SLEEP. AND THAT'S ALL I CAN REMEMBER.
I CAN ONLY REMEMBER...
HOW WE HELD OUR HANDS TOGETHER ...
ぎゅ…
GRASP...

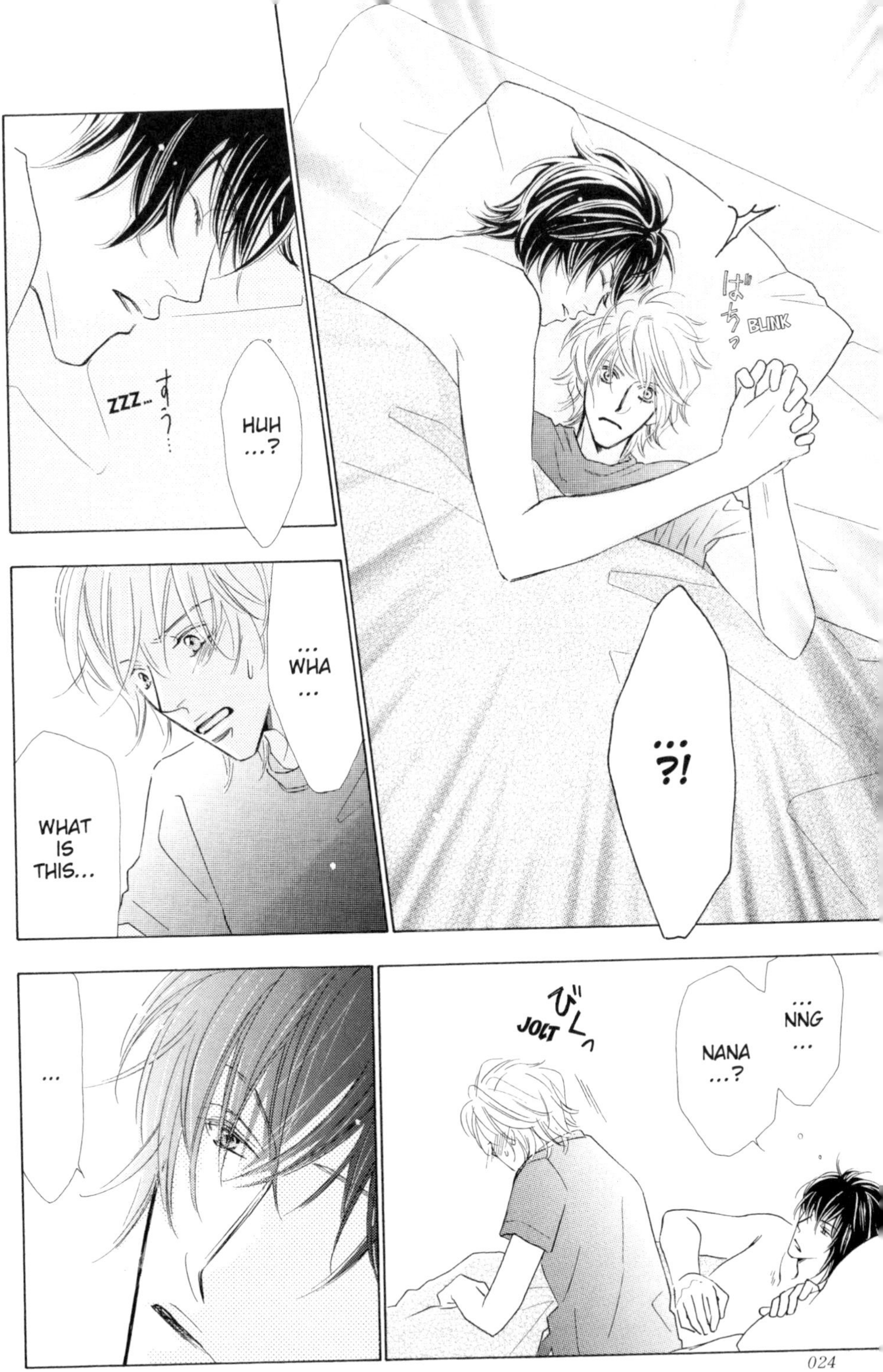
ばちっ
BLINK
...?!
HUH ...?
ZZZ... すぅ…
... WHA ...
WHAT IS THIS...
... NNG ...
NANA ...?
びくっ
JOLT
...

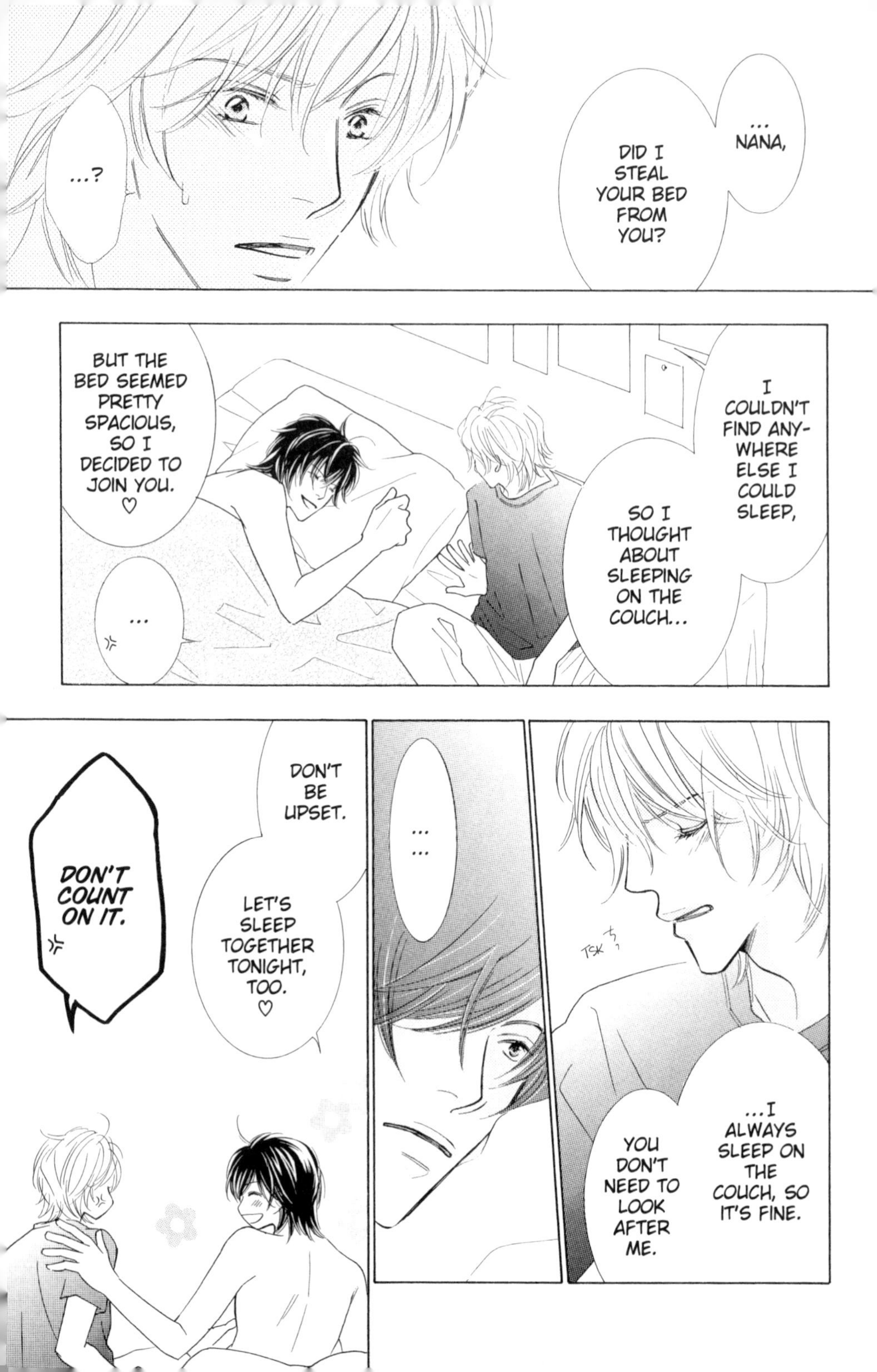
... NANA,
DID I STEAL YOUR BED FROM YOU?
...?
I COULDN'T FIND ANY-WHERE ELSE I COULD SLEEP,
SO I THOUGHT ABOUT SLEEPING ON THE COUCH...
BUT THE BED SEEMED PRETTY SPACIOUS, SO I DECIDED TO JOIN YOU. ♡
...
TSK
...I ALWAYS SLEEP ON THE COUCH, SO IT'S FINE.
YOU DON'T NEED TO LOOK AFTER ME.
... ...
DON'T BE UPSET.
LET'S SLEEP TOGETHER TONIGHT, TOO. ♡
DON'T COUNT ON IT.

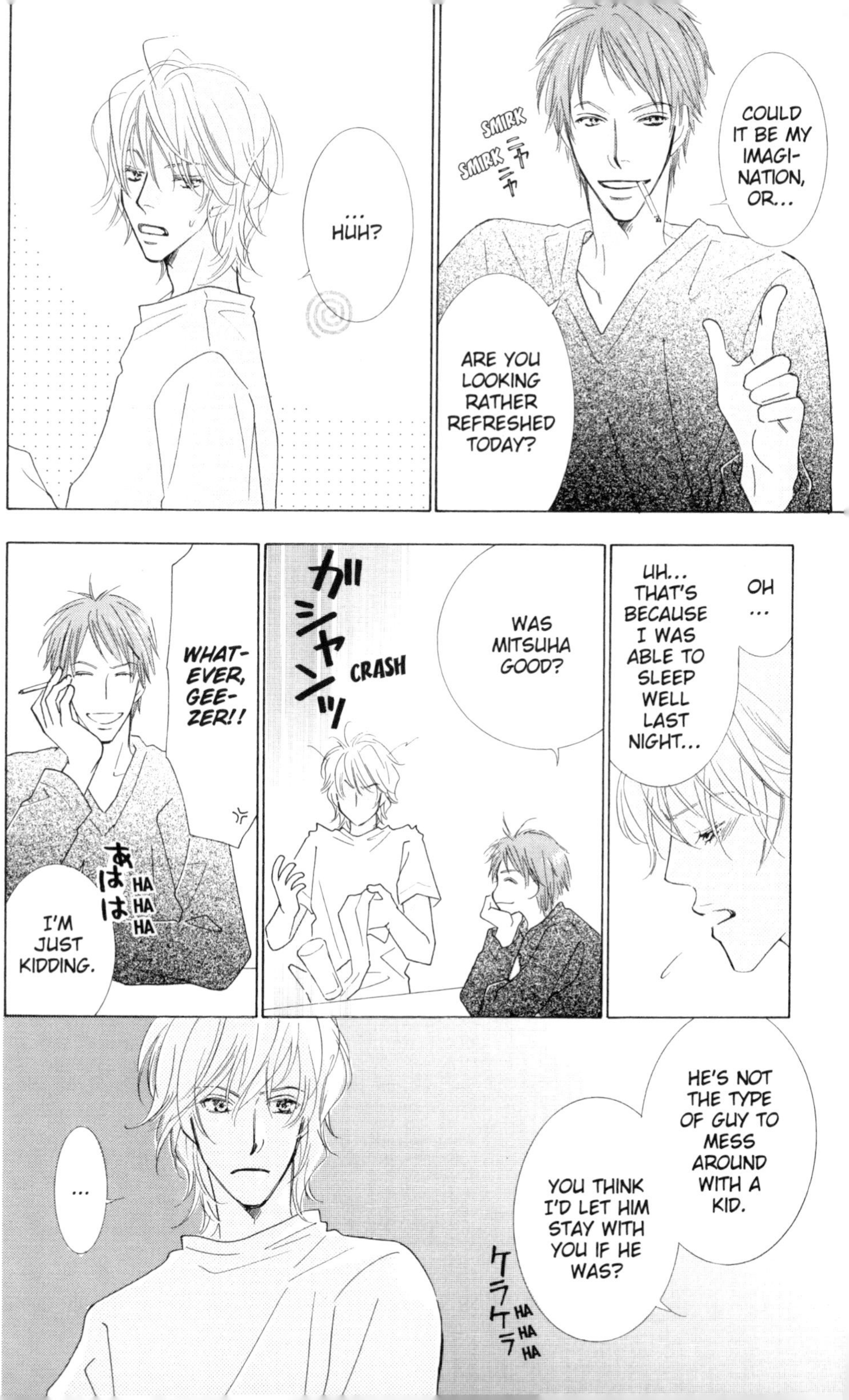
COULD IT BE MY IMAGI-NATION, OR...
ニヤニヤ SMIRK SMIRK
ARE YOU LOOKING RATHER REFRESHED TODAY?
... HUH?
OH ...
UH... THAT'S BECAUSE I WAS ABLE TO SLEEP WELL LAST NIGHT...
WAS MITSUHA GOOD?
ガシャンッ CRASH
WHAT-EVER, GEE-ZER!!
あはは HA HA HA
I'M JUST KIDDING.
HE'S NOT THE TYPE OF GUY TO MESS AROUND WITH A KID.
YOU THINK I'D LET HIM STAY WITH YOU IF HE WAS?
ケラケラ HA HA HA
...

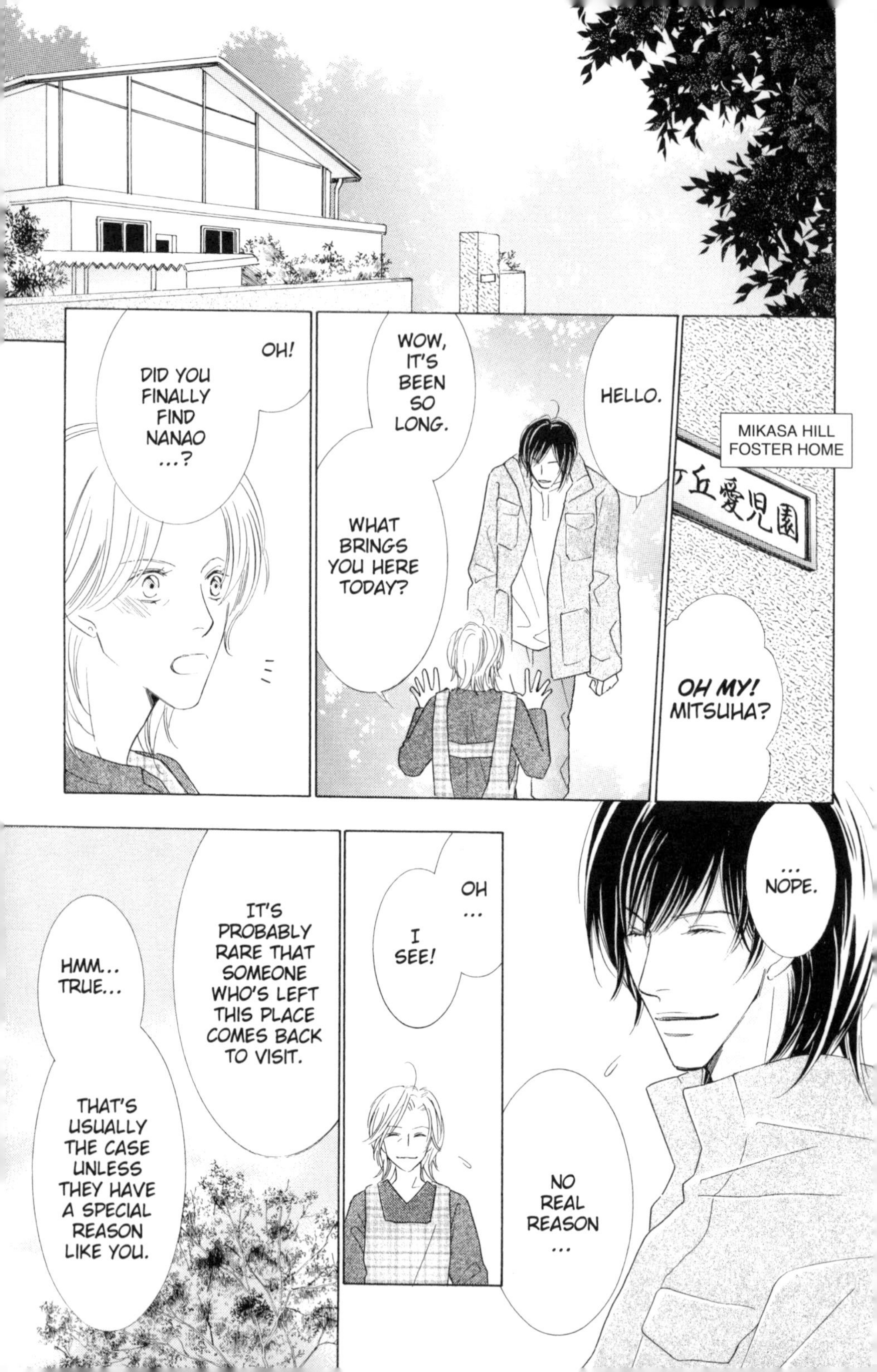
MIKASA HILL FOSTER HOME
丘愛児園
OH MY! MITSUHA?
HELLO.
WOW, IT'S BEEN SO LONG.
WHAT BRINGS YOU HERE TODAY?
OH!
DID YOU FINALLY FIND NANAO ...?
... NOPE.
NO REAL REASON ...
OH ... I SEE!
IT'S PROBABLY RARE THAT SOMEONE WHO'S LEFT THIS PLACE COMES BACK TO VISIT.
HMM... TRUE...
THAT'S USUALLY THE CASE UNLESS THEY HAVE A SPECIAL REASON LIKE YOU.

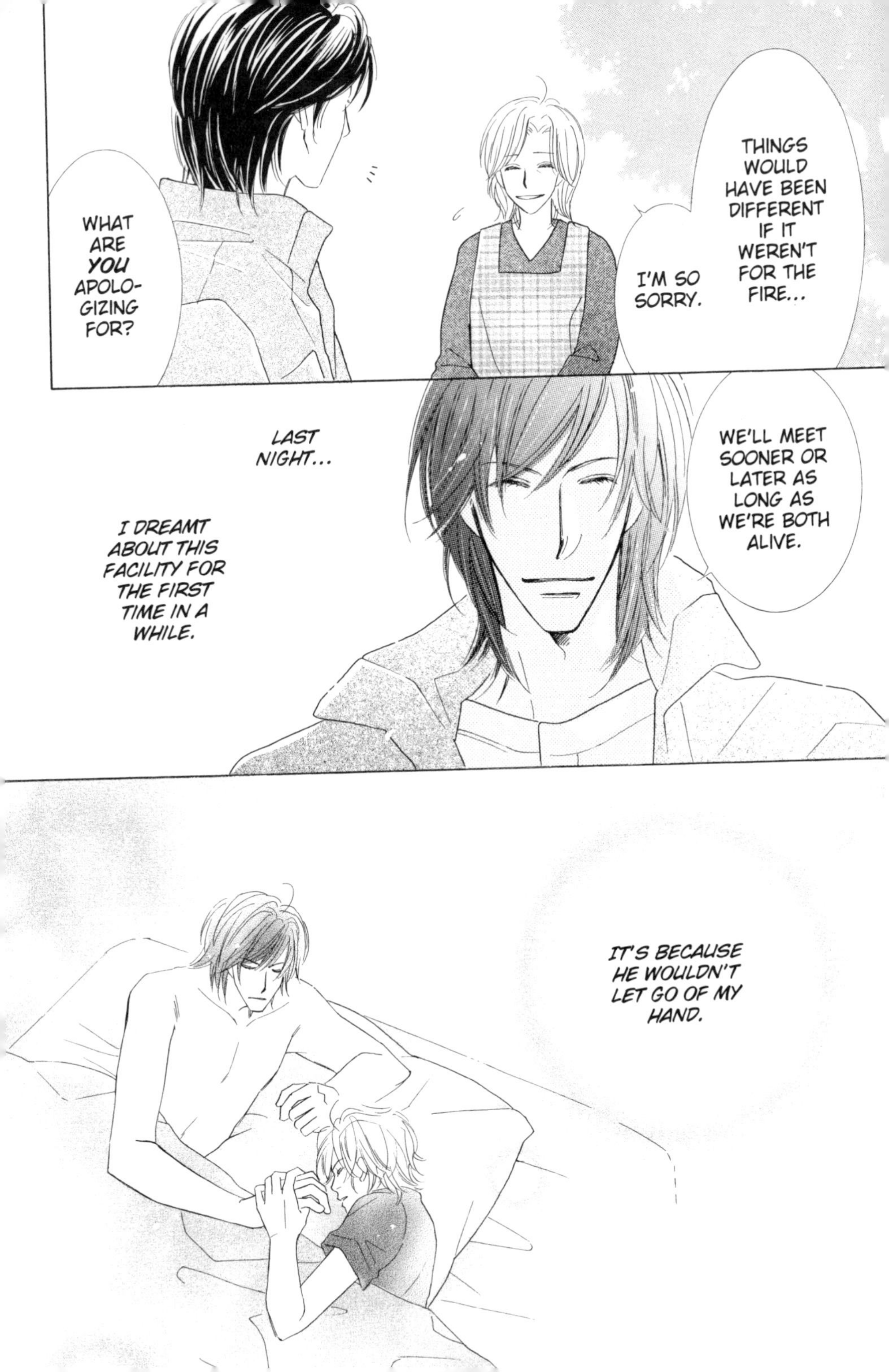
THINGS WOULD HAVE BEEN DIFFERENT IF IT WEREN'T FOR THE FIRE...
I'M SO SORRY.
WHAT ARE ***YOU*** APOLOGIZING FOR?
WE'LL MEET SOONER OR LATER AS LONG AS WE'RE BOTH ALIVE.
LAST NIGHT...
I DREAMT ABOUT THIS FACILITY FOR THE FIRST TIME IN A WHILE.
IT'S BECAUSE HE WOULDN'T LET GO OF MY HAND.

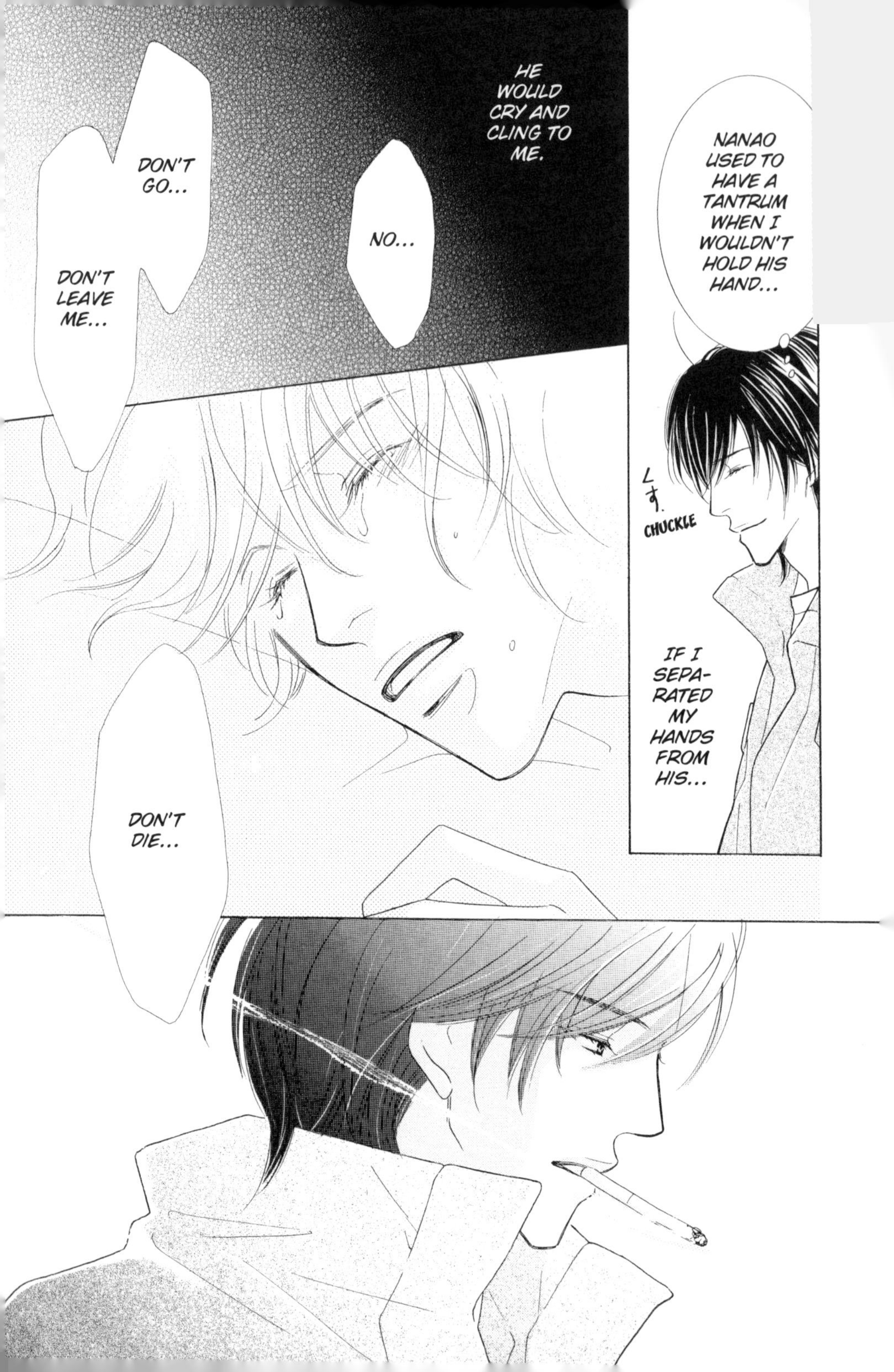
NANAO USED TO HAVE A TANTRUM WHEN I WOULDN'T HOLD HIS HAND...
くす.
CHUCKLE
IF I SEPARATED MY HANDS FROM HIS...
HE WOULD CRY AND CLING TO ME.
NO...
DON'T GO...
DON'T LEAVE ME...
DON'T DIE...

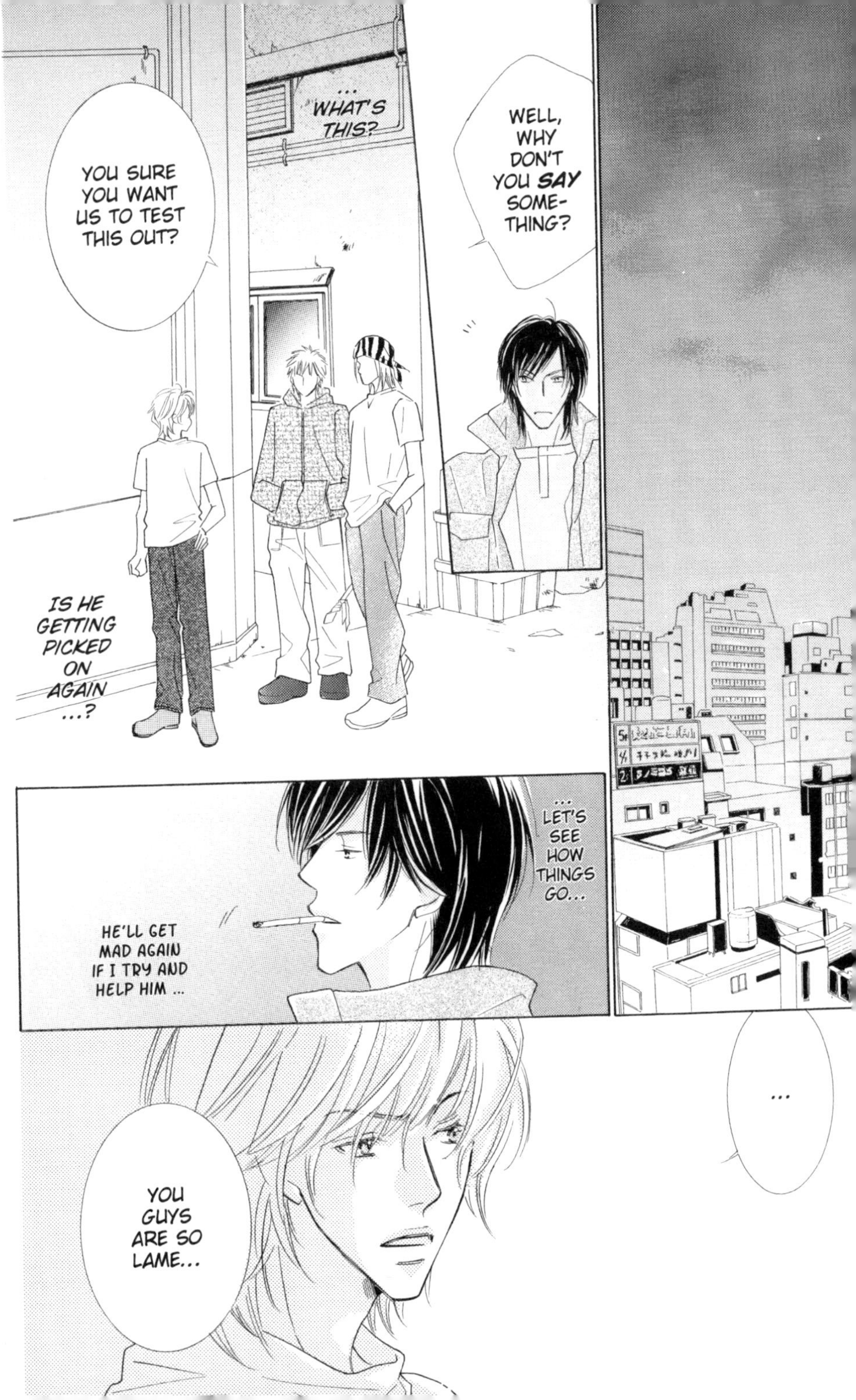
WELL, WHY DON'T YOU SAY SOMETHING?
...WHAT'S THIS?
YOU SURE YOU WANT US TO TEST THIS OUT?
IS HE GETTING PICKED ON AGAIN ...?
...LET'S SEE HOW THINGS GO...
HE'LL GET MAD AGAIN IF I TRY AND HELP HIM ...
...
YOU GUYS ARE SO LAME...

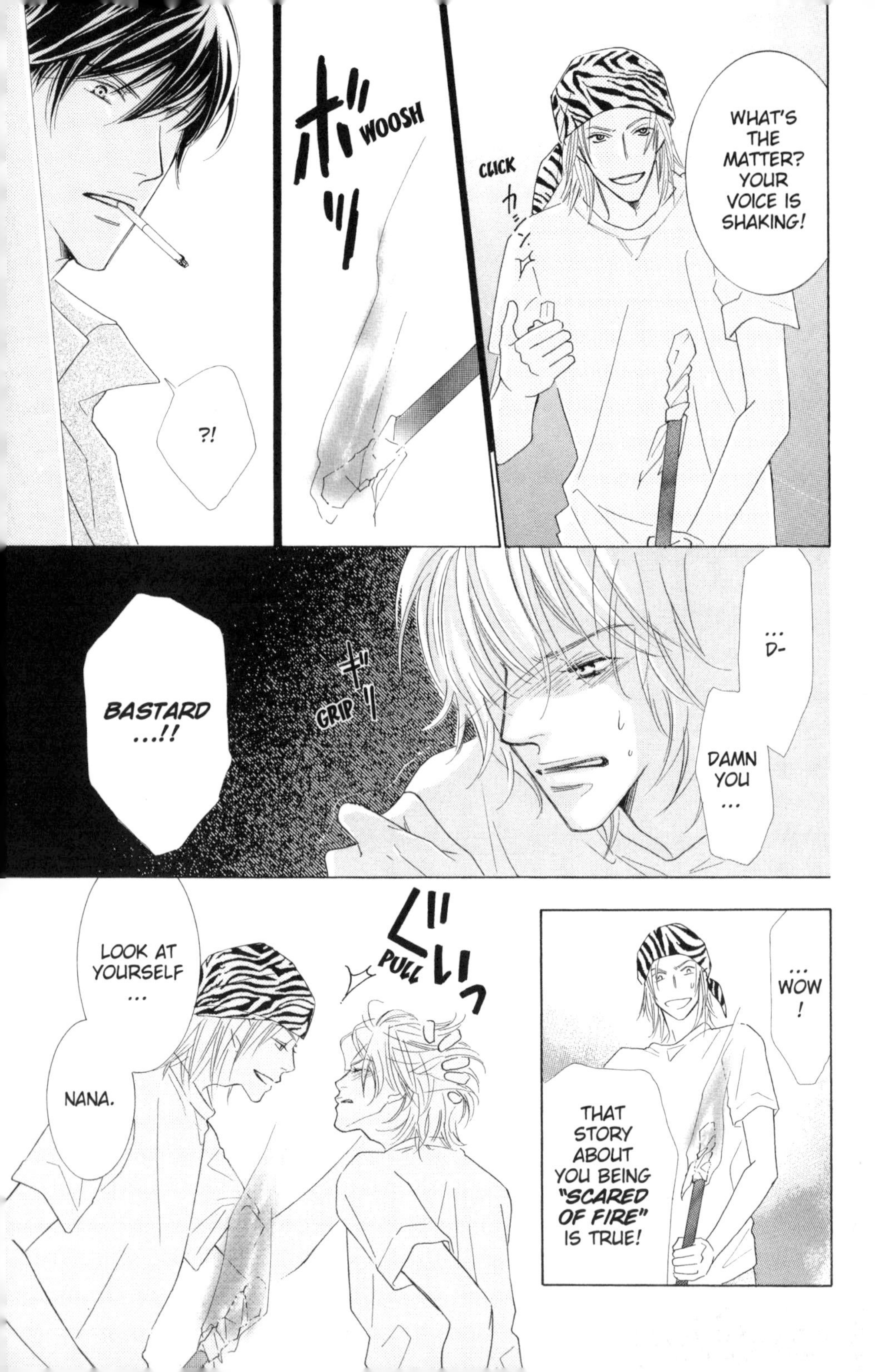
CLICK
WHAT'S THE MATTER? YOUR VOICE IS SHAKING!
ボッ
WOOSH
?!
... D-
DAMN YOU ...
ギリ
GRIP
BASTARD ...!!
... WOW!
THAT STORY ABOUT YOU BEING "SCARED OF FIRE" IS TRUE!
ぐいっ
PULL
LOOK AT YOURSELF ...
NANA.

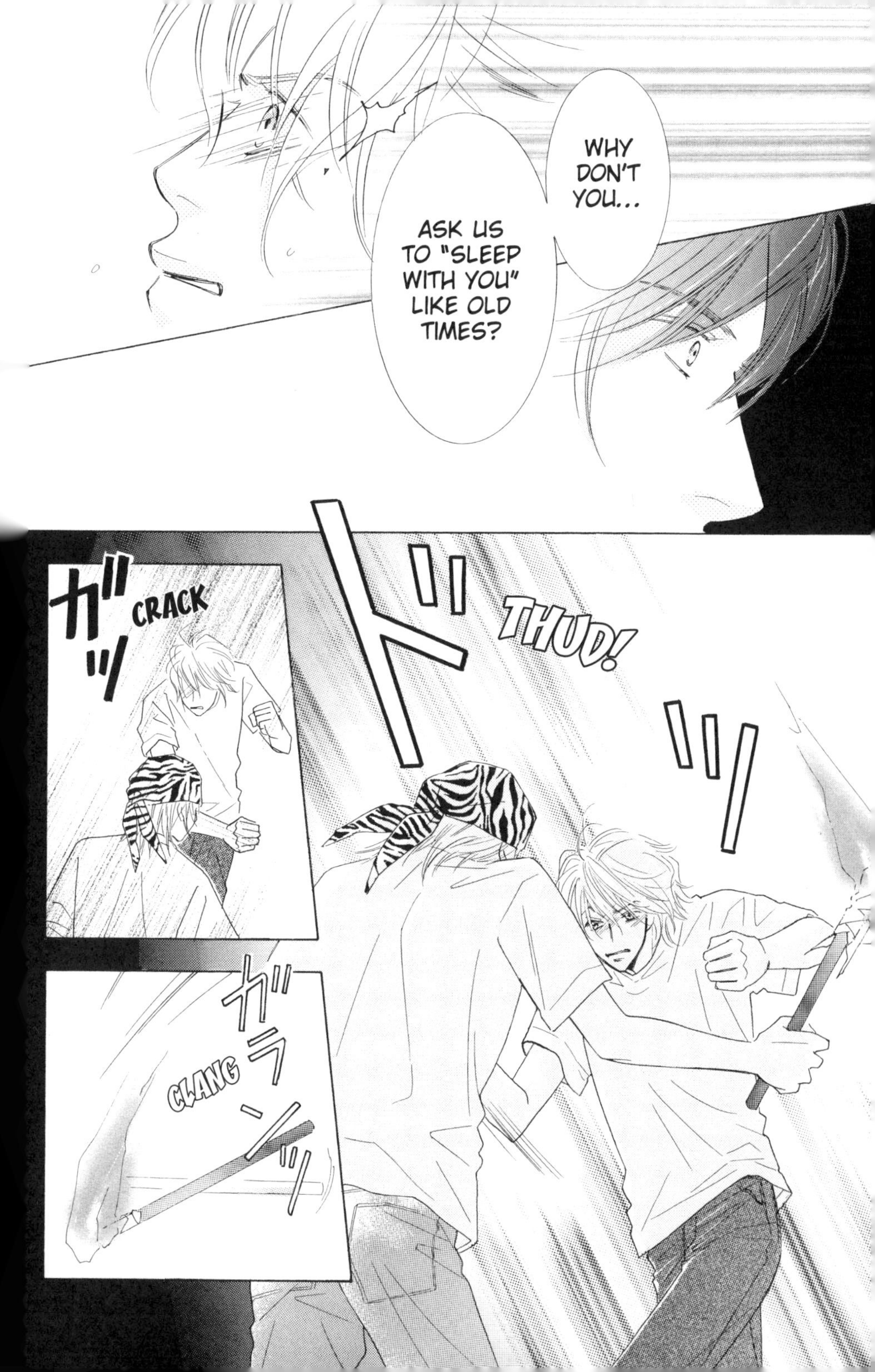
WHY DON'T YOU...
ASK US TO "SLEEP WITH YOU" LIKE OLD TIMES?
THUD!
CRACK
CLANG

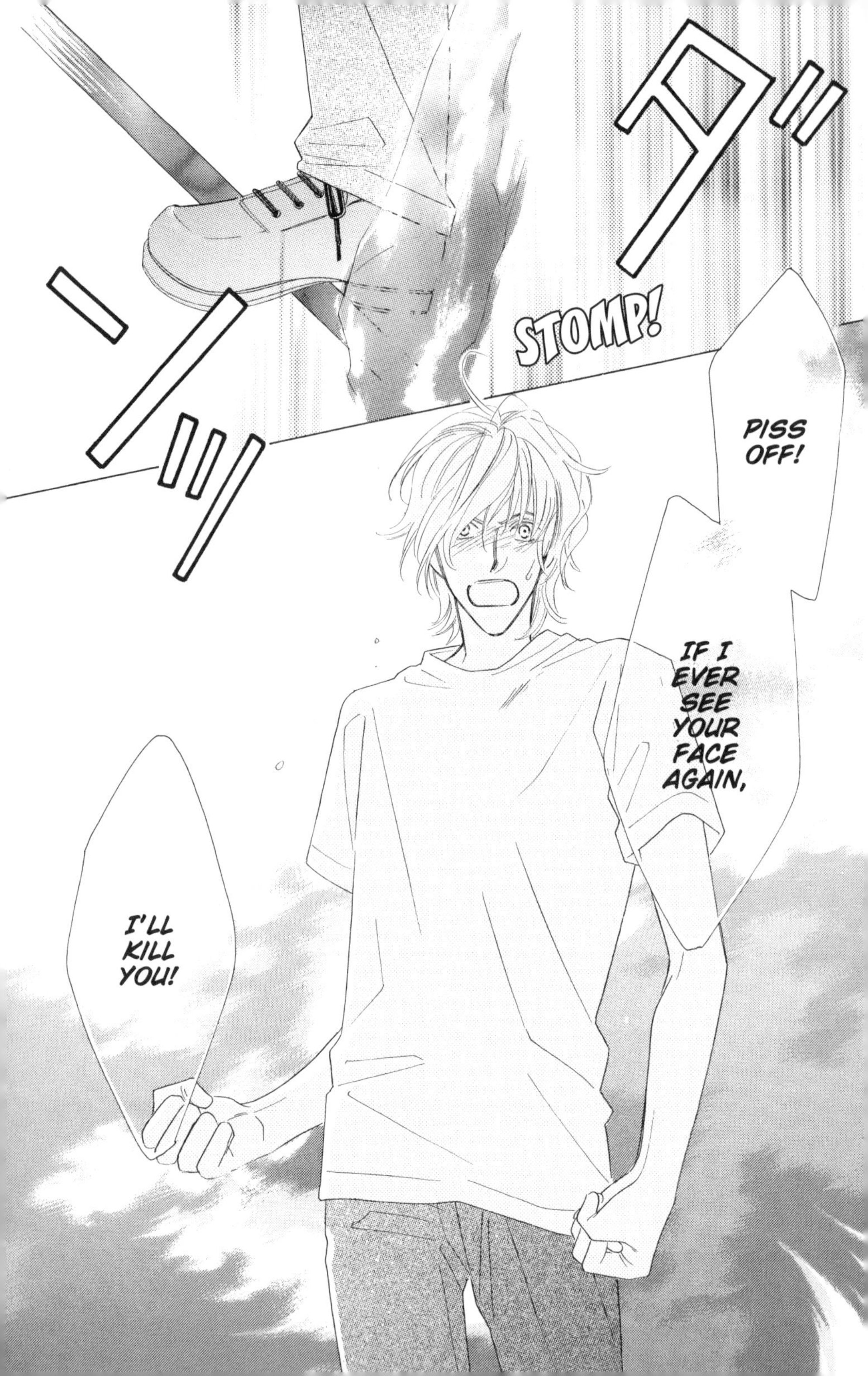

ダーン
STOMP!
ジ
PISS OFF!
IF I EVER SEE YOUR FACE AGAIN,
I'LL KILL YOU!

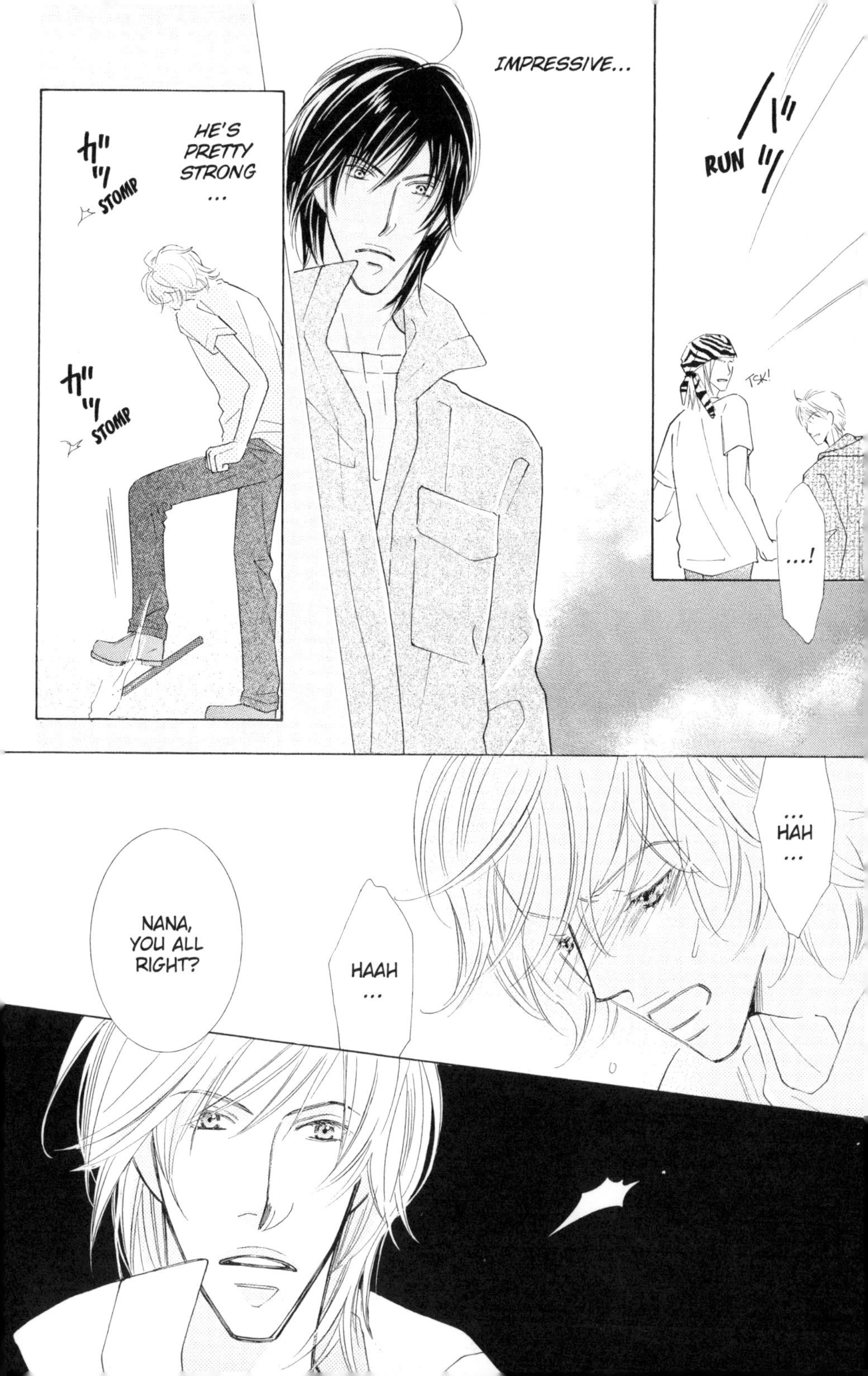
RUN
TSK!
...!
IMPRESSIVE...
HE'S PRETTY STRONG ...
ガッ STOMP
ガッ STOMP
... HAH ...
HAAH ...
NANA, YOU ALL RIGHT?

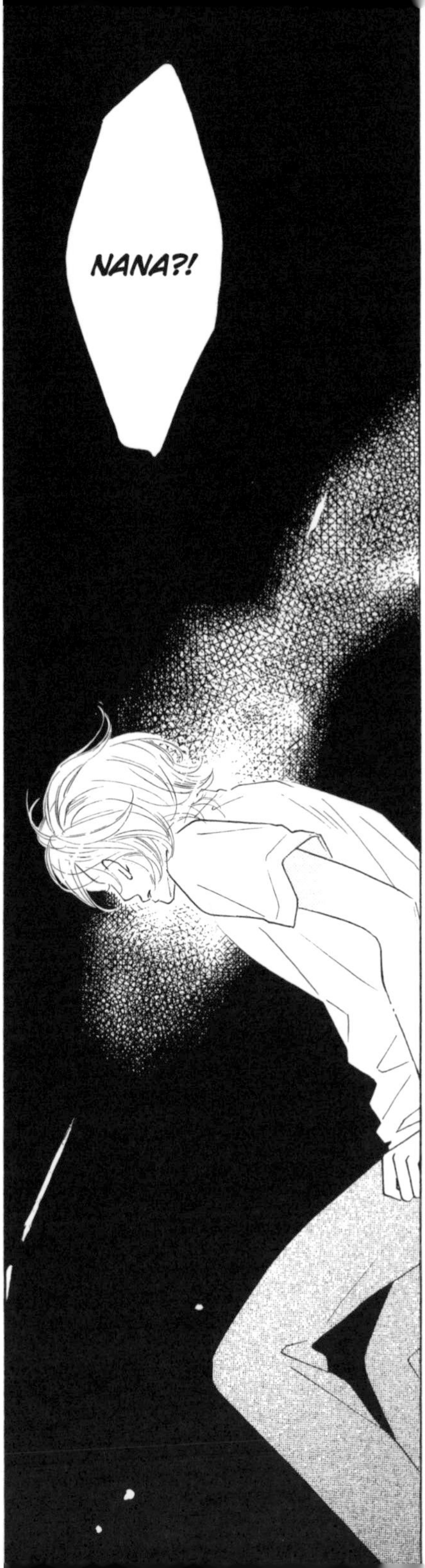
NANA?!
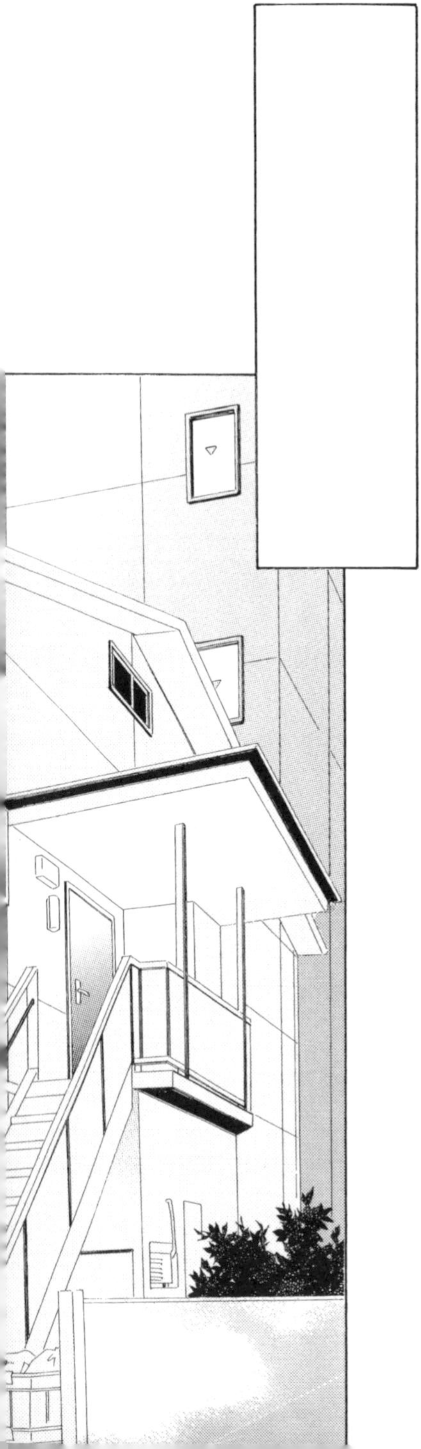

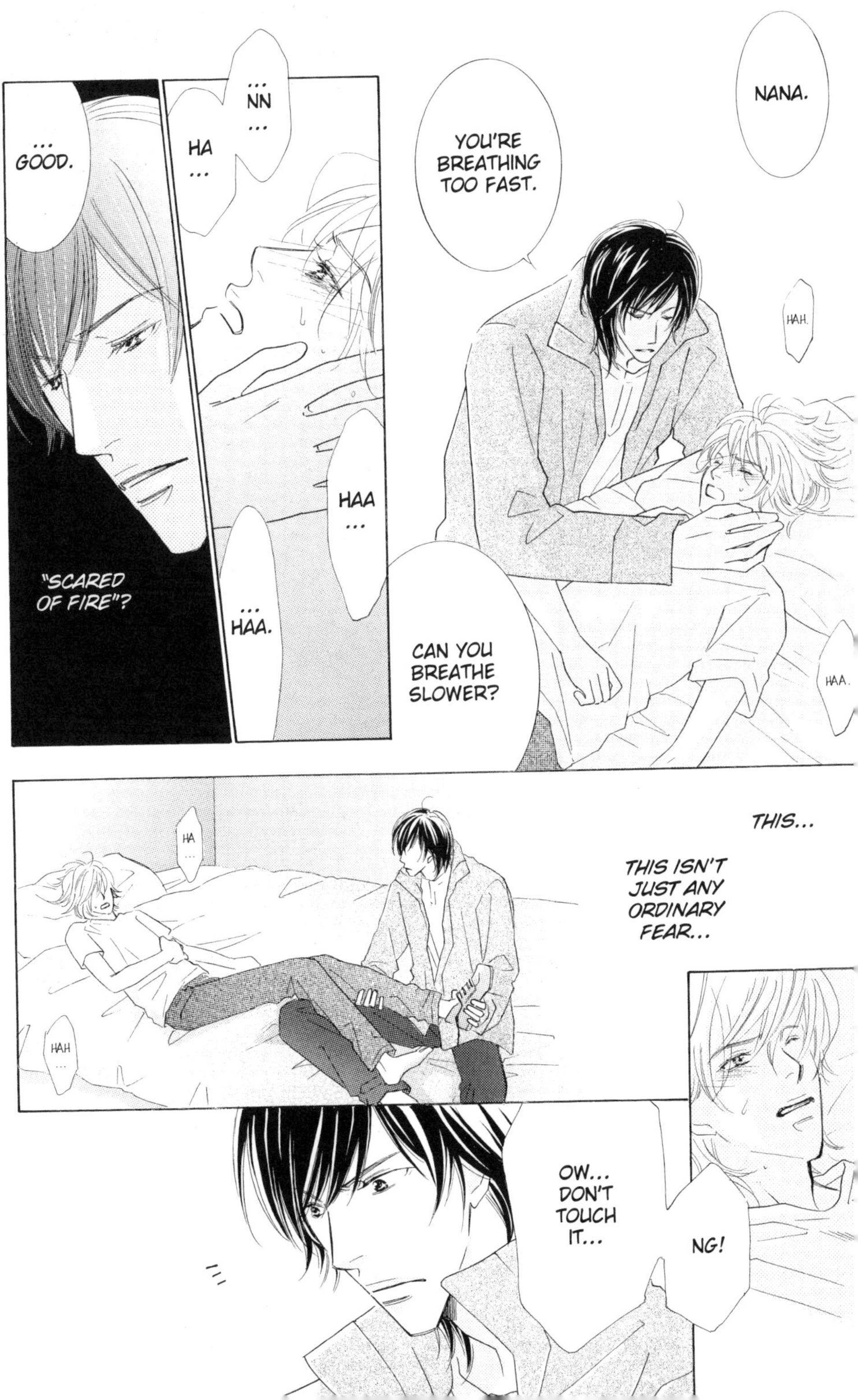
NANA.
YOU'RE BREATHING TOO FAST.
HAH.
CAN YOU BREATHE SLOWER?
HAA.
...NN...
HA...
HAA...
...HAA.
...GOOD.
"SCARED OF FIRE"?
THIS...
THIS ISN'T JUST ANY ORDINARY FEAR...
HA...
HAH...
NG!
OW... DON'T TOUCH IT...

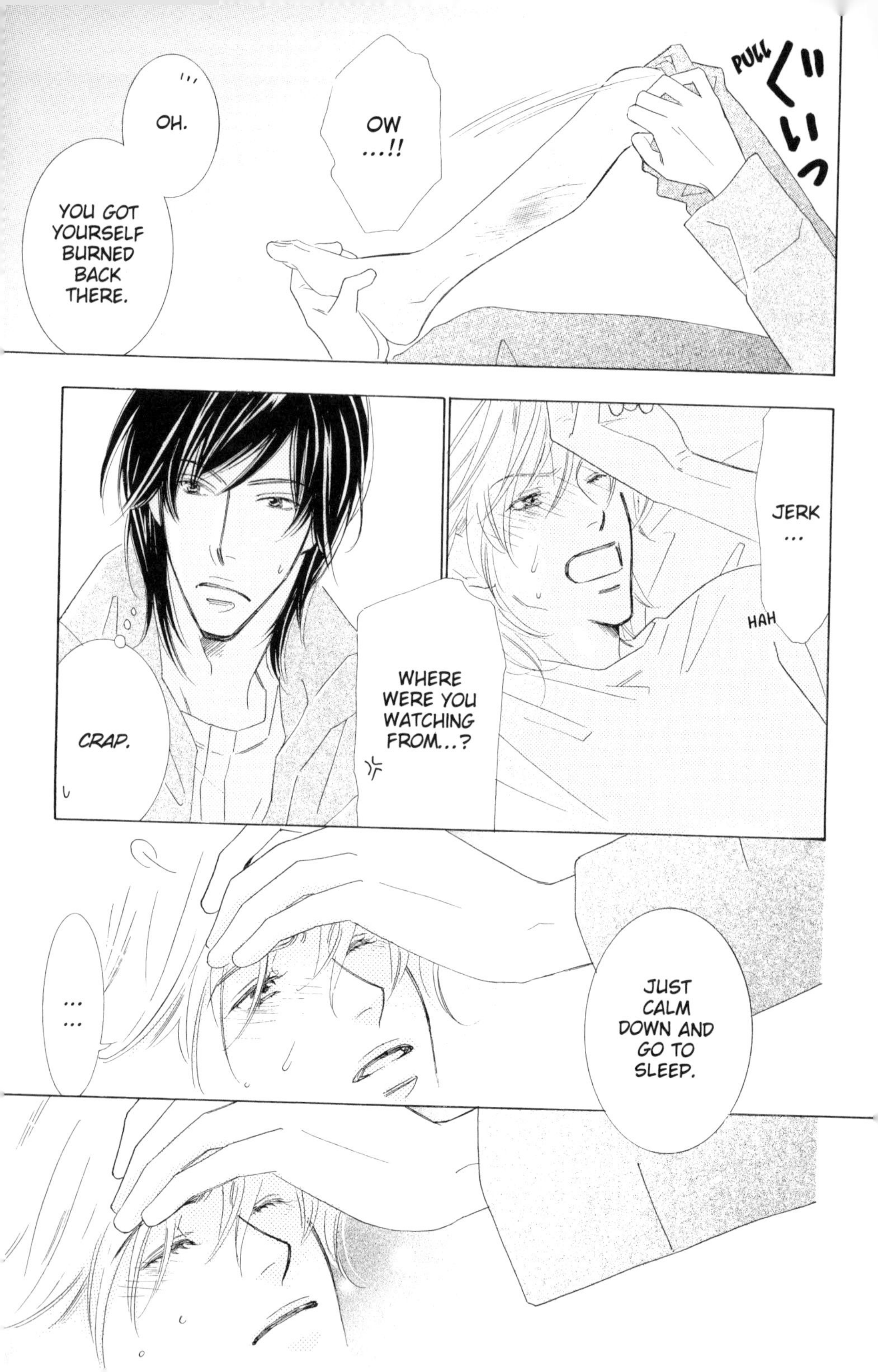
PULL
OW ...!!
OH.
YOU GOT YOURSELF BURNED BACK THERE.
JERK ...
HAH
WHERE WERE YOU WATCHING FROM...?
CRAP.
JUST CALM DOWN AND GO TO SLEEP.
... ...

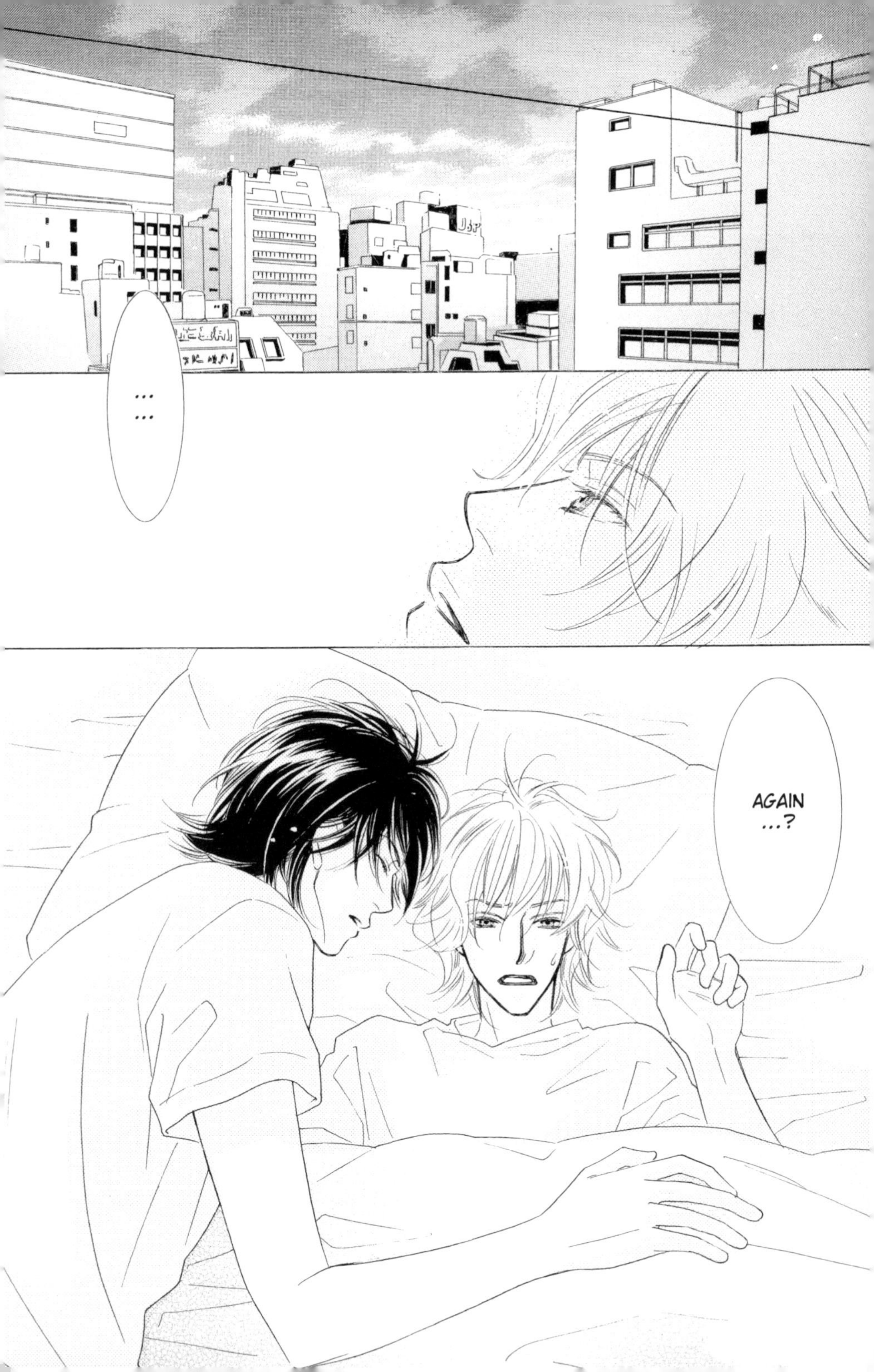
……
AGAIN …?

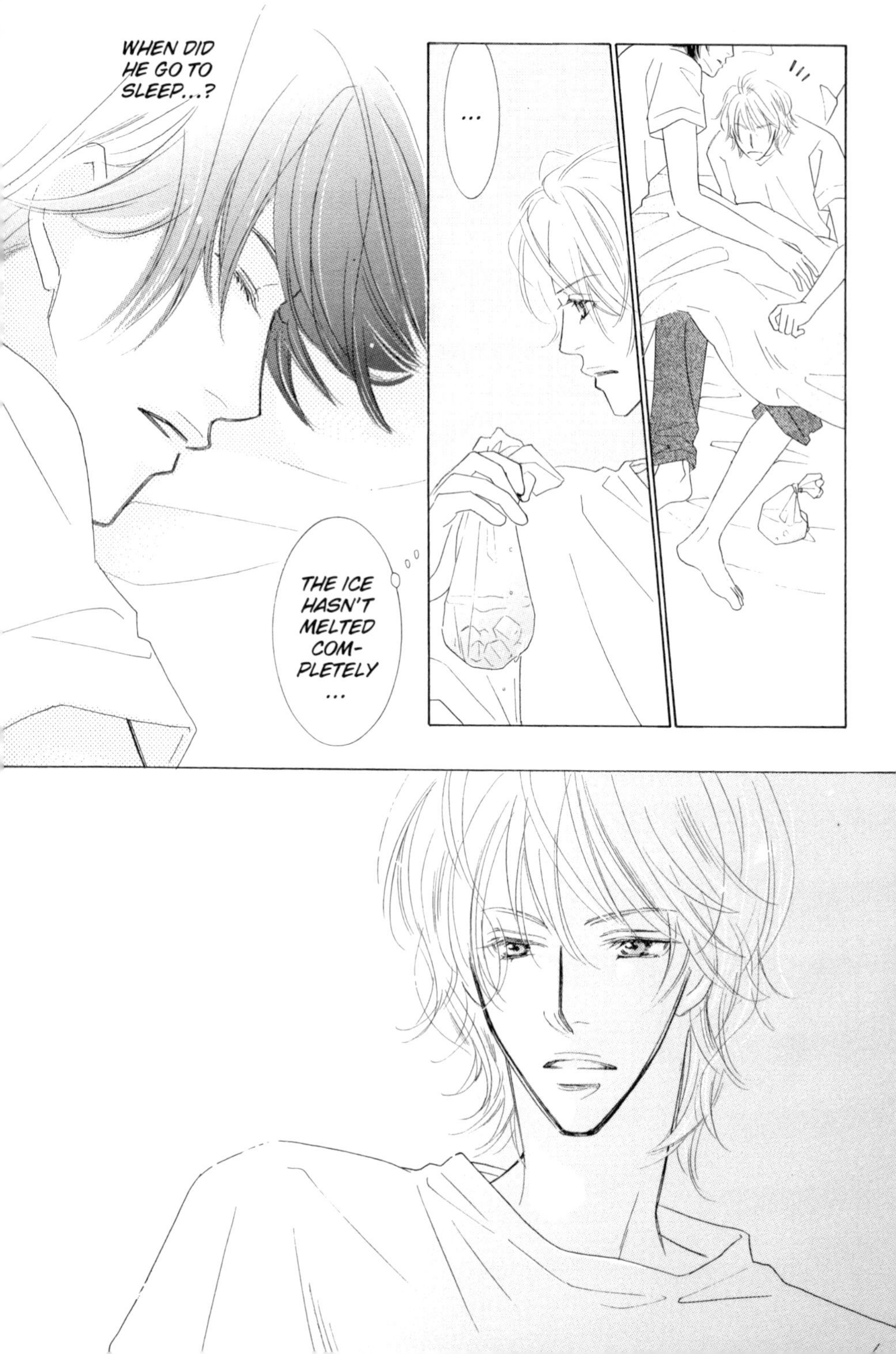
...
THE ICE HASN'T MELTED COMPLETELY...
WHEN DID HE GO TO SLEEP...?

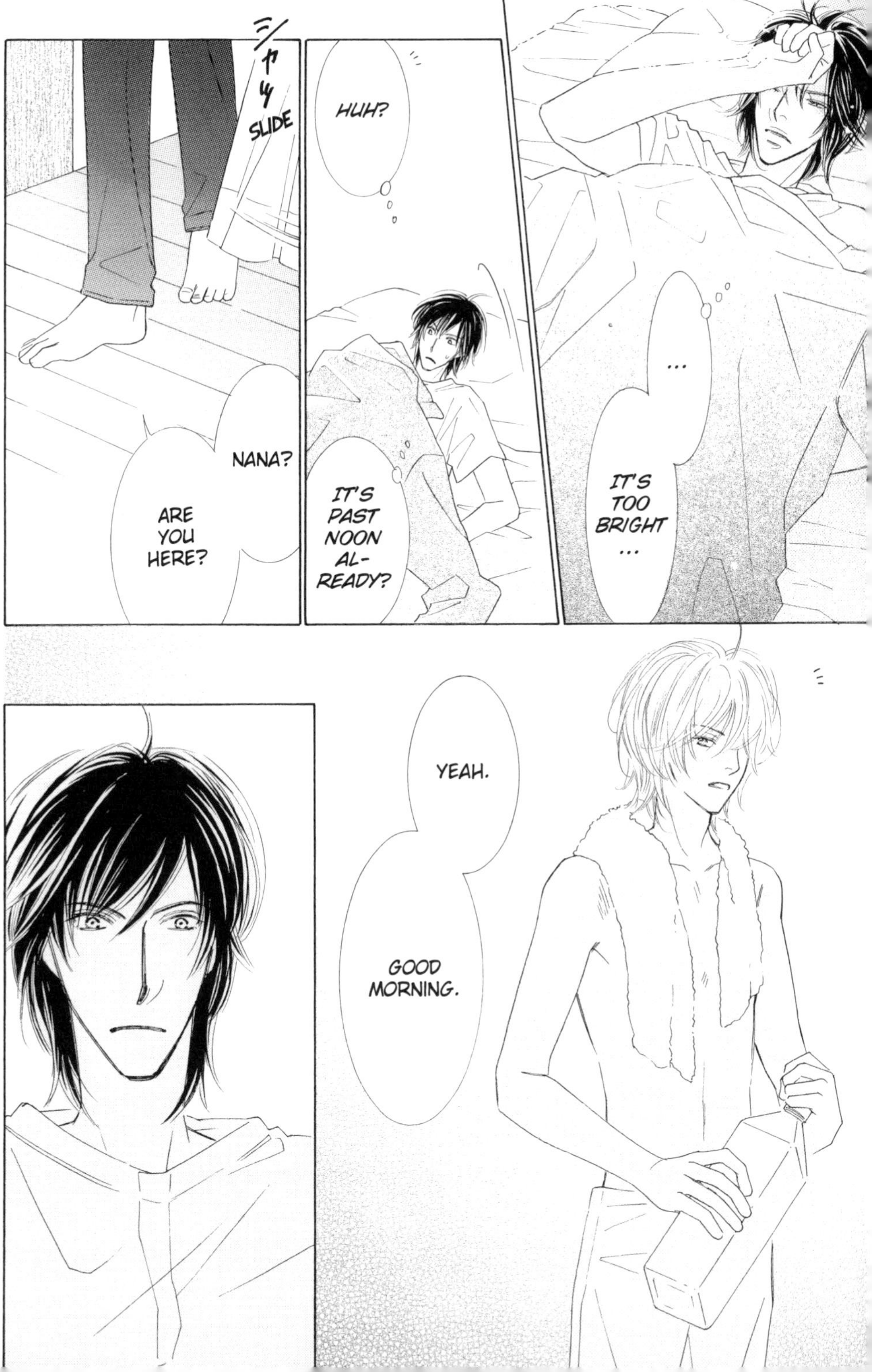
...
IT'S TOO BRIGHT ...
HUH?
IT'S PAST NOON AL-READY?
シャッ SLIDE
NANA?
ARE YOU HERE?
YEAH.
GOOD MORNING.

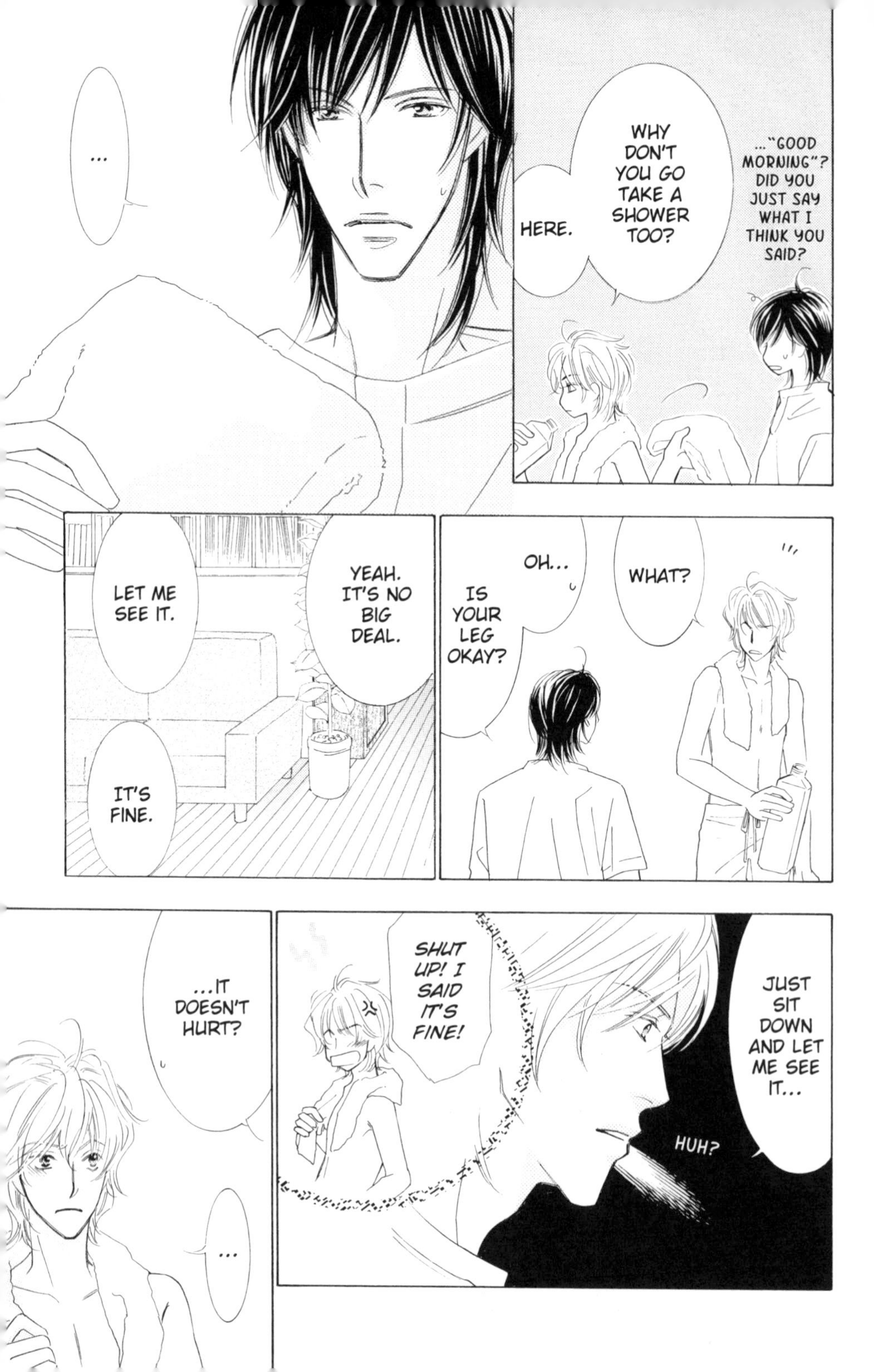
..."GOOD MORNING"? DID YOU JUST SAY WHAT I THINK YOU SAID?
WHY DON'T YOU GO TAKE A SHOWER TOO?
HERE.
...
WHAT?
OH...
IS YOUR LEG OKAY?
YEAH. IT'S NO BIG DEAL.
LET ME SEE IT.
IT'S FINE.
JUST SIT DOWN AND LET ME SEE IT...
HUH?
SHUT UP! I SAID IT'S FINE!
...IT DOESN'T HURT?
...

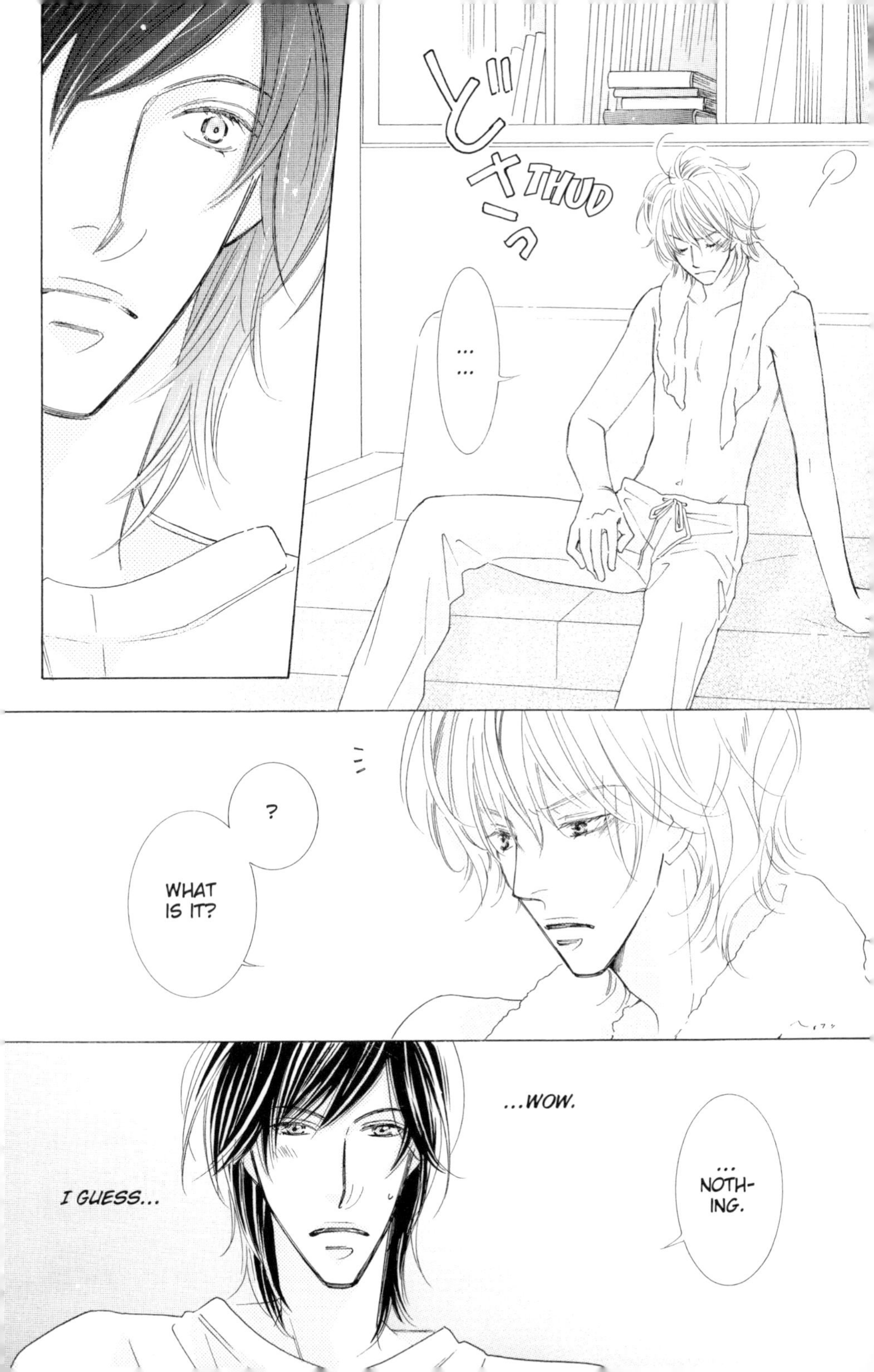

どさっ
THUD
……
?
WHAT IS IT?
... NOTH-ING.
...WOW.
I GUESS...

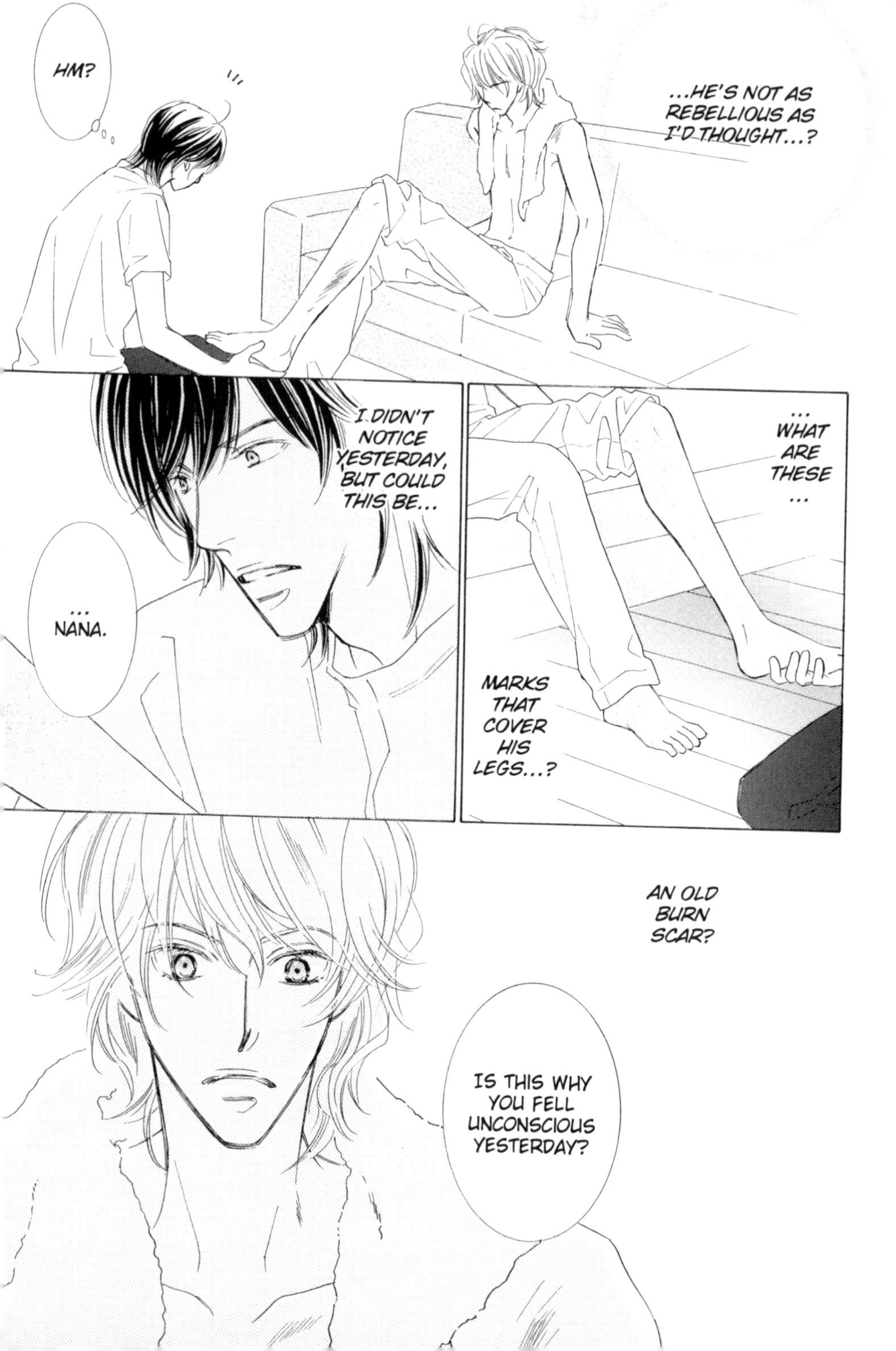
...HE'S NOT AS REBELLIOUS AS I'D THOUGHT...?
HM?
...WHAT ARE THESE...
MARKS THAT COVER HIS LEGS...?
I DIDN'T NOTICE YESTERDAY, BUT COULD THIS BE...
...NANA.
AN OLD BURN SCAR?
IS THIS WHY YOU FELL UNCONSCIOUS YESTERDAY?

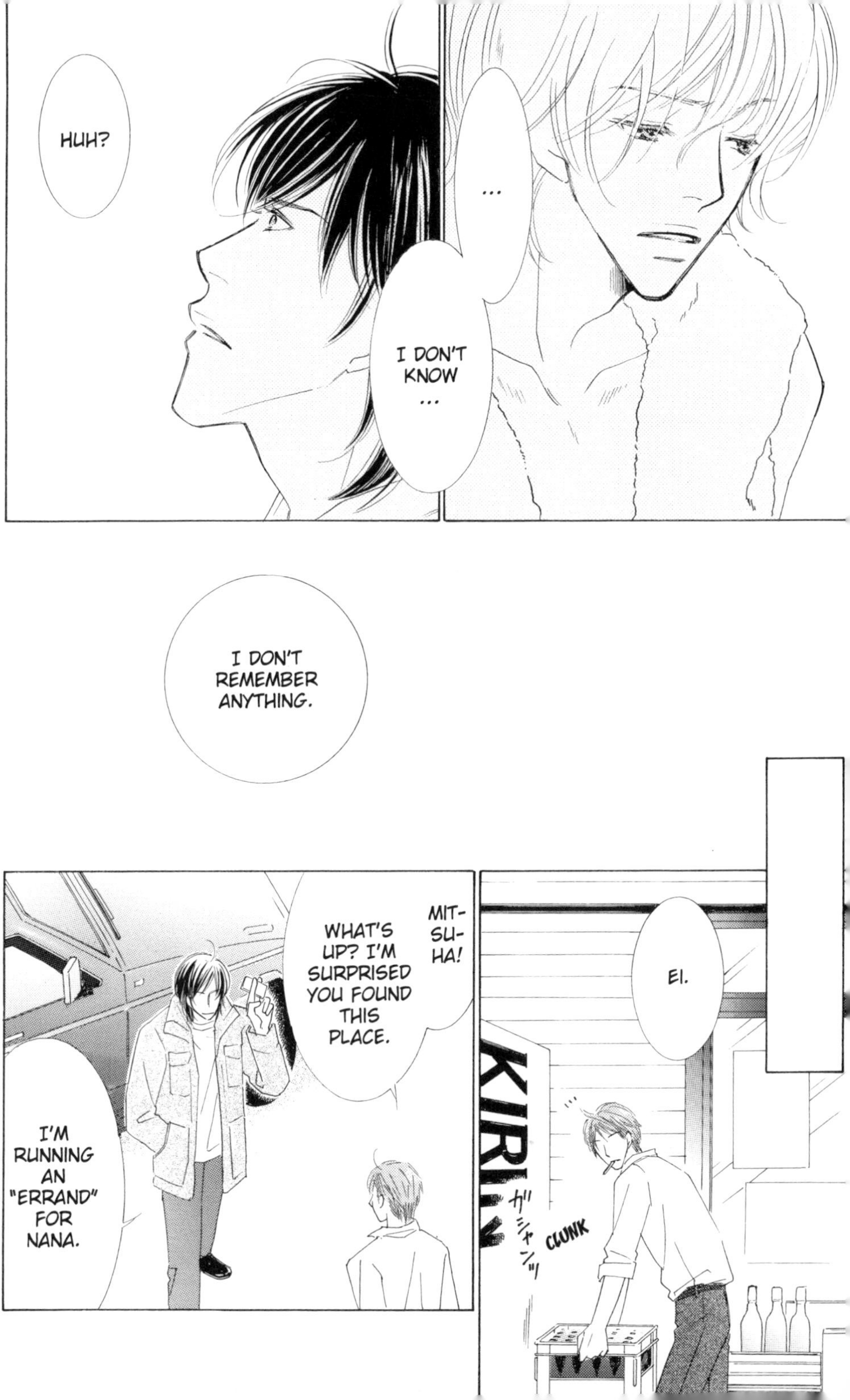
...
I DON'T KNOW ...
HUH?
I DON'T REMEMBER ANYTHING.
EI.
CLUNK
MIT-SU-HA!
WHAT'S UP? I'M SURPRISED YOU FOUND THIS PLACE.
I'M RUNNING AN "ERRAND" FOR NANA.

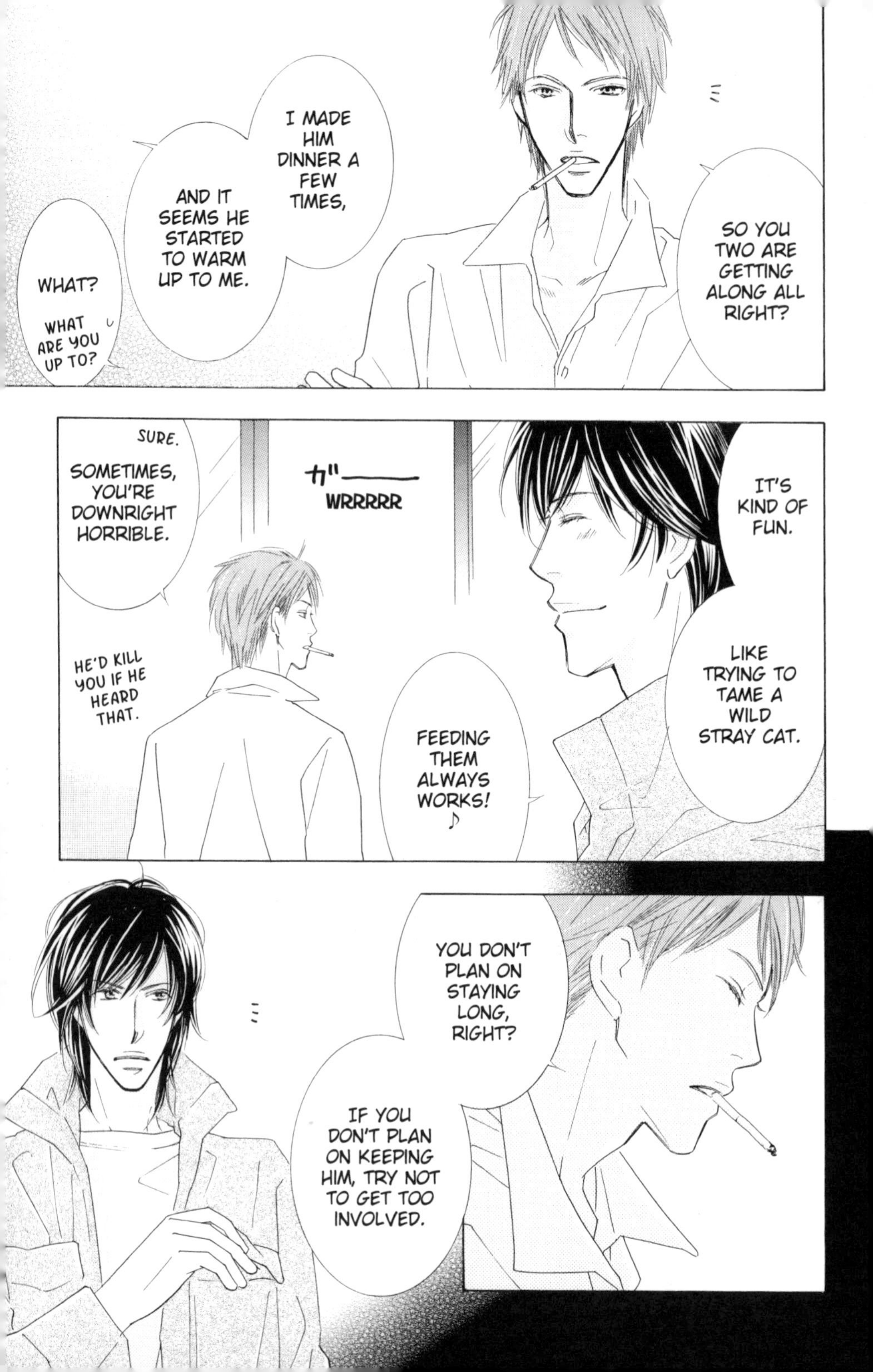
SO YOU TWO ARE GETTING ALONG ALL RIGHT?
I MADE HIM DINNER A FEW TIMES,
AND IT SEEMS HE STARTED TO WARM UP TO ME.
WHAT?
WHAT ARE YOU UP TO?
IT'S KIND OF FUN.
LIKE TRYING TO TAME A WILD STRAY CAT.
FEEDING THEM ALWAYS WORKS! ♪
ガ"——
WRRRRR
SURE.
SOMETIMES, YOU'RE DOWNRIGHT HORRIBLE.
HE'D KILL YOU IF HE HEARD THAT.
YOU DON'T PLAN ON STAYING LONG, RIGHT?
IF YOU DON'T PLAN ON KEEPING HIM, TRY NOT TO GET TOO INVOLVED.

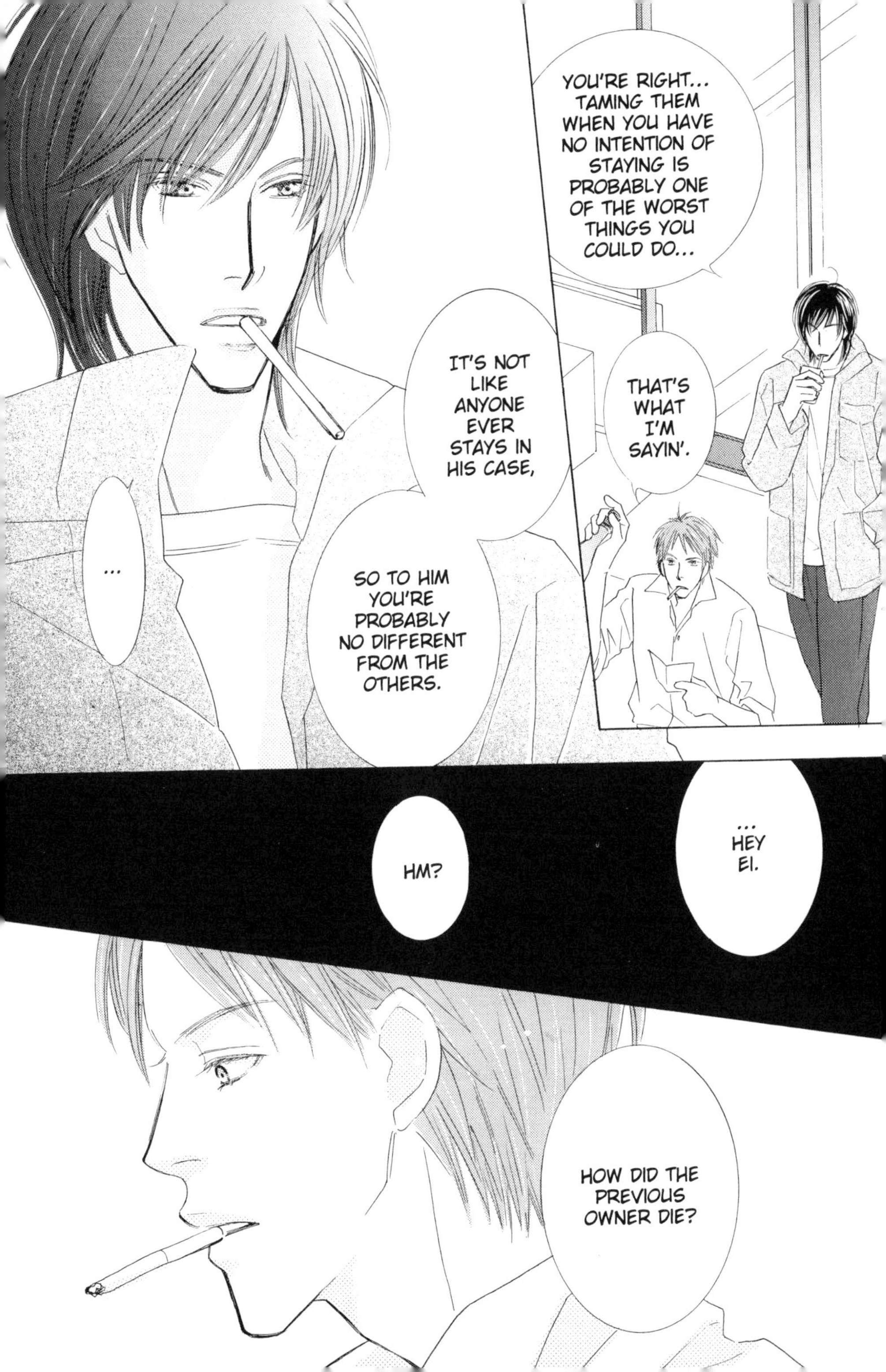
YOU'RE RIGHT... TAMING THEM WHEN YOU HAVE NO INTENTION OF STAYING IS PROBABLY ONE OF THE WORST THINGS YOU COULD DO...
THAT'S WHAT I'M SAYIN'.
IT'S NOT LIKE ANYONE EVER STAYS IN HIS CASE,
SO TO HIM YOU'RE PROBABLY NO DIFFERENT FROM THE OTHERS.
...
... HEY EI.
HM?
HOW DID THE PREVIOUS OWNER DIE?

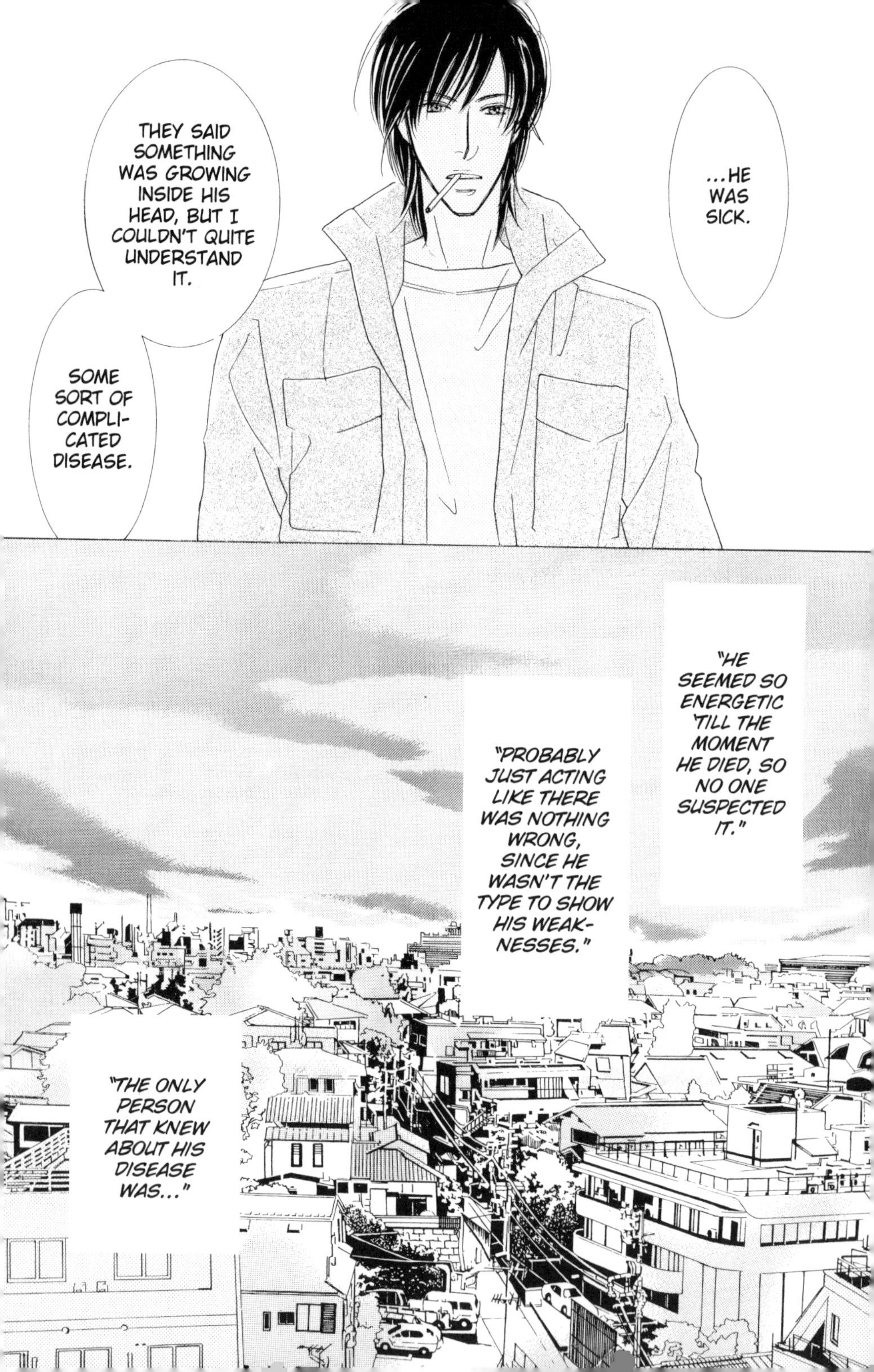
...HE WAS SICK.
THEY SAID SOMETHING WAS GROWING INSIDE HIS HEAD, BUT I COULDN'T QUITE UNDERSTAND IT.
SOME SORT OF COMPLI-CATED DISEASE.
"HE SEEMED SO ENERGETIC 'TILL THE MOMENT HE DIED, SO NO ONE SUSPECTED IT."
"PROBABLY JUST ACTING LIKE THERE WAS NOTHING WRONG, SINCE HE WASN'T THE TYPE TO SHOW HIS WEAK-NESSES."
"THE ONLY PERSON THAT KNEW ABOUT HIS DISEASE WAS..."

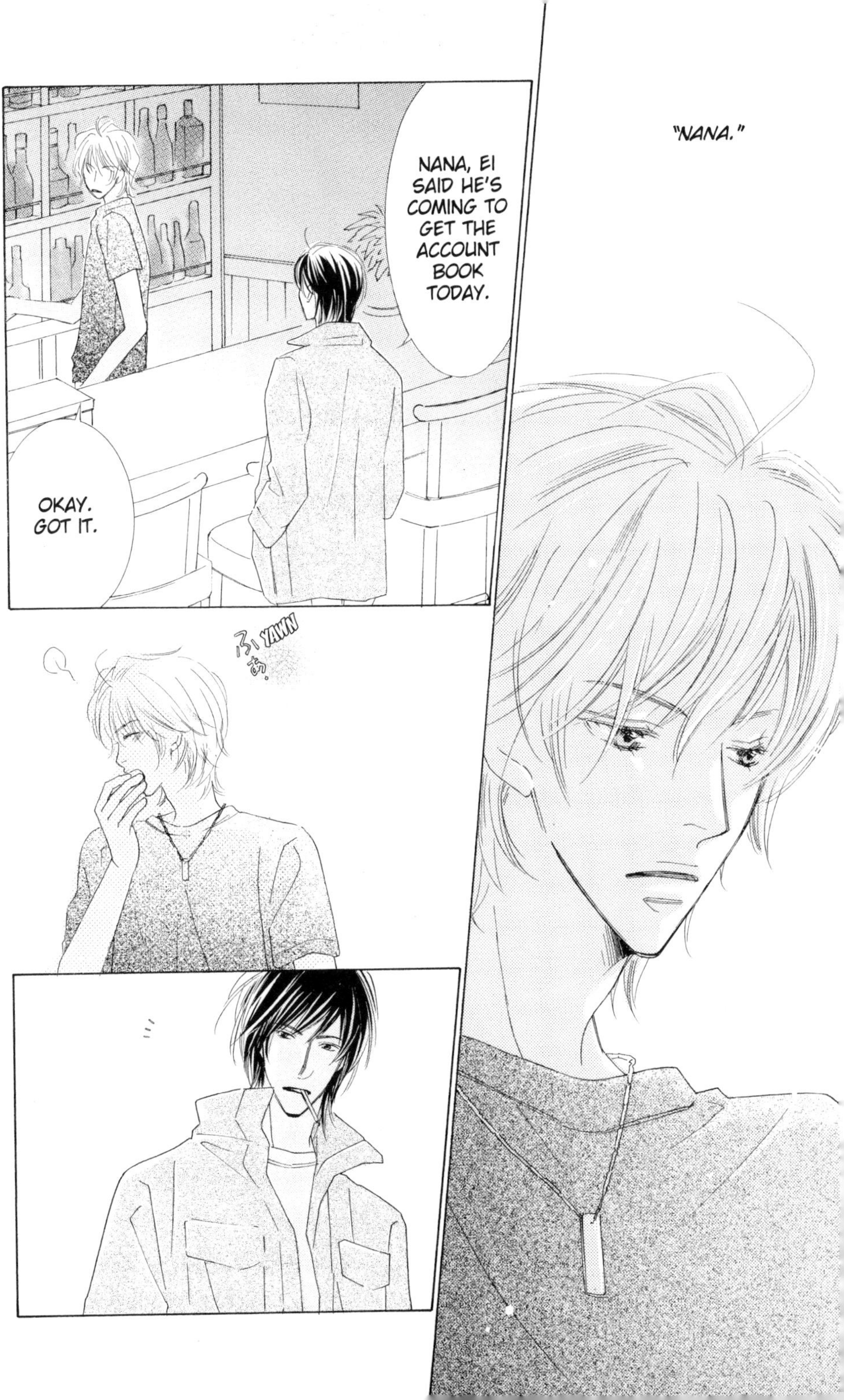
"NANA."
NANA, EI SAID HE'S COMING TO GET THE ACCOUNT BOOK TODAY.
OKAY. GOT IT.
YAWN

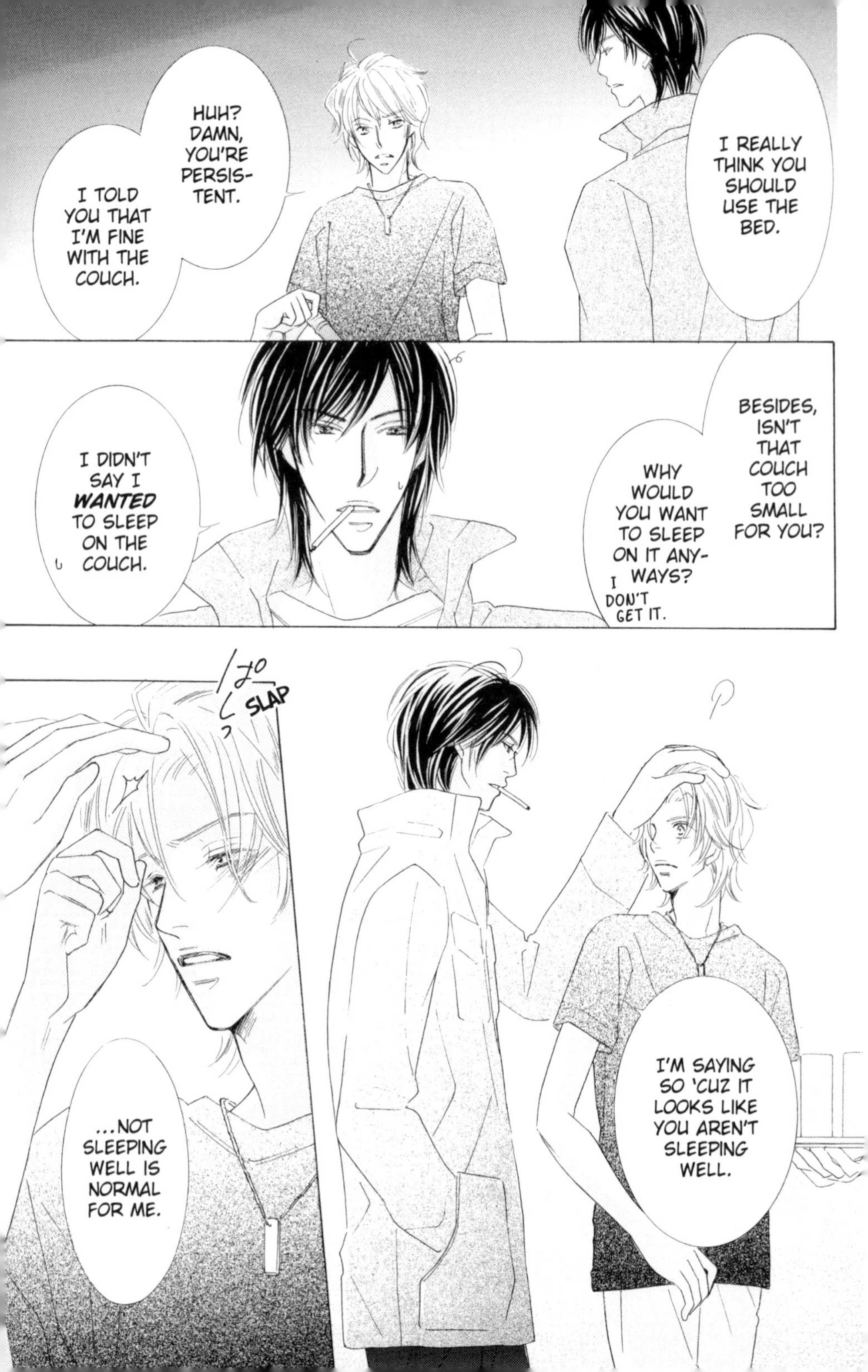
I REALLY THINK YOU SHOULD USE THE BED.
HUH? DAMN, YOU'RE PERSIST-TENT.
I TOLD YOU THAT I'M FINE WITH THE COUCH.
BESIDES, ISN'T THAT COUCH TOO SMALL FOR YOU?
WHY WOULD YOU WANT TO SLEEP ON IT ANY-WAYS?
I DON'T GET IT.
I DIDN'T SAY I WANTED TO SLEEP ON THE COUCH.
I'M SAYING SO 'CUZ IT LOOKS LIKE YOU AREN'T SLEEPING WELL.
SLAP
...NOT SLEEPING WELL IS NORMAL FOR ME.

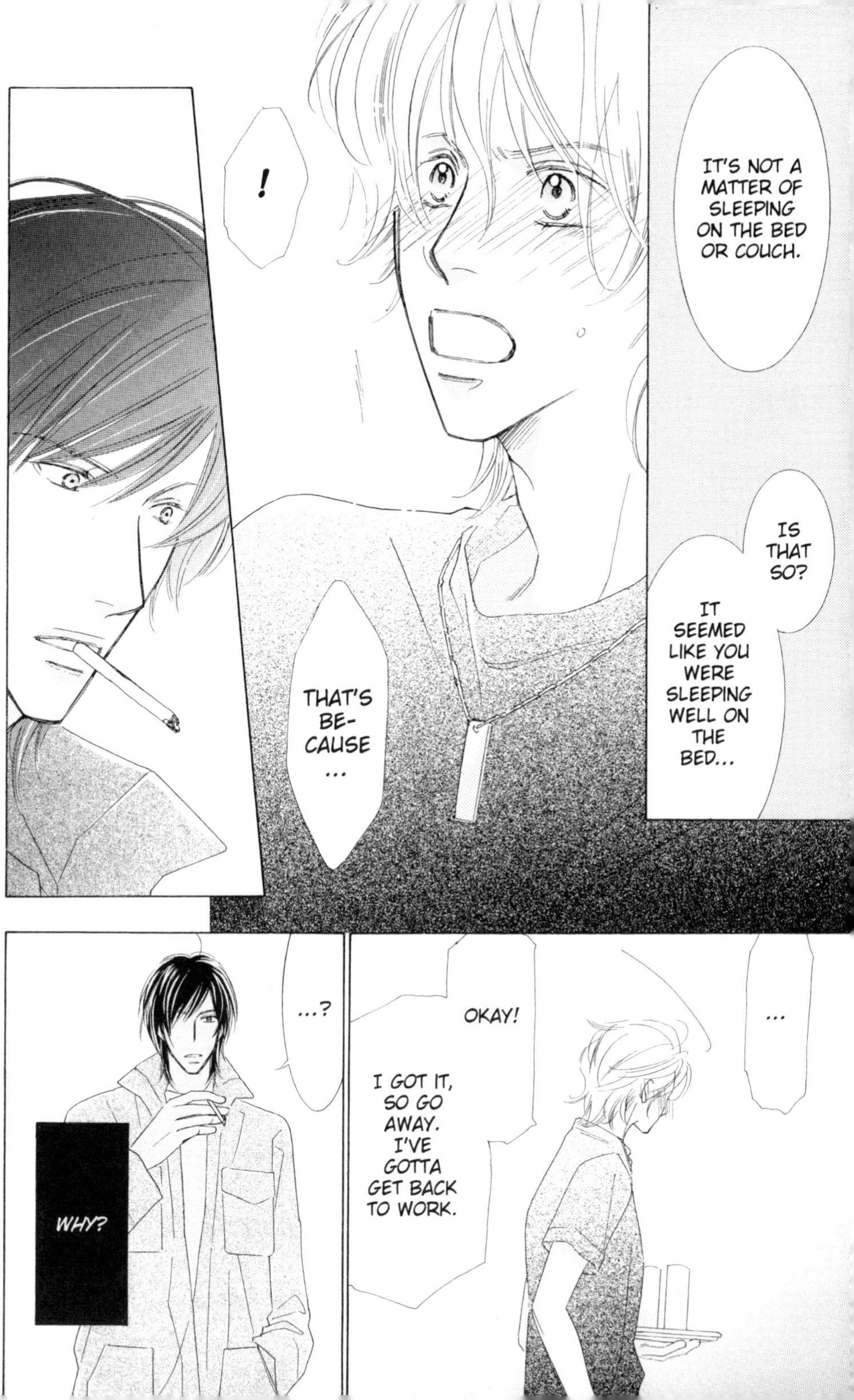
IT'S NOT A MATTER OF SLEEPING ON THE BED OR COUCH.
IS THAT SO?
IT SEEMED LIKE YOU WERE SLEEPING WELL ON THE BED...
!
THAT'S BE-CAUSE ...
...
OKAY!
I GOT IT, SO GO AWAY. I'VE GOTTA GET BACK TO WORK.
...?
WHY?

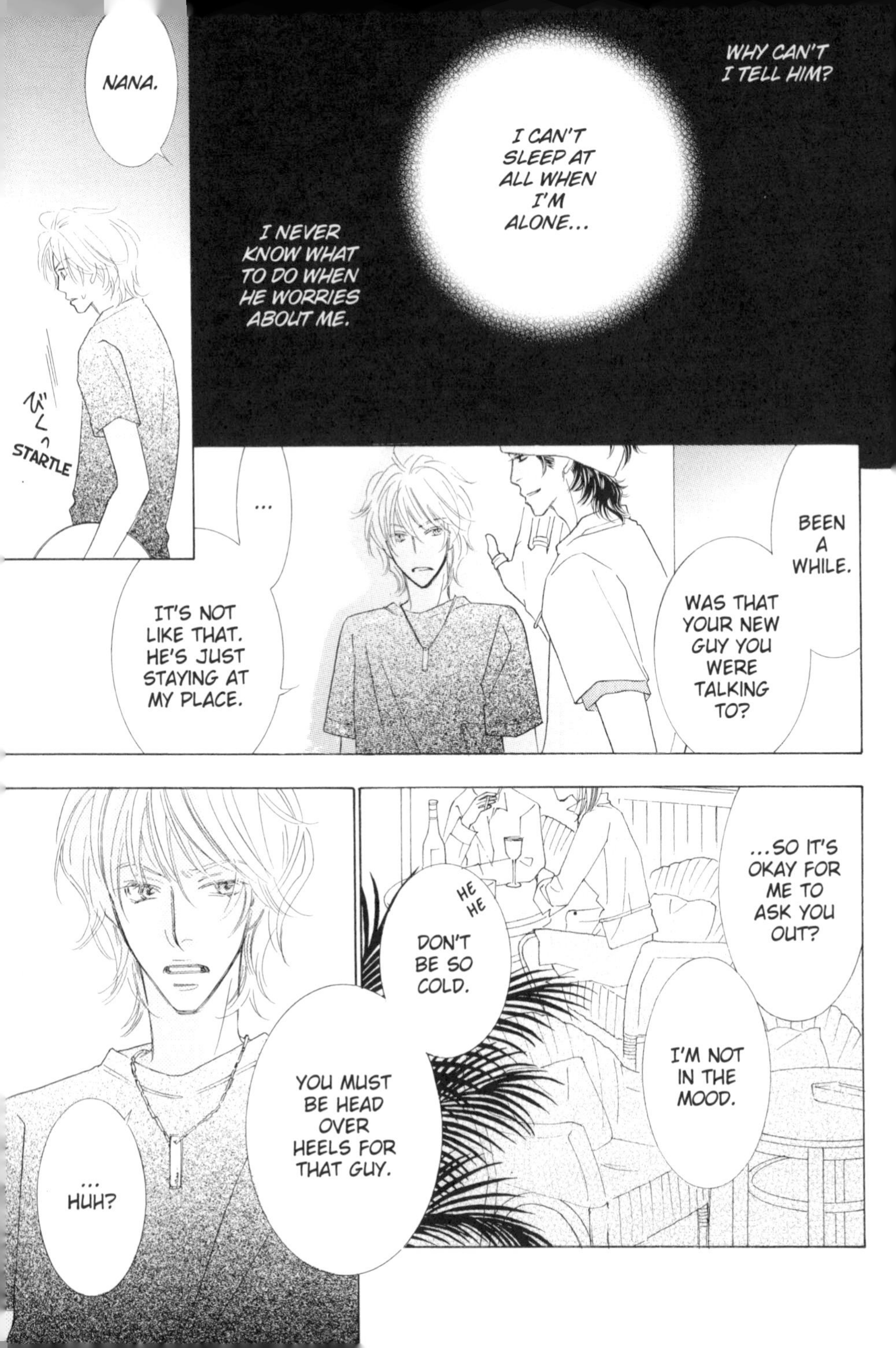
WHY CAN'T I TELL HIM?
I CAN'T SLEEP AT ALL WHEN I'M ALONE...
I NEVER KNOW WHAT TO DO WHEN HE WORRIES ABOUT ME.
BEEN A WHILE.
WAS THAT YOUR NEW GUY YOU WERE TALKING TO?
...
IT'S NOT LIKE THAT. HE'S JUST STAYING AT MY PLACE.
NANA.
びくっ
STARTLE
...SO IT'S OKAY FOR ME TO ASK YOU OUT?
I'M NOT IN THE MOOD.
HE HE
DON'T BE SO COLD.
YOU MUST BE HEAD OVER HEELS FOR THAT GUY.
... HUH?

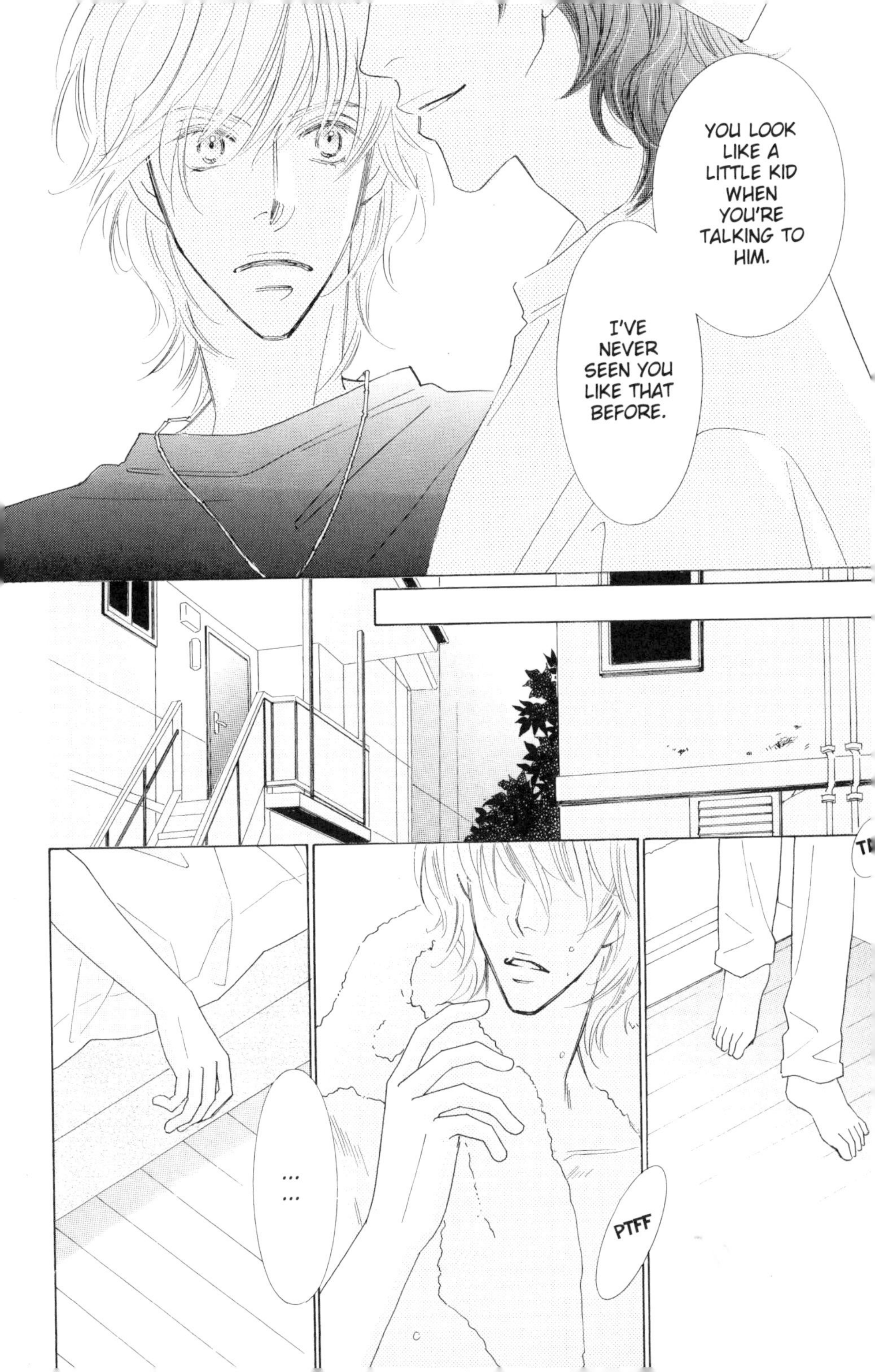
YOU LOOK LIKE A LITTLE KID WHEN YOU'RE TALKING TO HIM.
I'VE NEVER SEEN YOU LIKE THAT BEFORE.
PTFF
... ...

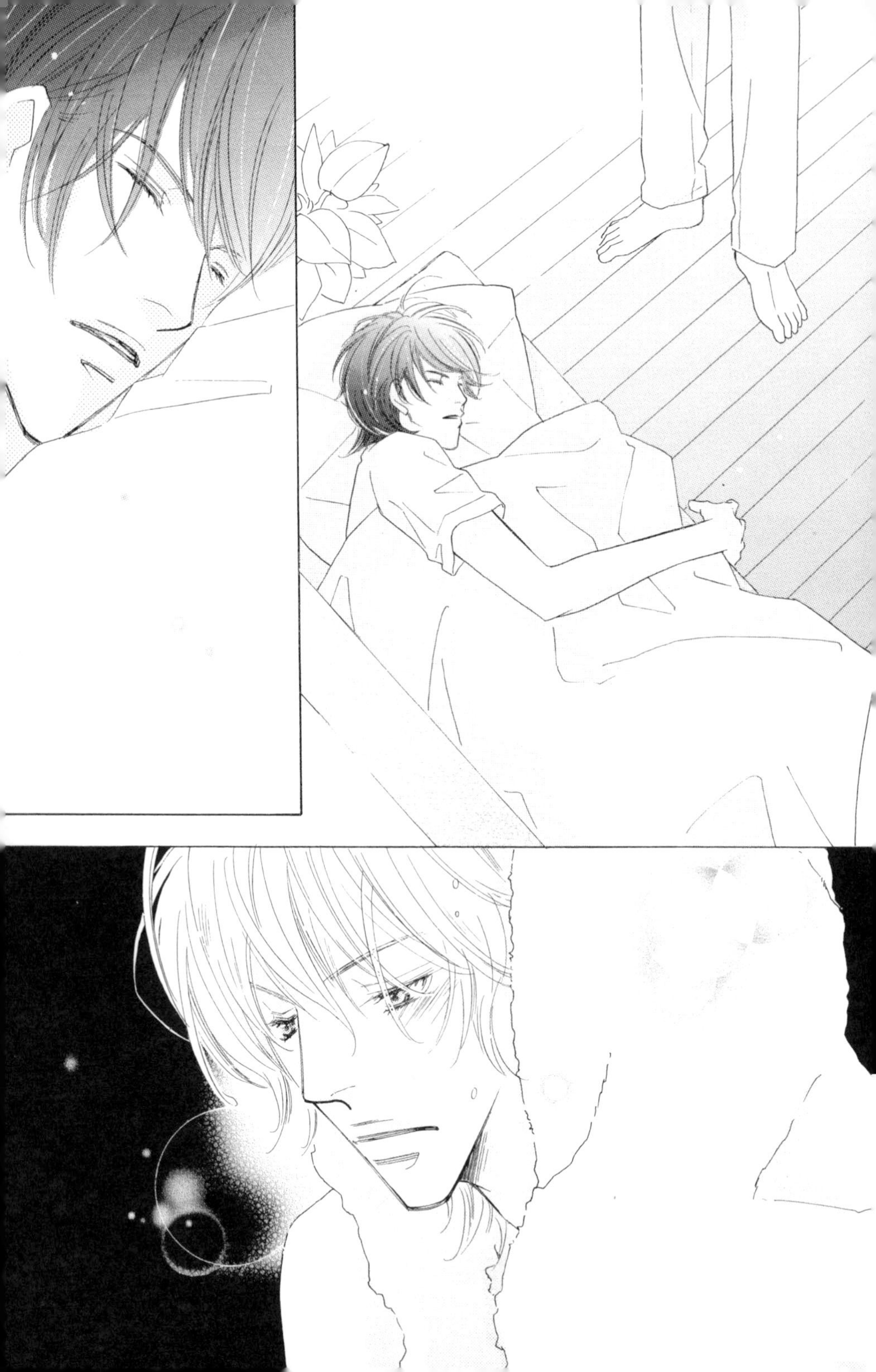

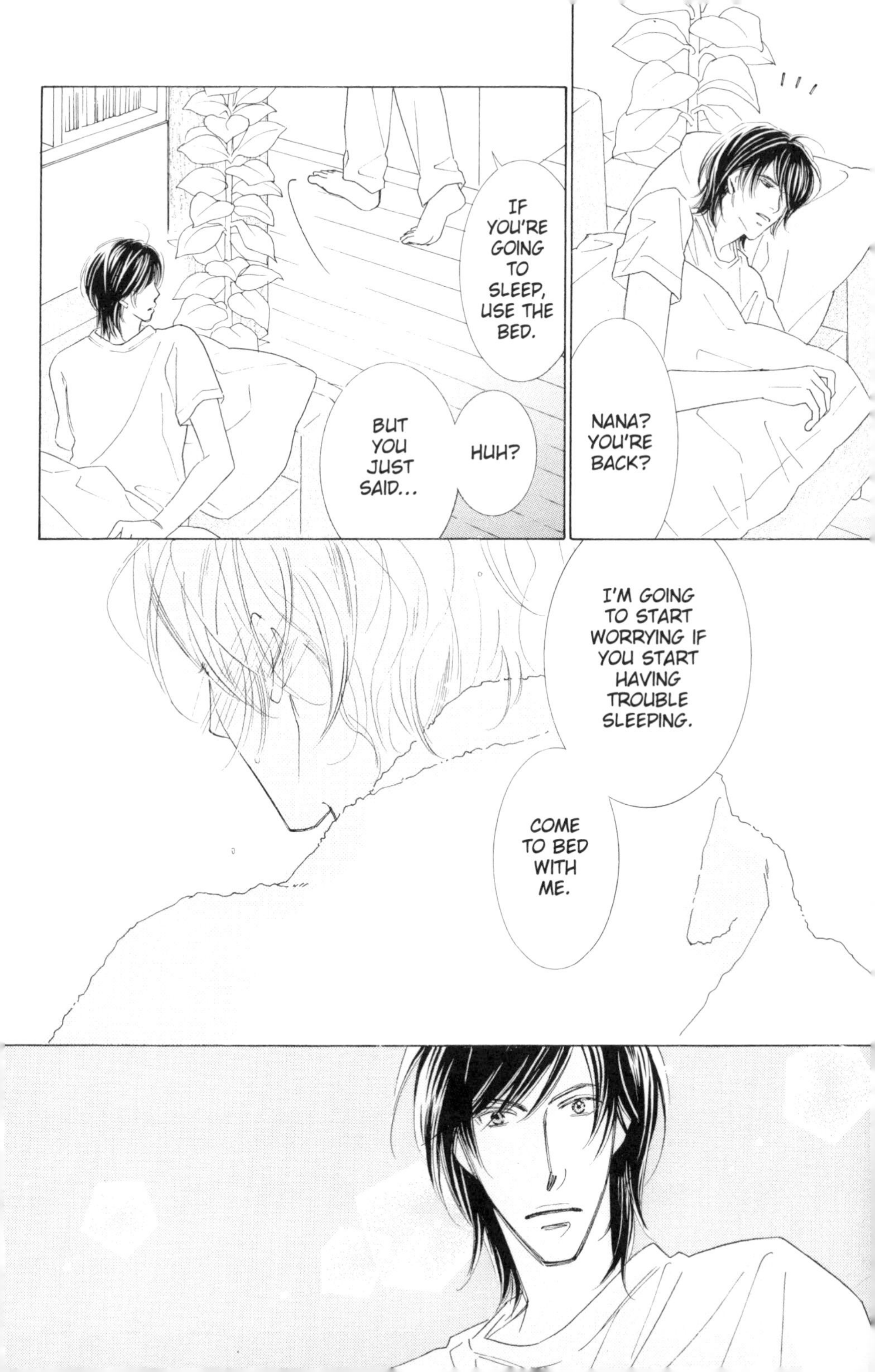
NANA? YOU'RE BACK?
IF YOU'RE GOING TO SLEEP, USE THE BED.
HUH?
BUT YOU JUST SAID...
I'M GOING TO START WORRYING IF YOU START HAVING TROUBLE SLEEPING.
COME TO BED WITH ME.

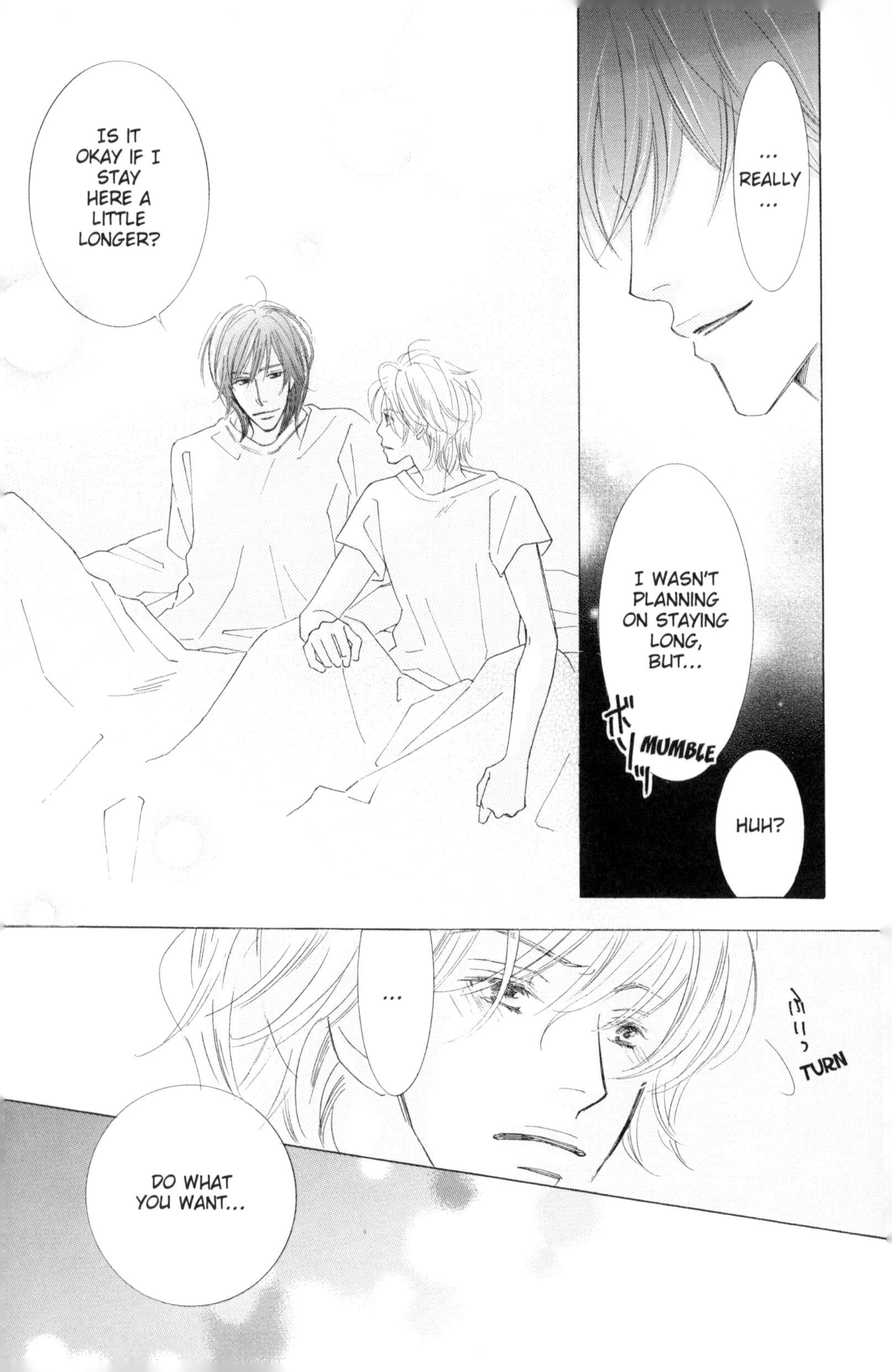
...REALLY...
I WASN'T PLANNING ON STAYING LONG, BUT...
MUMBLE
HUH?
IS IT OKAY IF I STAY HERE A LITTLE LONGER?
...
TURN
DO WHAT YOU WANT...

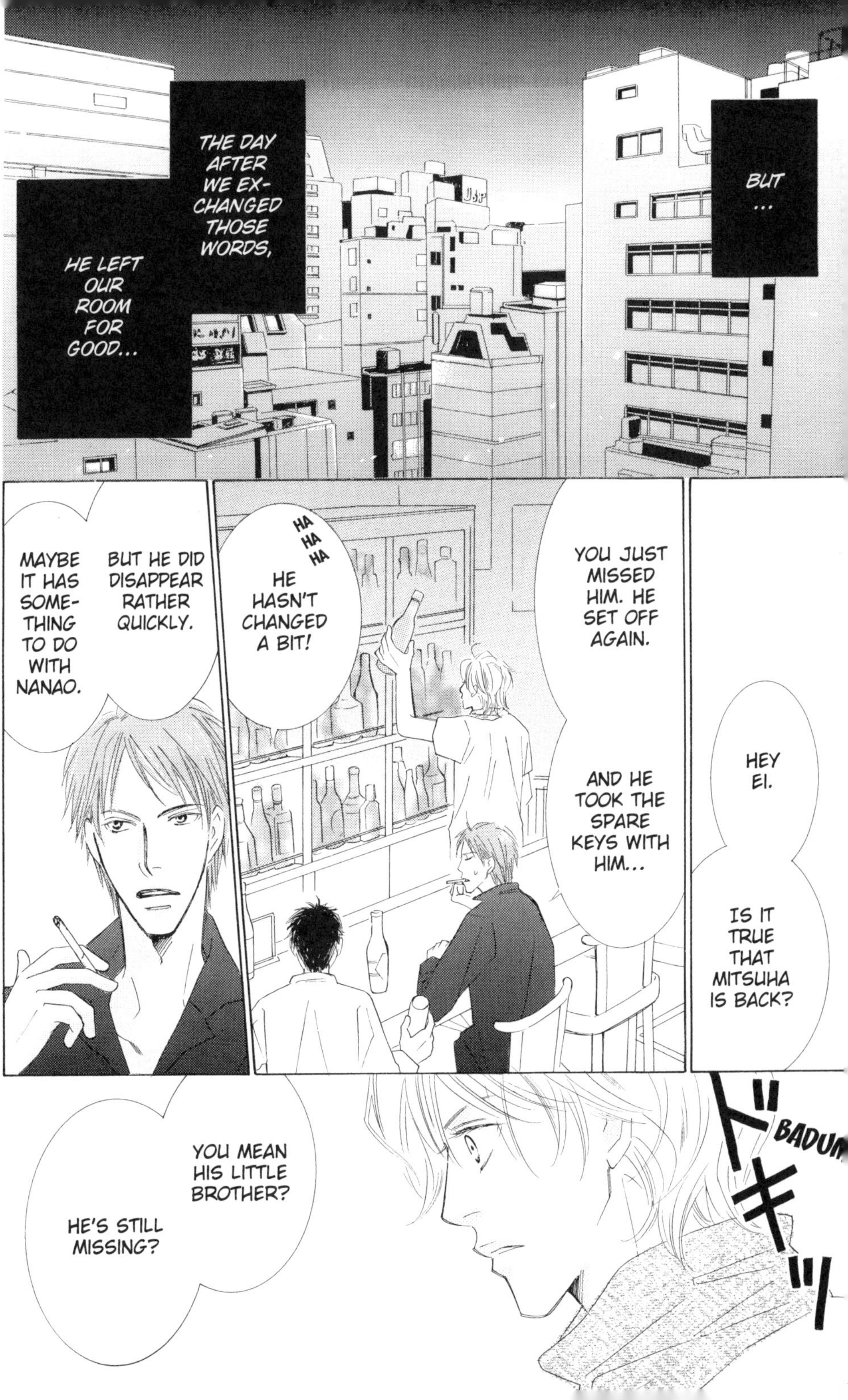
BUT …
THE DAY AFTER WE EX-CHANGED THOSE WORDS,
HE LEFT OUR ROOM FOR GOOD…
HEY EI.
IS IT TRUE THAT MITSUHA IS BACK?
YOU JUST MISSED HIM. HE SET OFF AGAIN.
AND HE TOOK THE SPARE KEYS WITH HIM…
HA HA HA
HE HASN'T CHANGED A BIT!
BUT HE DID DISAPPEAR RATHER QUICKLY.
MAYBE IT HAS SOME-THING TO DO WITH NANAO.
ドキッ
BADUM
YOU MEAN HIS LITTLE BROTHER?
HE'S STILL MISSING?

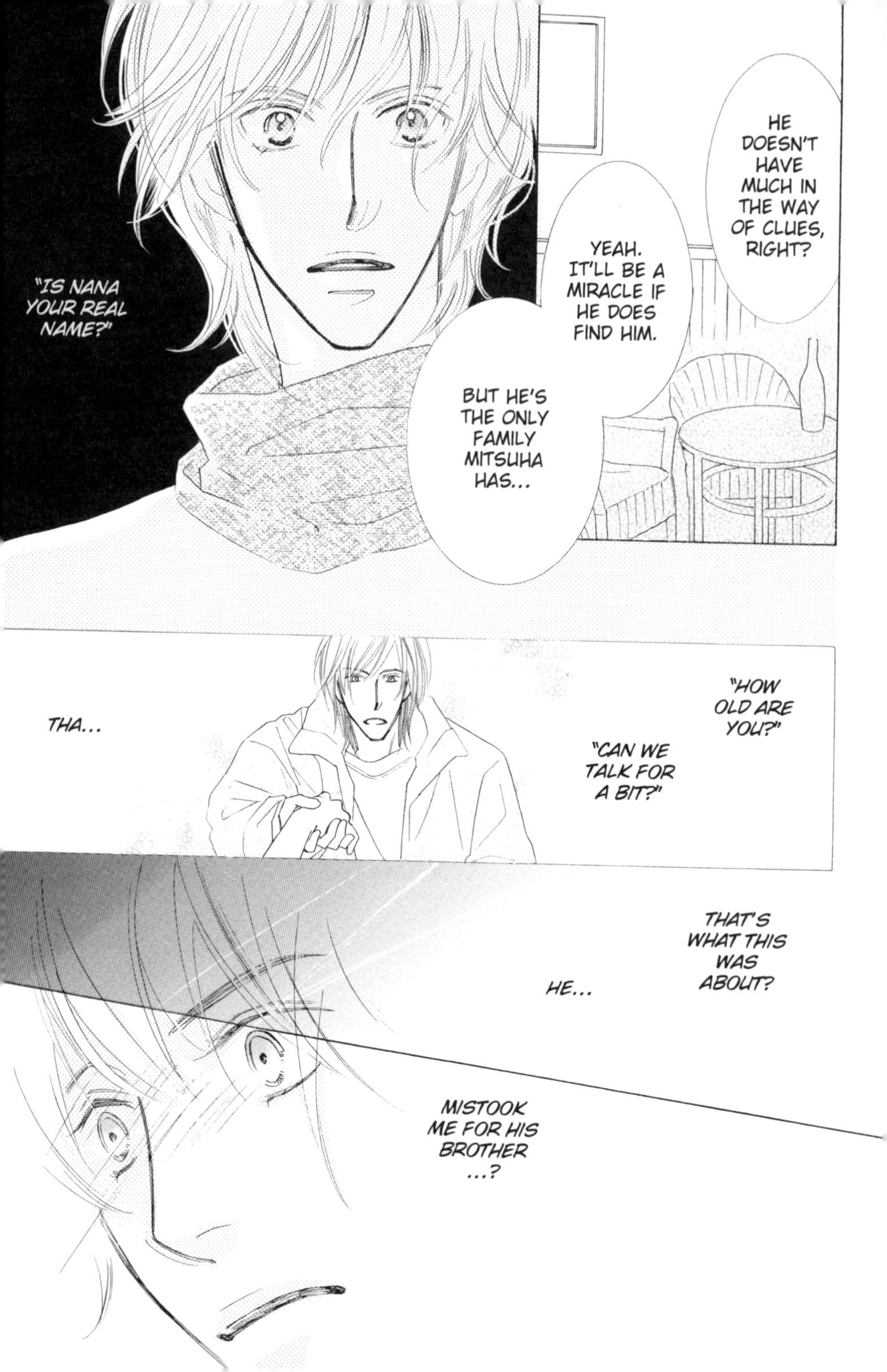
HE DOESN'T HAVE MUCH IN THE WAY OF CLUES, RIGHT?
YEAH. IT'LL BE A MIRACLE IF HE DOES FIND HIM.
BUT HE'S THE ONLY FAMILY MITSUHA HAS...
"IS NANA YOUR REAL NAME?"
"HOW OLD ARE YOU?"
"CAN WE TALK FOR A BIT?"
THA...
THAT'S WHAT THIS WAS ABOUT?
HE...
MISTOOK ME FOR HIS BROTHER ...?

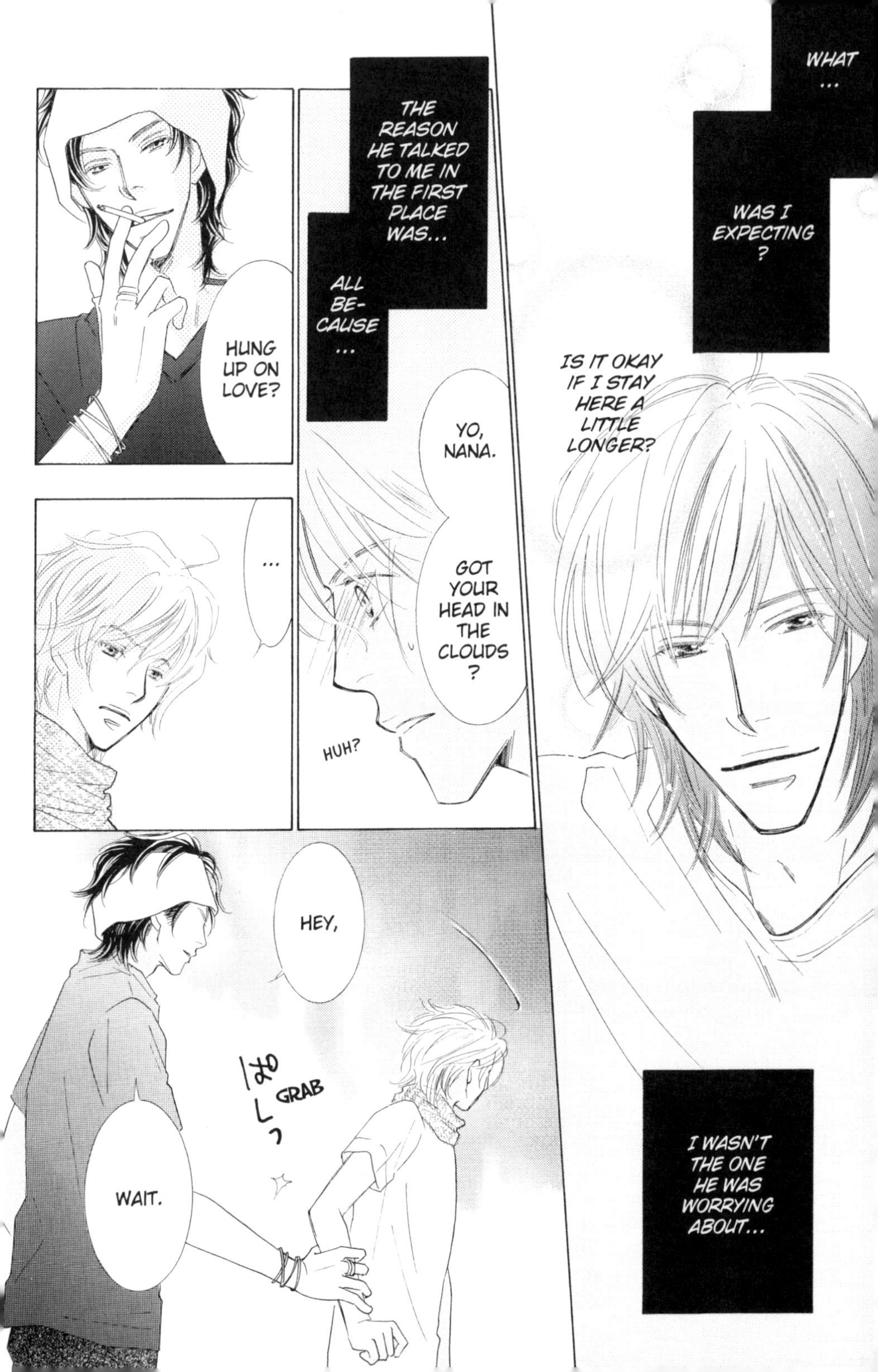
WHAT...
WAS I EXPECTING?
IS IT OKAY IF I STAY HERE A LITTLE LONGER?
I WASN'T THE ONE HE WAS WORRYING ABOUT...
THE REASON HE TALKED TO ME IN THE FIRST PLACE WAS...
ALL BE-CAUSE...
HUNG UP ON LOVE?
YO, NANA.
GOT YOUR HEAD IN THE CLOUDS?
HUH?
...
HEY,
GRAB
WAIT.

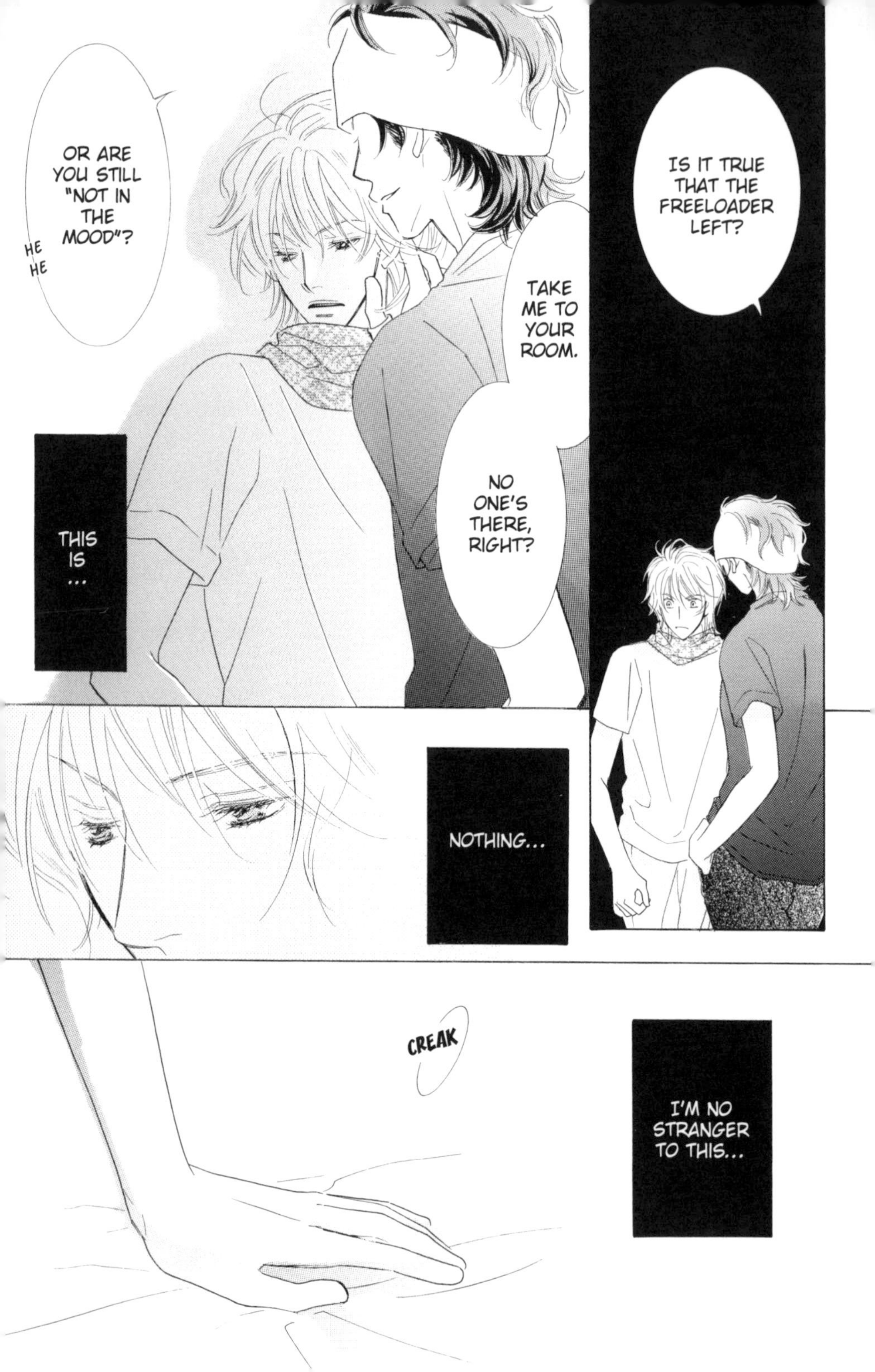
IS IT TRUE THAT THE FREELOADER LEFT?
TAKE ME TO YOUR ROOM.
NO ONE'S THERE, RIGHT?
OR ARE YOU STILL "NOT IN THE MOOD"?
HE HE
THIS IS...
NOTHING...
I'M NO STRANGER TO THIS...
CREAK

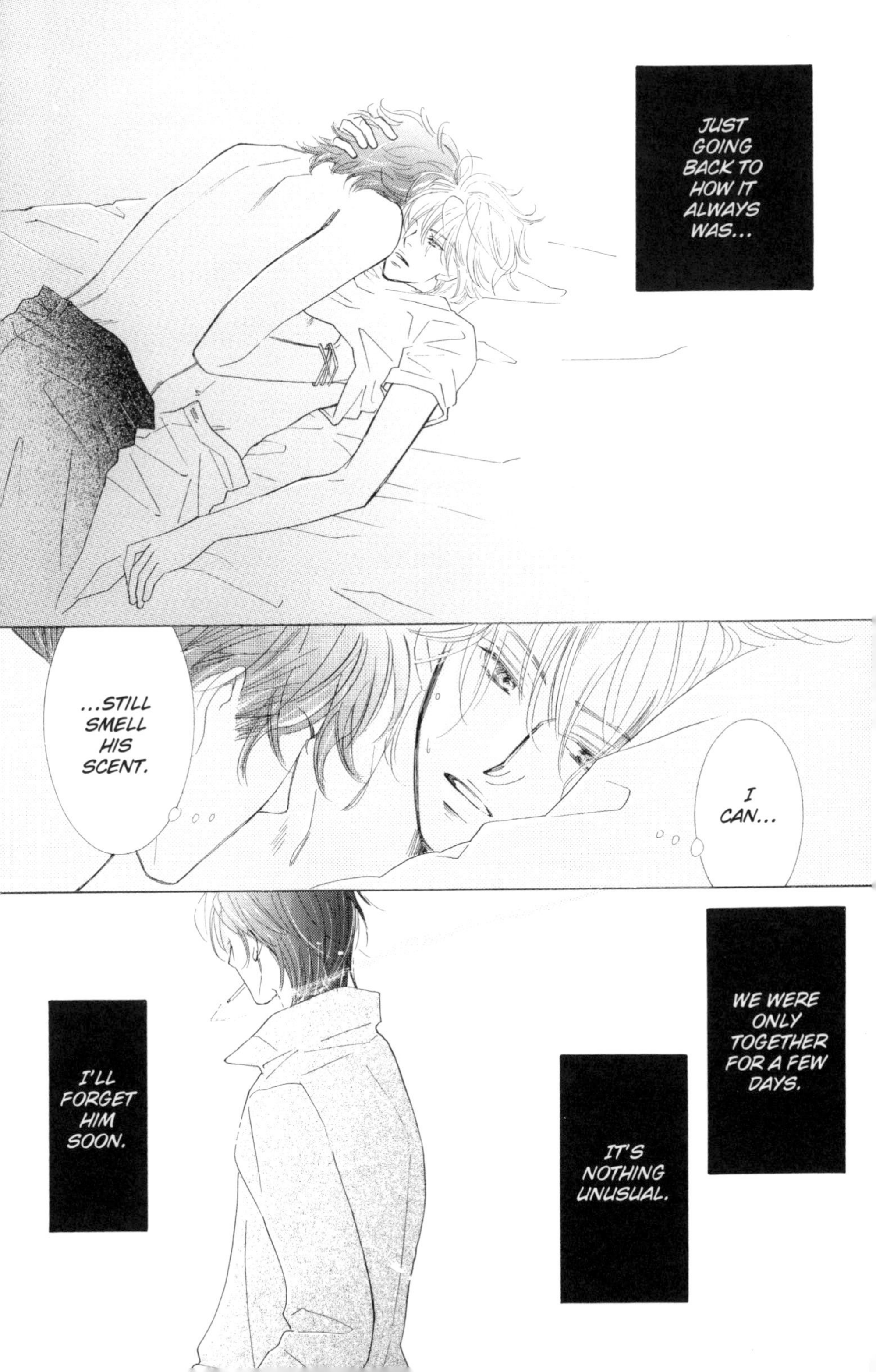
JUST GOING BACK TO HOW IT ALWAYS WAS...
I CAN...
...STILL SMELL HIS SCENT.
WE WERE ONLY TOGETHER FOR A FEW DAYS.
IT'S NOTHING UNUSUAL.
I'LL FORGET HIM SOON.

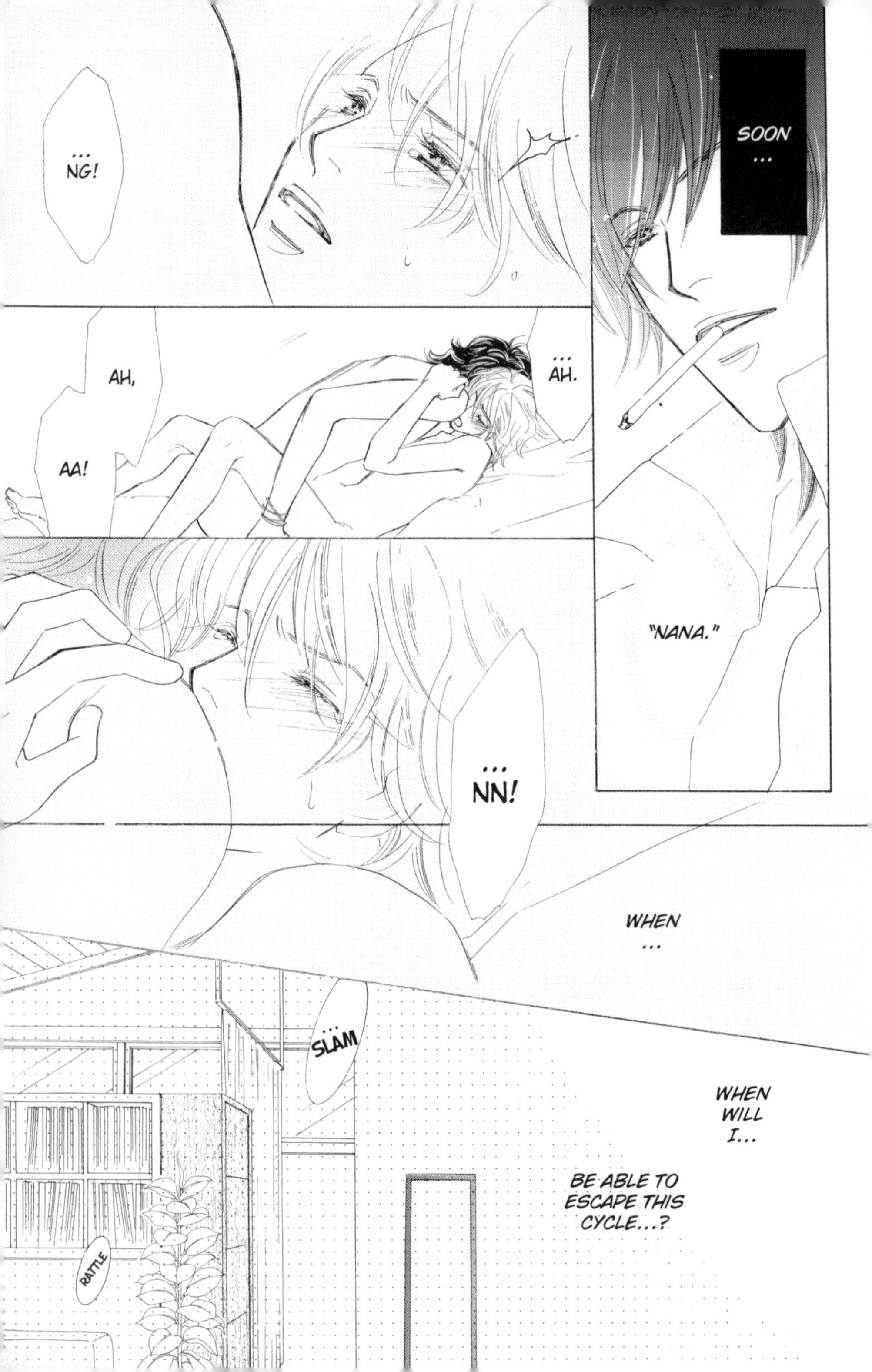
SOON ...
"NANA."
...NG!
...AH.
AH,
AA!
...NN!
WHEN ...
WHEN WILL I...
BE ABLE TO ESCAPE THIS CYCLE...?
...SLAM
RATTLE

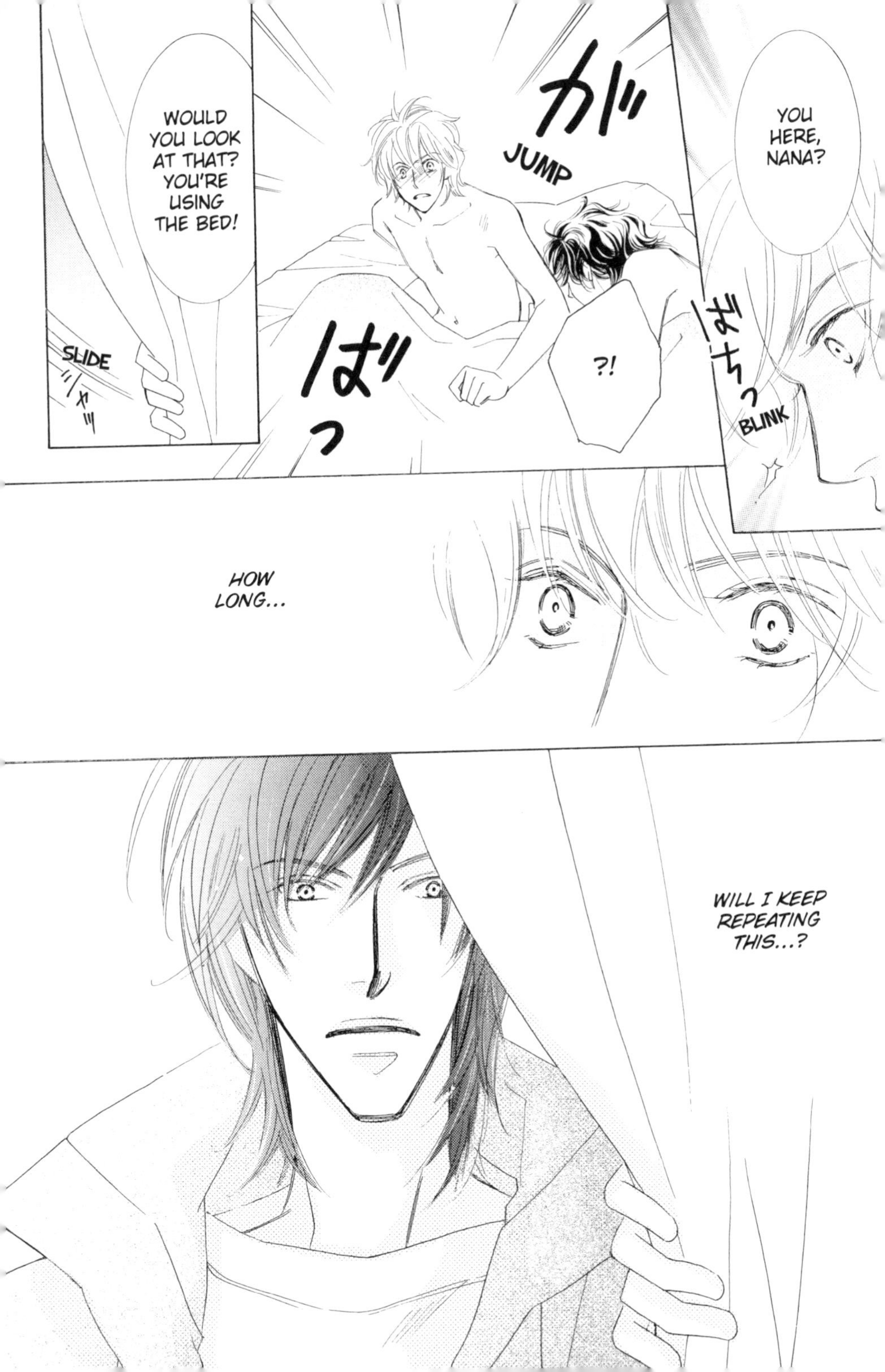
YOU HERE, NANA?
BLINK
JUMP
?!
WOULD YOU LOOK AT THAT? YOU'RE USING THE BED!
SLIDE
HOW LONG...
WILL I KEEP REPEATING THIS...?

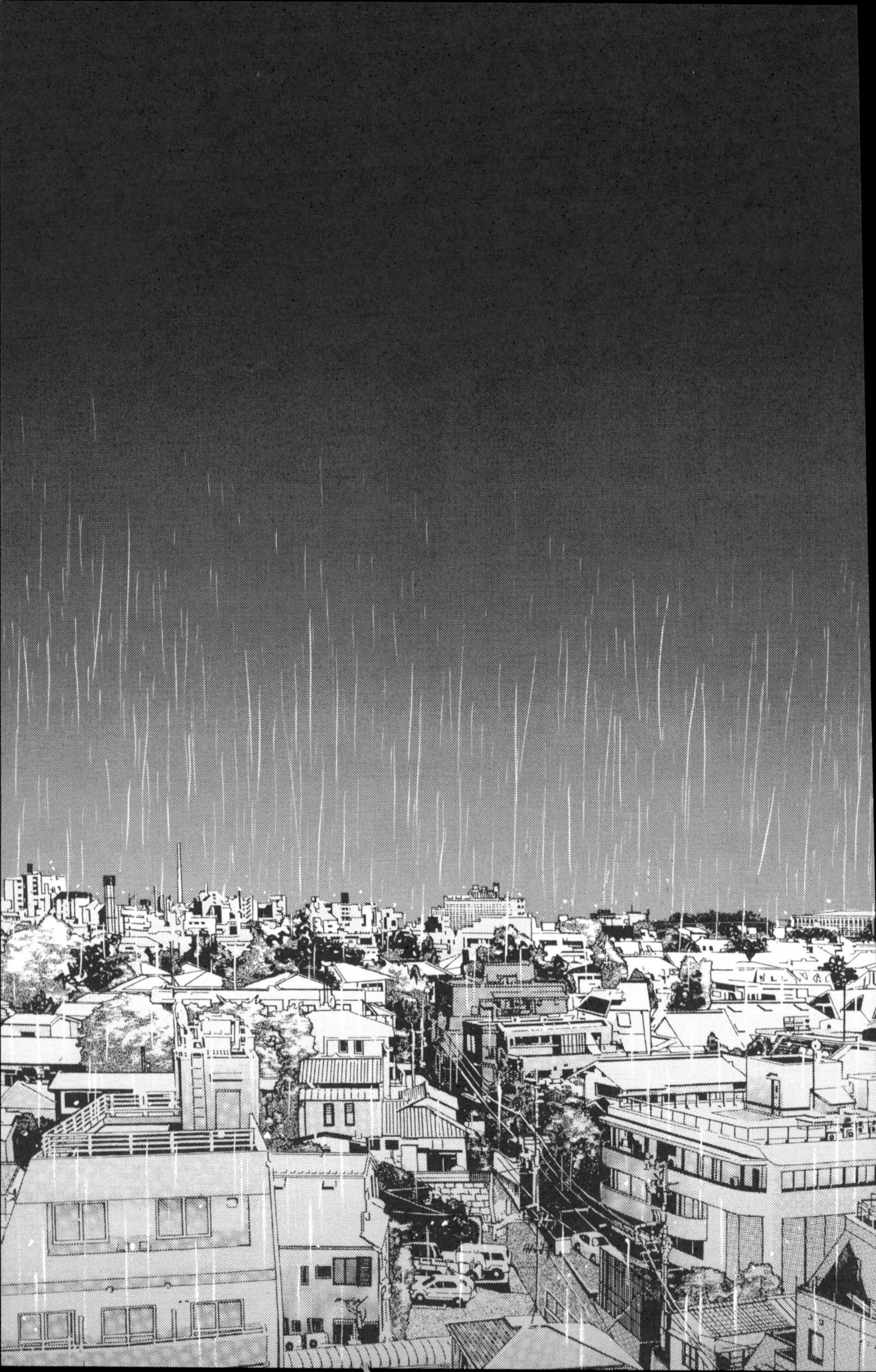

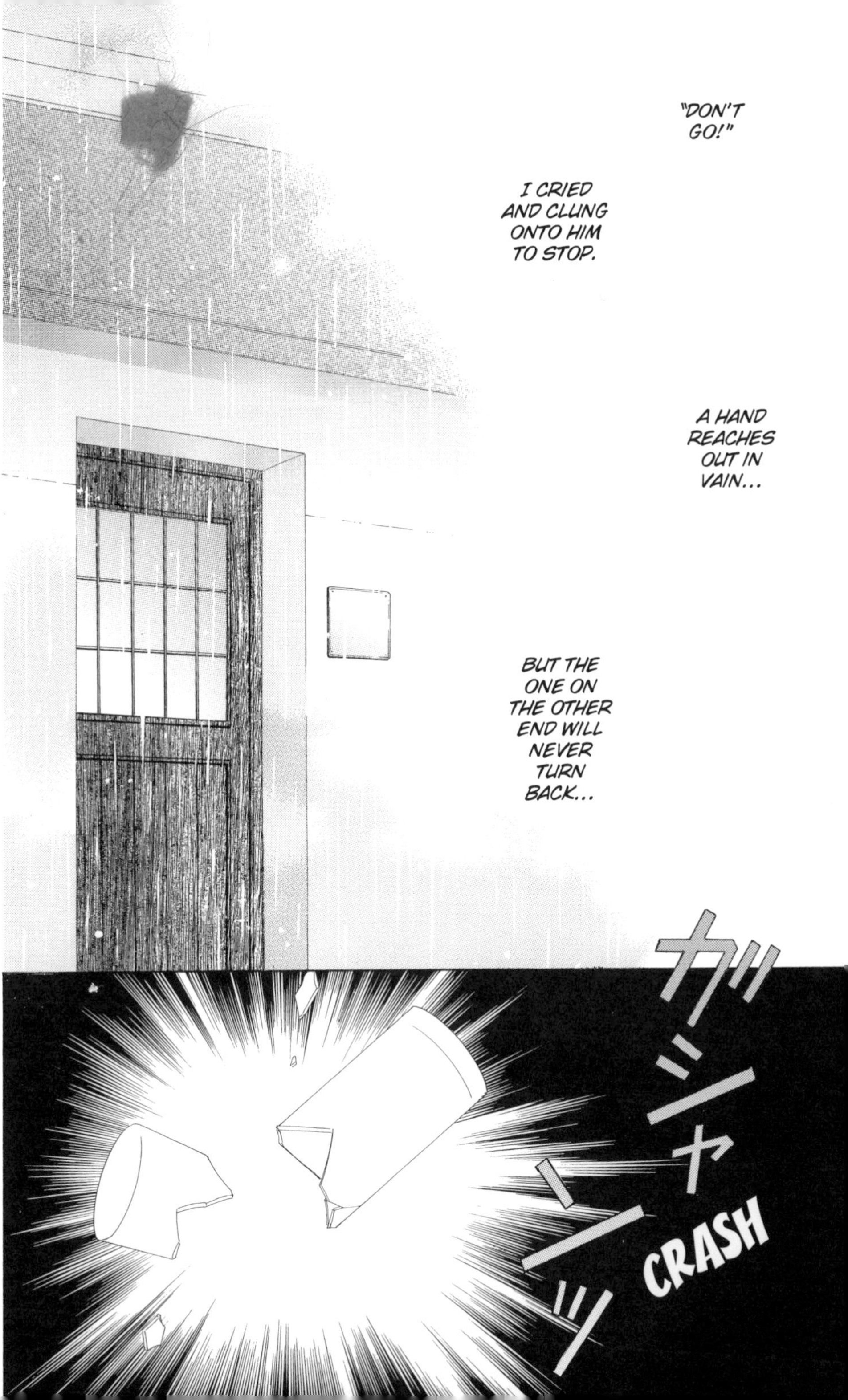
"DON'T GO!"
I CRIED AND CLUNG ONTO HIM TO STOP.
A HAND REACHES OUT IN VAIN...
BUT THE ONE ON THE OTHER END WILL NEVER TURN BACK...
ガシャーンッ
CRASH

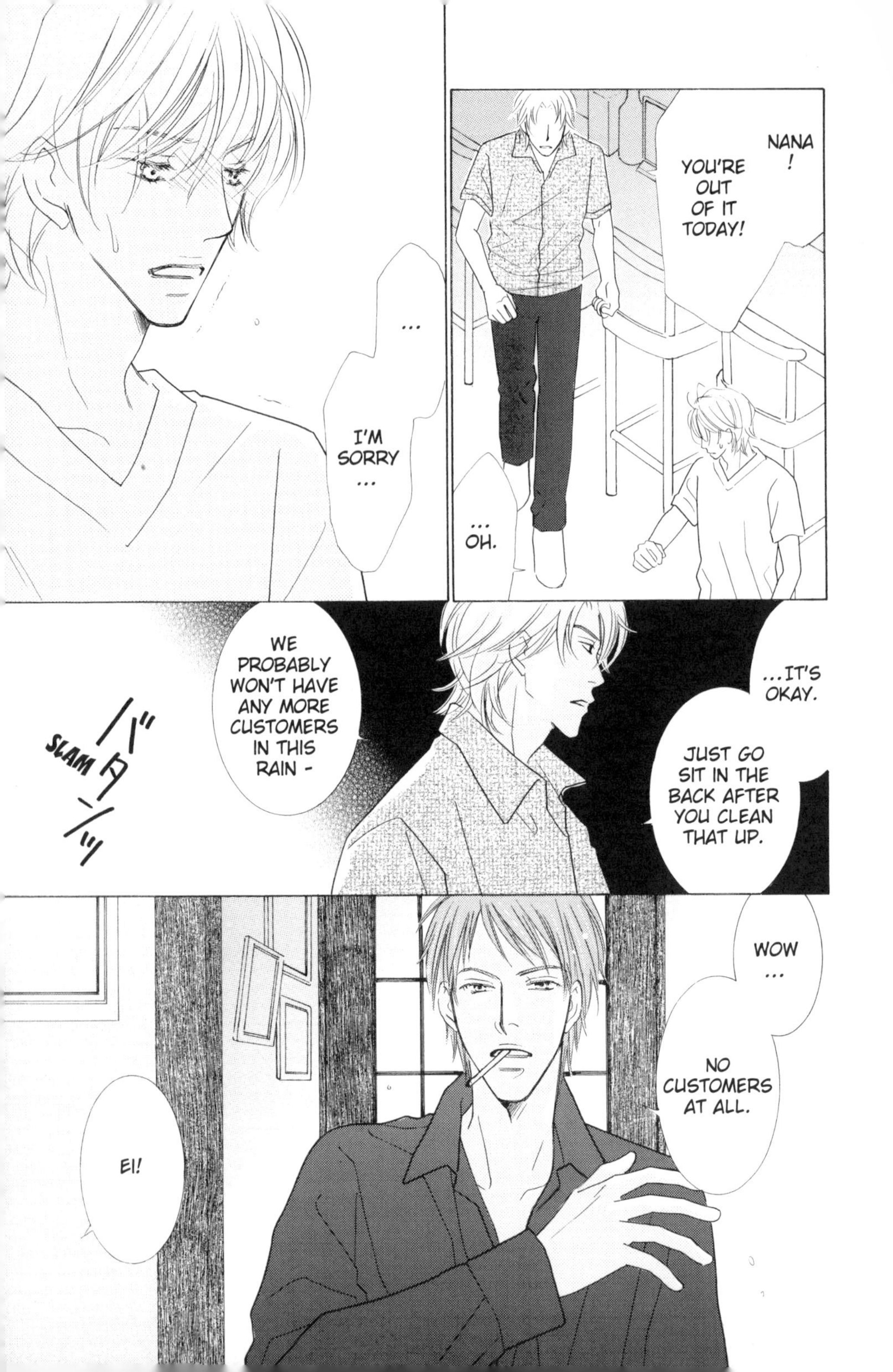
NANA!
YOU'RE OUT OF IT TODAY!
...OH.
...
I'M SORRY...
...IT'S OKAY.
JUST GO SIT IN THE BACK AFTER YOU CLEAN THAT UP.
WE PROBABLY WON'T HAVE ANY MORE CUSTOMERS IN THIS RAIN -
バタンッ
SLAM
WOW...
NO CUSTOMERS AT ALL.
EI!

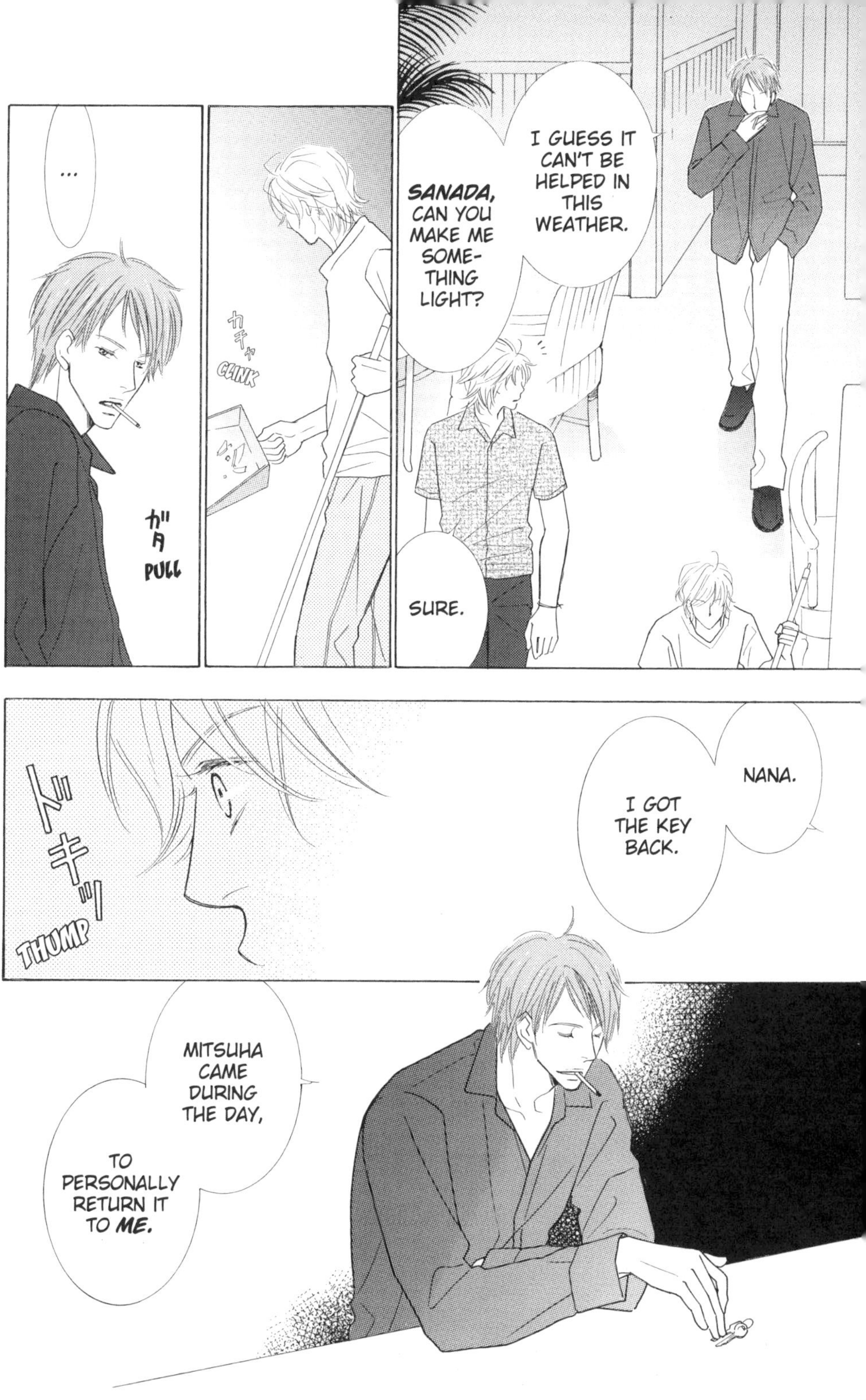

I GUESS IT CAN'T BE HELPED IN THIS WEATHER.
SANADA, CAN YOU MAKE ME SOME-THING LIGHT?
SURE.
カチャ
CLINK
...
ガタ
PULL
NANA.
I GOT THE KEY BACK.
ドキッ
THUMP
MITSUHA CAME DURING THE DAY,
TO PERSONALLY RETURN IT TO ME.

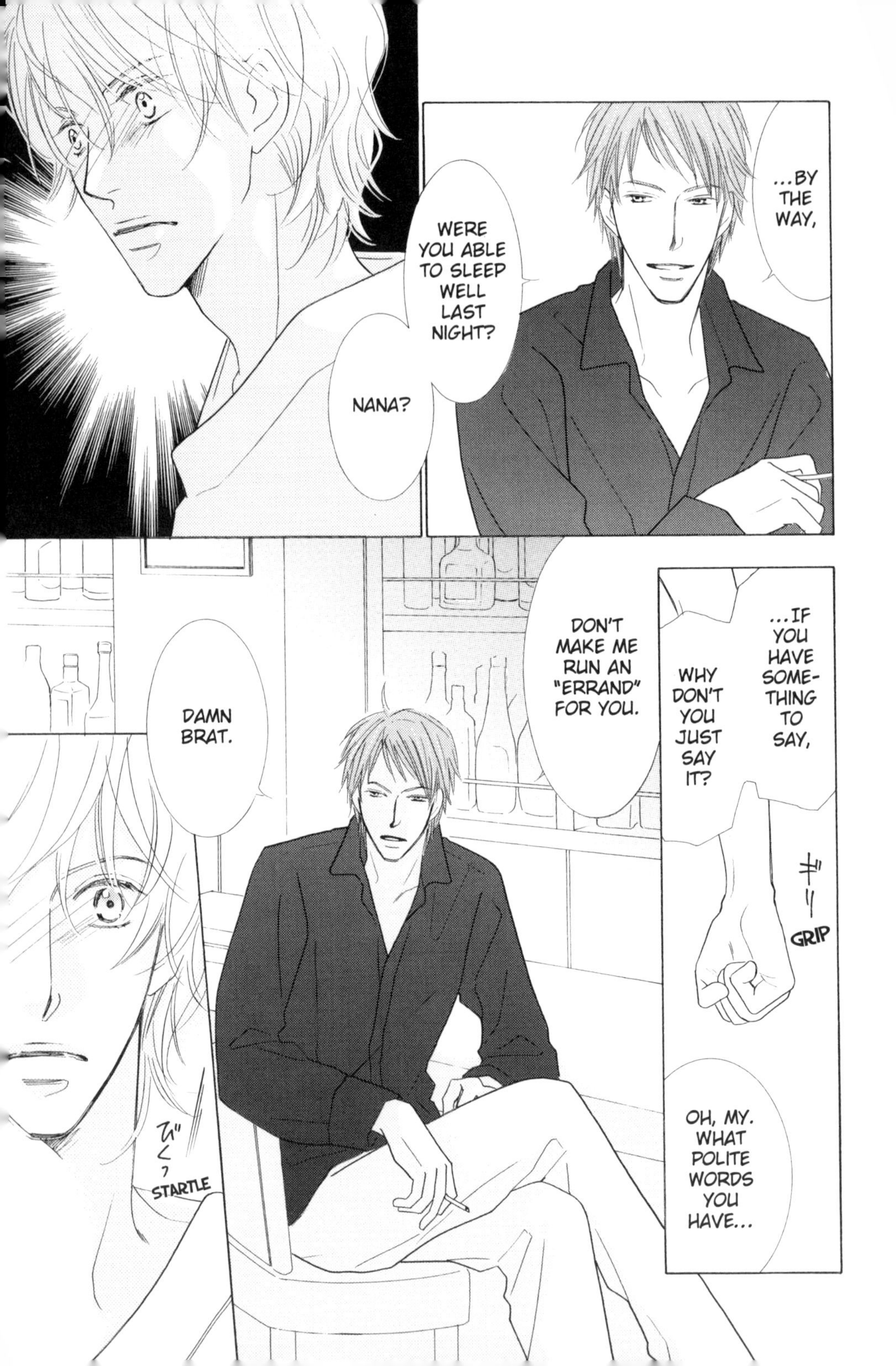
...BY THE WAY,
WERE YOU ABLE TO SLEEP WELL LAST NIGHT?
NANA?
...IF YOU HAVE SOMETHING TO SAY,
WHY DON'T YOU JUST SAY IT?
ギリ
GRIP
OH, MY. WHAT POLITE WORDS YOU HAVE...
DON'T MAKE ME RUN AN "ERRAND" FOR YOU.
DAMN BRAT.
びくっ
STARTLE

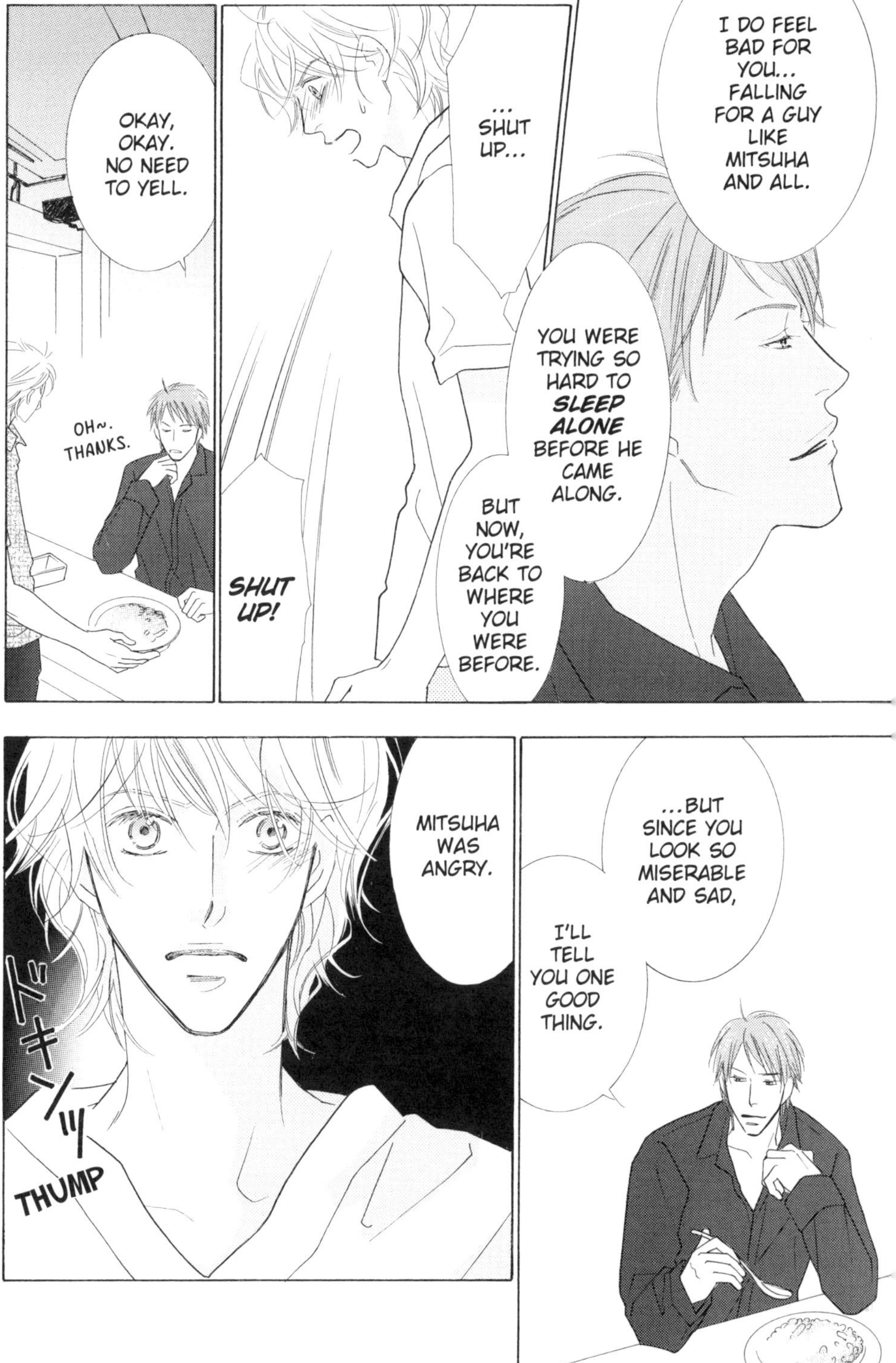
I DO FEEL BAD FOR YOU... FALLING FOR A GUY LIKE MITSUHA AND ALL.
YOU WERE TRYING SO HARD TO **SLEEP ALONE** BEFORE HE CAME ALONG.
BUT NOW, YOU'RE BACK TO WHERE YOU WERE BEFORE.
... SHUT UP...
SHUT UP!
OKAY, OKAY. NO NEED TO YELL.
OH~. THANKS.
...BUT SINCE YOU LOOK SO MISERABLE AND SAD,
I'LL TELL YOU ONE GOOD THING.
MITSUHA WAS ANGRY.
ドキンッ
THUMP

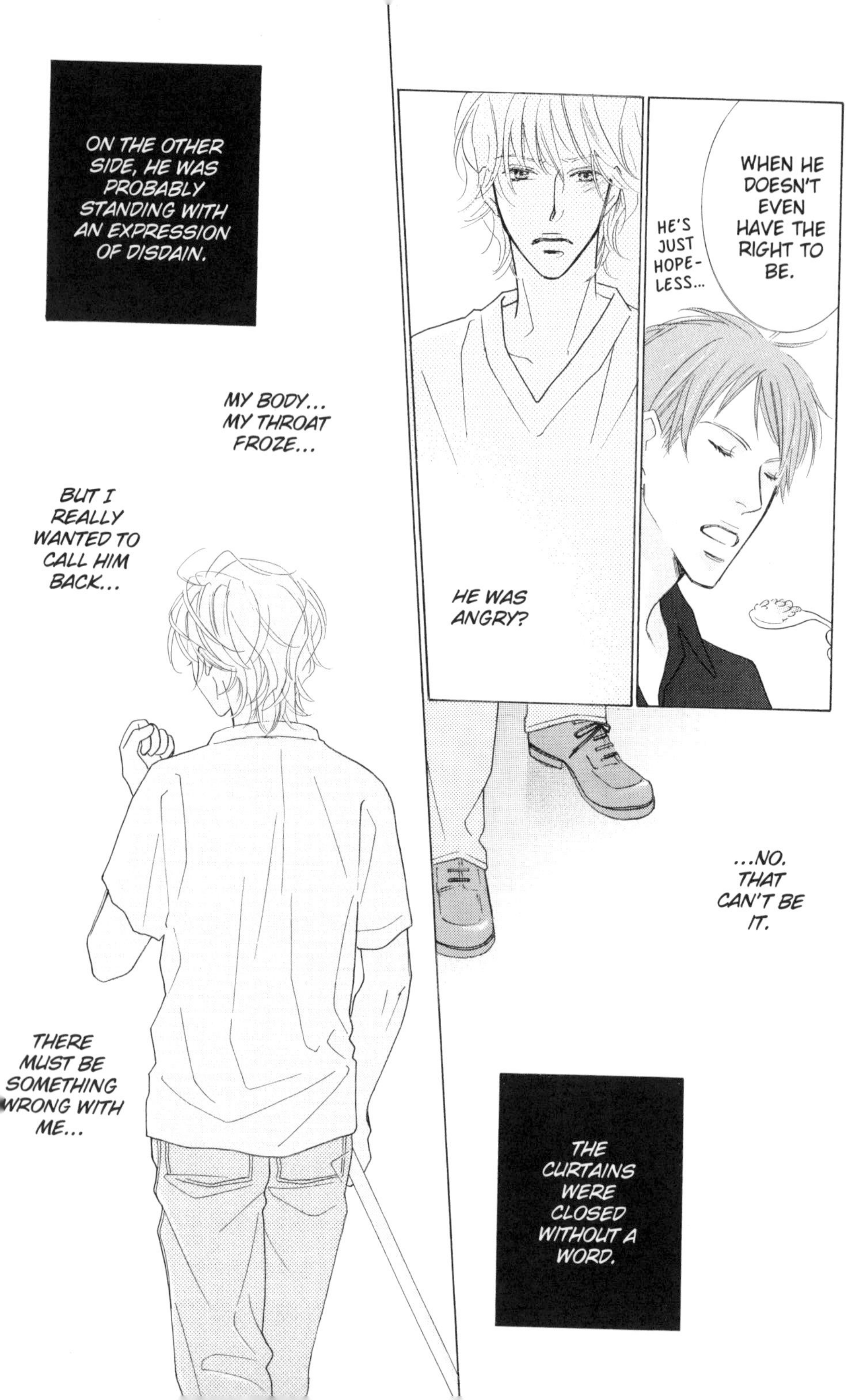
WHEN HE DOESN'T EVEN HAVE THE RIGHT TO BE.
HE'S JUST HOPE-LESS...
HE WAS ANGRY?
...NO. THAT CAN'T BE IT.
THE CURTAINS WERE CLOSED WITHOUT A WORD.
ON THE OTHER SIDE, HE WAS PROBABLY STANDING WITH AN EXPRESSION OF DISDAIN.
MY BODY... MY THROAT FROZE...
BUT I REALLY WANTED TO CALL HIM BACK...
THERE MUST BE SOMETHING WRONG WITH ME...

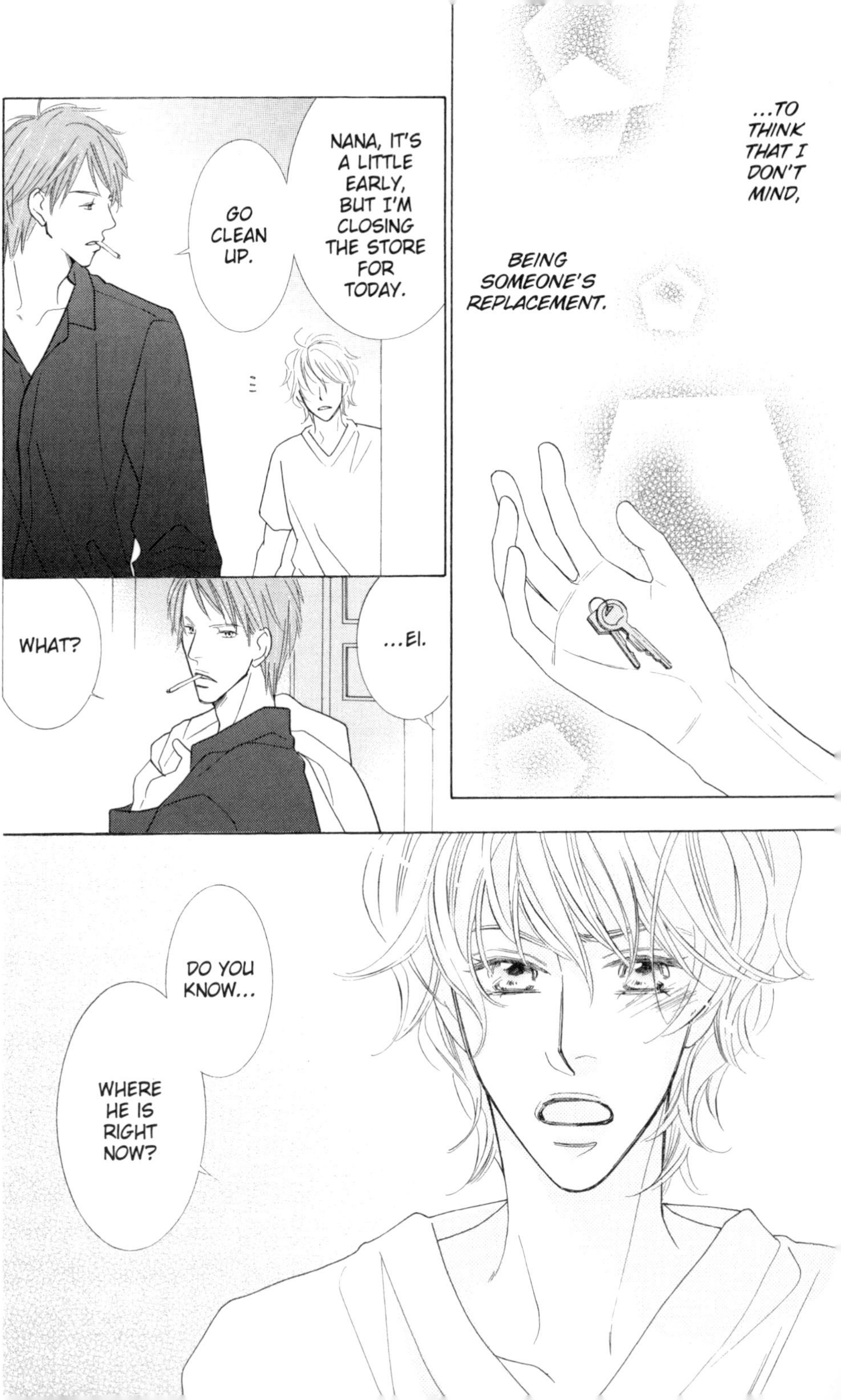
...TO THINK THAT I DON'T MIND,
BEING SOMEONE'S REPLACEMENT.
NANA, IT'S A LITTLE EARLY, BUT I'M CLOSING THE STORE FOR TODAY.
GO CLEAN UP.
...EI.
WHAT?
DO YOU KNOW...
WHERE HE IS RIGHT NOW?

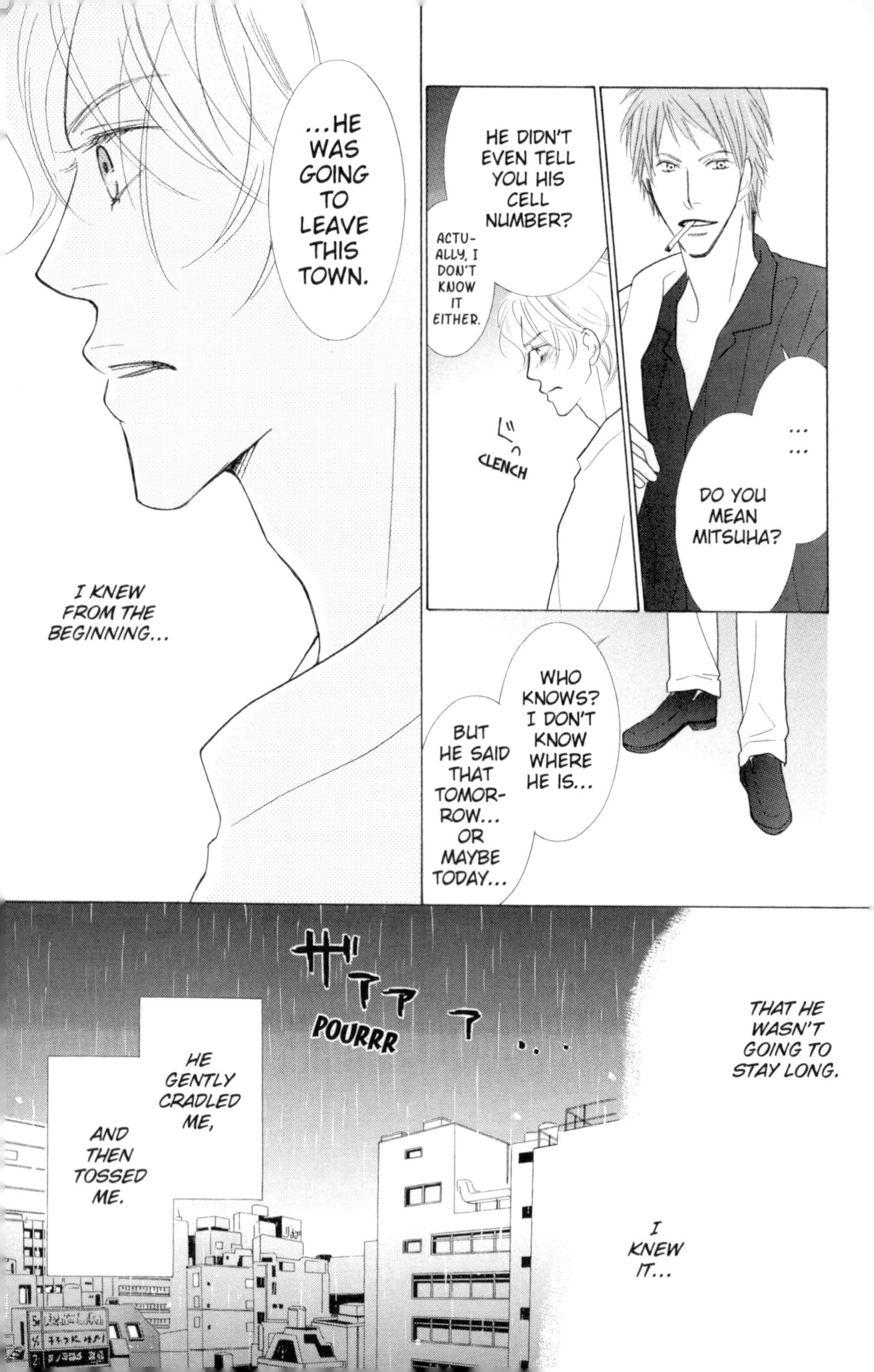

......
DO YOU MEAN MITSUHA?
HE DIDN'T EVEN TELL YOU HIS CELL NUMBER?
ACTU-ALLY, I DON'T KNOW IT EITHER.
CLENCH
WHO KNOWS? I DON'T KNOW WHERE HE IS...
BUT HE SAID THAT TOMOR-ROW... OR MAYBE TODAY...
...HE WAS GOING TO LEAVE THIS TOWN.
I KNEW FROM THE BEGINNING...
THAT HE WASN'T GOING TO STAY LONG.
I KNEW IT...
ザァァァ
POURRR
HE GENTLY CRADLED ME,
AND THEN TOSSED ME.

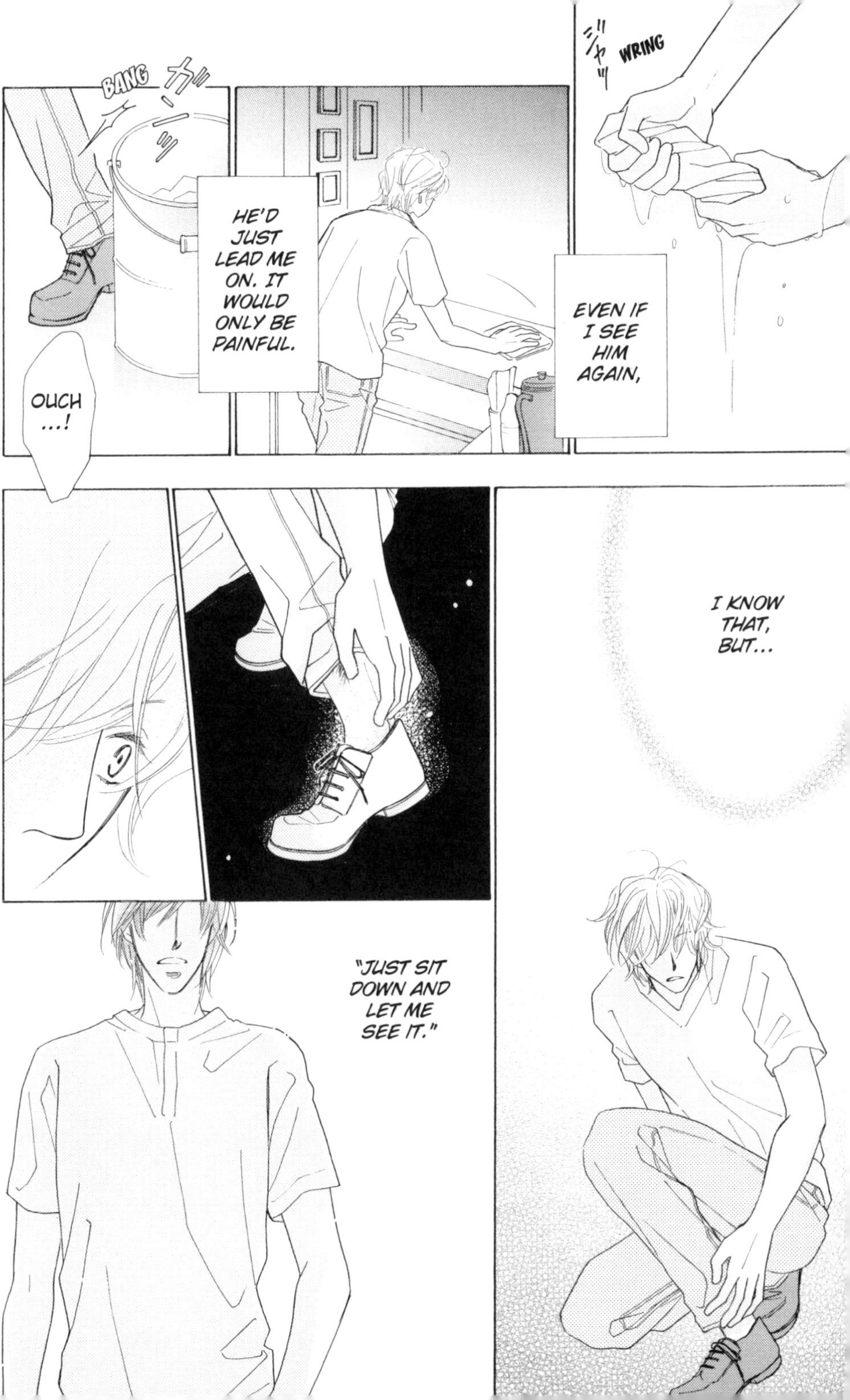
WRING
EVEN IF I SEE HIM AGAIN,
HE'D JUST LEAD ME ON. IT WOULD ONLY BE PAINFUL.
BANG
OUCH ...!
I KNOW THAT, BUT...
"JUST SIT DOWN AND LET ME SEE IT."

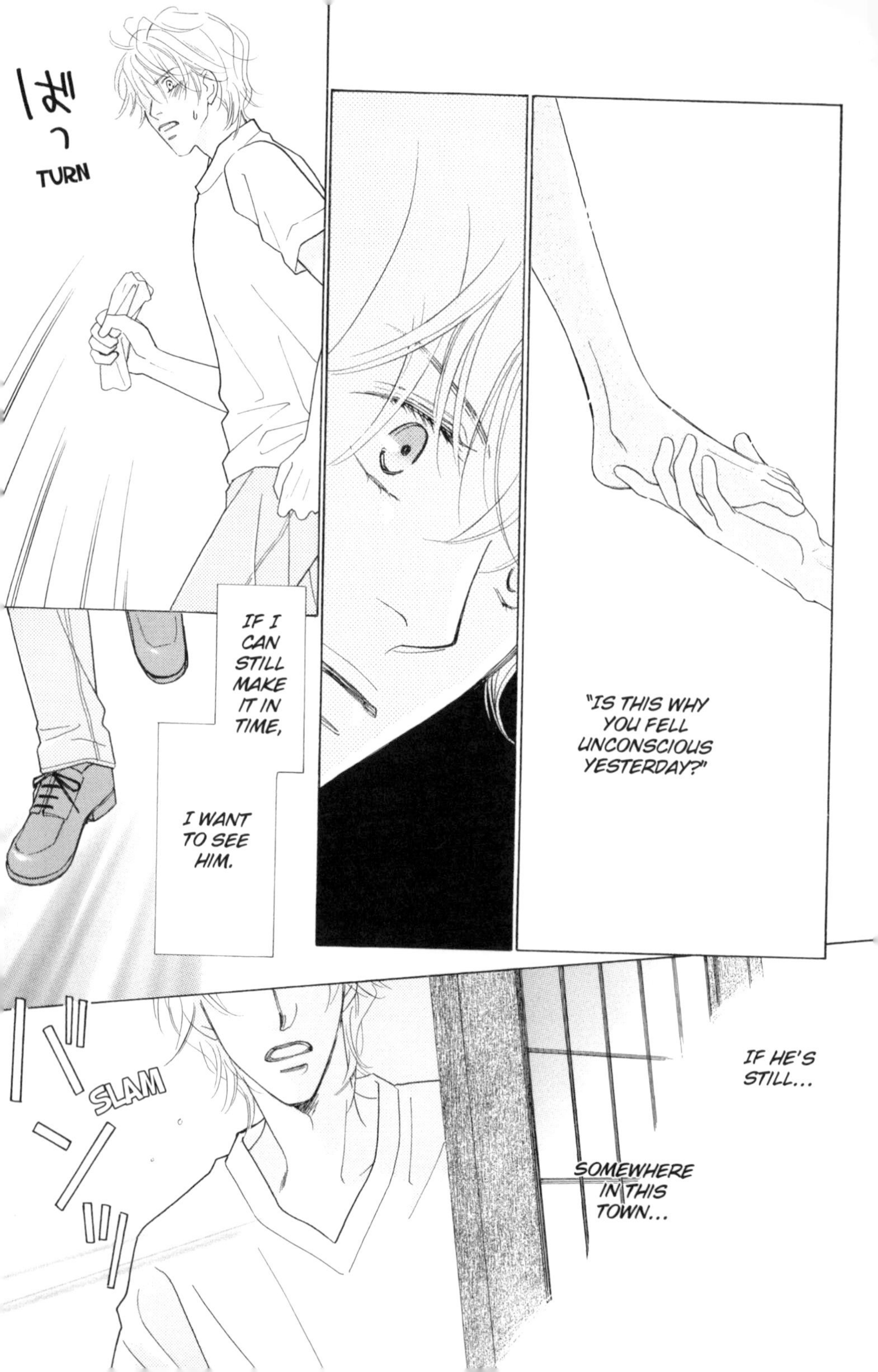
"IS THIS WHY YOU FELL UNCONSCIOUS YESTERDAY?"
ぱっ
TURN
IF I CAN STILL MAKE IT IN TIME,
I WANT TO SEE HIM.
IF HE'S STILL...
SOMEWHERE IN THIS TOWN...
SLAM

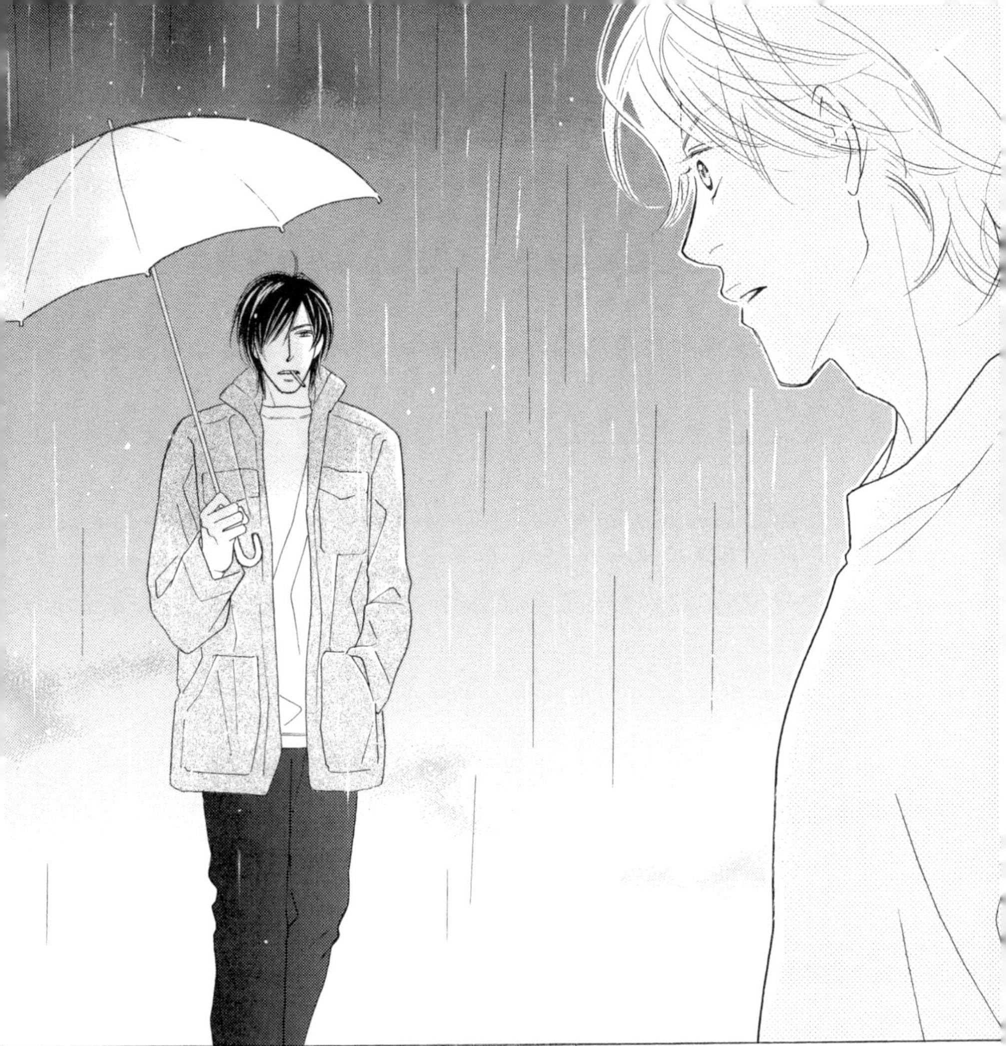
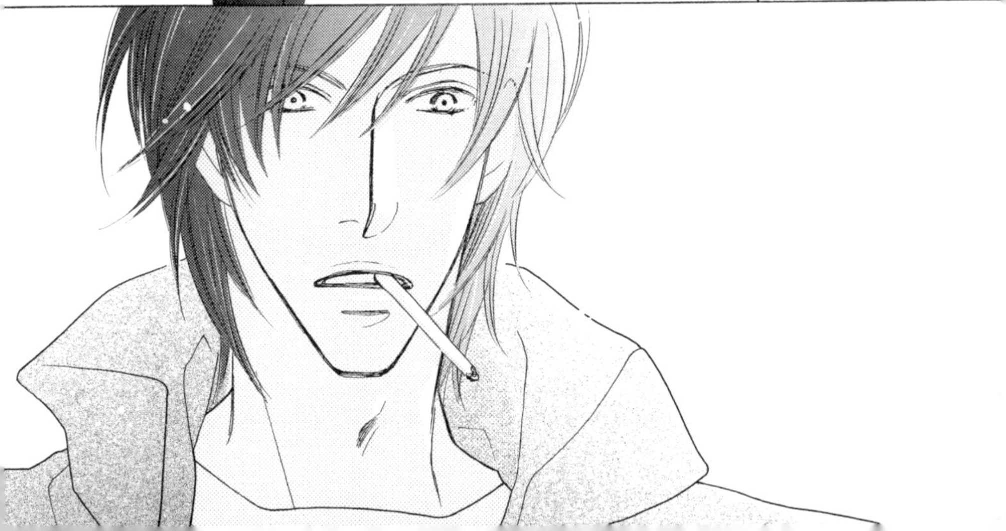

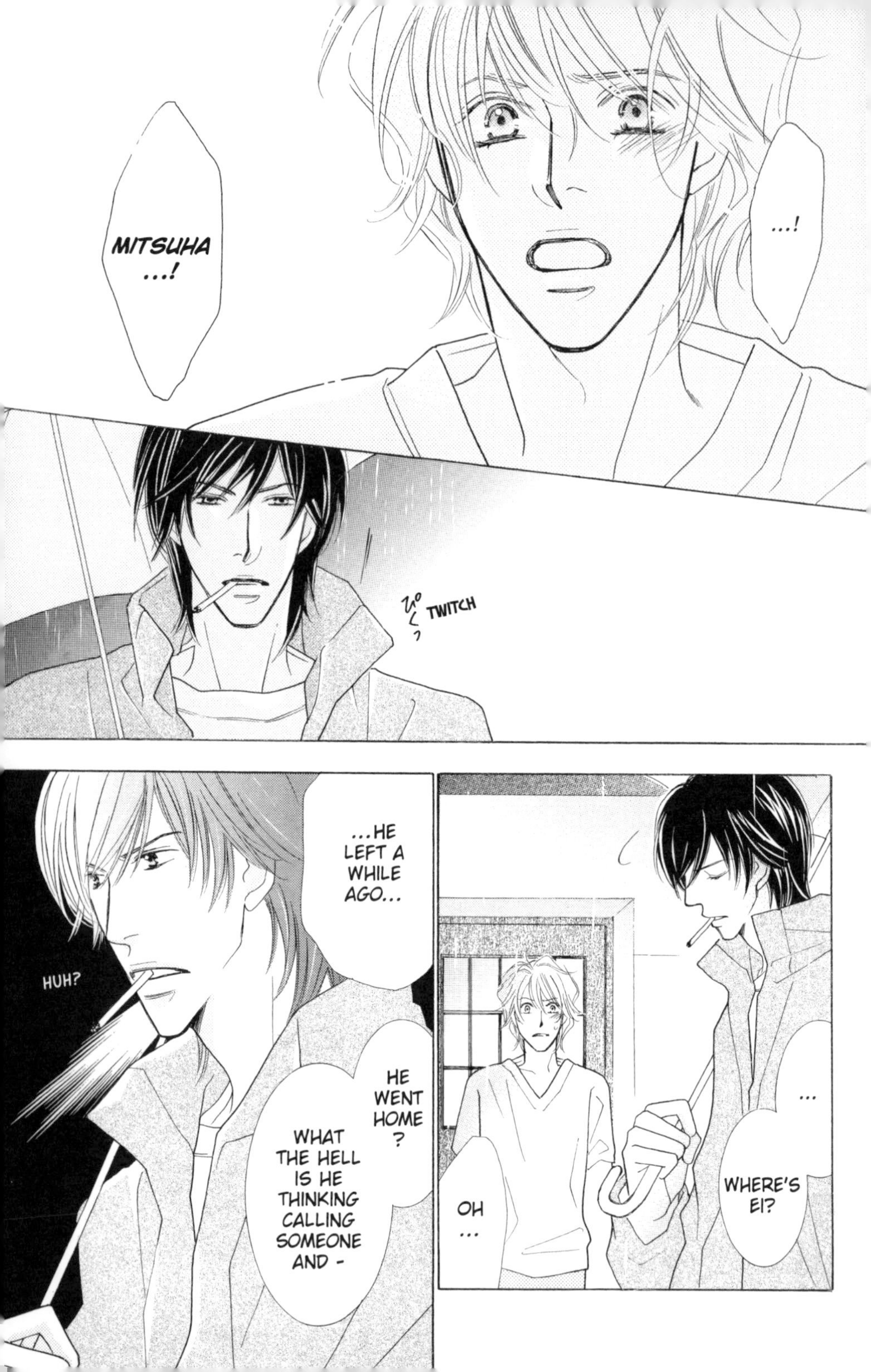
...!
MITSUHA ...!
TWITCH
...
WHERE'S EI?
OH ...
...HE LEFT A WHILE AGO...
HE WENT HOME?
WHAT THE HELL IS HE THINKING CALLING SOMEONE AND -
HUH?

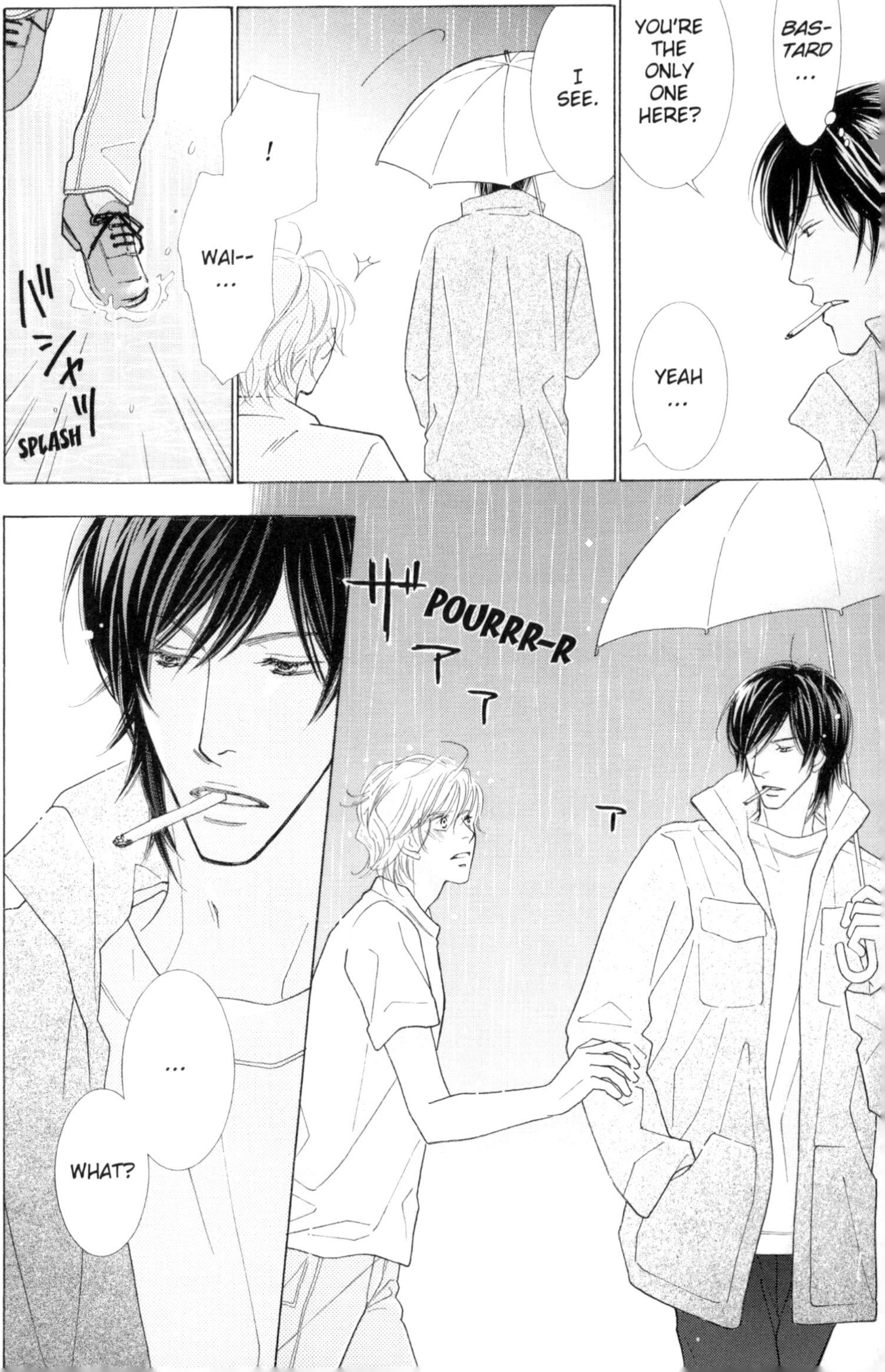
BAS-TARD...
YOU'RE THE ONLY ONE HERE?
YEAH...
I SEE.
!
WAI--...
バシャッ
SPLASH
ザアアア
POURRRR-R
...
WHAT?

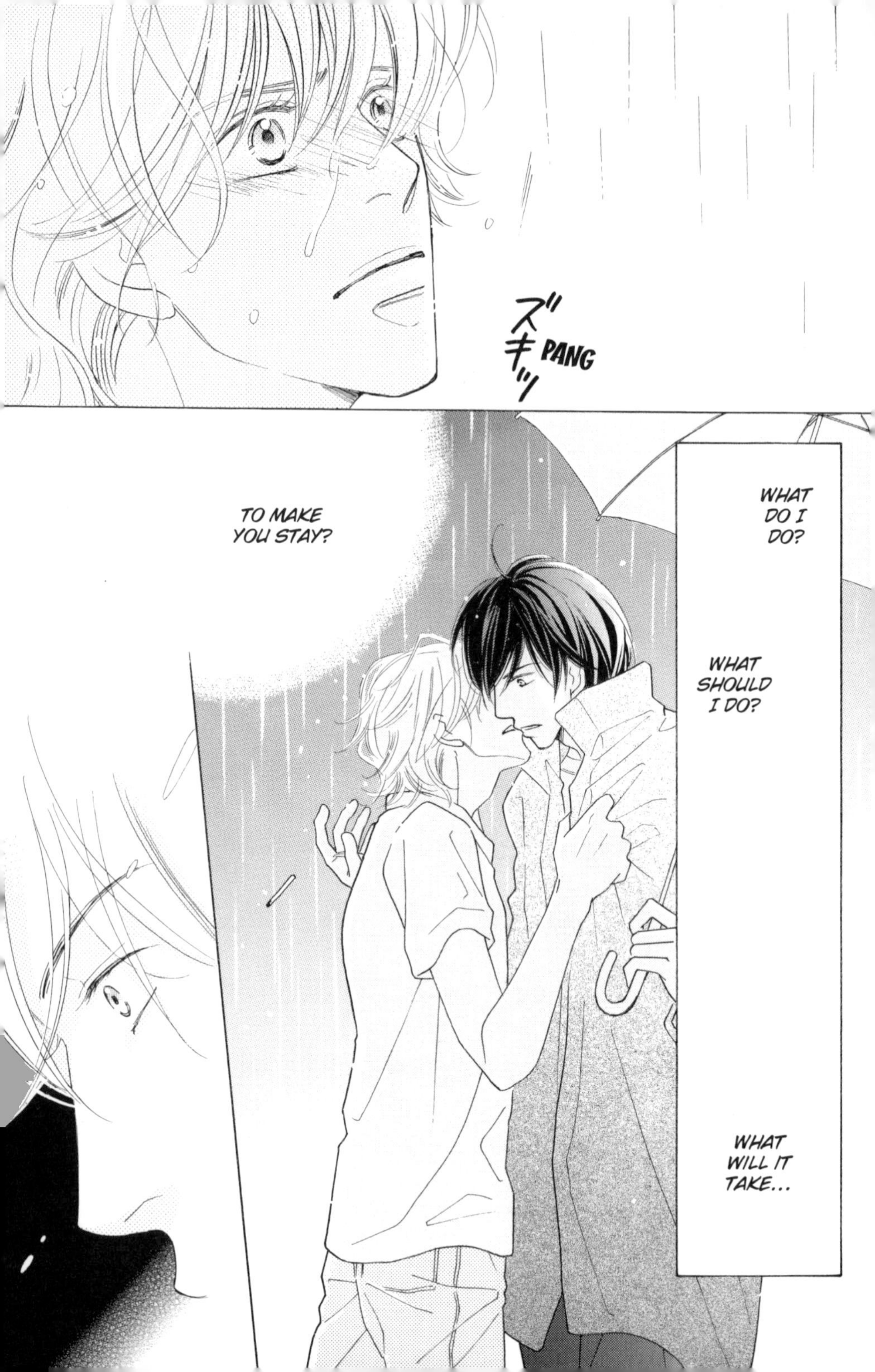
ズキッ
PANG
WHAT DO I DO?
WHAT SHOULD I DO?
WHAT WILL IT TAKE...
TO MAKE YOU STAY?

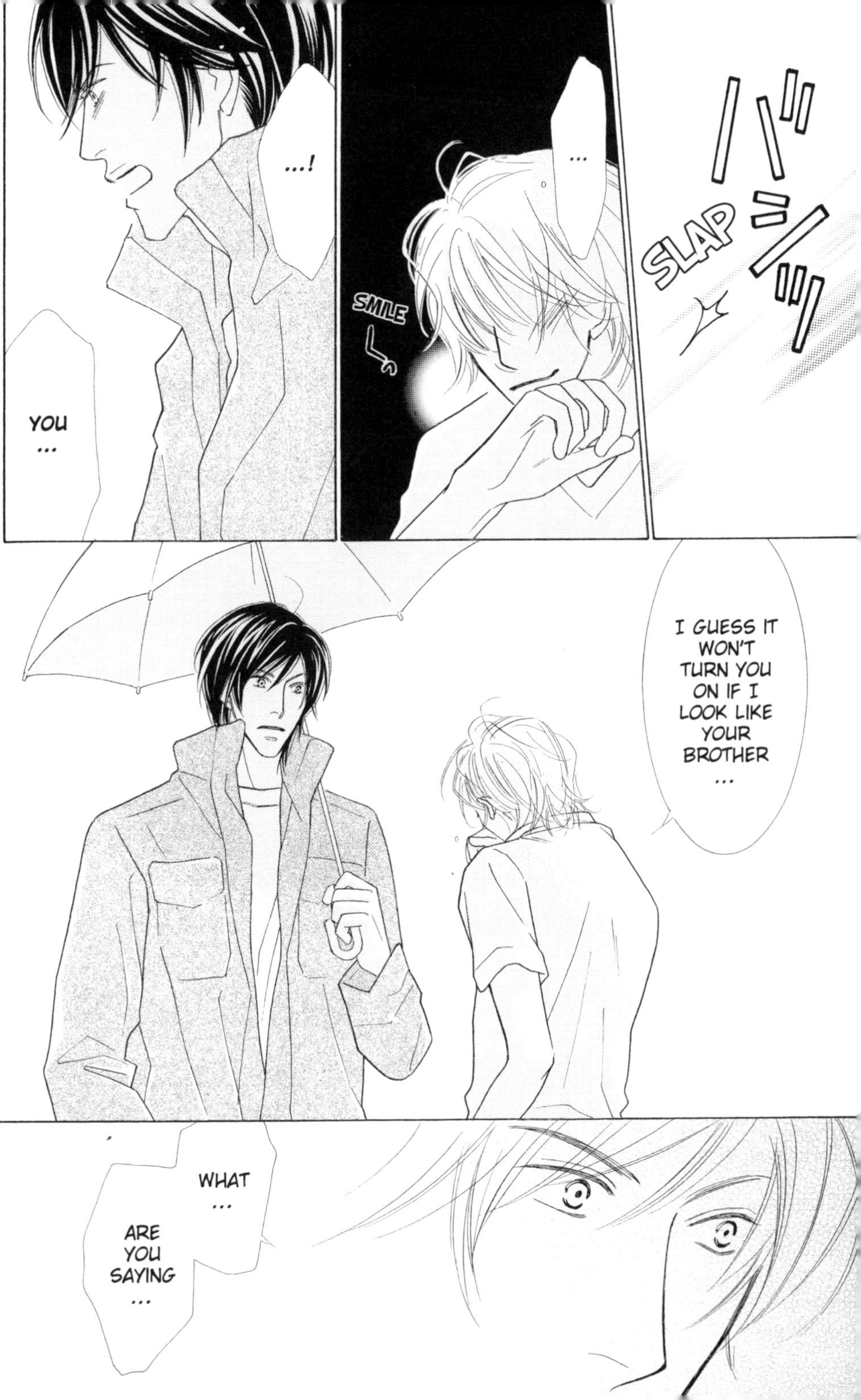
SLAP
...
SMILE
...!
YOU ...
I GUESS IT WON'T TURN YOU ON IF I LOOK LIKE YOUR BROTHER ...
WHAT ...
ARE YOU SAYING ...

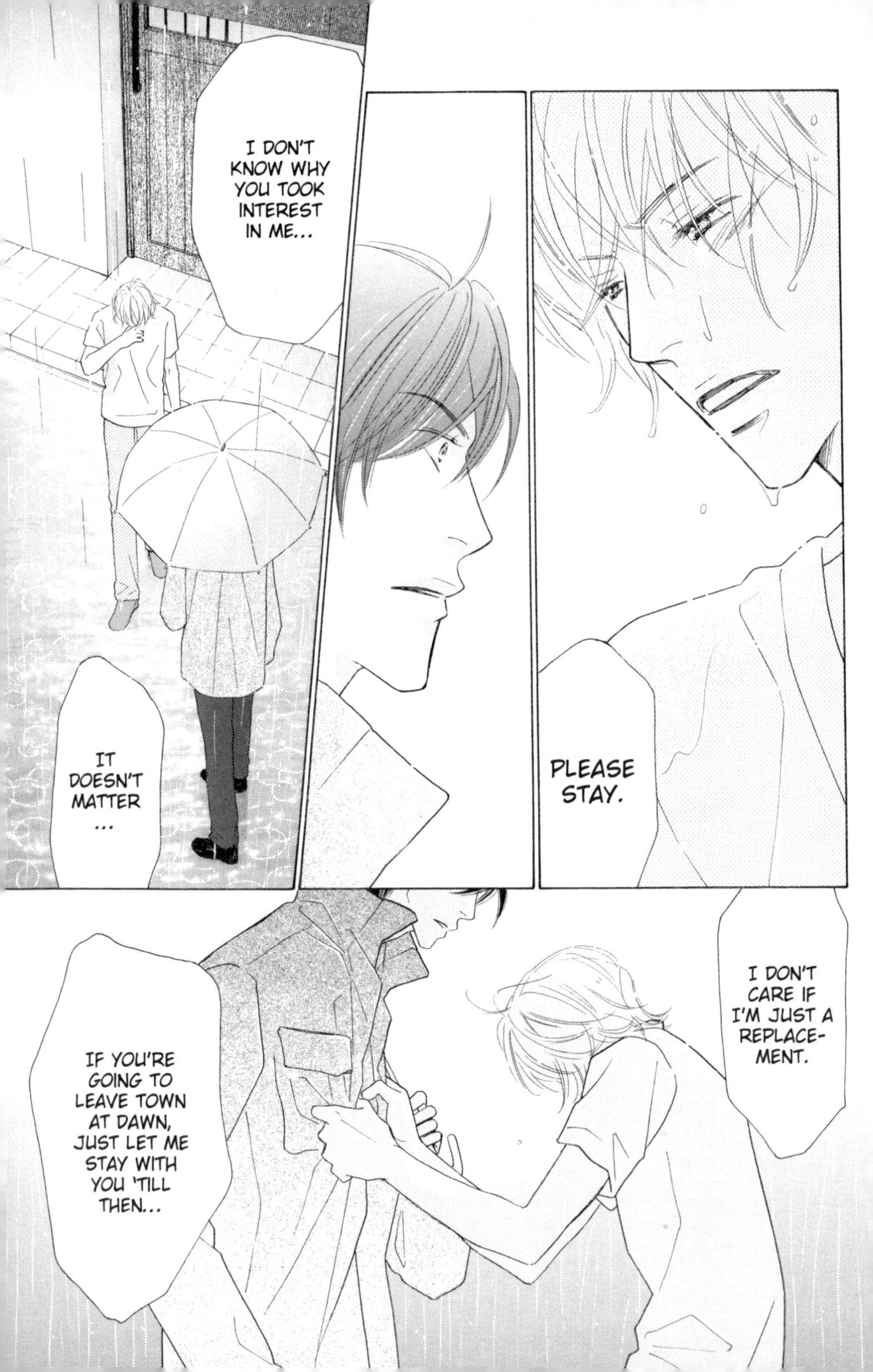
PLEASE STAY.
I DON'T KNOW WHY YOU TOOK INTEREST IN ME...
IT DOESN'T MATTER...
I DON'T CARE IF I'M JUST A REPLACE-MENT.
IF YOU'RE GOING TO LEAVE TOWN AT DAWN, JUST LET ME STAY WITH YOU 'TILL THEN...

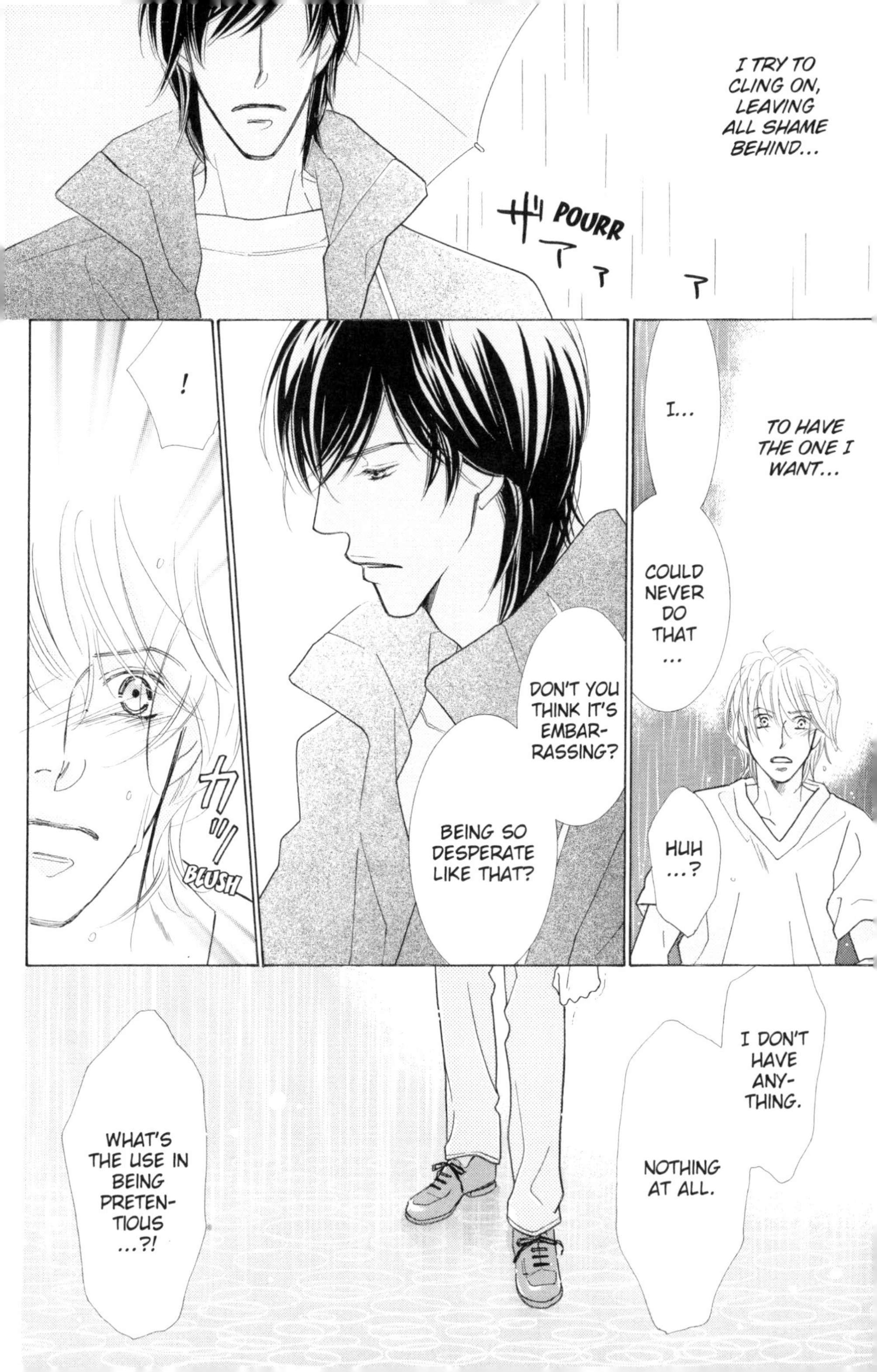
I TRY TO CLING ON, LEAVING ALL SHAME BEHIND...
ザァァァ POURR
TO HAVE THE ONE I WANT...
I...
COULD NEVER DO THAT...
HUH...?
DON'T YOU THINK IT'S EMBARRASSING?
BEING SO DESPERATE LIKE THAT?
!
カッ BLUSH
I DON'T HAVE ANYTHING.
NOTHING AT ALL.
WHAT'S THE USE IN BEING PRETENTIOUS...?!

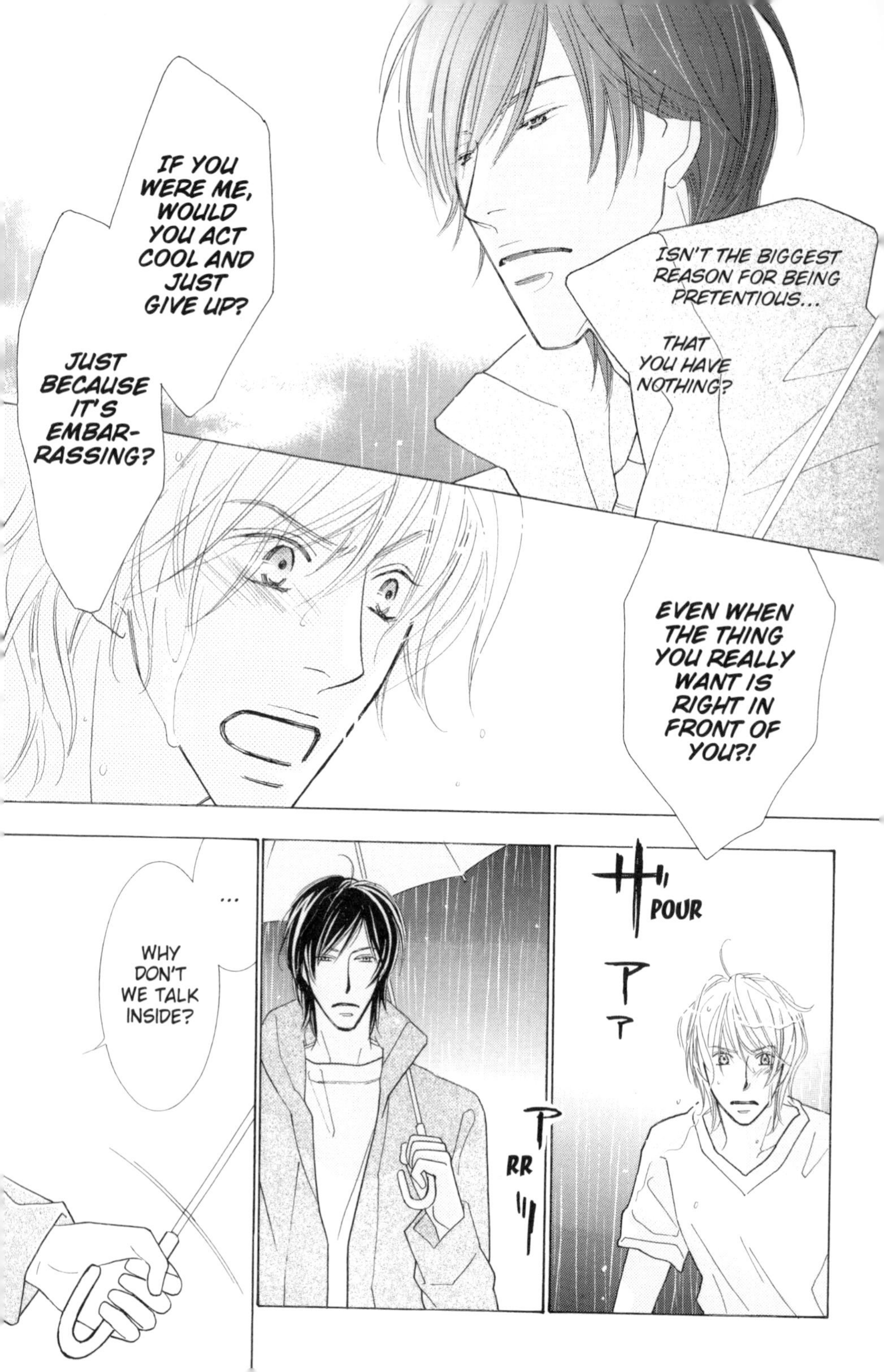
ISN'T THE BIGGEST REASON FOR BEING PRETENTIOUS...
THAT YOU HAVE NOTHING?
IF YOU WERE ME, WOULD YOU ACT COOL AND JUST GIVE UP?
JUST BECAUSE IT'S EMBARRASSING?
EVEN WHEN THE THING YOU REALLY WANT IS RIGHT IN FRONT OF YOU?!
POUR
RR
...
WHY DON'T WE TALK INSIDE?

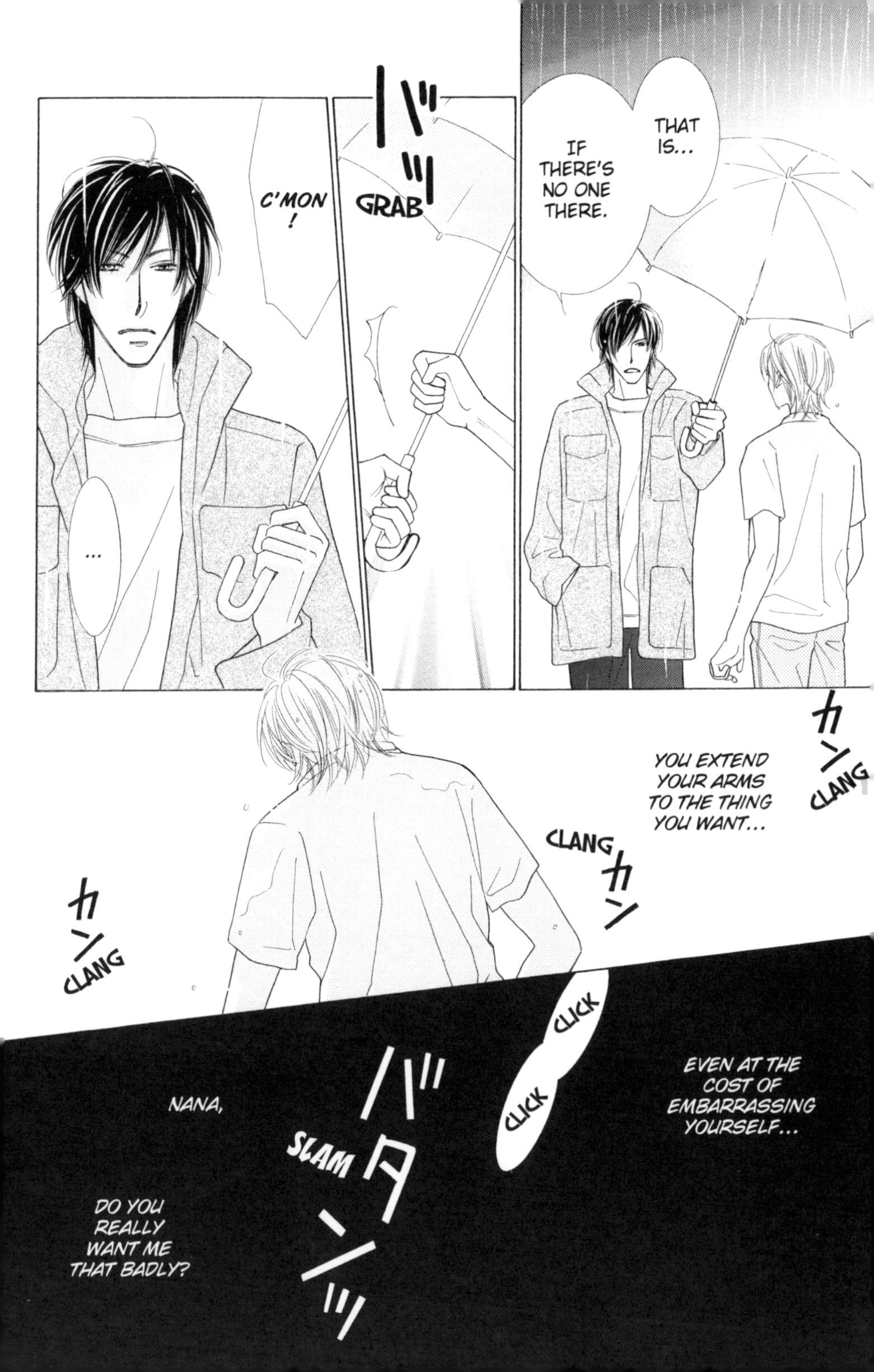
THAT IS...
IF THERE'S NO ONE THERE.
バッ
GRAB
C'MON!
...
カン
CLANG
YOU EXTEND YOUR ARMS TO THE THING YOU WANT...
CLANG
カン
カン
CLANG
EVEN AT THE COST OF EMBARRASSING YOURSELF...
CLICK
CLICK
バタンッ
SLAM
NANA,
DO YOU REALLY WANT ME THAT BADLY?

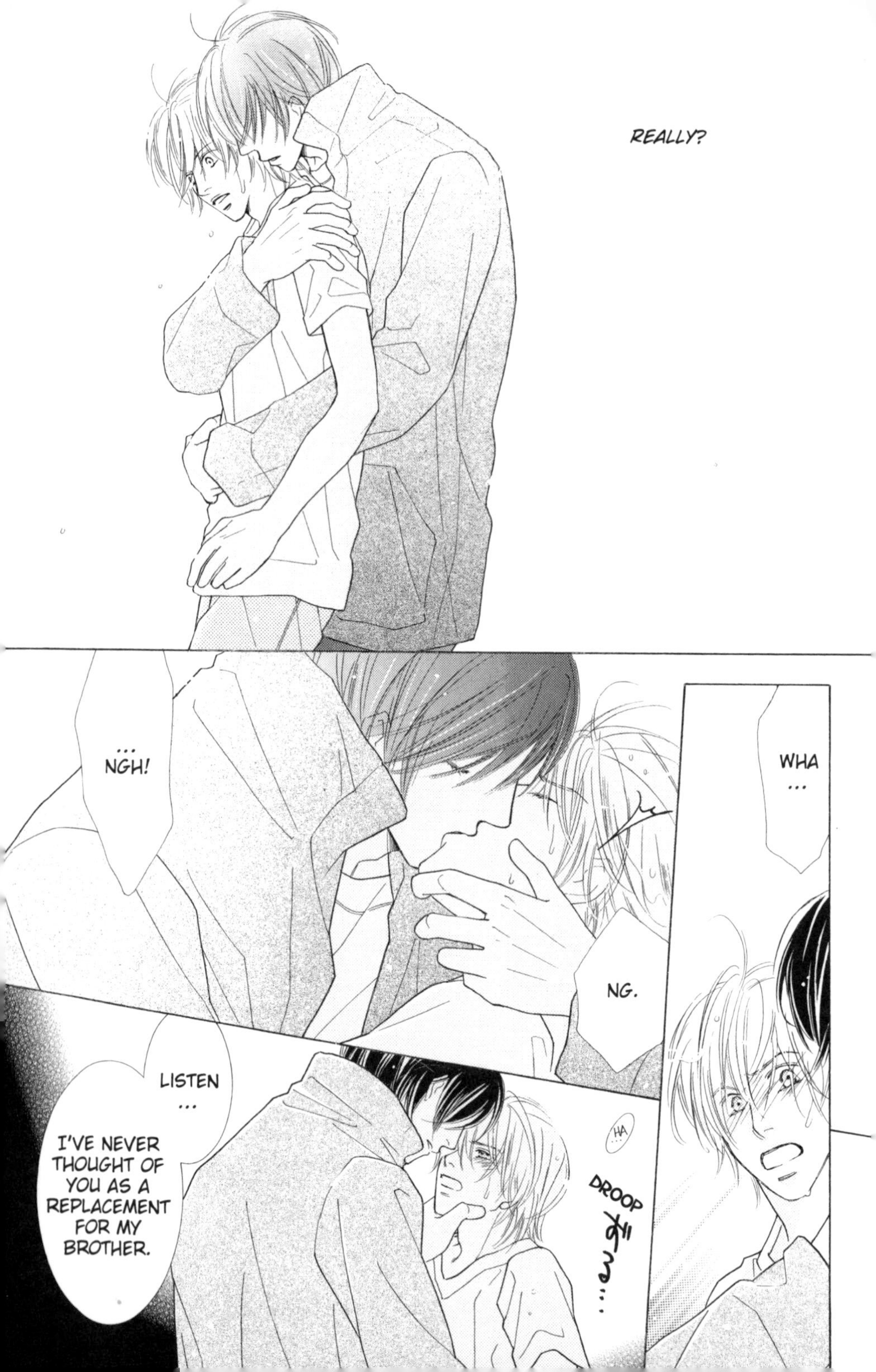
REALLY?
WHA ...
... NGH!
NG.
HA ...
DROOP
LISTEN ...
I'VE NEVER THOUGHT OF YOU AS A REPLACEMENT FOR MY BROTHER.

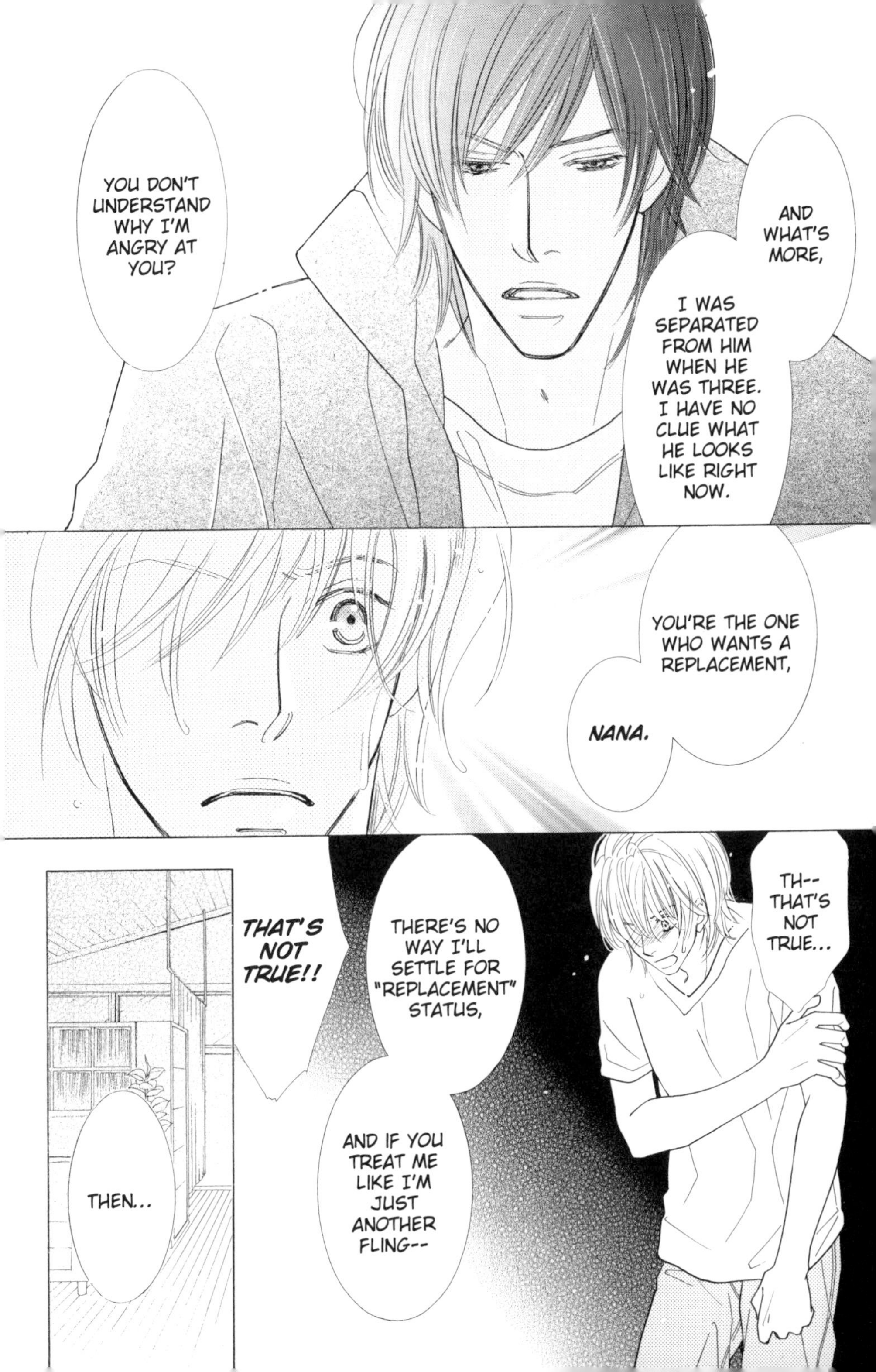
AND WHAT'S MORE,
I WAS SEPARATED FROM HIM WHEN HE WAS THREE. I HAVE NO CLUE WHAT HE LOOKS LIKE RIGHT NOW.
YOU DON'T UNDERSTAND WHY I'M ANGRY AT YOU?
YOU'RE THE ONE WHO WANTS A REPLACEMENT,
NANA.
TH-- THAT'S NOT TRUE...
THERE'S NO WAY I'LL SETTLE FOR "REPLACEMENT" STATUS,
THAT'S NOT TRUE!!
AND IF YOU TREAT ME LIKE I'M JUST ANOTHER FLING--
THEN...

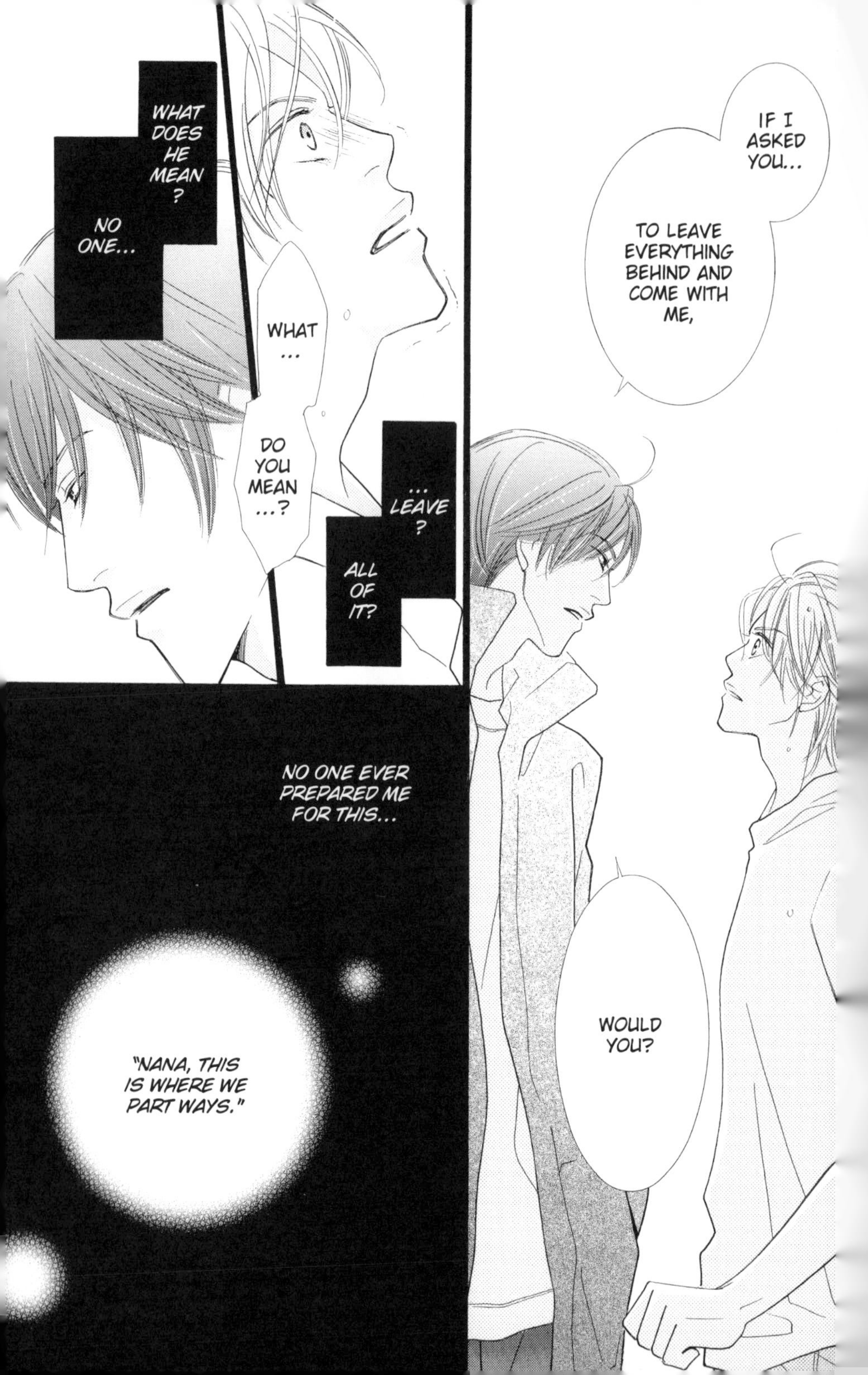
IF I ASKED YOU...
TO LEAVE EVERYTHING BEHIND AND COME WITH ME,
WOULD YOU?
...LEAVE?
ALL OF IT?
WHAT...
DO YOU MEAN...?
WHAT DOES HE MEAN?
NO ONE...
NO ONE EVER PREPARED ME FOR THIS...
"NANA, THIS IS WHERE WE PART WAYS."

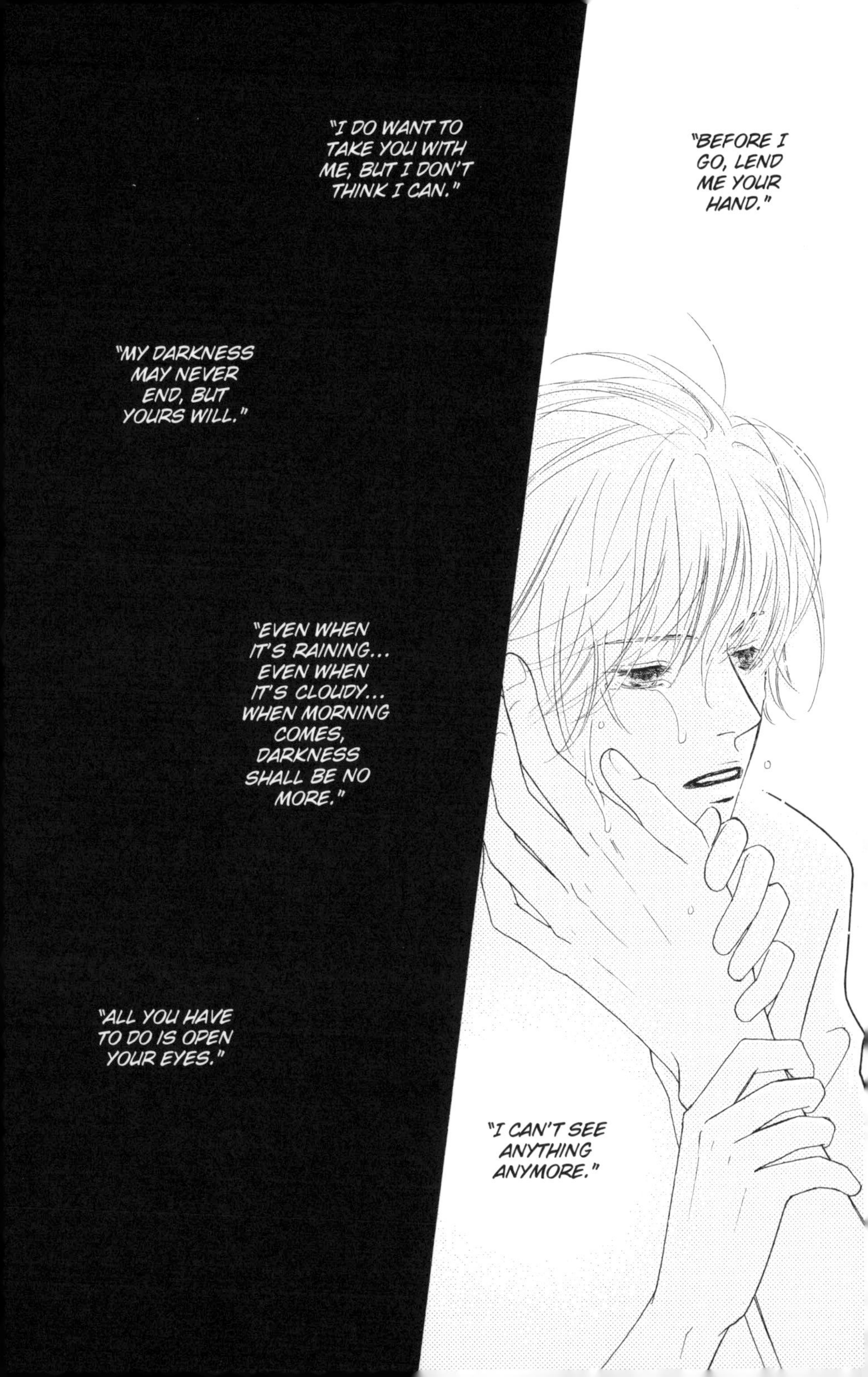
"BEFORE I GO, LEND ME YOUR HAND."
"I CAN'T SEE ANYTHING ANYMORE."
"I DO WANT TO TAKE YOU WITH ME, BUT I DON'T THINK I CAN."
"MY DARKNESS MAY NEVER END, BUT YOURS WILL."
"EVEN WHEN IT'S RAINING... EVEN WHEN IT'S CLOUDY... WHEN MORNING COMES, DARKNESS SHALL BE NO MORE."
"ALL YOU HAVE TO DO IS OPEN YOUR EYES."

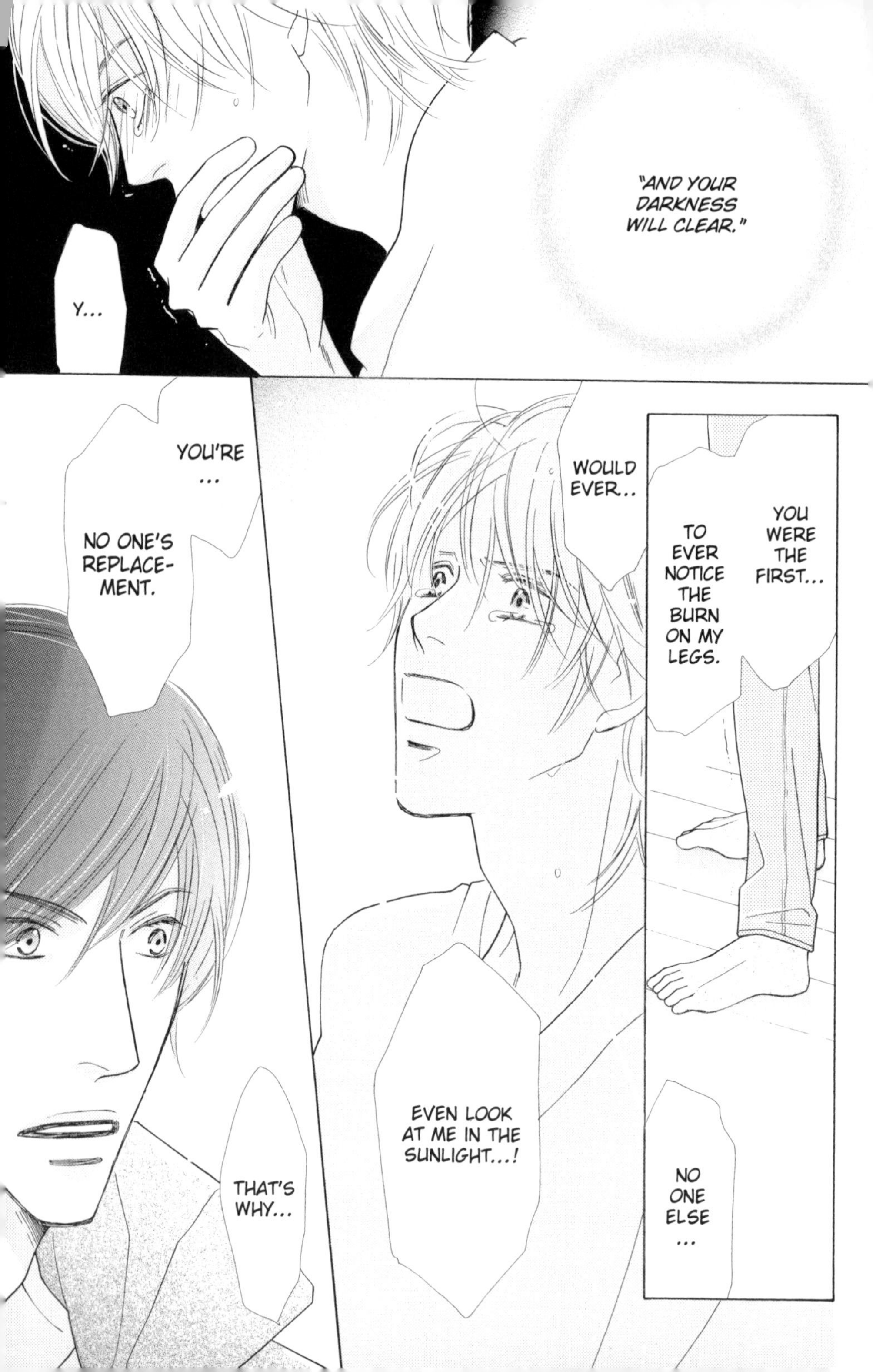
"AND YOUR DARKNESS WILL CLEAR."
Y...
YOU WERE THE FIRST...
TO EVER NOTICE THE BURN ON MY LEGS.
NO ONE ELSE ...
WOULD EVER...
EVEN LOOK AT ME IN THE SUNLIGHT...!
YOU'RE ...
NO ONE'S REPLACE-MENT.
THAT'S WHY...

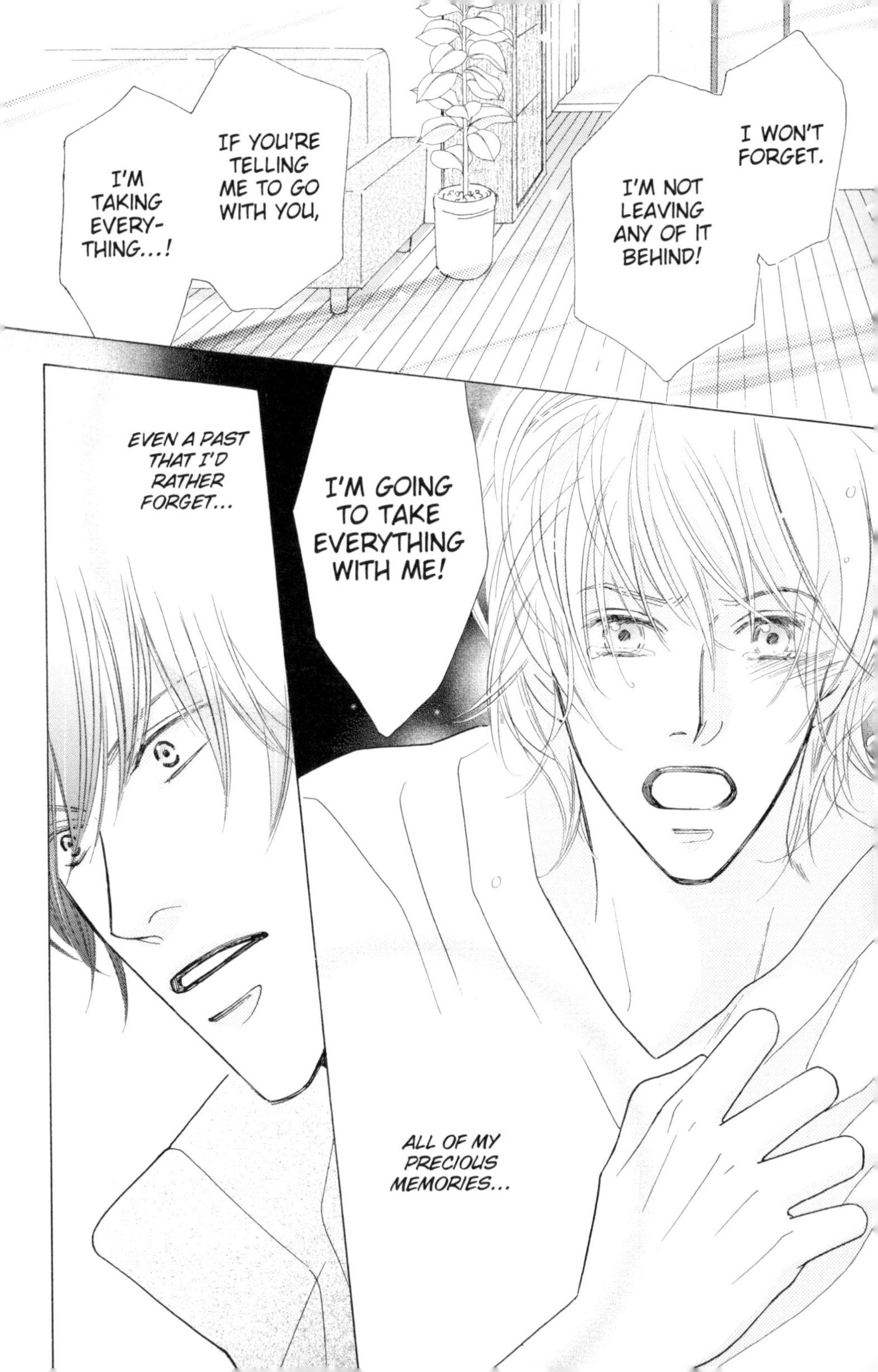
I WON'T FORGET.
I'M NOT LEAVING ANY OF IT BEHIND!
IF YOU'RE TELLING ME TO GO WITH YOU,
I'M TAKING EVERY-THING...!
I'M GOING TO TAKE EVERYTHING WITH ME!
EVEN A PAST THAT I'D RATHER FORGET...
ALL OF MY PRECIOUS MEMORIES...

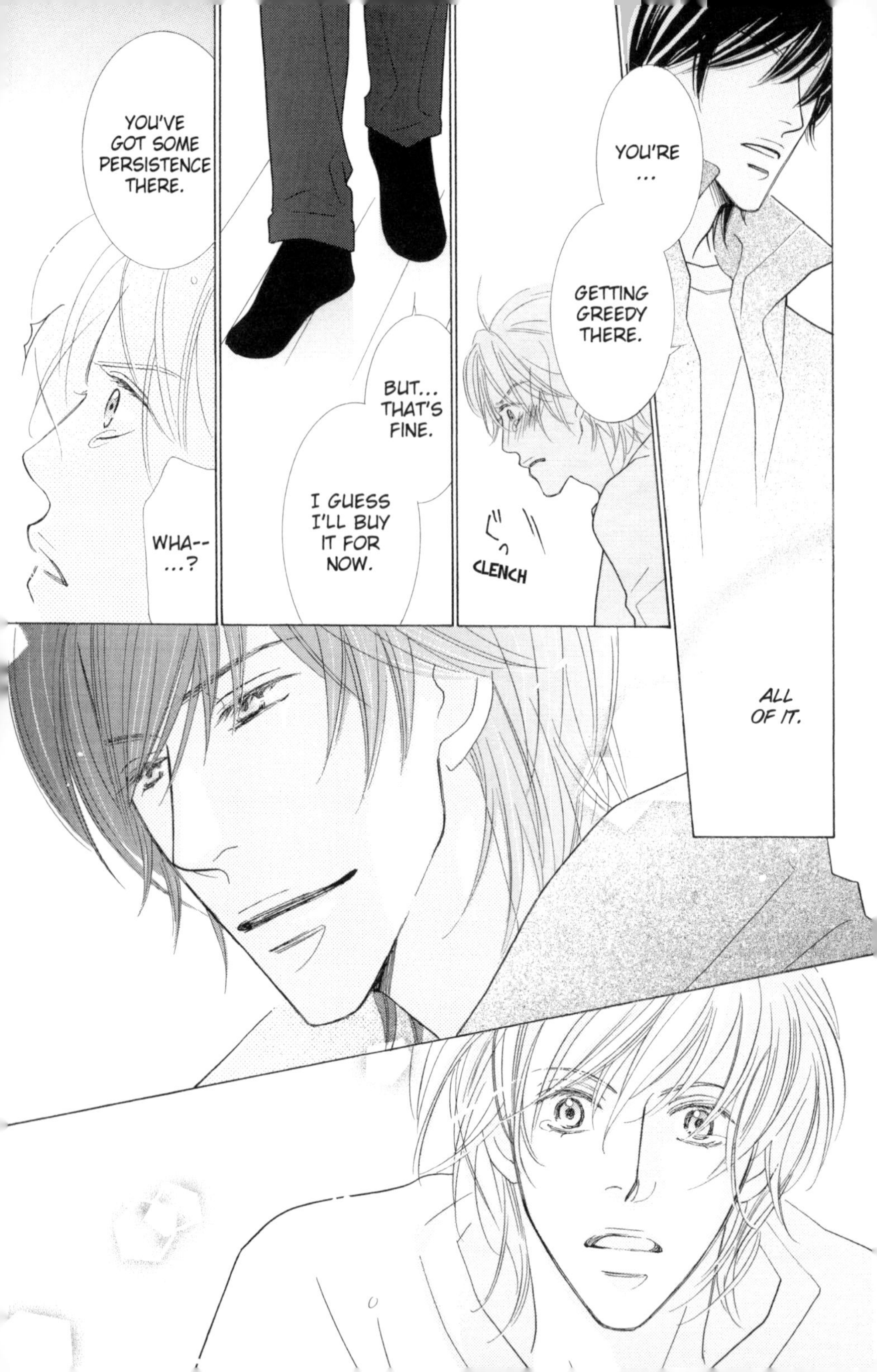
YOU'RE ...
GETTING GREEDY THERE.
ALL OF IT.
CLENCH
BUT... THAT'S FINE.
I GUESS I'LL BUY IT FOR NOW.
YOU'VE GOT SOME PERSISTENCE THERE.
WHA-- ...?

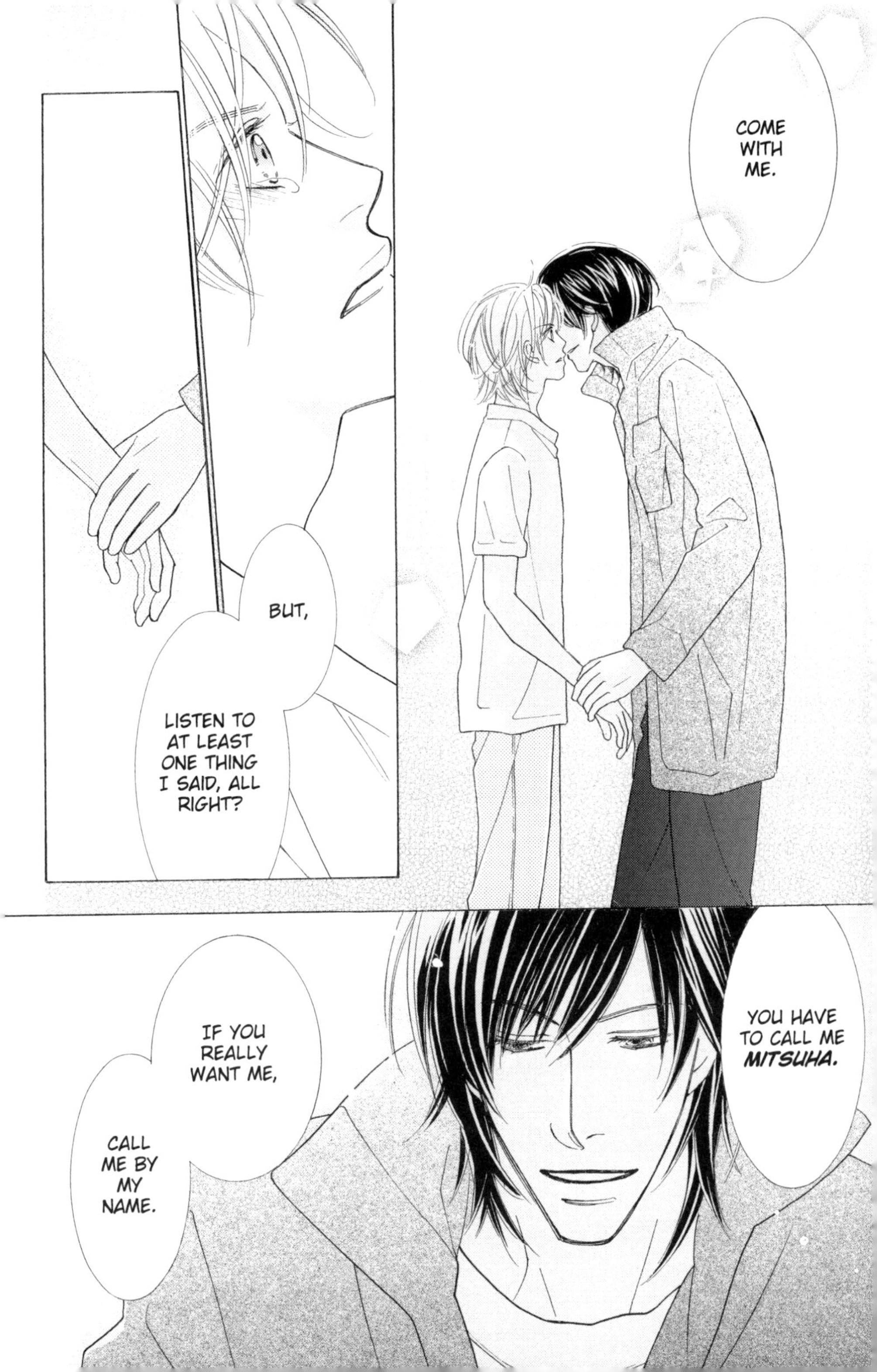
COME WITH ME.
BUT,
LISTEN TO AT LEAST ONE THING I SAID, ALL RIGHT?
YOU HAVE TO CALL ME **MITSUHA.**
IF YOU REALLY WANT ME,
CALL ME BY MY NAME.

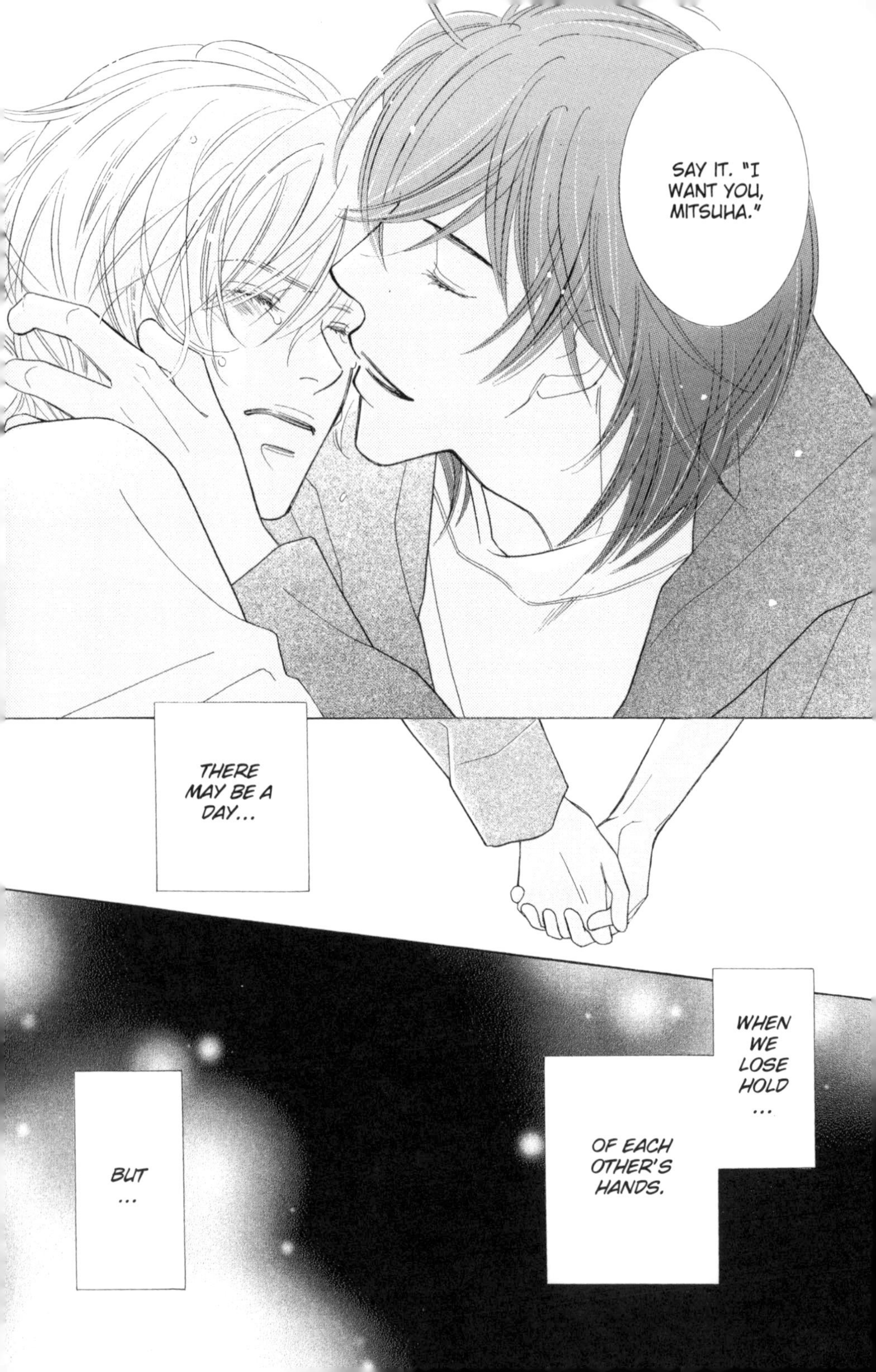
SAY IT. "I WANT YOU, MITSUHA."
THERE MAY BE A DAY...
WHEN WE LOSE HOLD...
OF EACH OTHER'S HANDS.
BUT...

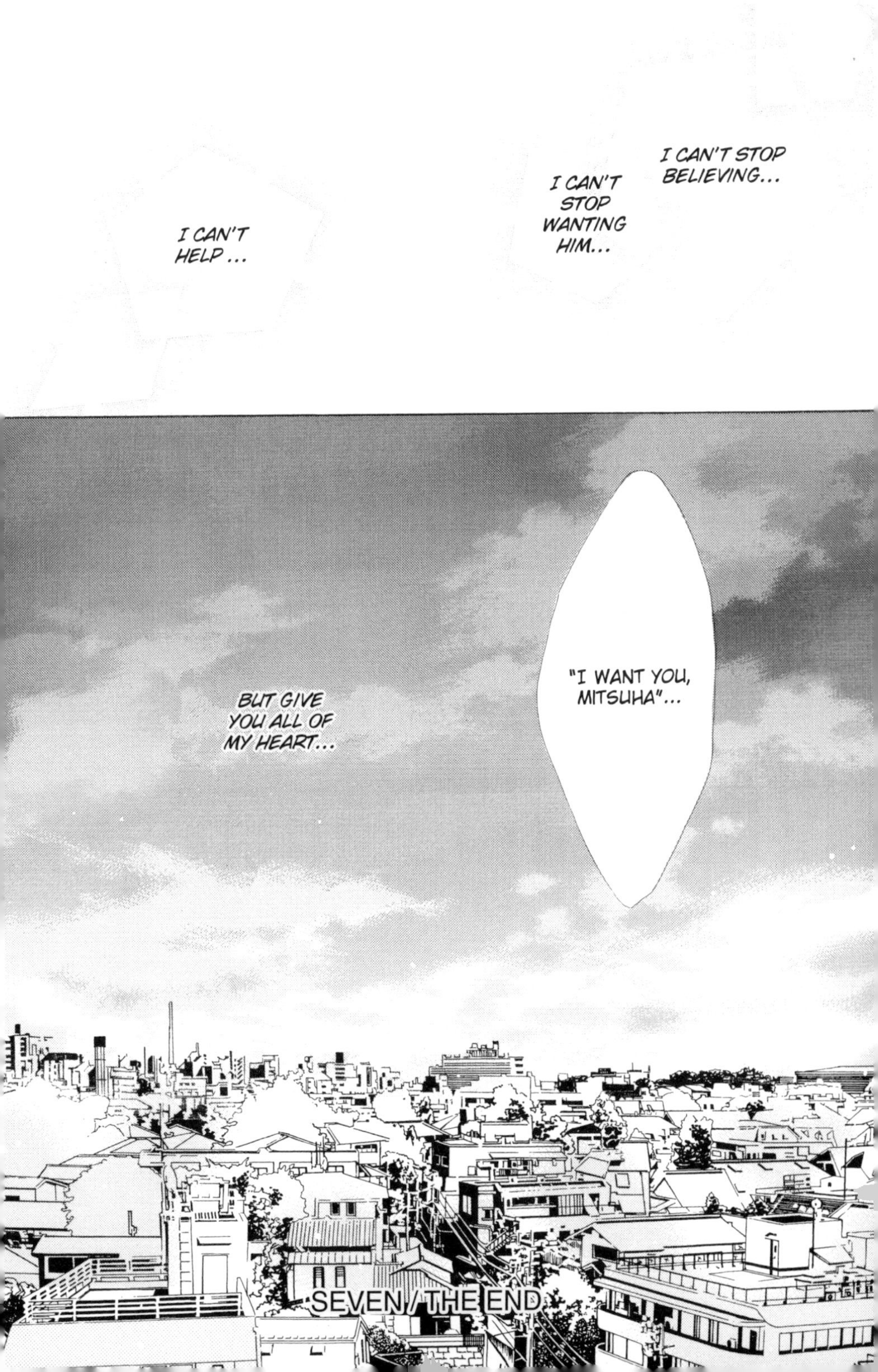
I CAN'T STOP BELIEVING...
I CAN'T STOP WANTING HIM...
I CAN'T HELP...
"I WANT YOU, MITSUHA"...
BUT GIVE YOU ALL OF MY HEART...
SEVEN / THE END

白日の真下

はくじつのました

WITHIN PLAIN VIEW

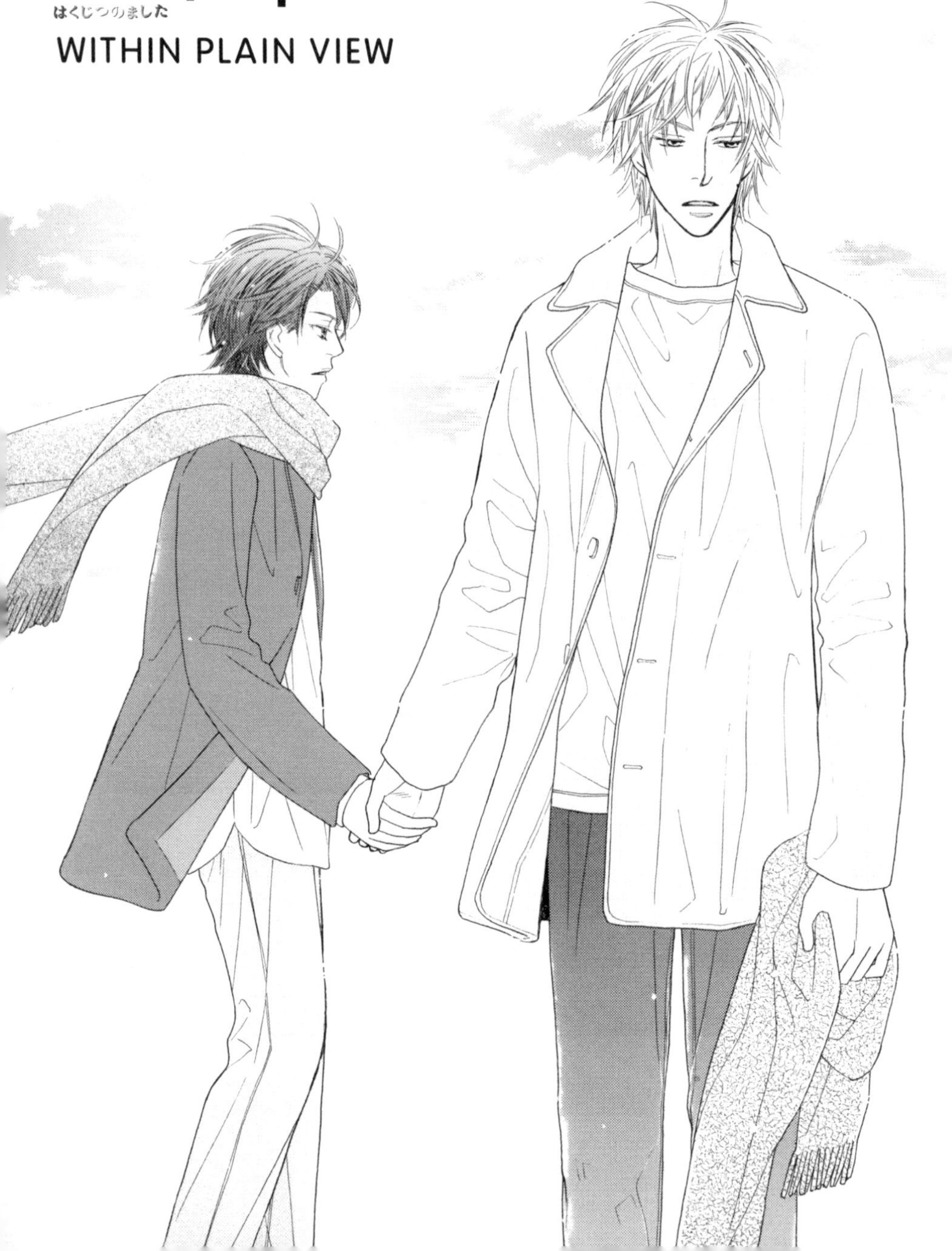

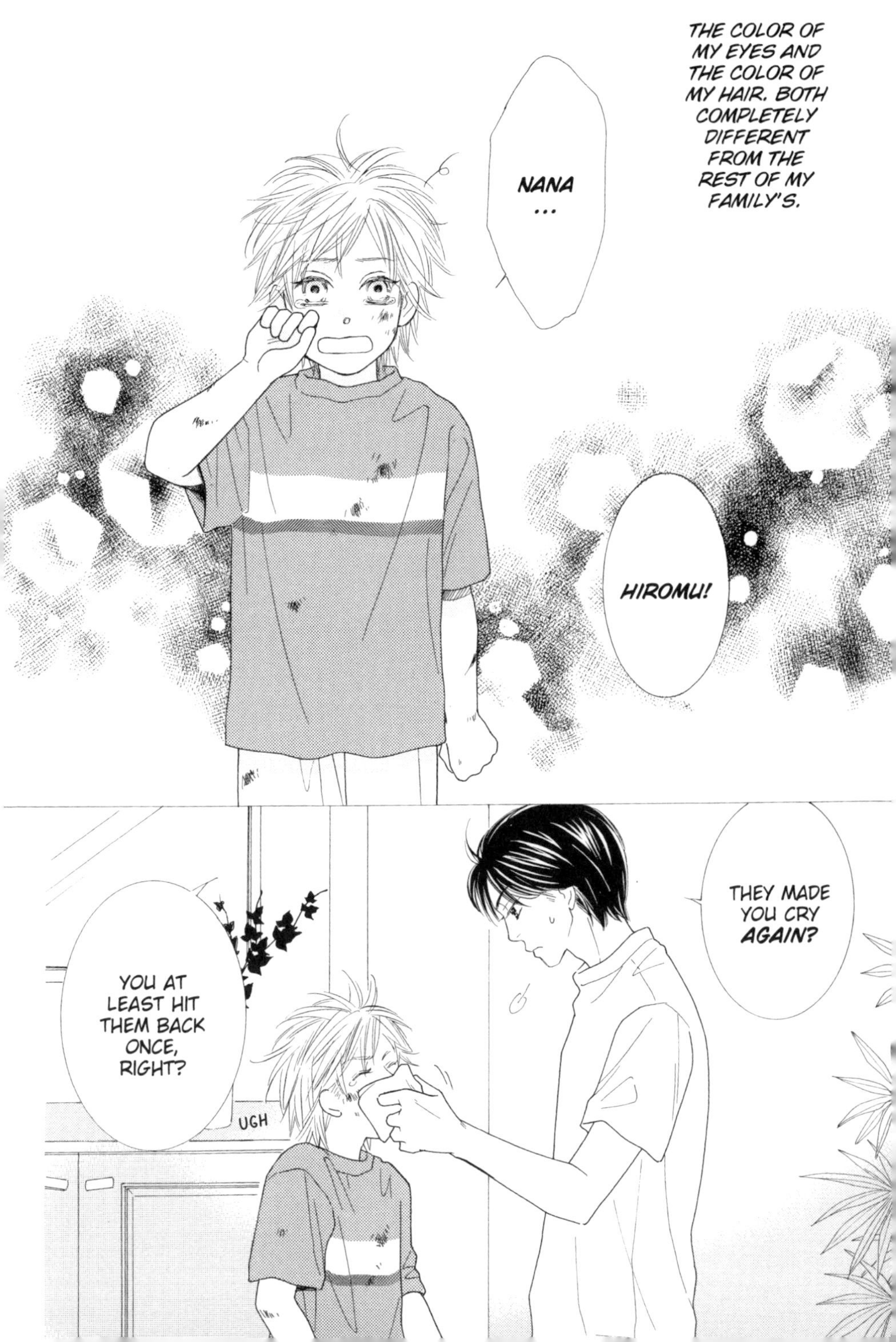
THE COLOR OF MY EYES AND THE COLOR OF MY HAIR. BOTH COMPLETELY DIFFERENT FROM THE REST OF MY FAMILY'S.
NANA...
HIROMU!
THEY MADE YOU CRY AGAIN?
UGH
YOU AT LEAST HIT THEM BACK ONCE, RIGHT?

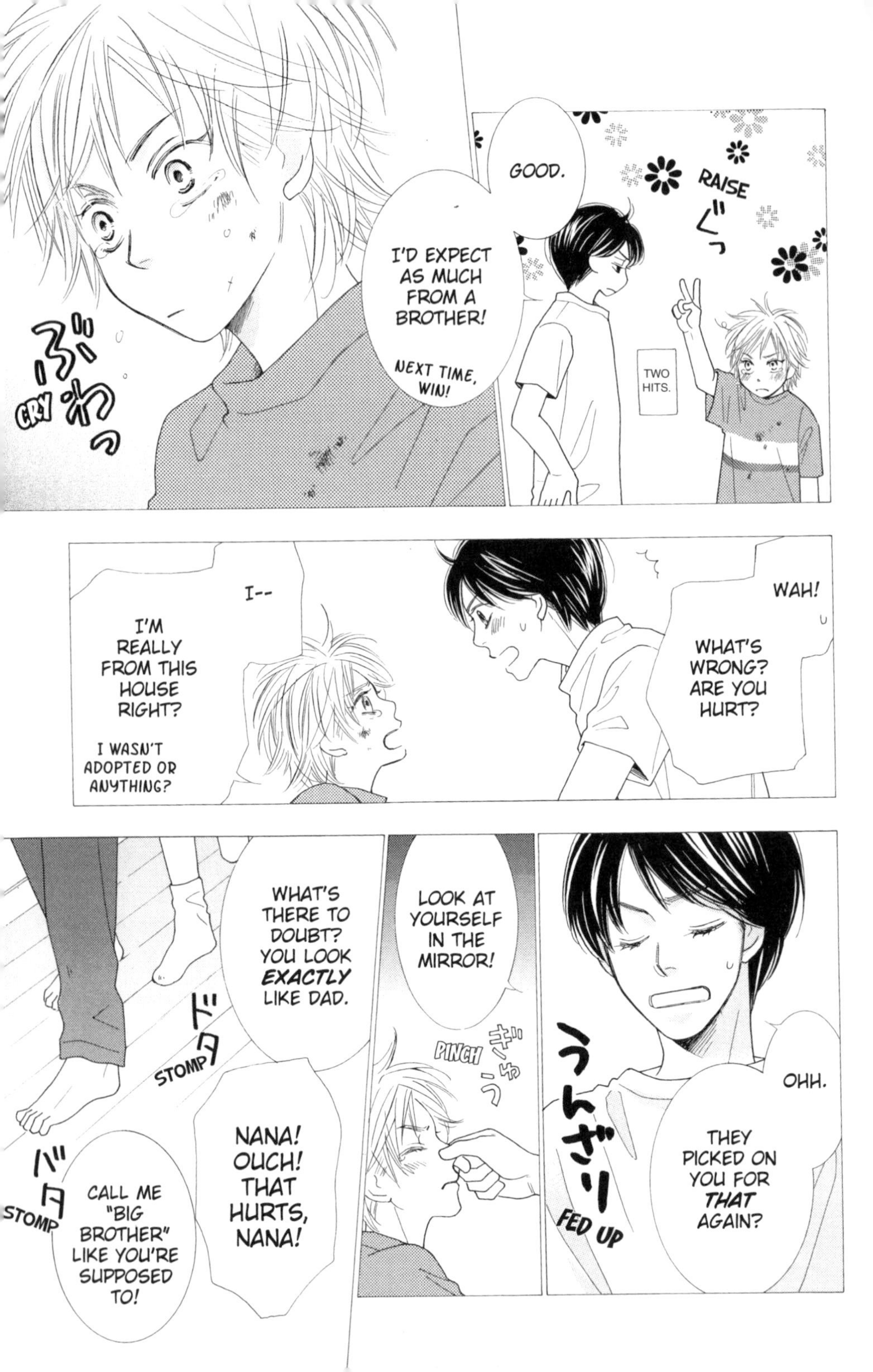
GOOD.
I'D EXPECT AS MUCH FROM A BROTHER!
NEXT TIME, WIN!
RAISE
ぐっ
TWO HITS.
ぶわっ
CRY
WAH!
WHAT'S WRONG? ARE YOU HURT?
I--
I'M REALLY FROM THIS HOUSE RIGHT?
I WASN'T ADOPTED OR ANYTHING?
OHH.
THEY PICKED ON YOU FOR *THAT* AGAIN?
うんざり
FED UP
LOOK AT YOURSELF IN THE MIRROR!
ぎゅう
PINCH
WHAT'S THERE TO DOUBT? YOU LOOK ***EXACTLY*** LIKE DAD.
ドタ
STOMP
NANA! OUCH! THAT HURTS, NANA!
バタ
STOMP
CALL ME "BIG BROTHER" LIKE YOU'RE SUPPOSED TO!

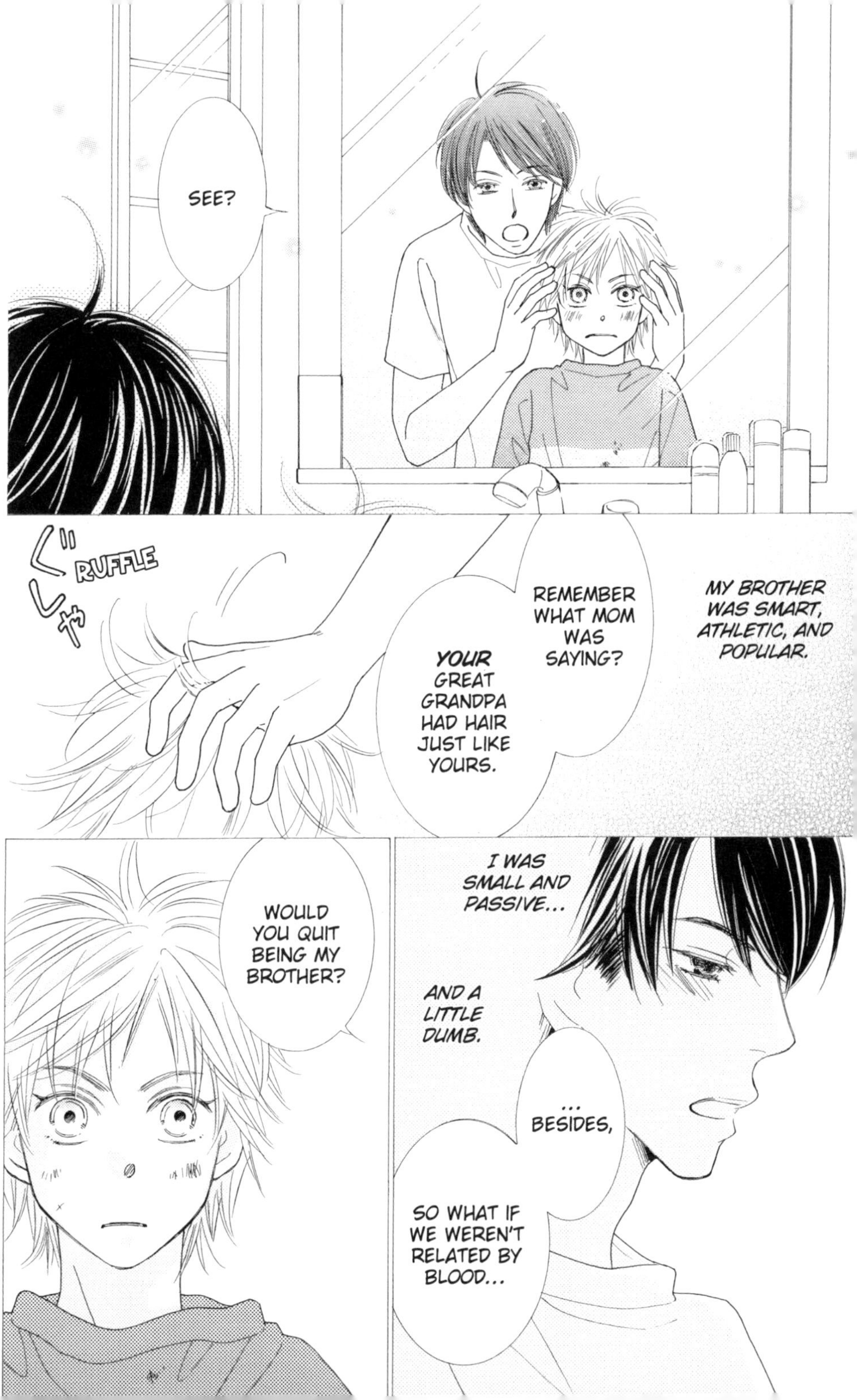
SEE?
MY BROTHER WAS SMART, ATHLETIC, AND POPULAR.
REMEMBER WHAT MOM WAS SAYING?
YOUR GREAT GRANDPA HAD HAIR JUST LIKE YOURS.
くしゃ RUFFLE
I WAS SMALL AND PASSIVE...
AND A LITTLE DUMB.
... BESIDES,
SO WHAT IF WE WEREN'T RELATED BY BLOOD...
WOULD YOU QUIT BEING MY BROTHER?

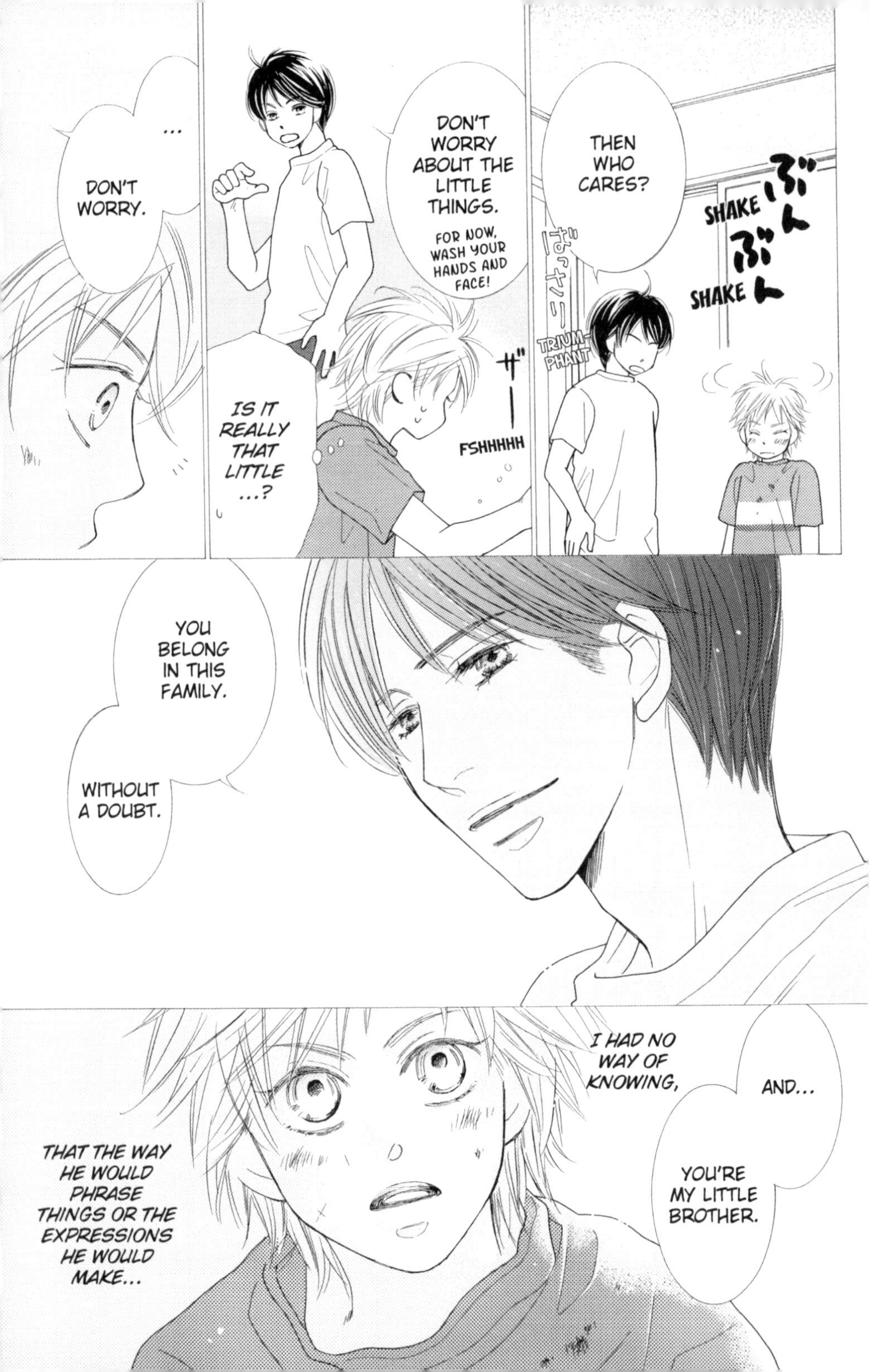
ぶん ぶん
SHAKE SHAKE
THEN WHO CARES?
ぱっさり
TRIUM-PHANT
DON'T WORRY ABOUT THE LITTLE THINGS.
FOR NOW, WASH YOUR HANDS AND FACE!
ザー
FSHHHHH
IS IT REALLY THAT LITTLE ...?
... DON'T WORRY.
YOU BELONG IN THIS FAMILY.
WITHOUT A DOUBT.
AND...
YOU'RE MY LITTLE BROTHER.
I HAD NO WAY OF KNOWING,
THAT THE WAY HE WOULD PHRASE THINGS OR THE EXPRESSIONS HE WOULD MAKE...

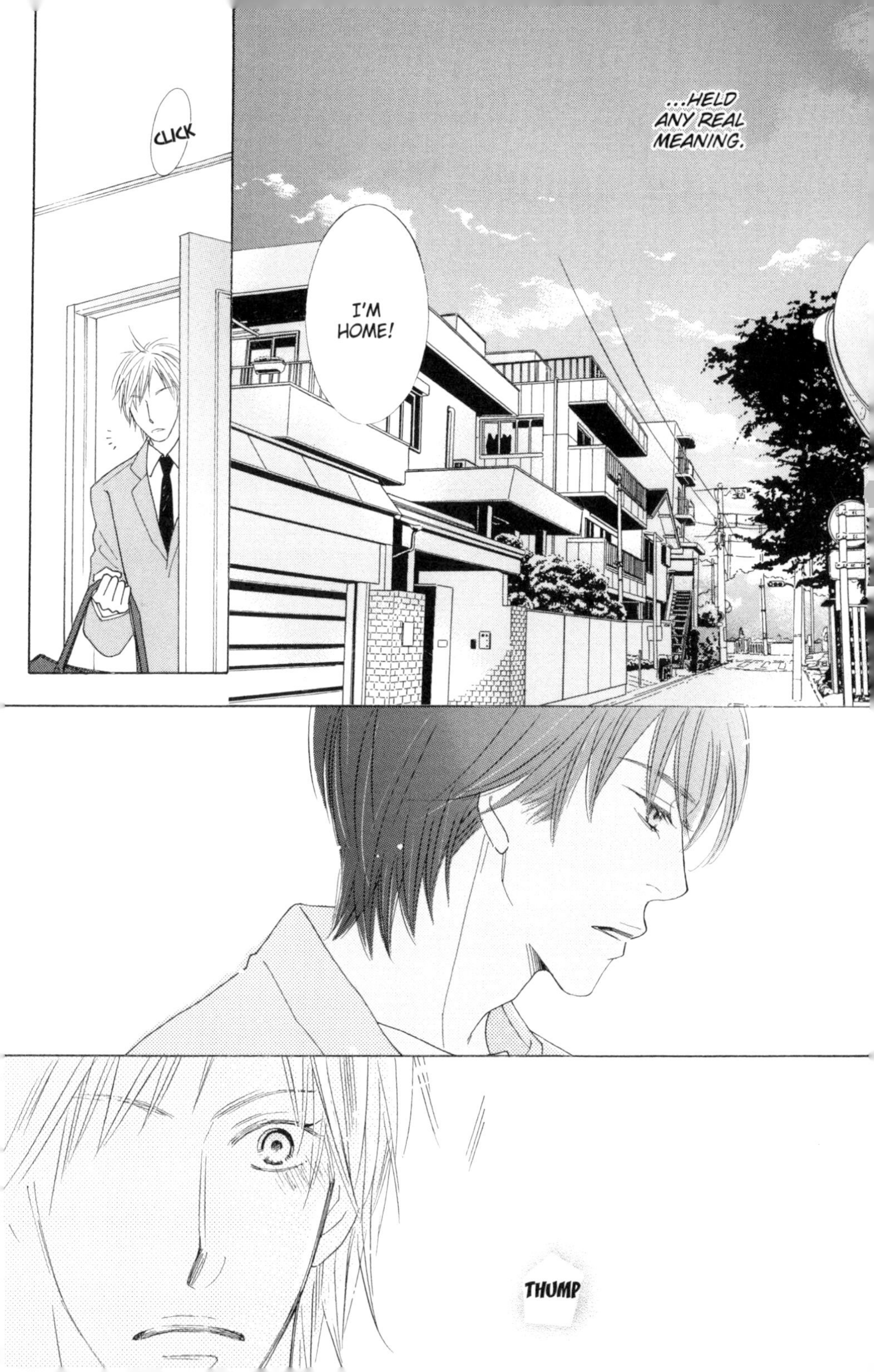
...HELD ANY REAL MEANING.
I'M HOME!
CLICK
THUMP

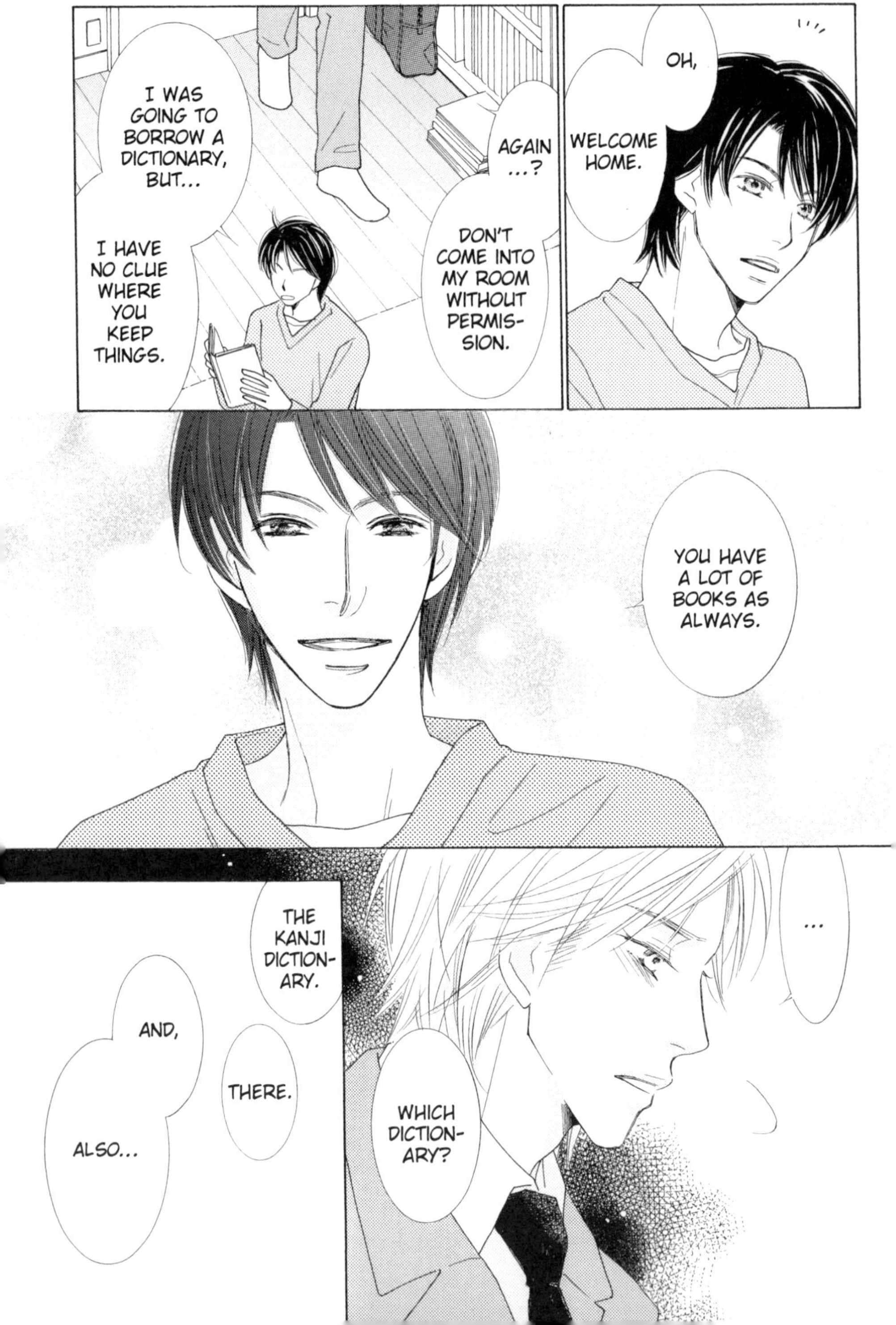
OH,
WELCOME HOME.
AGAIN ...?
DON'T COME INTO MY ROOM WITHOUT PERMIS-SION.
I WAS GOING TO BORROW A DICTIONARY, BUT...
I HAVE NO CLUE WHERE YOU KEEP THINGS.
YOU HAVE A LOT OF BOOKS AS ALWAYS.
...
WHICH DICTION-ARY?
THE KANJI DICTION-ARY.
THERE.
AND,
ALSO...

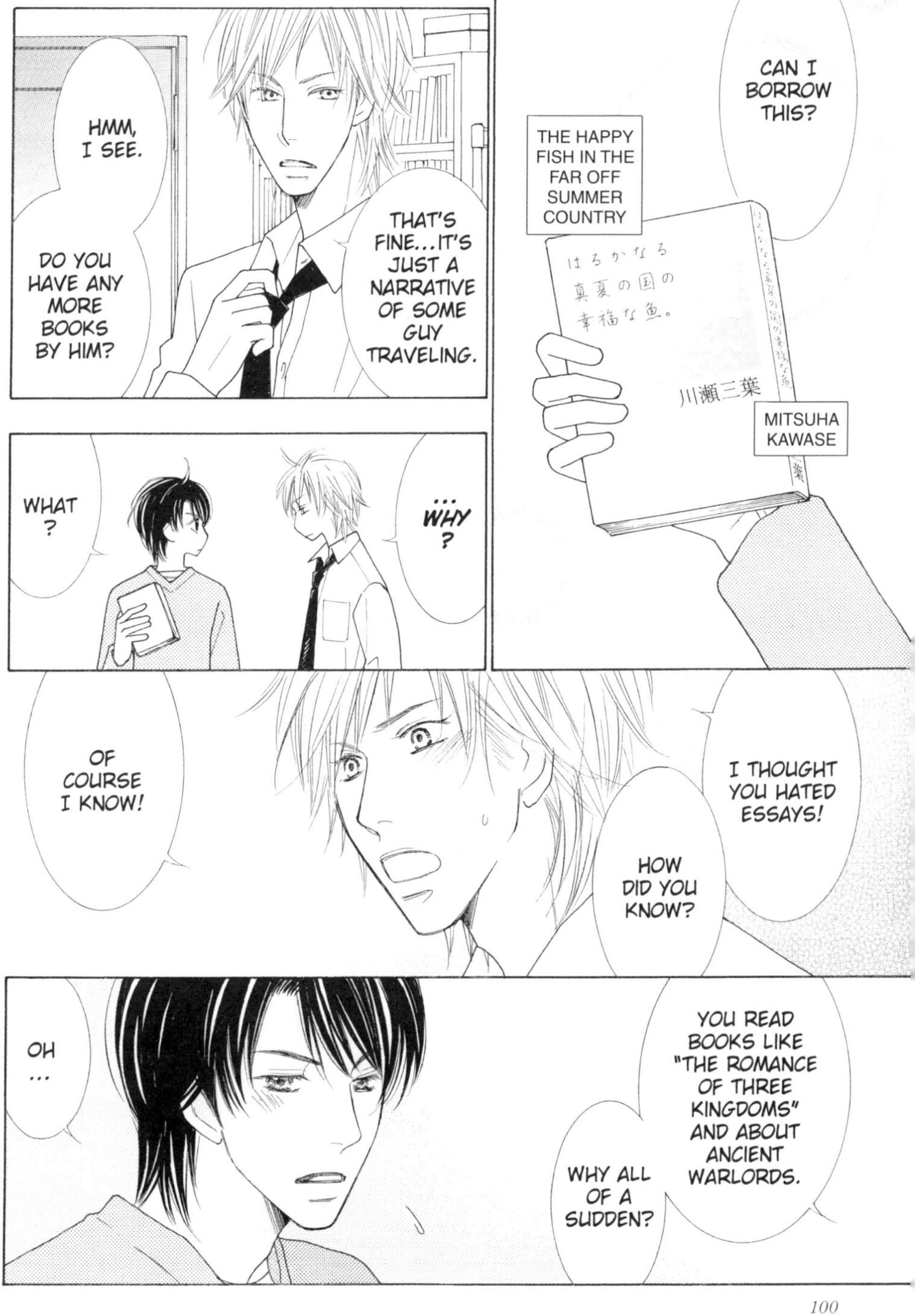
CAN I BORROW THIS?
THE HAPPY FISH IN THE FAR OFF SUMMER COUNTRY
はるかなる真夏の国の幸福な魚。
川瀬三葉
MITSUHA KAWASE
THAT'S FINE...IT'S JUST A NARRATIVE OF SOME GUY TRAVELING.
HMM, I SEE.
DO YOU HAVE ANY MORE BOOKS BY HIM?
... *WHY* ?
WHAT ?
I THOUGHT YOU HATED ESSAYS!
HOW DID YOU KNOW?
OF COURSE I KNOW!
YOU READ BOOKS LIKE "THE ROMANCE OF THREE KINGDOMS" AND ABOUT ANCIENT WARLORDS.
WHY ALL OF A SUDDEN?
OH ...

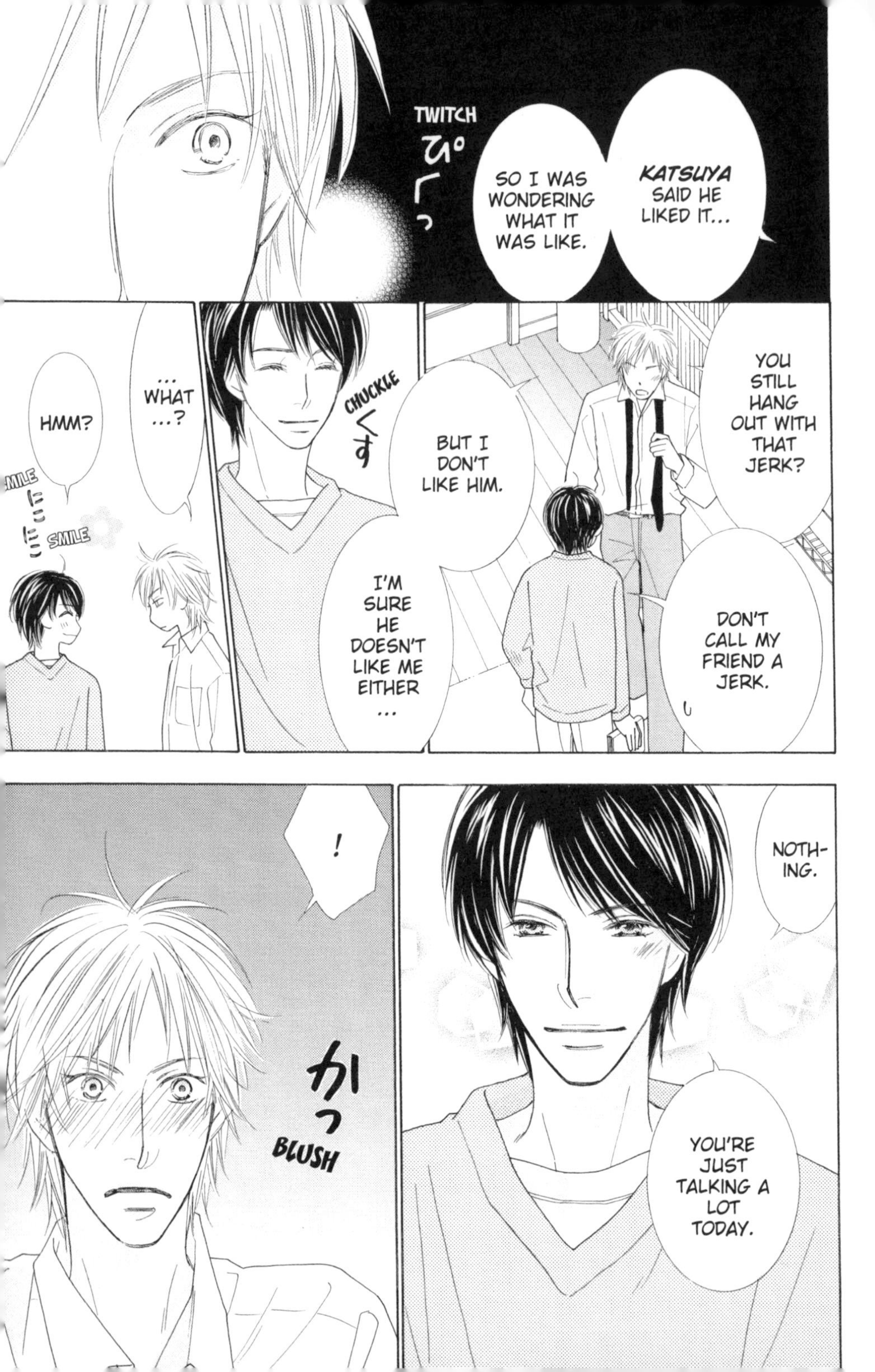
KATSUYA SAID HE LIKED IT...
SO I WAS WONDERING WHAT IT WAS LIKE.
TWITCH
ぴくっ
YOU STILL HANG OUT WITH THAT JERK?
DON'T CALL MY FRIEND A JERK.
BUT I DON'T LIKE HIM.
CHUCKLE
くす
I'M SURE HE DOESN'T LIKE ME EITHER...
...WHAT...?
HMM?
SMILE
にこ
にこ
SMILE
NOTHING.
YOU'RE JUST TALKING A LOT TODAY.
!
かっ
BLUSH

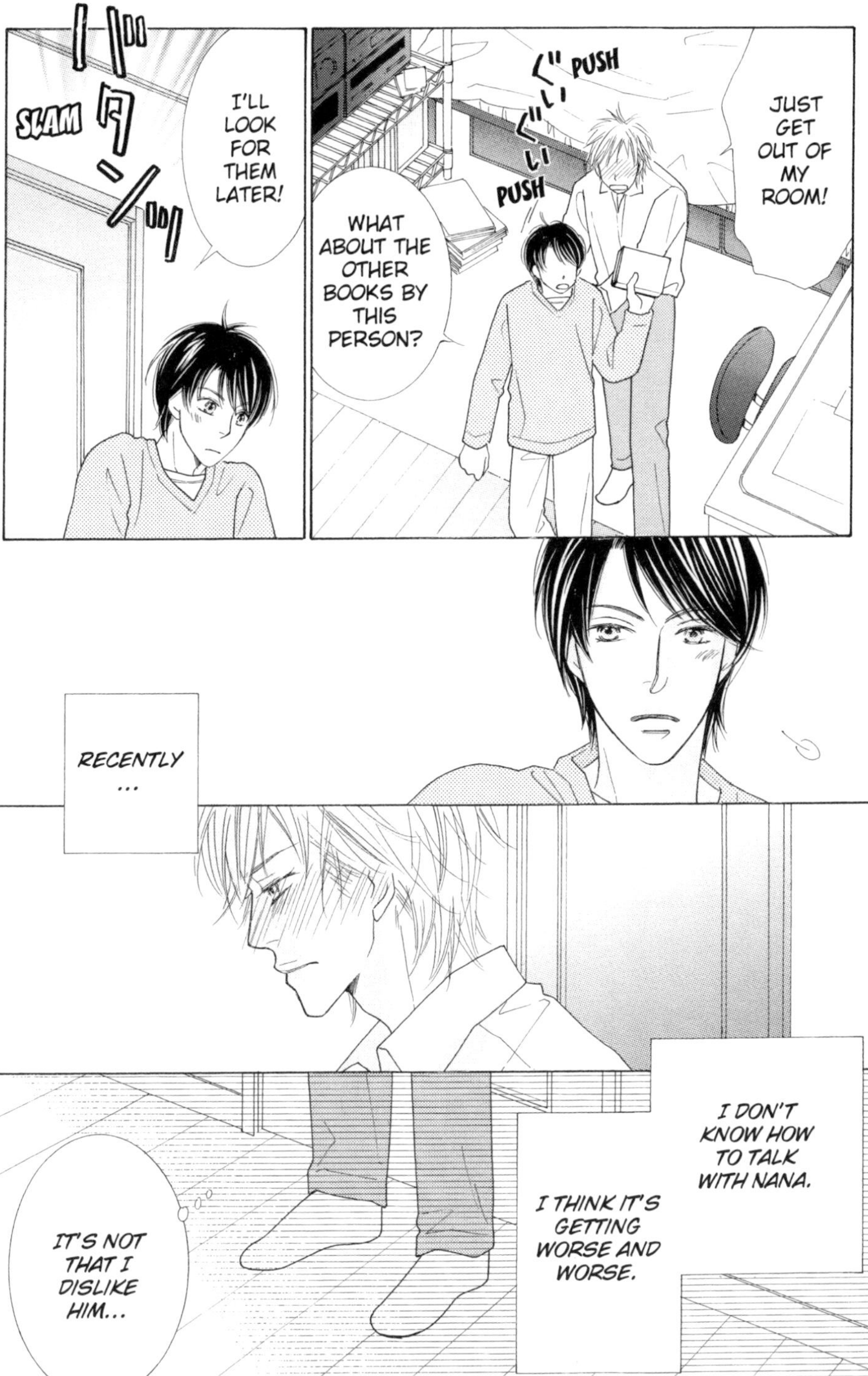
JUST GET OUT OF MY ROOM!
PUSH
PUSH
WHAT ABOUT THE OTHER BOOKS BY THIS PERSON?
I'LL LOOK FOR THEM LATER!
SLAM
RECENTLY...
I DON'T KNOW HOW TO TALK WITH NANA.
I THINK IT'S GETTING WORSE AND WORSE.
IT'S NOT THAT I DISLIKE HIM...

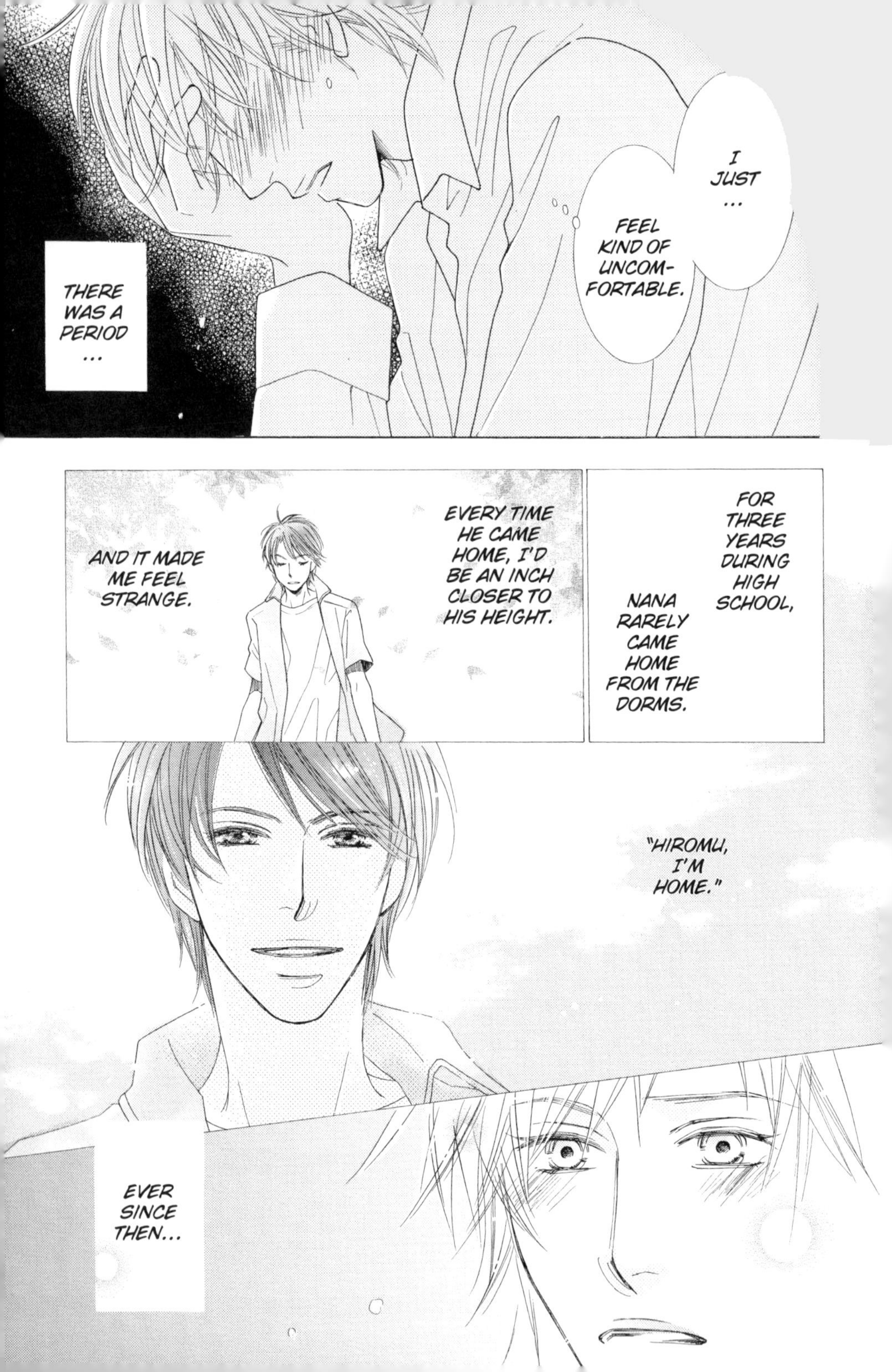
I JUST ... FEEL KIND OF UNCOM-FORTABLE.
THERE WAS A PERIOD ...
FOR THREE YEARS DURING HIGH SCHOOL,
NANA RARELY CAME HOME FROM THE DORMS.
EVERY TIME HE CAME HOME, I'D BE AN INCH CLOSER TO HIS HEIGHT.
AND IT MADE ME FEEL STRANGE.
"HIROMU, I'M HOME."
EVER SINCE THEN...

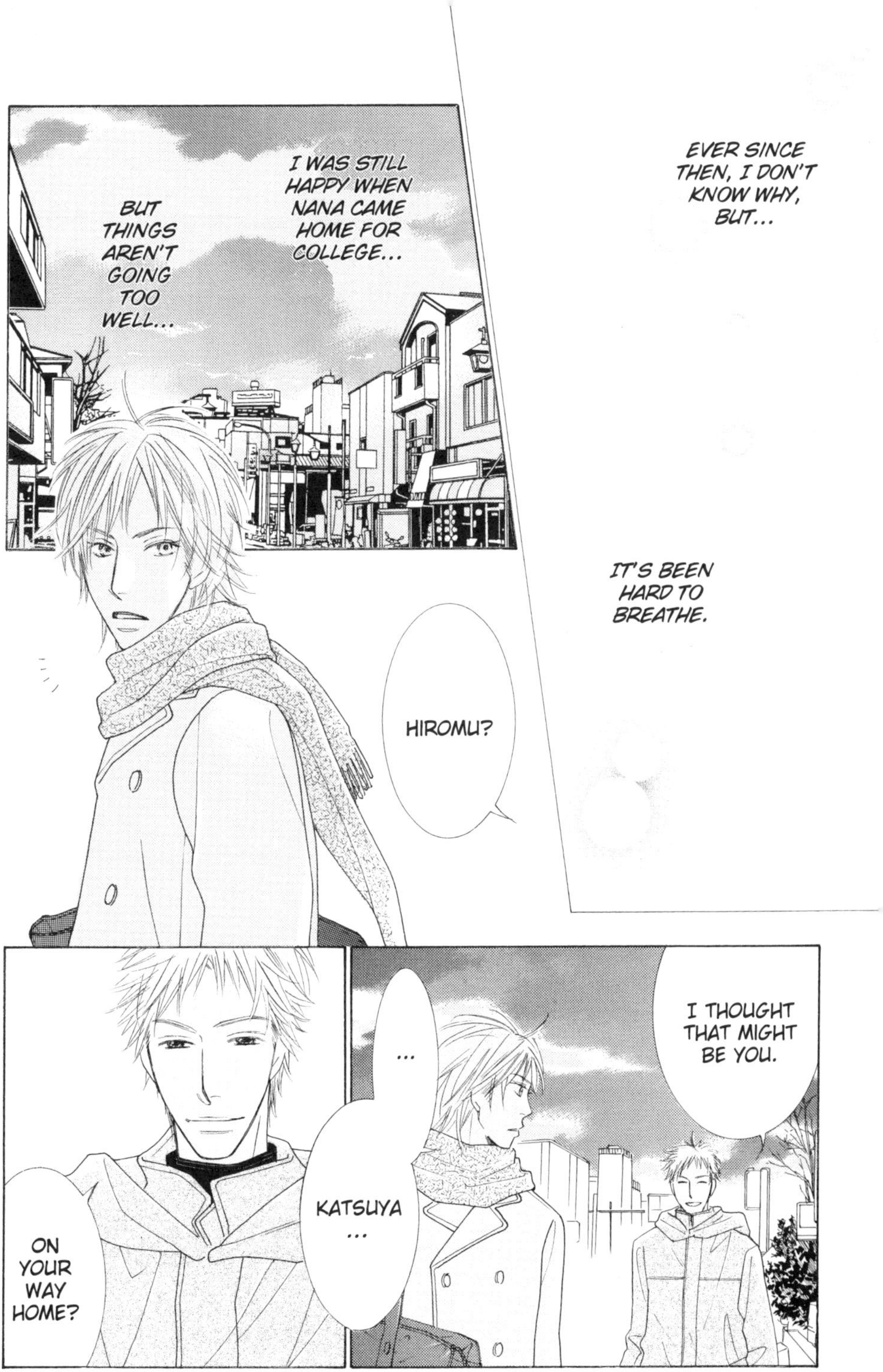
EVER SINCE THEN, I DON'T KNOW WHY, BUT...
IT'S BEEN HARD TO BREATHE.
I WAS STILL HAPPY WHEN NANA CAME HOME FOR COLLEGE...
BUT THINGS AREN'T GOING TOO WELL...
HIROMU?
I THOUGHT THAT MIGHT BE YOU.
...
KATSUYA...
ON YOUR WAY HOME?

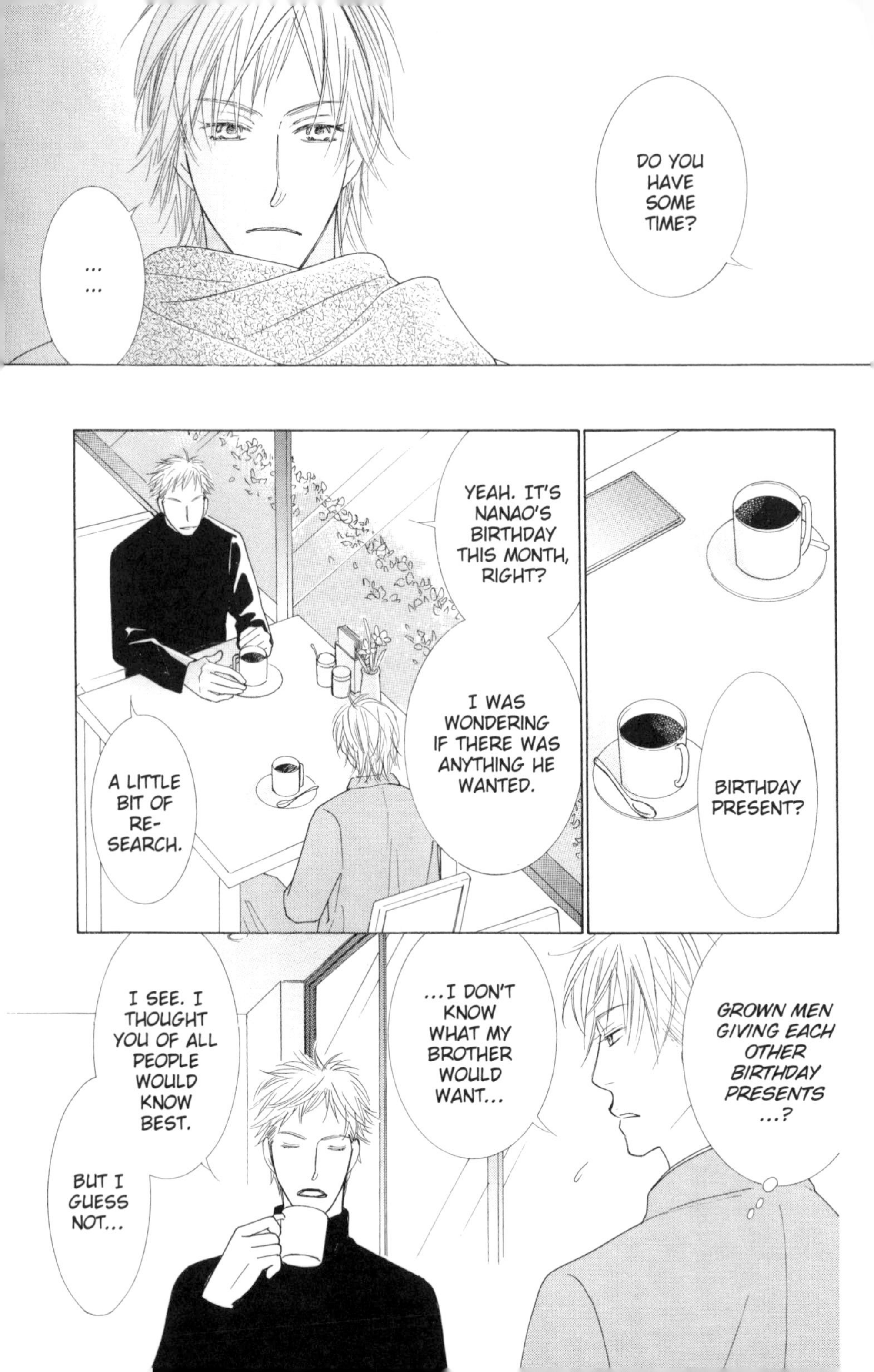
DO YOU HAVE SOME TIME?
……
BIRTHDAY PRESENT?
YEAH. IT'S NANAO'S BIRTHDAY THIS MONTH, RIGHT?
I WAS WONDERING IF THERE WAS ANYTHING HE WANTED.
A LITTLE BIT OF RE-SEARCH.
GROWN MEN GIVING EACH OTHER BIRTHDAY PRESENTS …?
…I DON'T KNOW WHAT MY BROTHER WOULD WANT…
I SEE. I THOUGHT YOU OF ALL PEOPLE WOULD KNOW BEST.
BUT I GUESS NOT…

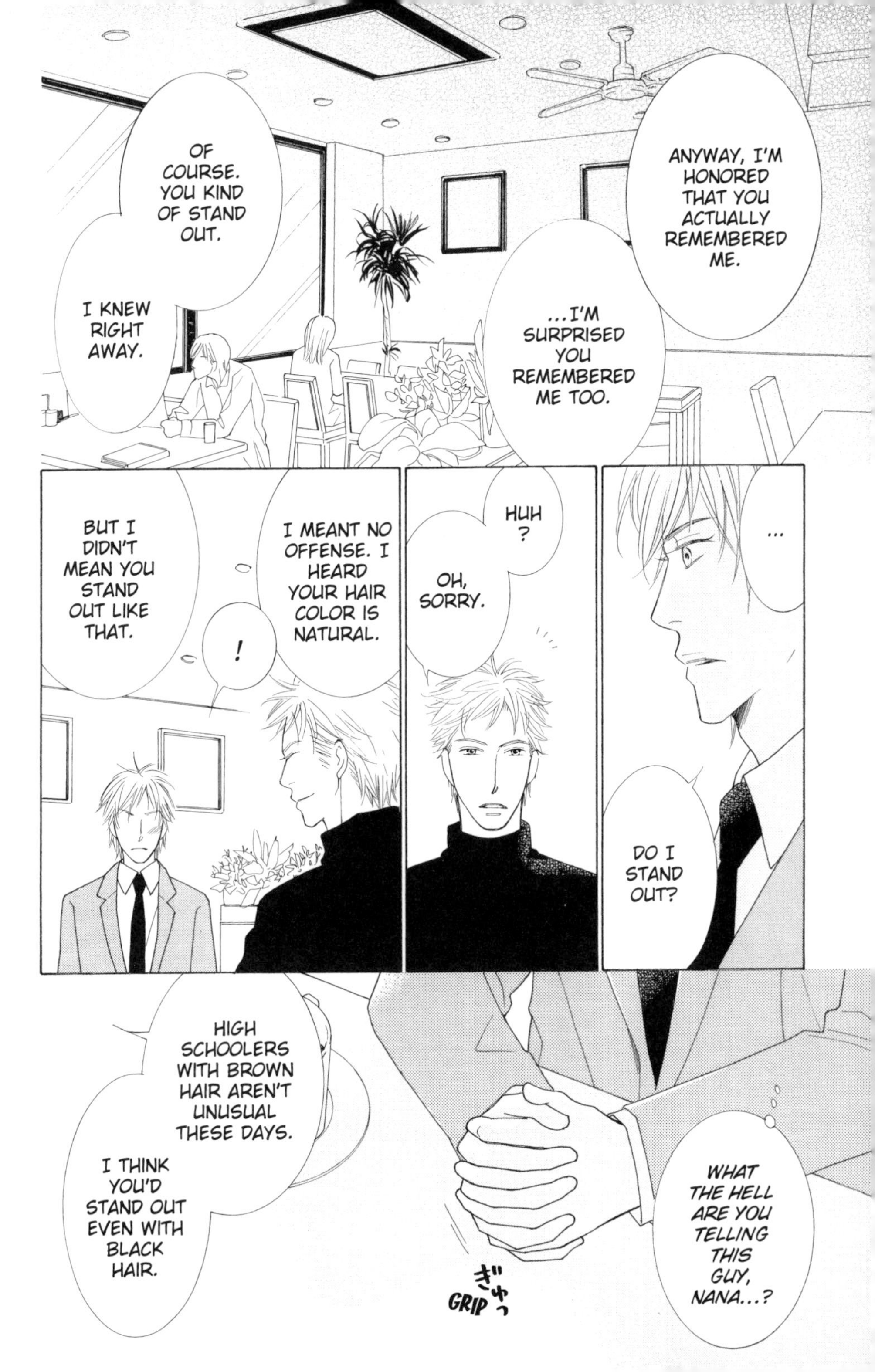
ANYWAY, I'M HONORED THAT YOU ACTUALLY REMEMBERED ME.
...I'M SURPRISED YOU REMEMBERED ME TOO.
OF COURSE. YOU KIND OF STAND OUT.
I KNEW RIGHT AWAY.
...
DO I STAND OUT?
HUH?
OH, SORRY.
I MEANT NO OFFENSE. I HEARD YOUR HAIR COLOR IS NATURAL.
!
BUT I DIDN'T MEAN YOU STAND OUT LIKE THAT.
HIGH SCHOOLERS WITH BROWN HAIR AREN'T UNUSUAL THESE DAYS.
I THINK YOU'D STAND OUT EVEN WITH BLACK HAIR.
ぎゅっ
GRIP
WHAT THE HELL ARE YOU TELLING THIS GUY, NANA...?

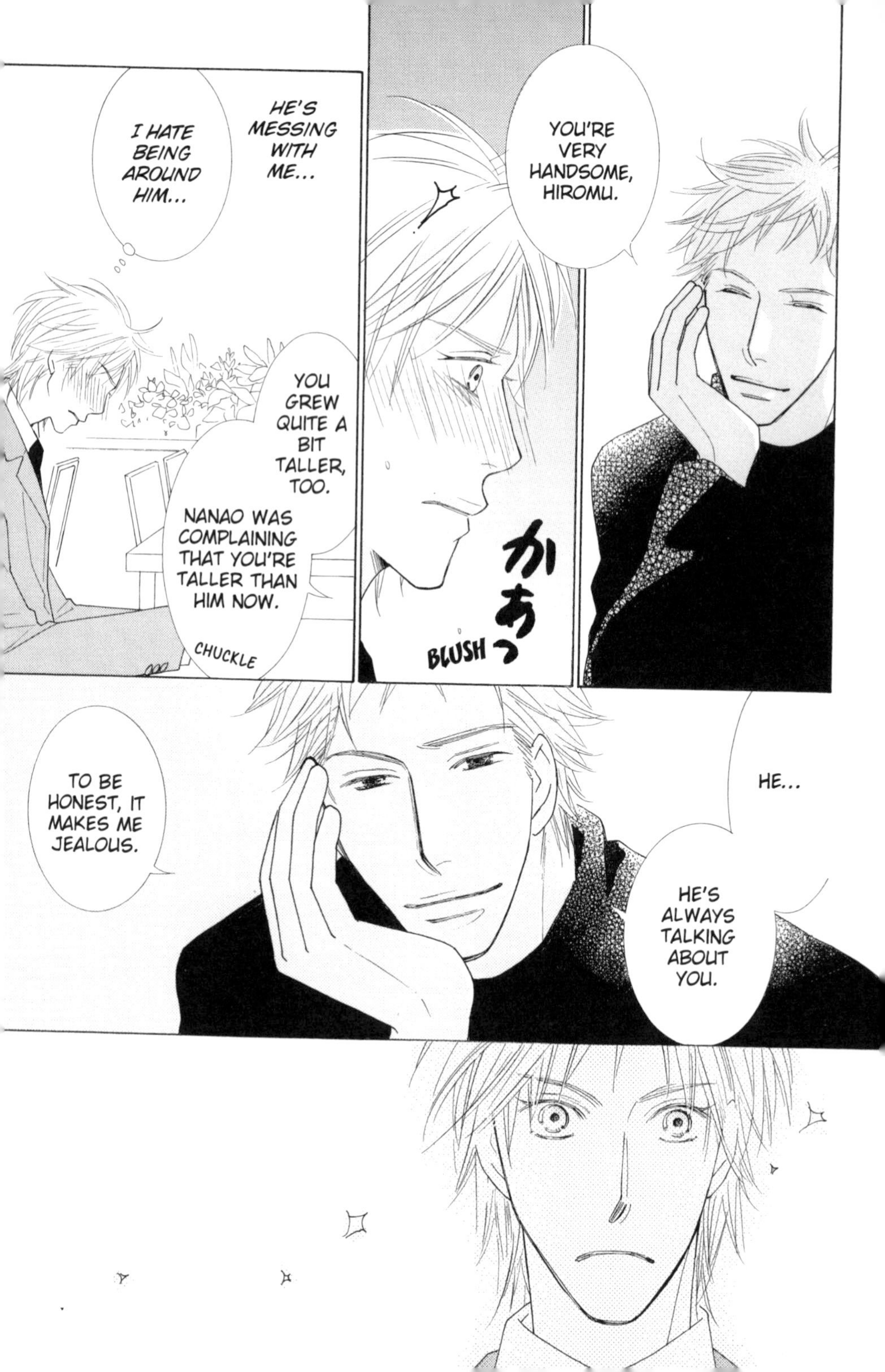
YOU'RE VERY HANDSOME, HIROMU.
かあっ
BLUSH
HE'S MESSING WITH ME...
I HATE BEING AROUND HIM...
YOU GREW QUITE A BIT TALLER, TOO.
NANAO WAS COMPLAINING THAT YOU'RE TALLER THAN HIM NOW.
CHUCKLE
HE...
HE'S ALWAYS TALKING ABOUT YOU.
TO BE HONEST, IT MAKES ME JEALOUS.

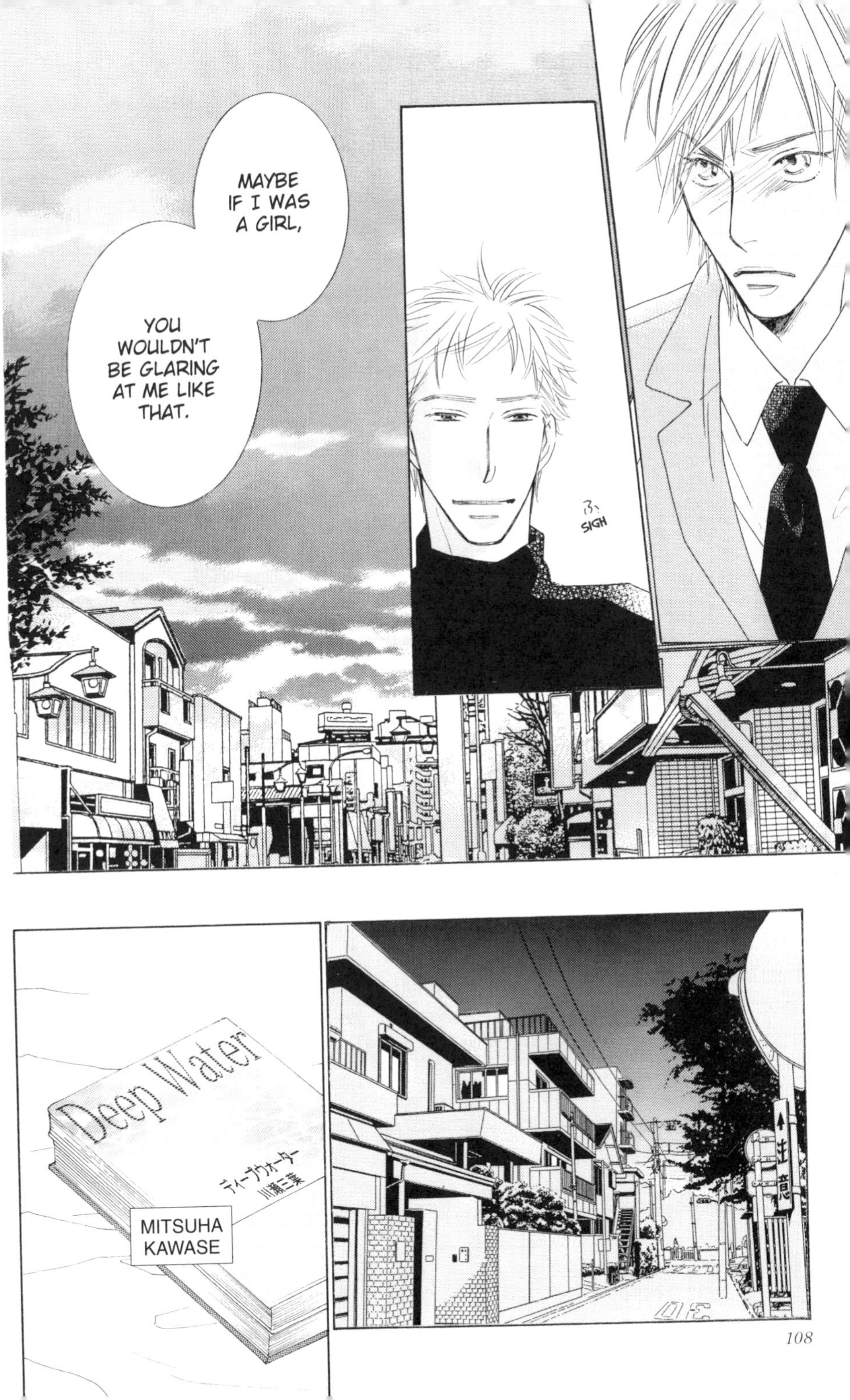
ふ
SIGH
MAYBE IF I WAS A GIRL,
YOU WOULDN'T BE GLARING AT ME LIKE THAT.
Deep Water
ディープウォーター
川瀬三葉
MITSUHA KAWASE

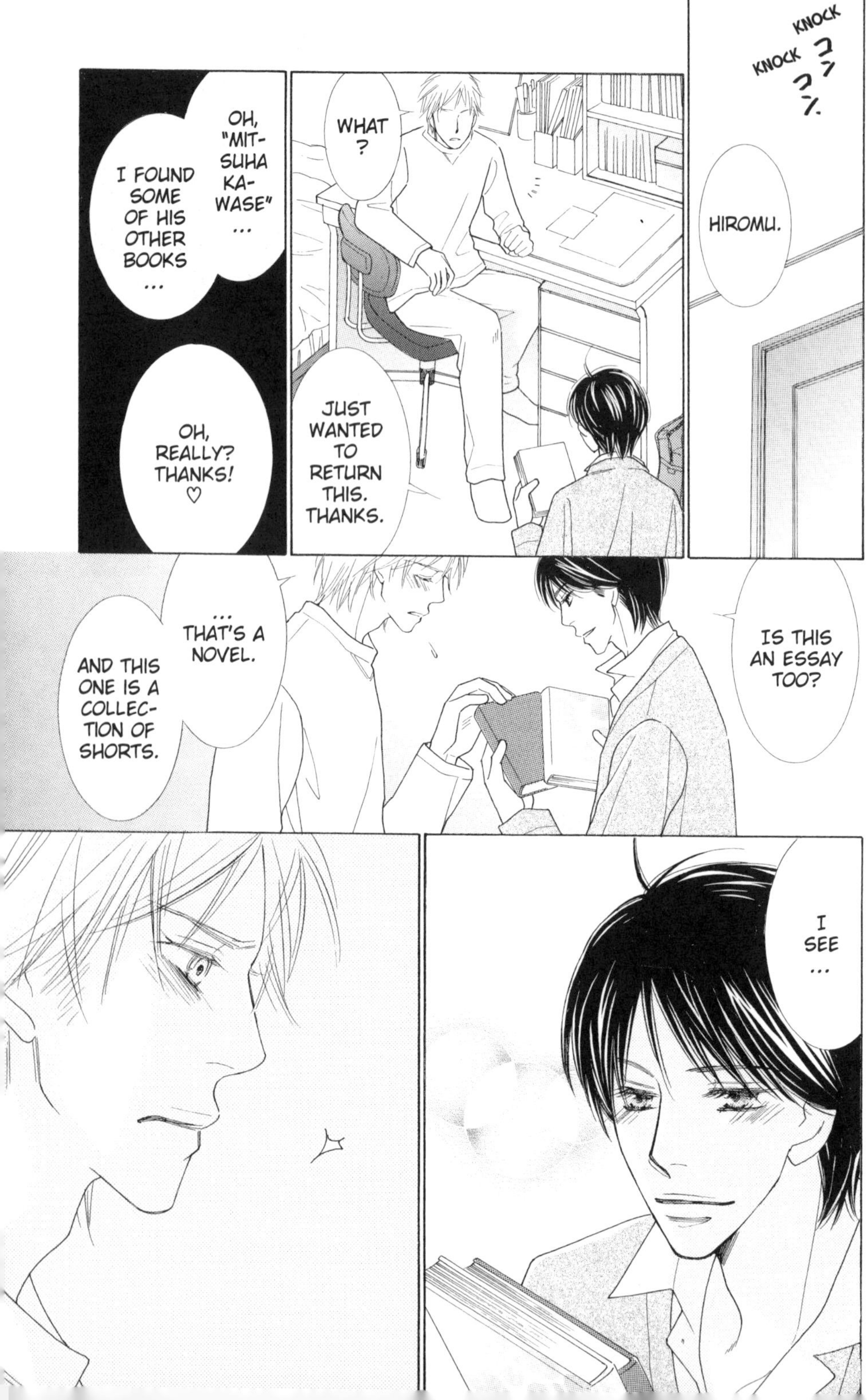
KNOCK
KNOCK
HIROMU.
WHAT?
JUST WANTED TO RETURN THIS. THANKS.
OH, "MIT-SUHA KA-WASE"...
I FOUND SOME OF HIS OTHER BOOKS...
OH, REALLY? THANKS! ♡
IS THIS AN ESSAY TOO?
...THAT'S A NOVEL.
AND THIS ONE IS A COLLEC-TION OF SHORTS.
I SEE...

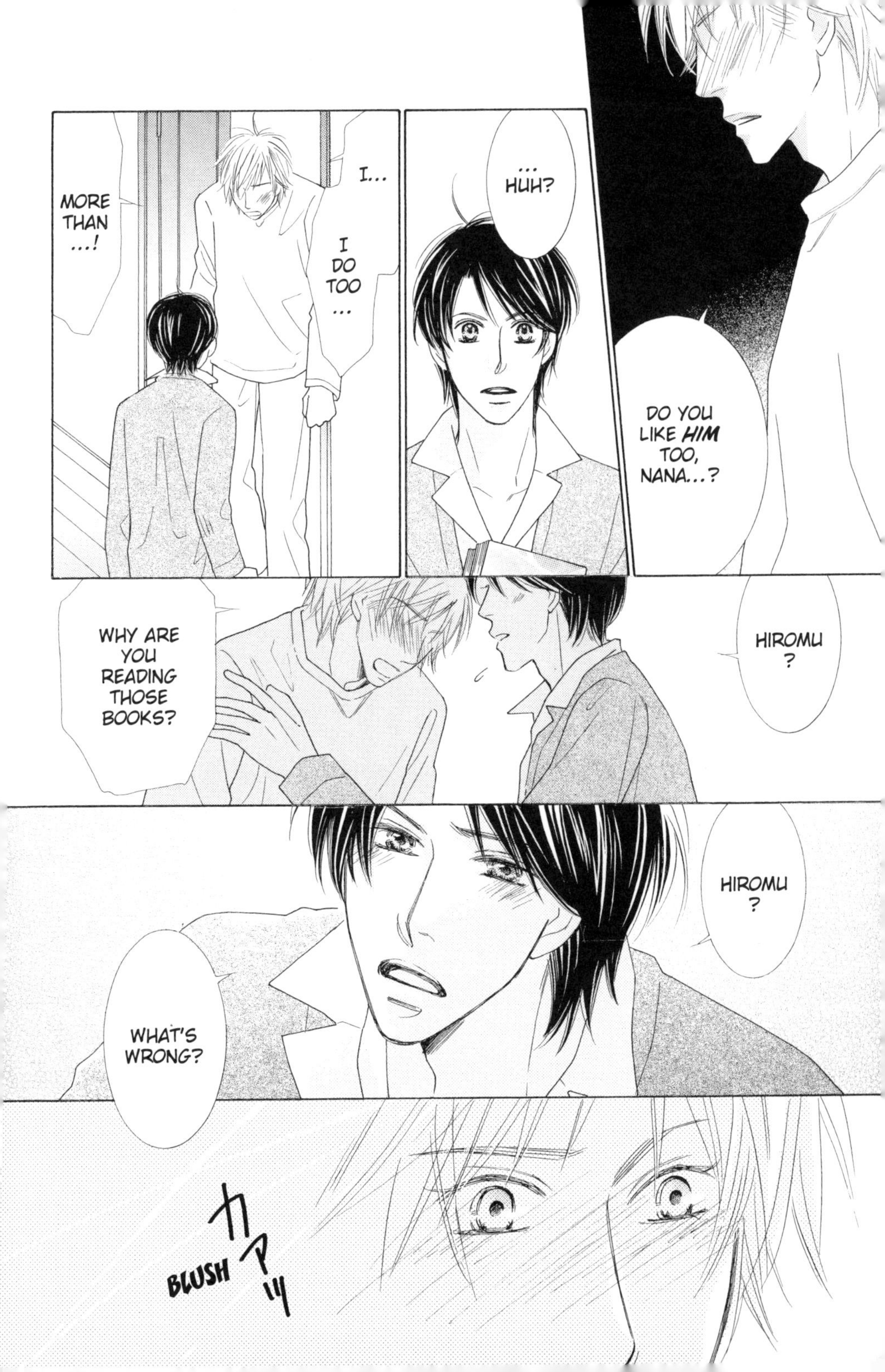
DO YOU LIKE *HIM* TOO, NANA...?
...HUH?
I...
I DO TOO...
MORE THAN...!
HIROMU?
WHY ARE YOU READING THOSE BOOKS?
HIROMU?
WHAT'S WRONG?
カアッ
BLUSH

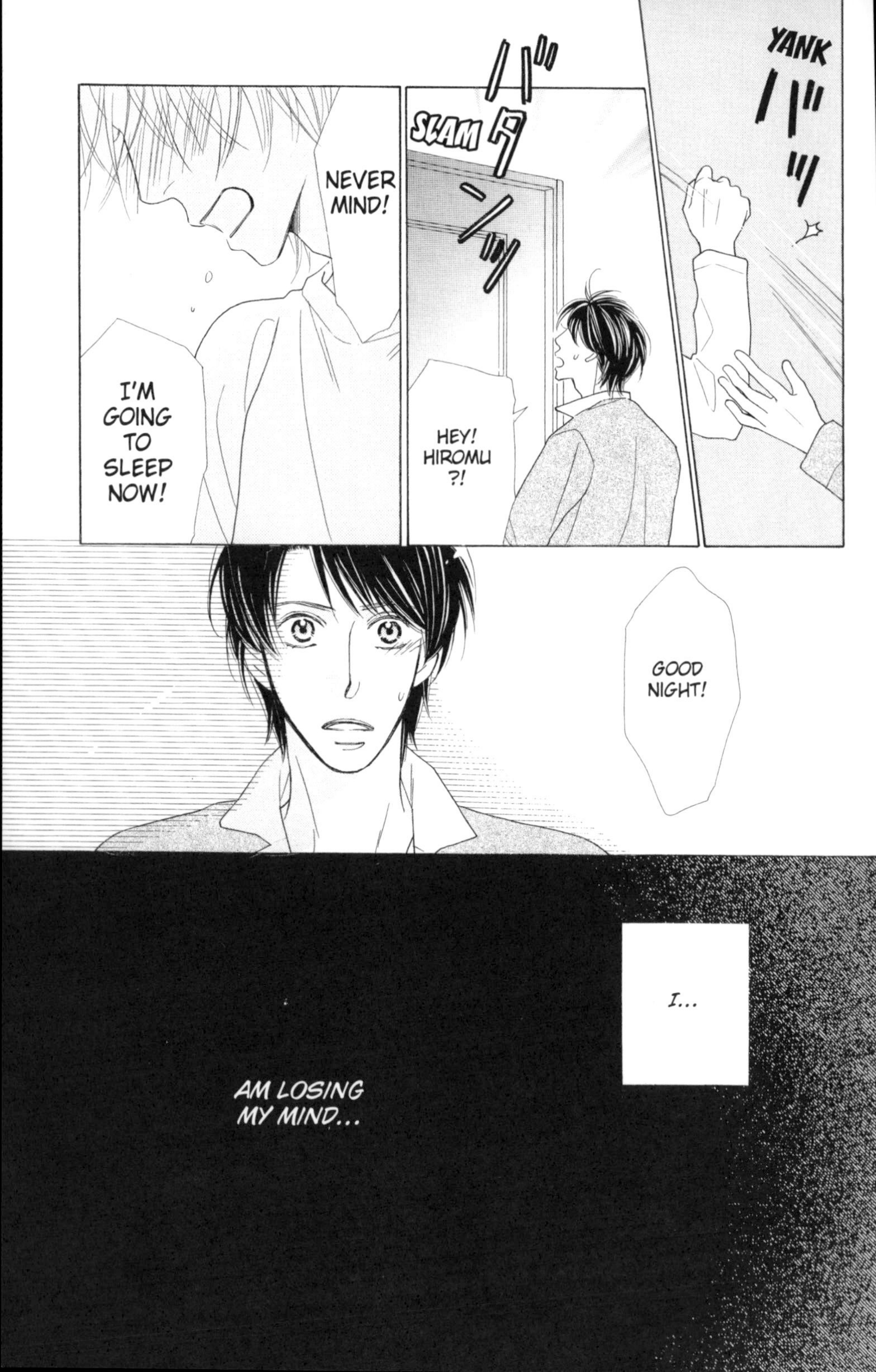
YANK
SLAM
HEY! HIROMU?!
NEVER MIND!
I'M GOING TO SLEEP NOW!
GOOD NIGHT!
I...
AM LOSING MY MIND...

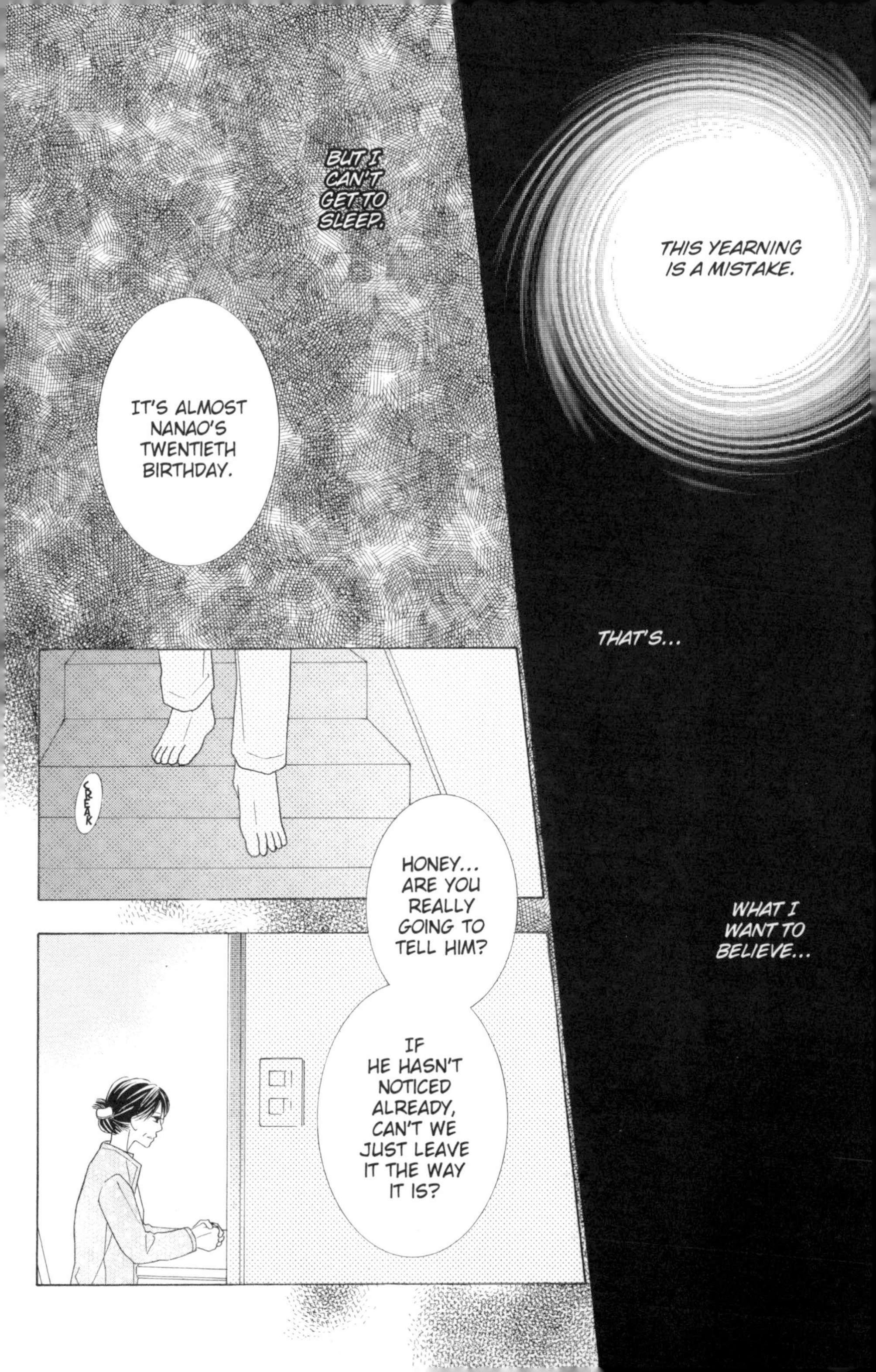
THIS YEARNING IS A MISTAKE.
THAT'S...
WHAT I WANT TO BELIEVE...
BUT I CAN'T GET TO SLEEP.
IT'S ALMOST NANAO'S TWENTIETH BIRTHDAY.
CREAK
HONEY... ARE YOU REALLY GOING TO TELL HIM?
IF HE HASN'T NOTICED ALREADY, CAN'T WE JUST LEAVE IT THE WAY IT IS?

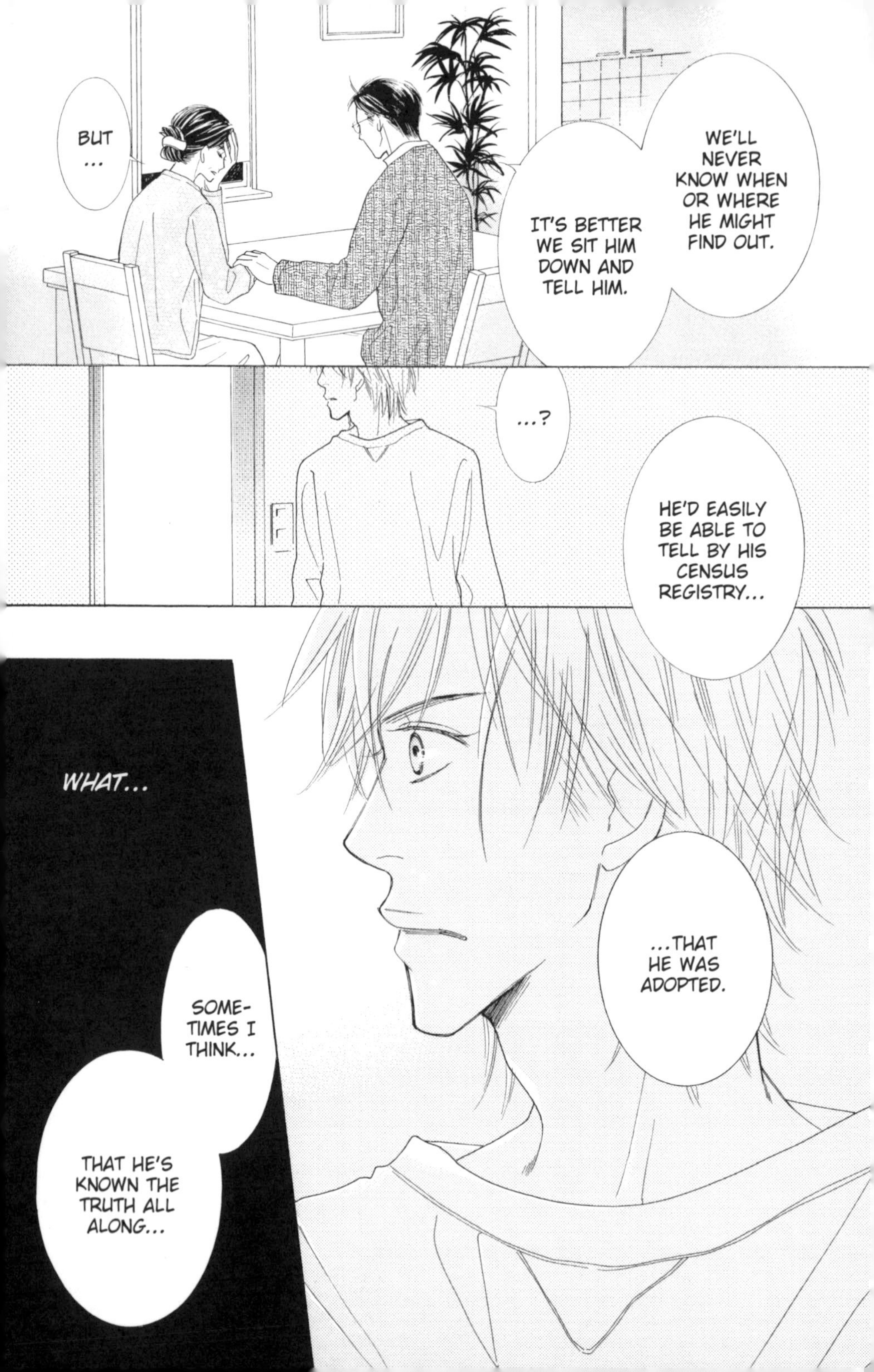
WE'LL NEVER KNOW WHEN OR WHERE HE MIGHT FIND OUT.
IT'S BETTER WE SIT HIM DOWN AND TELL HIM.
BUT ...
...?
HE'D EASILY BE ABLE TO TELL BY HIS CENSUS REGISTRY...
...THAT HE WAS ADOPTED.
WHAT...
SOME-TIMES I THINK...
THAT HE'S KNOWN THE TRUTH ALL ALONG...

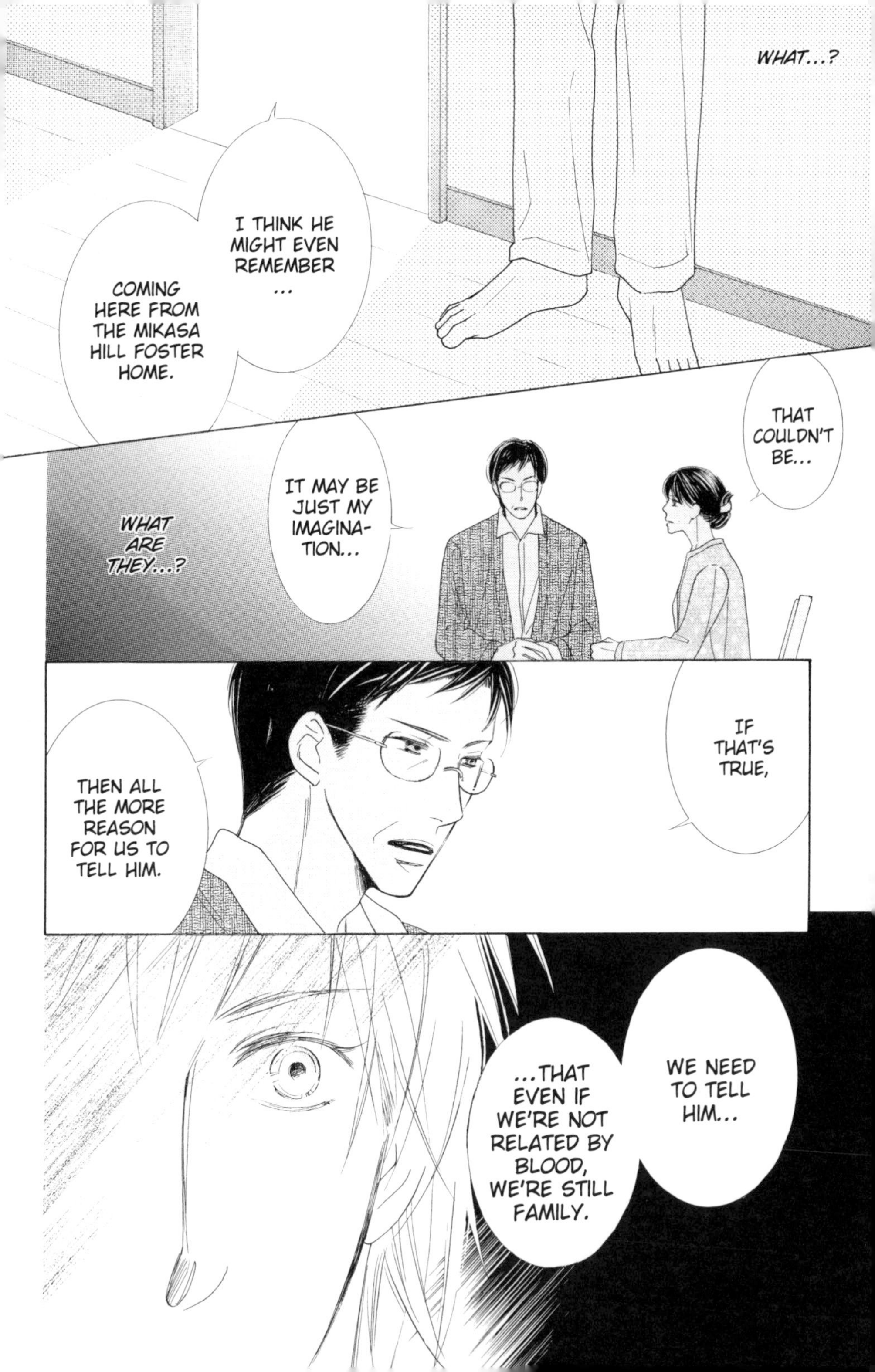
WHAT...?
I THINK HE MIGHT EVEN REMEMBER ...
COMING HERE FROM THE MIKASA HILL FOSTER HOME.
THAT COULDN'T BE...
IT MAY BE JUST MY IMAGINA-TION...
WHAT ARE THEY...?
IF THAT'S TRUE,
THEN ALL THE MORE REASON FOR US TO TELL HIM.
WE NEED TO TELL HIM...
...THAT EVEN IF WE'RE NOT RELATED BY BLOOD, WE'RE STILL FAMILY.

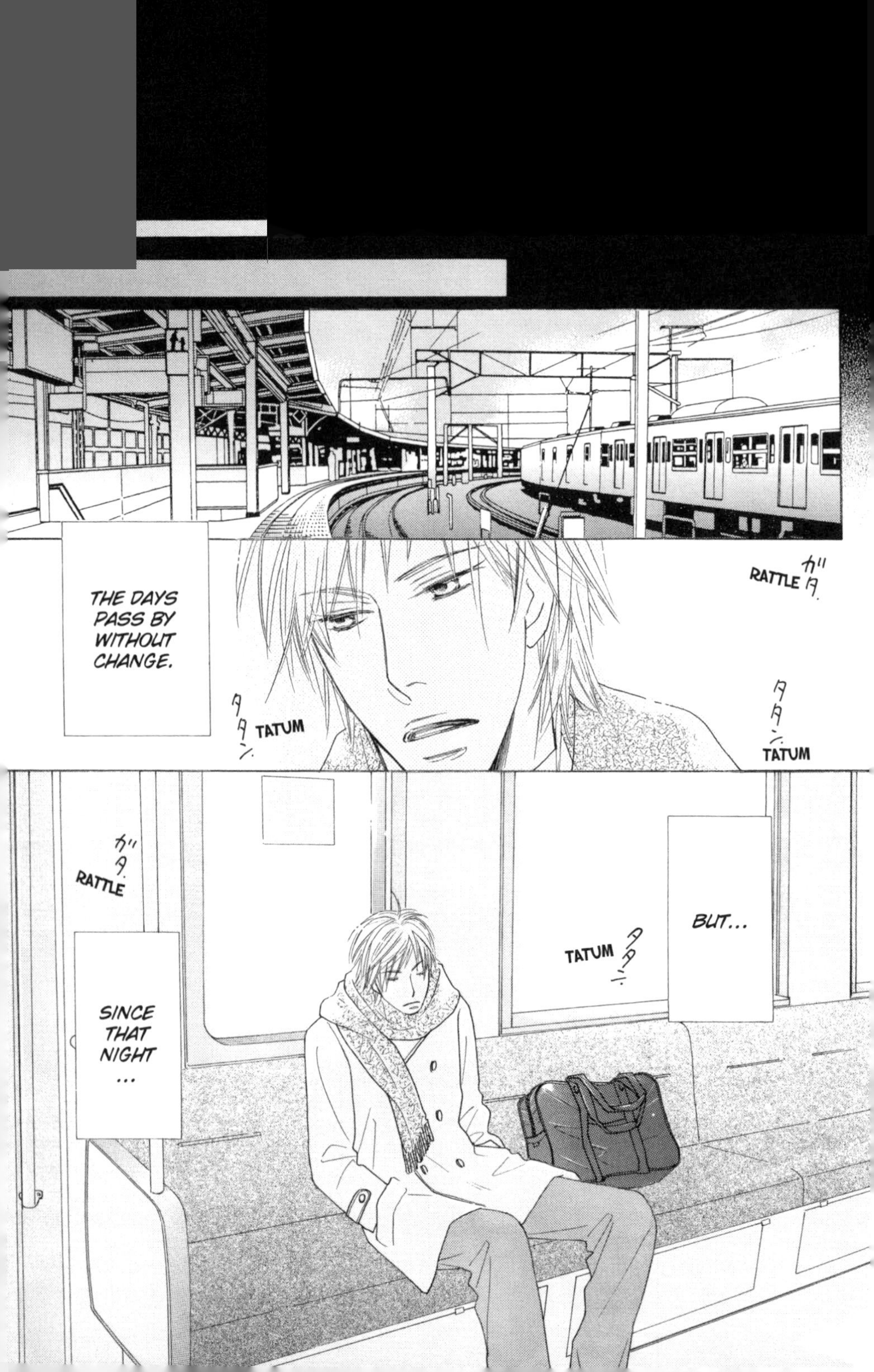

RATTLE ガタ
TATUM タタン
THE DAYS PASS BY WITHOUT CHANGE.
TATUM タタン
BUT...
TATUM タタン
RATTLE ガタ
SINCE THAT NIGHT ...

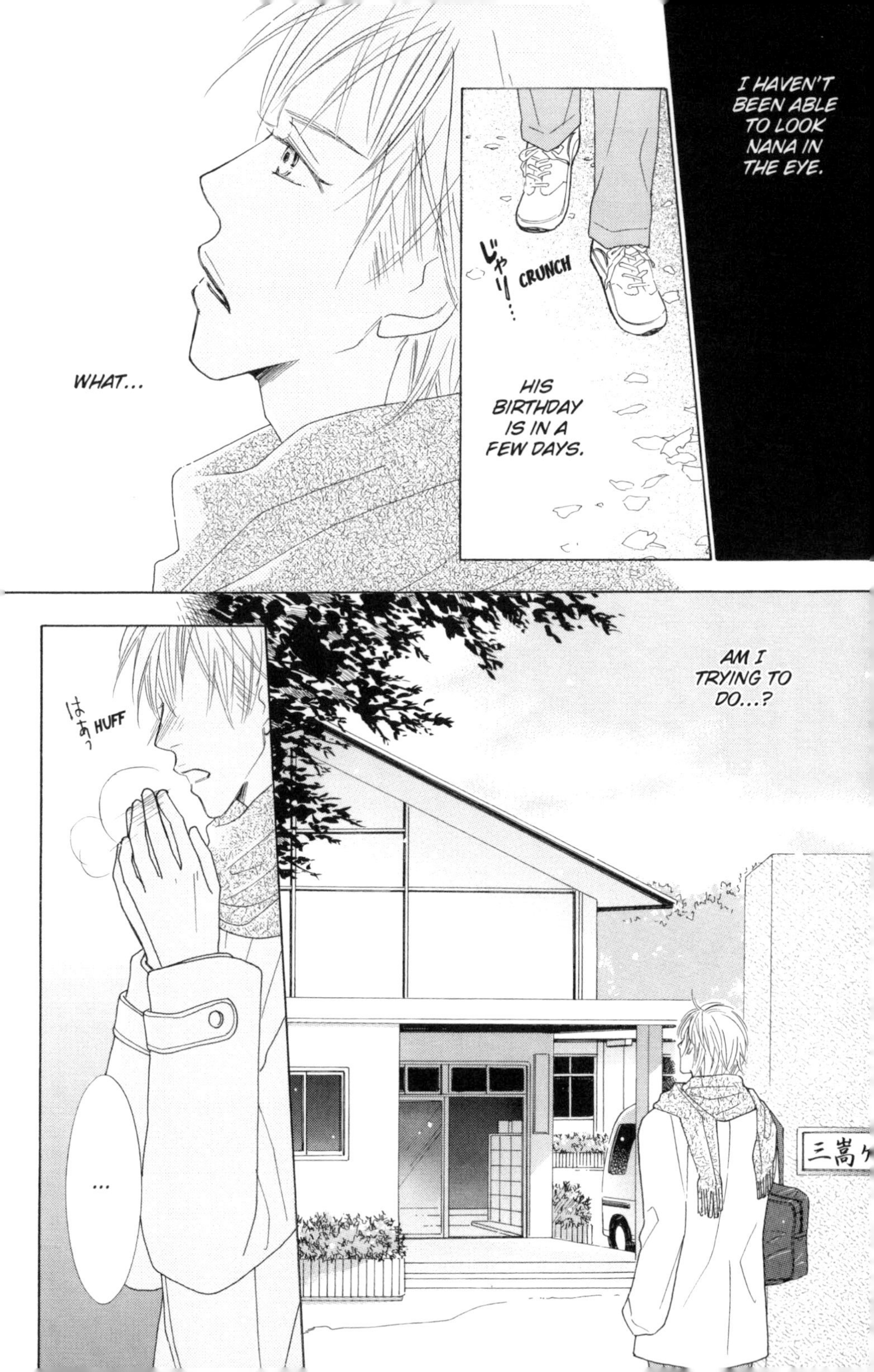
I HAVEN'T BEEN ABLE TO LOOK NANA IN THE EYE.
じゃり… CRUNCH
HIS BIRTHDAY IS IN A FEW DAYS.
WHAT...
AM I TRYING TO DO...?
はあっ HUFF
...

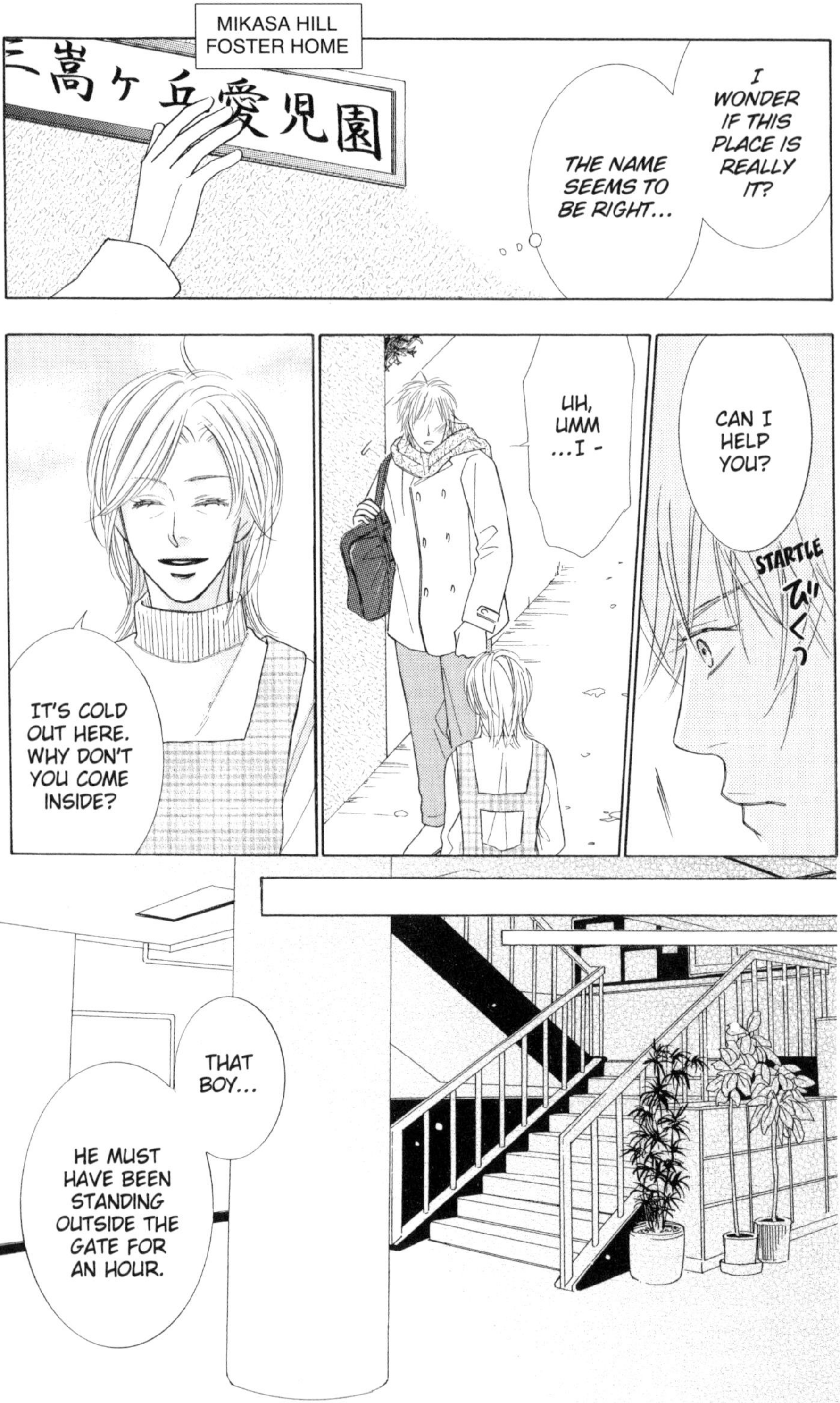
MIKASA HILL FOSTER HOME
三嵩ヶ丘愛児園
I WONDER IF THIS PLACE IS REALLY IT?
THE NAME SEEMS TO BE RIGHT...
CAN I HELP YOU?
STARTLE
びくっ
UH, UMM ...I -
IT'S COLD OUT HERE. WHY DON'T YOU COME INSIDE?
THAT BOY...
HE MUST HAVE BEEN STANDING OUTSIDE THE GATE FOR AN HOUR.

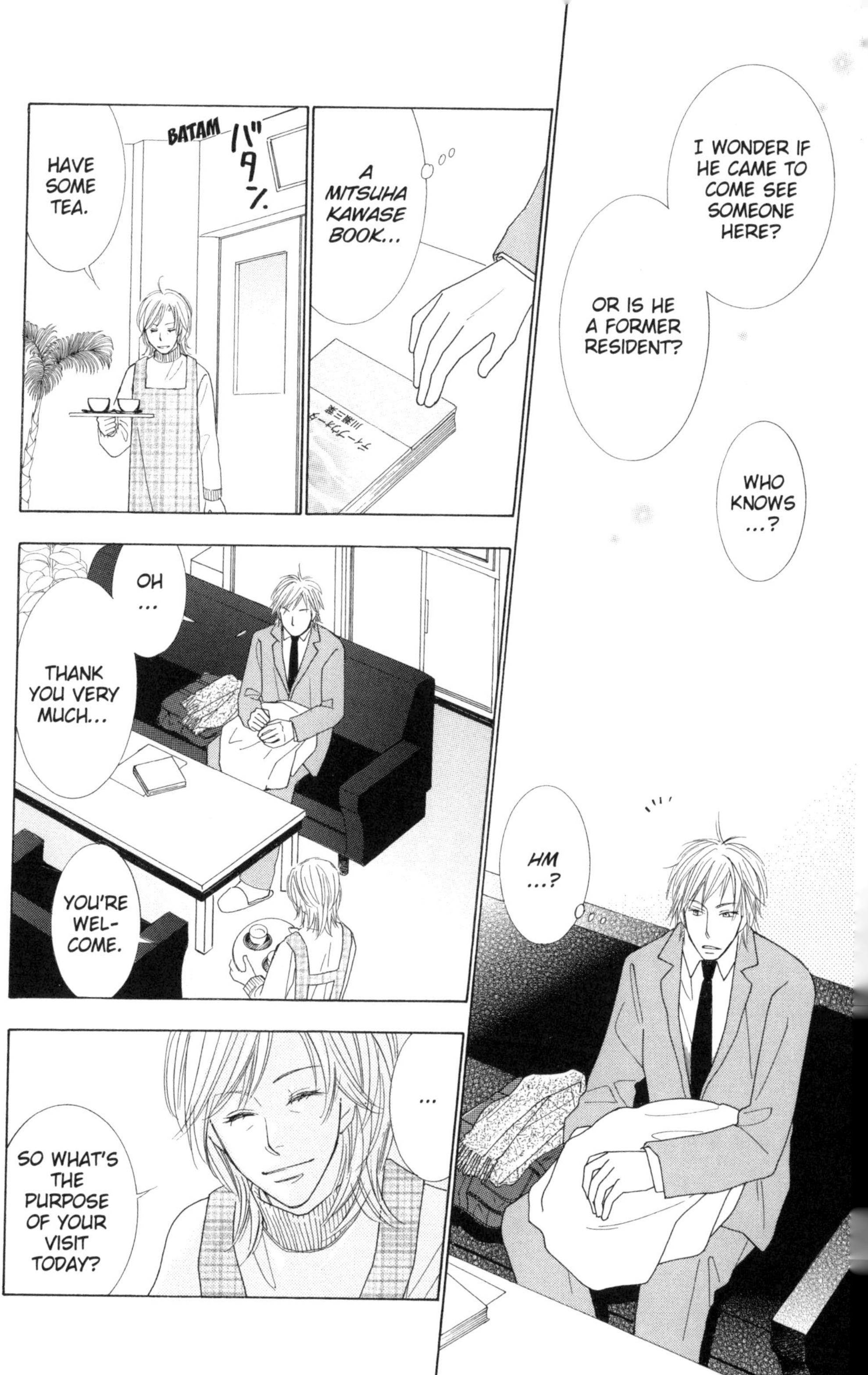
I WONDER IF HE CAME TO COME SEE SOMEONE HERE?
OR IS HE A FORMER RESIDENT?
WHO KNOWS...?
HM...?
A MITSUHA KAWASE BOOK...
バタン
BATAM
HAVE SOME TEA.
OH...
THANK YOU VERY MUCH...
YOU'RE WEL-COME.
...
SO WHAT'S THE PURPOSE OF YOUR VISIT TODAY?

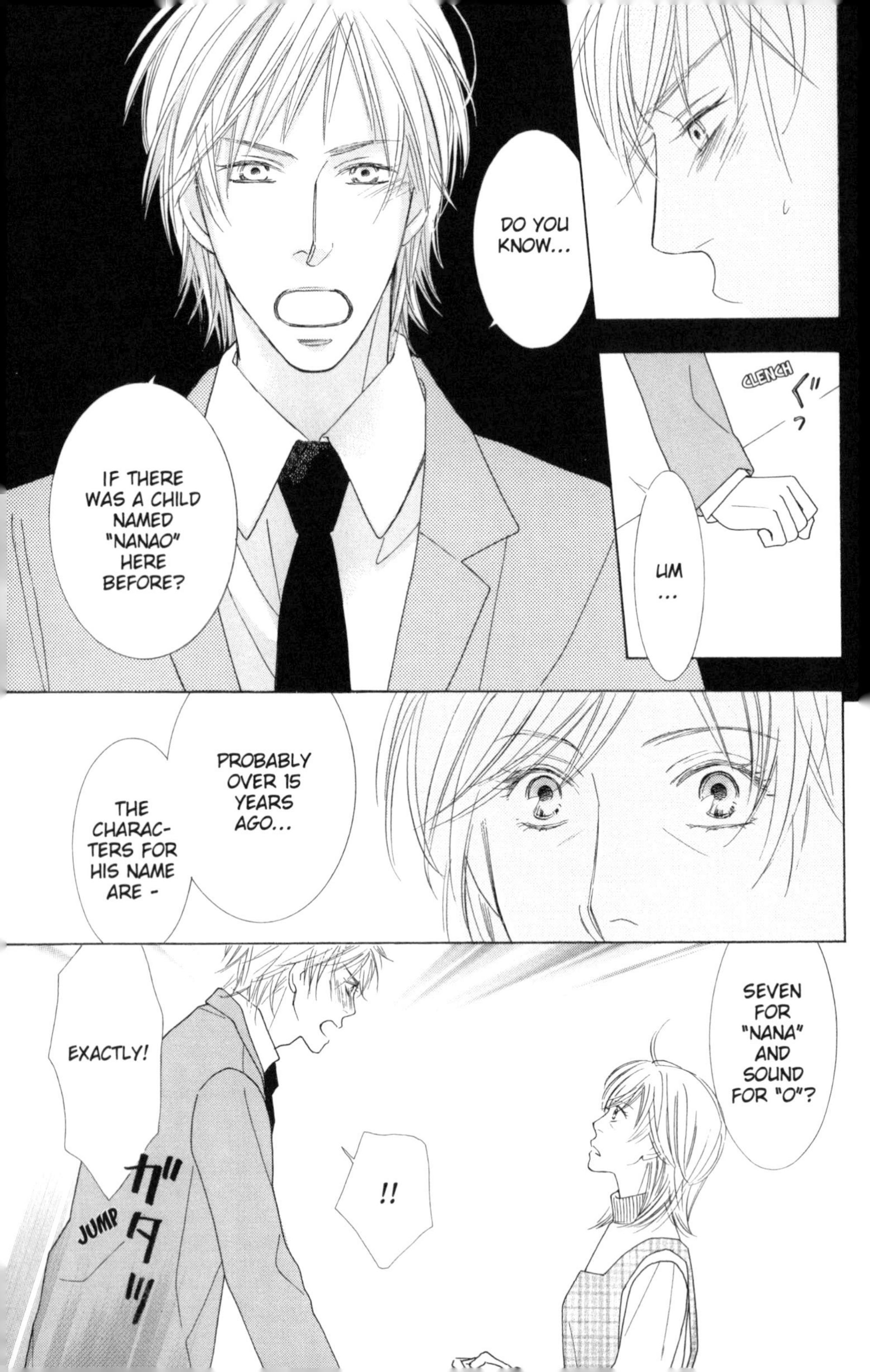
DO YOU KNOW...
IF THERE WAS A CHILD NAMED "NANAO" HERE BEFORE?
CLENCH
UM ...
PROBABLY OVER 15 YEARS AGO...
THE CHARAC-TERS FOR HIS NAME ARE -
SEVEN FOR "NANA" AND SOUND FOR "O"?
!!
EXACTLY!
ガタッ
JUMP

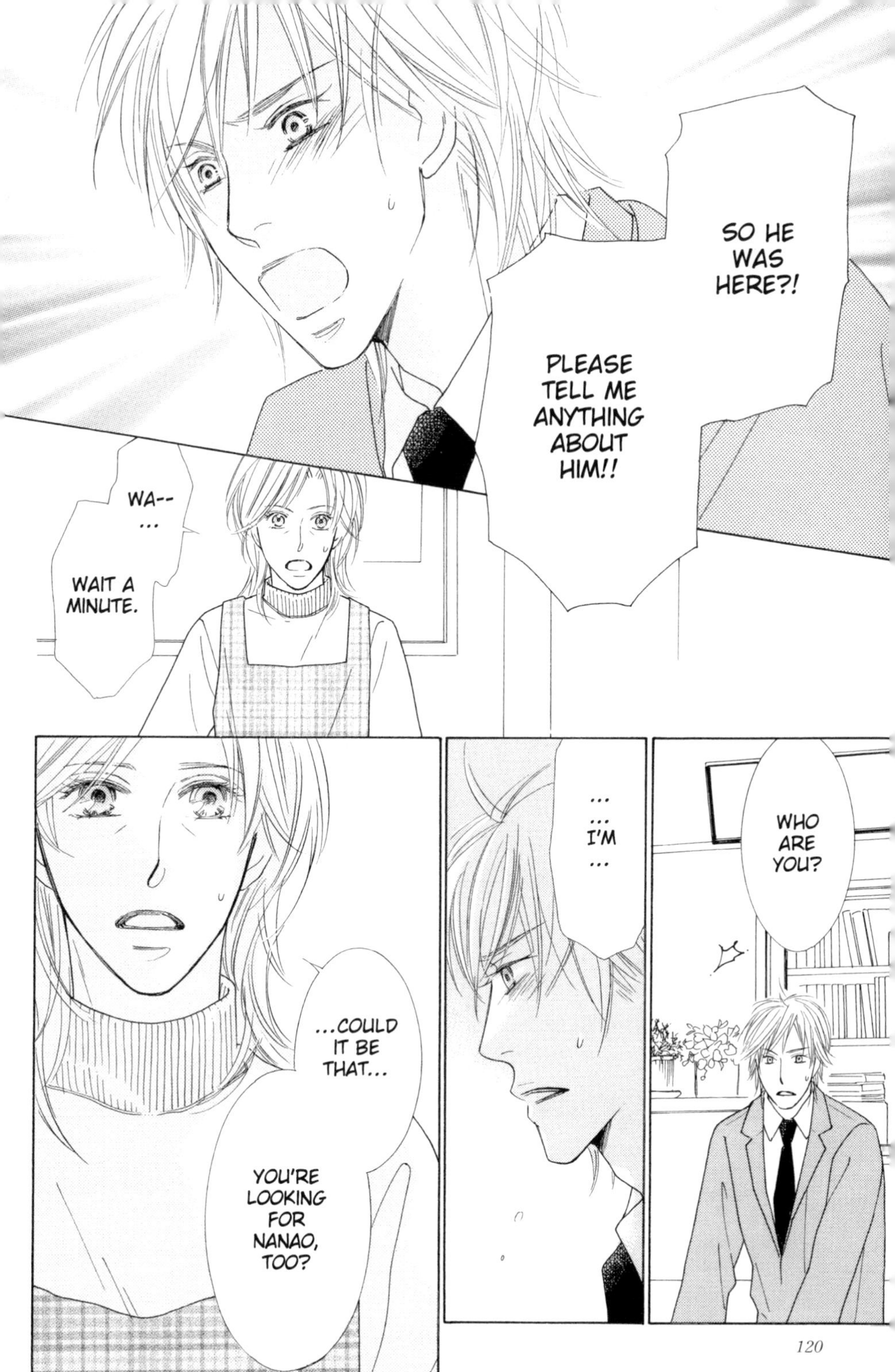
SO HE WAS HERE?!
PLEASE TELL ME ANYTHING ABOUT HIM!!
WA-- ...
WAIT A MINUTE.
WHO ARE YOU?
... ... I'M ...
...COULD IT BE THAT...
YOU'RE LOOKING FOR NANAO, TOO?

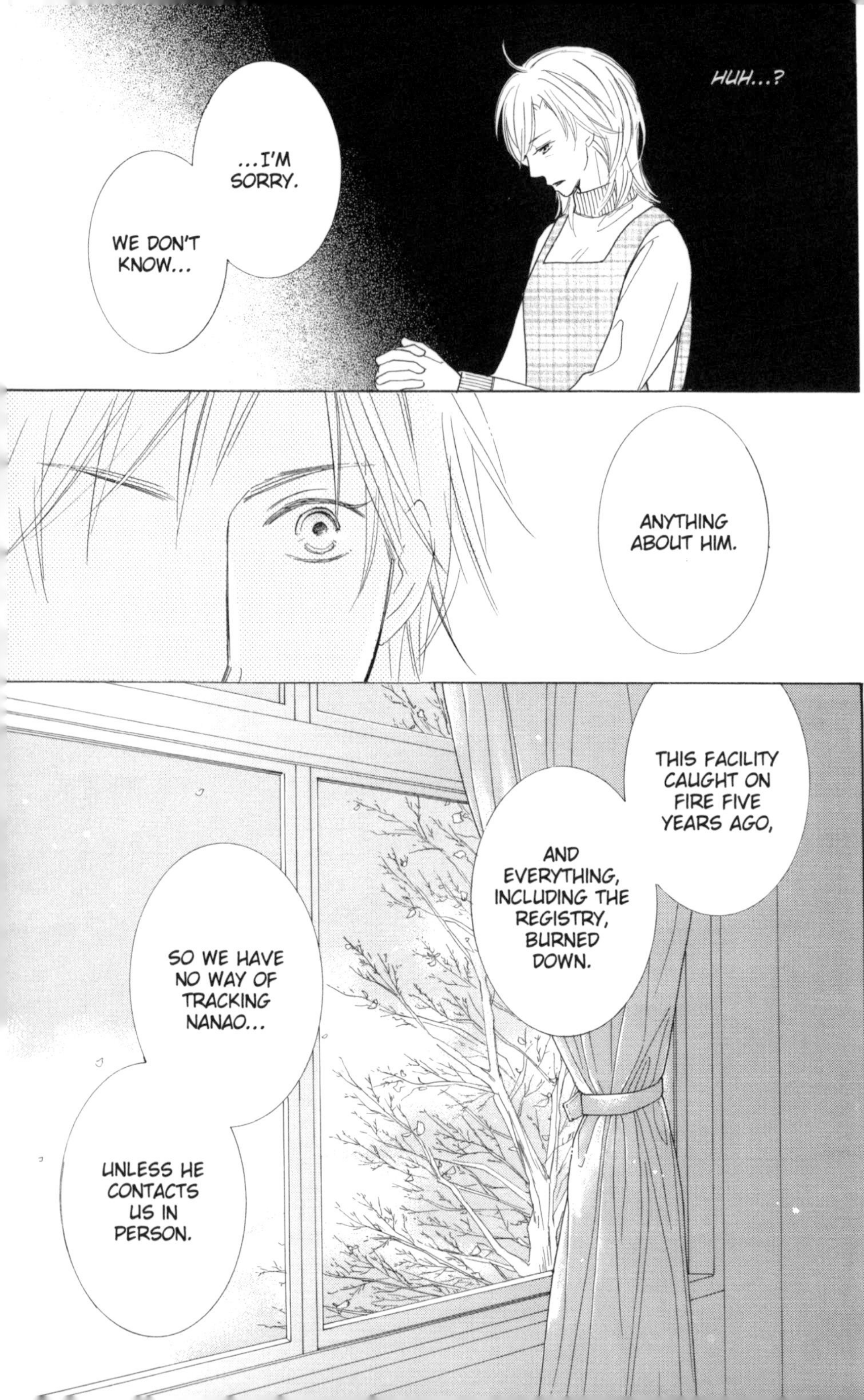
HUH...?
...I'M SORRY.
WE DON'T KNOW...
ANYTHING ABOUT HIM.
THIS FACILITY CAUGHT ON FIRE FIVE YEARS AGO,
AND EVERYTHING, INCLUDING THE REGISTRY, BURNED DOWN.
SO WE HAVE NO WAY OF TRACKING NANAO...
UNLESS HE CONTACTS US IN PERSON.

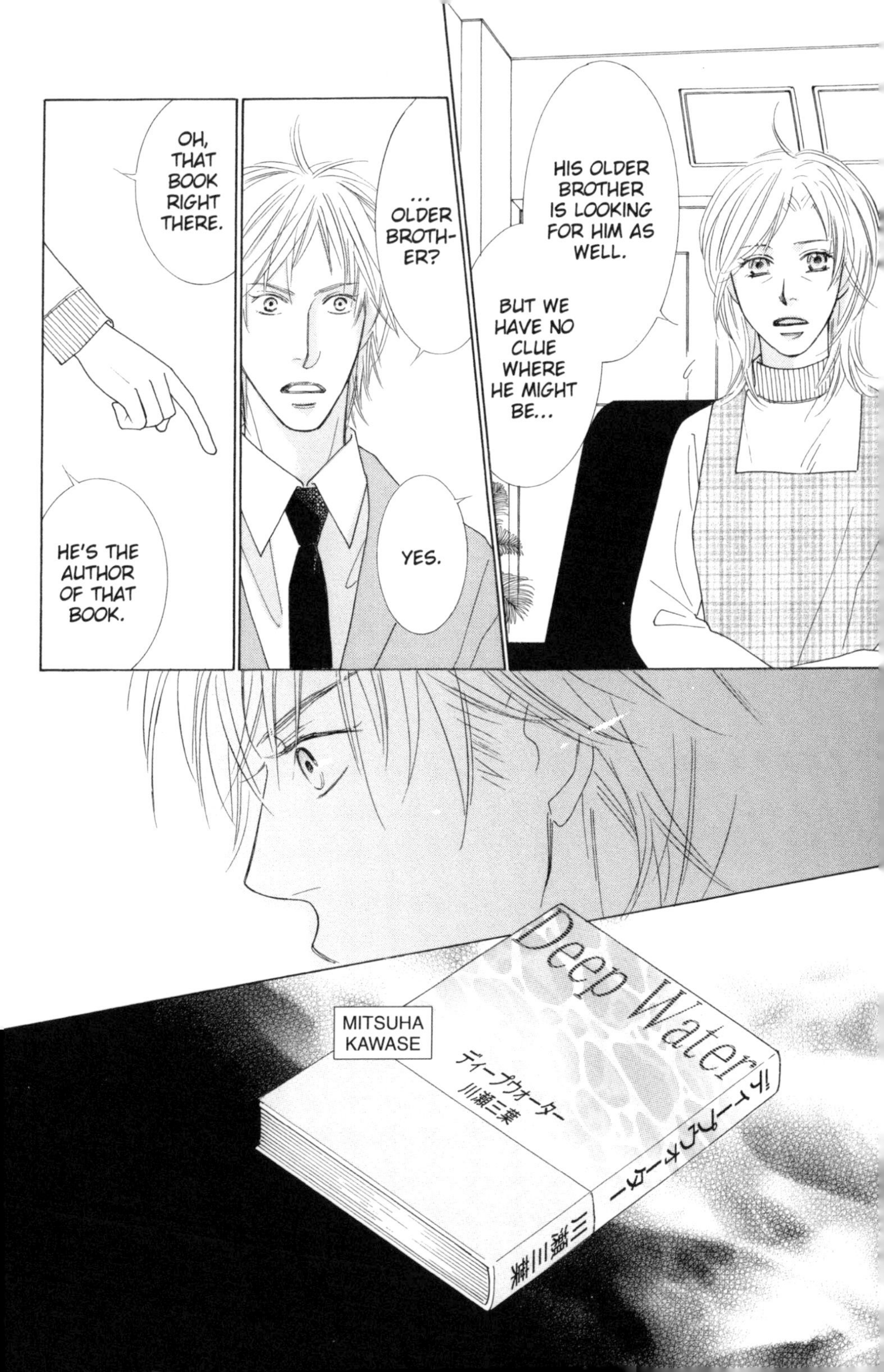
HIS OLDER BROTHER IS LOOKING FOR HIM AS WELL.
BUT WE HAVE NO CLUE WHERE HE MIGHT BE...
... OLDER BROTH-ER?
YES.
OH, THAT BOOK RIGHT THERE.
HE'S THE AUTHOR OF THAT BOOK.
Deep Water
MITSUHA KAWASE
ディープウォーター
川瀬三葉
ディープウォーター
川瀬三葉

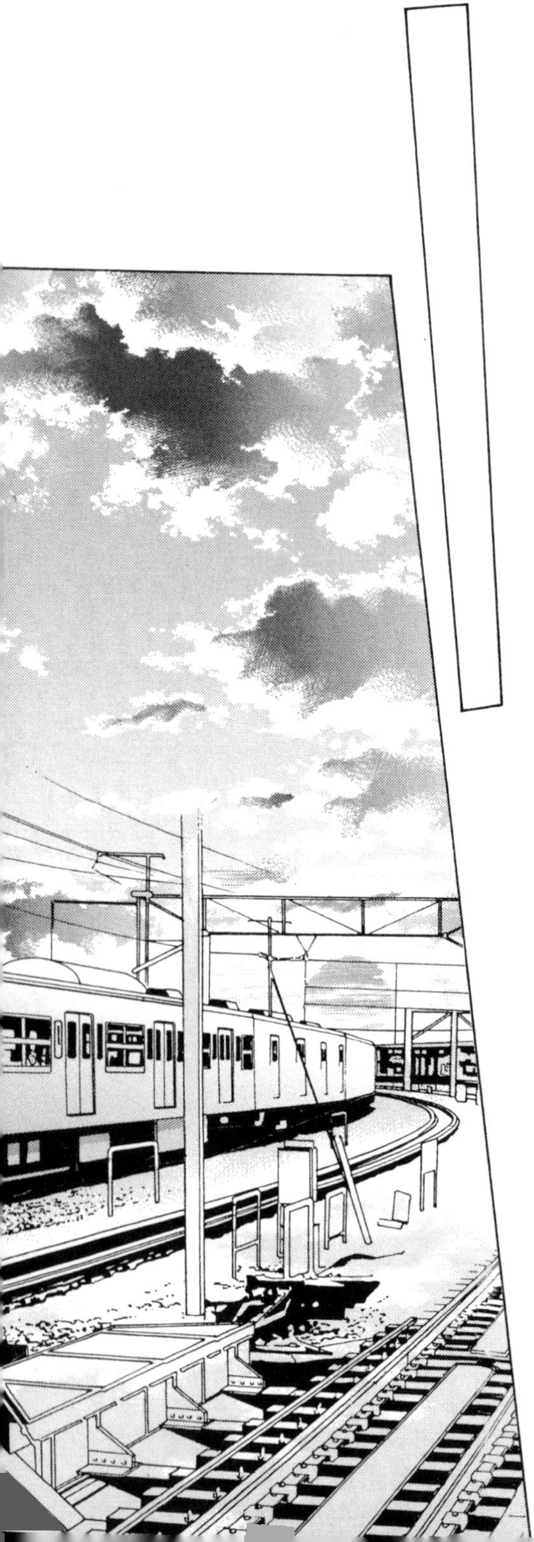

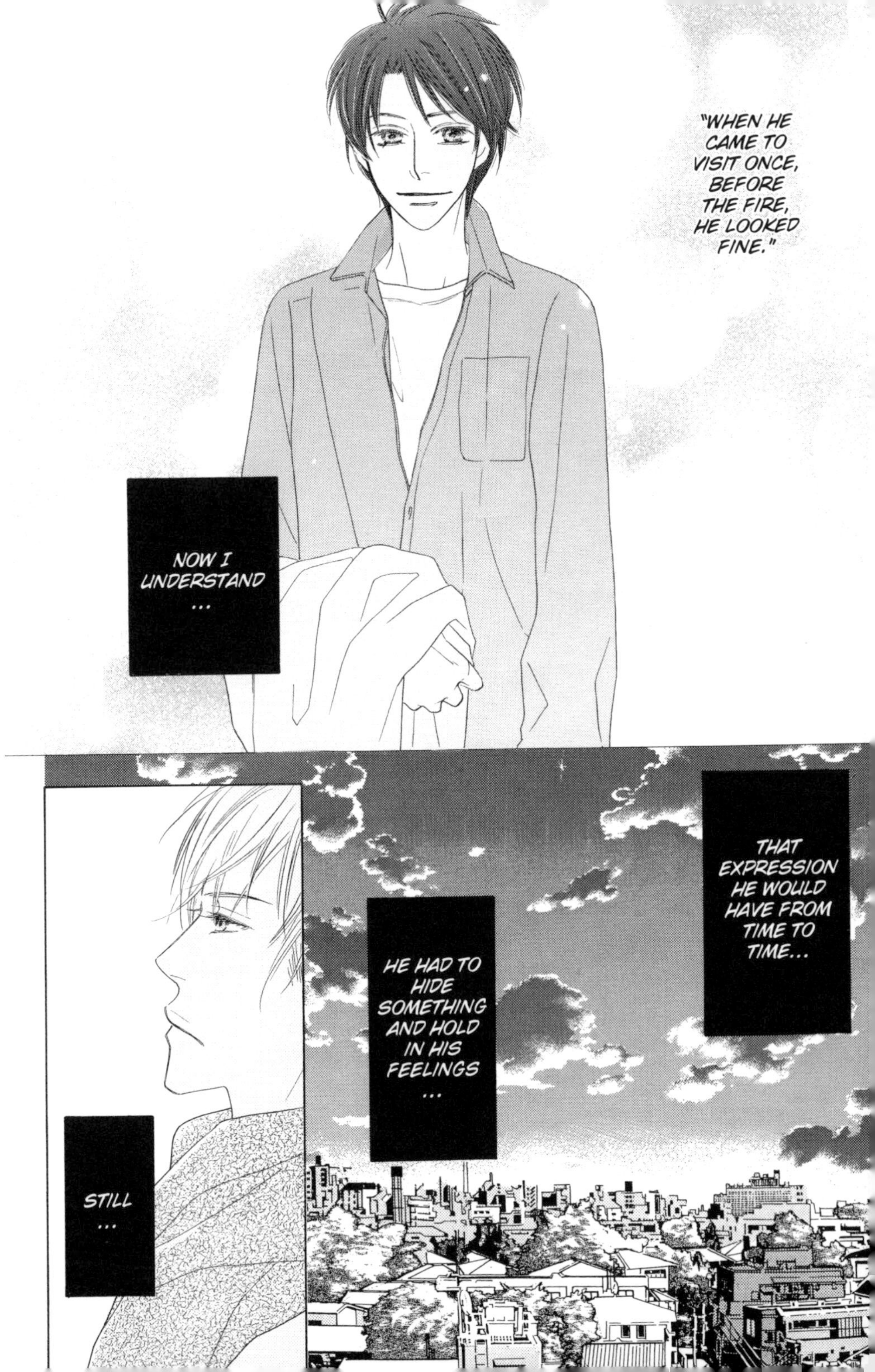
"WHEN HE CAME TO VISIT ONCE, BEFORE THE FIRE, HE LOOKED FINE."
NOW I UNDERSTAND ...
THAT EXPRESSION HE WOULD HAVE FROM TIME TO TIME...
HE HAD TO HIDE SOMETHING AND HOLD IN HIS FEELINGS ...
STILL ...

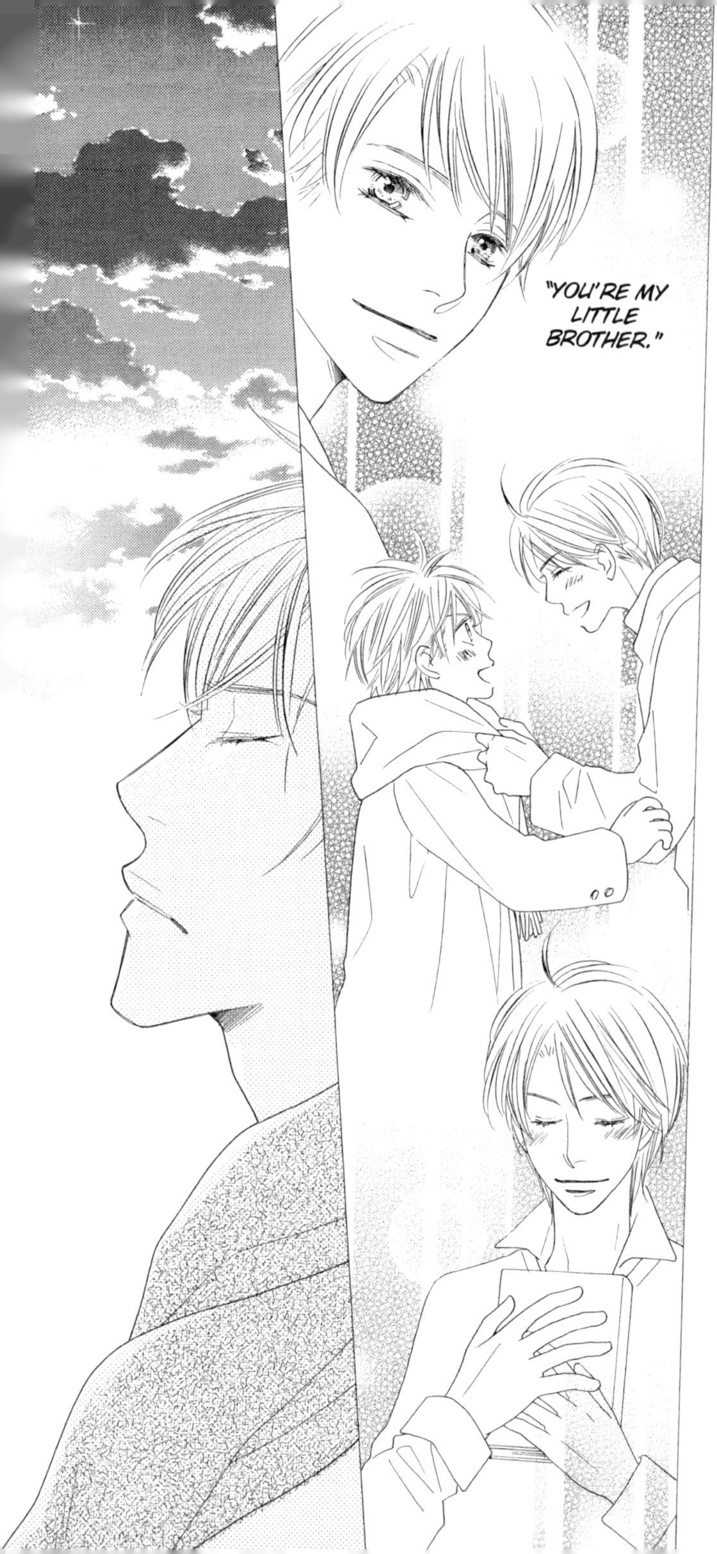
"YOU'RE MY LITTLE BROTHER."

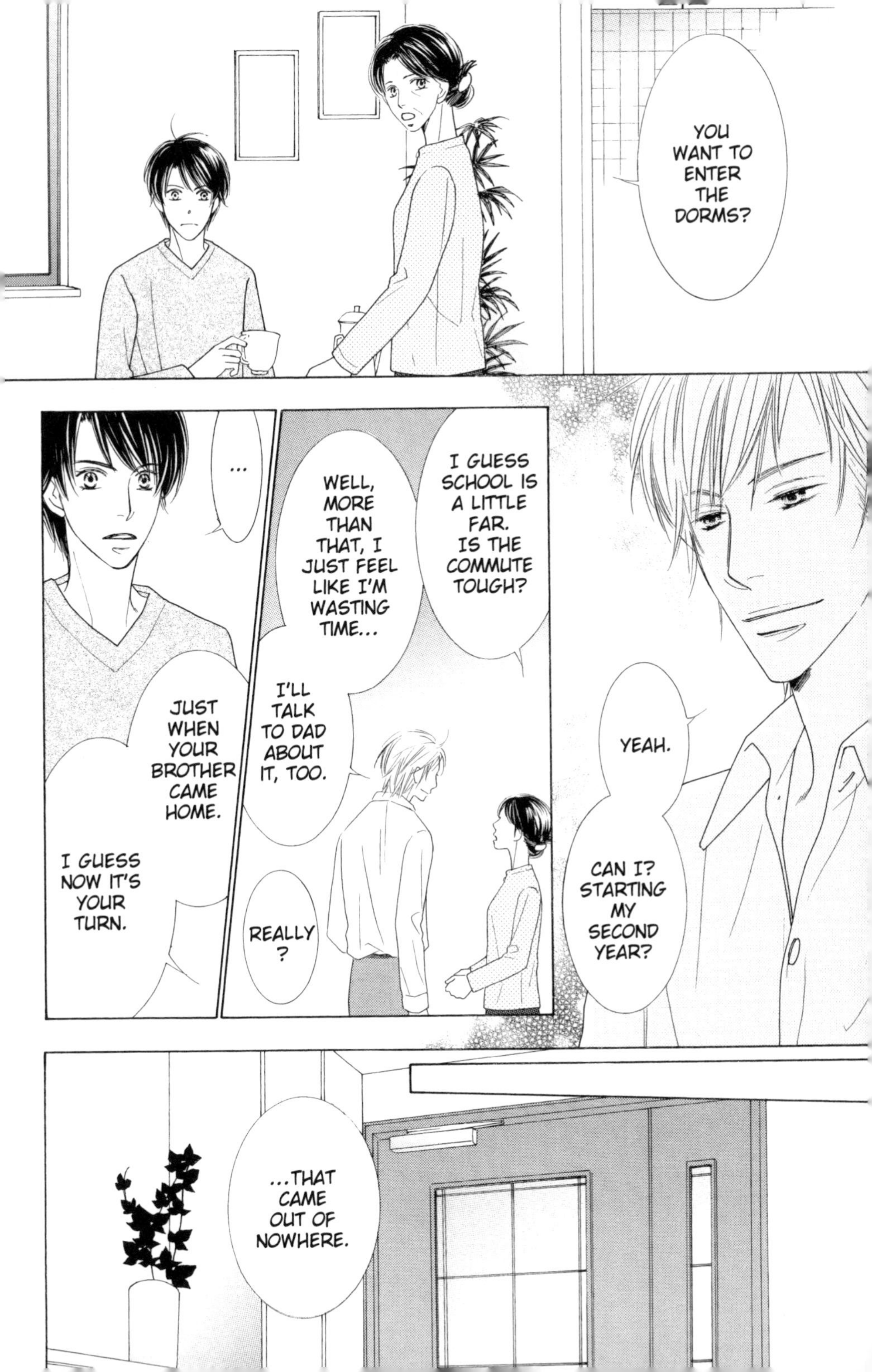
YOU WANT TO ENTER THE DORMS?
YEAH.
CAN I? STARTING MY SECOND YEAR?
I GUESS SCHOOL IS A LITTLE FAR. IS THE COMMUTE TOUGH?
WELL, MORE THAN THAT, I JUST FEEL LIKE I'M WASTING TIME...
I'LL TALK TO DAD ABOUT IT, TOO.
REALLY?
...
JUST WHEN YOUR BROTHER CAME HOME.
I GUESS NOW IT'S YOUR TURN.
...THAT CAME OUT OF NOWHERE.

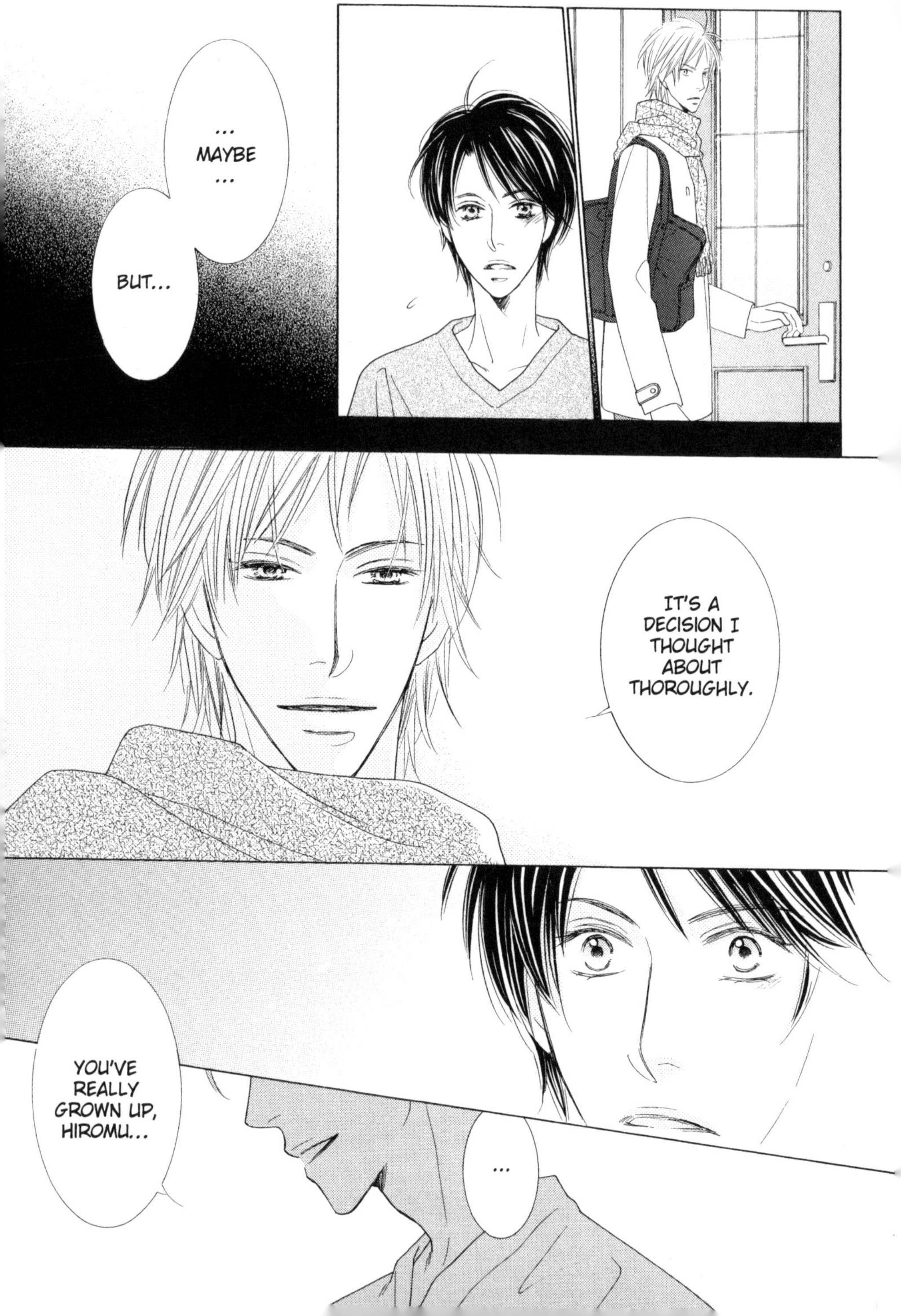

...MAYBE...
BUT...
IT'S A DECISION I THOUGHT ABOUT THOROUGHLY.
YOU'VE REALLY GROWN UP, HIROMU...
...

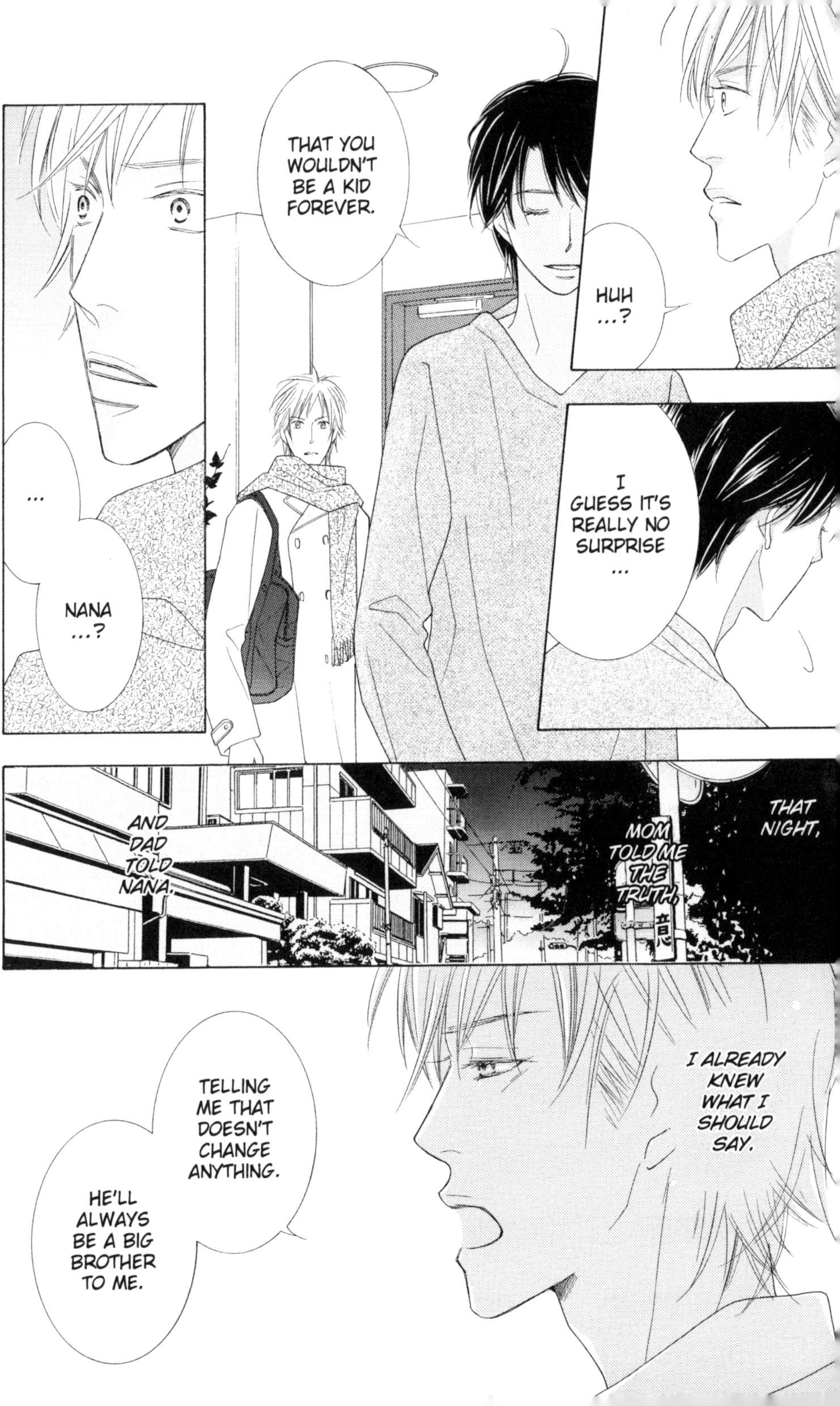
HUH ...?
I GUESS IT'S REALLY NO SURPRISE ...
THAT YOU WOULDN'T BE A KID FOREVER.
...
NANA ...?
THAT NIGHT,
MOM TOLD ME THE TRUTH,
AND DAD TOLD NANA.
I ALREADY KNEW WHAT I SHOULD SAY.
TELLING ME THAT DOESN'T CHANGE ANYTHING.
HE'LL ALWAYS BE A BIG BROTHER TO ME.

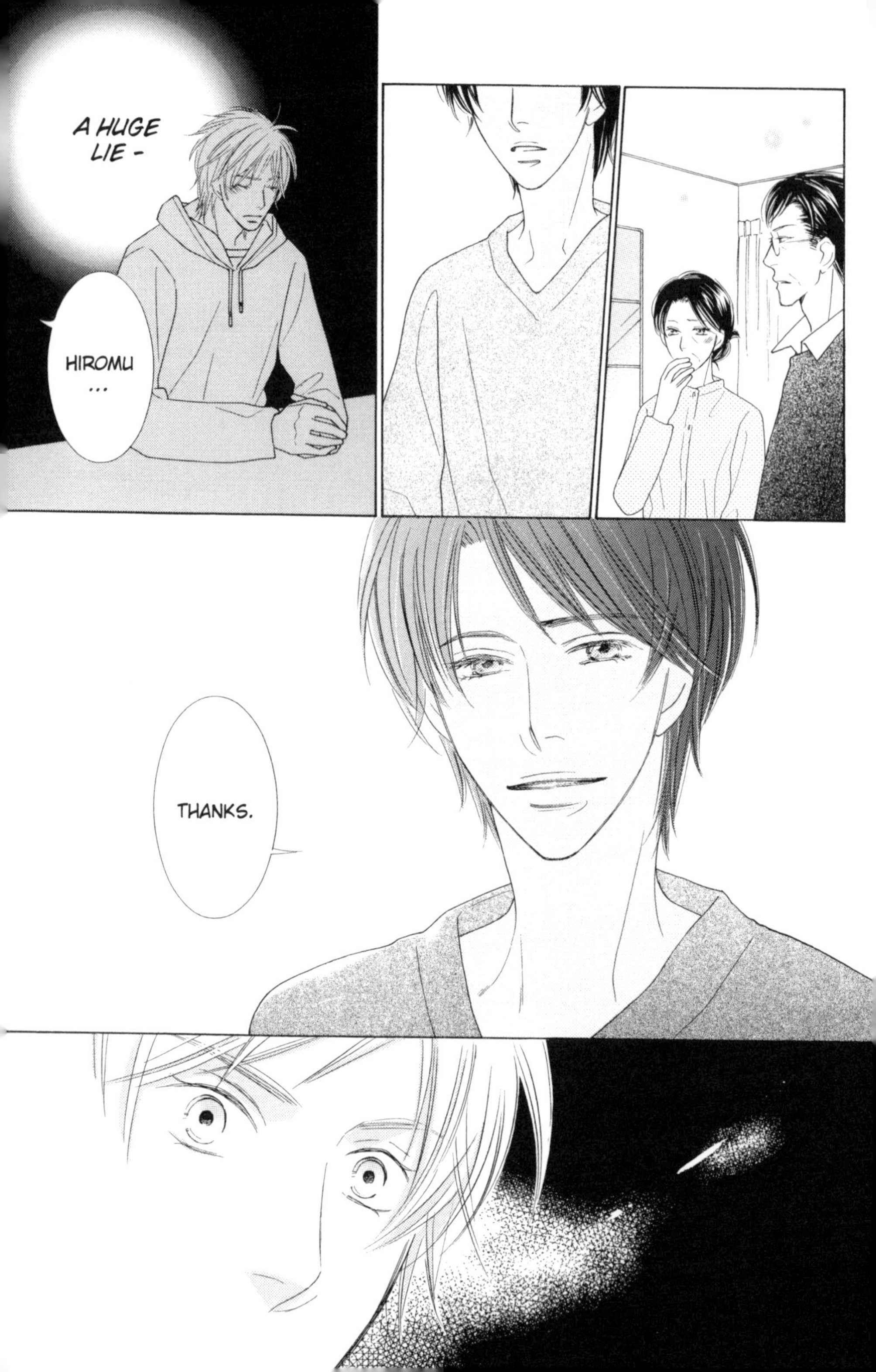
A HUGE LIE -
HIROMU ...
THANKS.

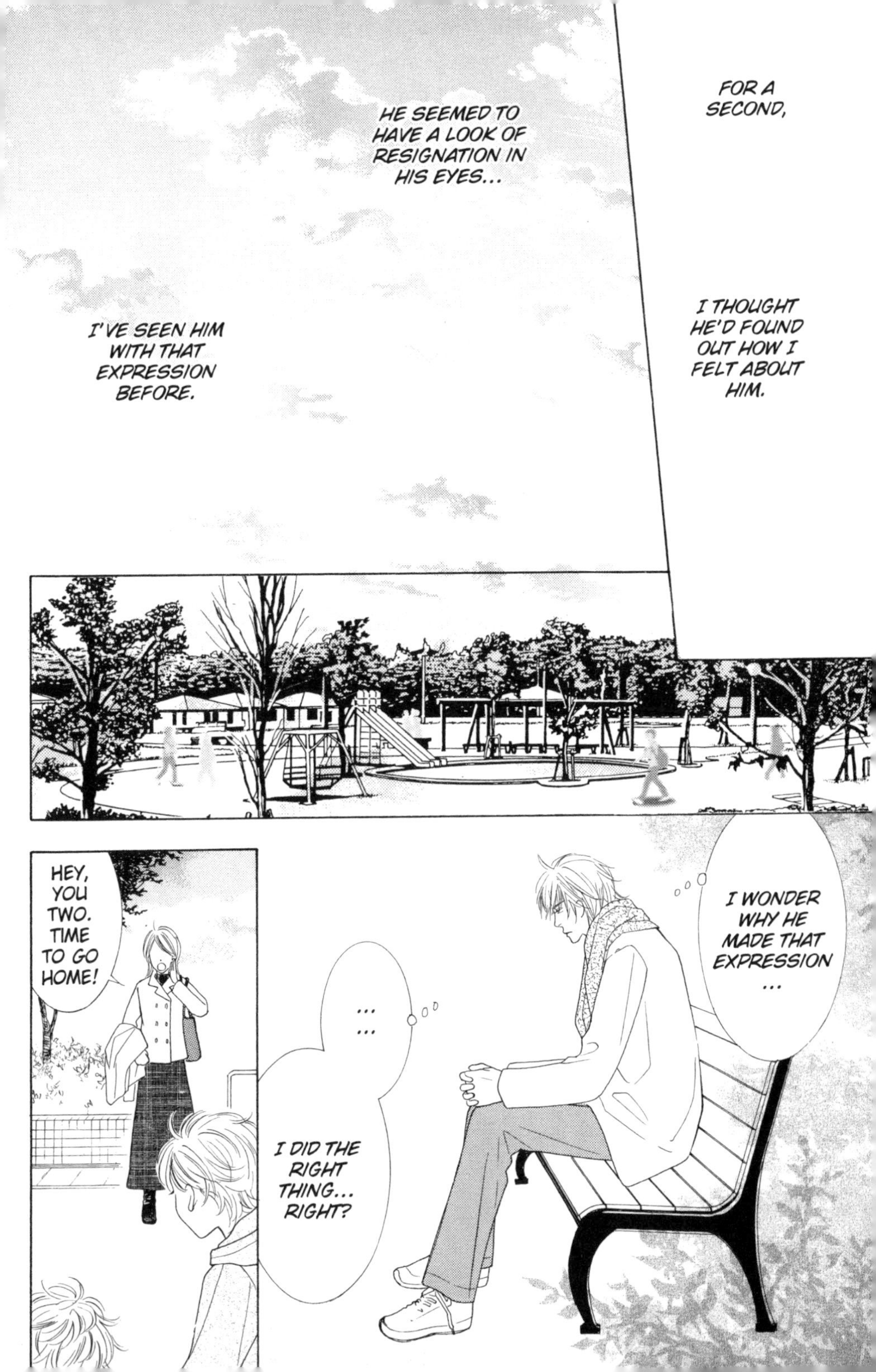
FOR A SECOND,
I THOUGHT HE'D FOUND OUT HOW I FELT ABOUT HIM.
HE SEEMED TO HAVE A LOOK OF RESIGNATION IN HIS EYES...
I'VE SEEN HIM WITH THAT EXPRESSION BEFORE.
I WONDER WHY HE MADE THAT EXPRESSION ...
... ...
I DID THE RIGHT THING... RIGHT?
HEY, YOU TWO. TIME TO GO HOME!

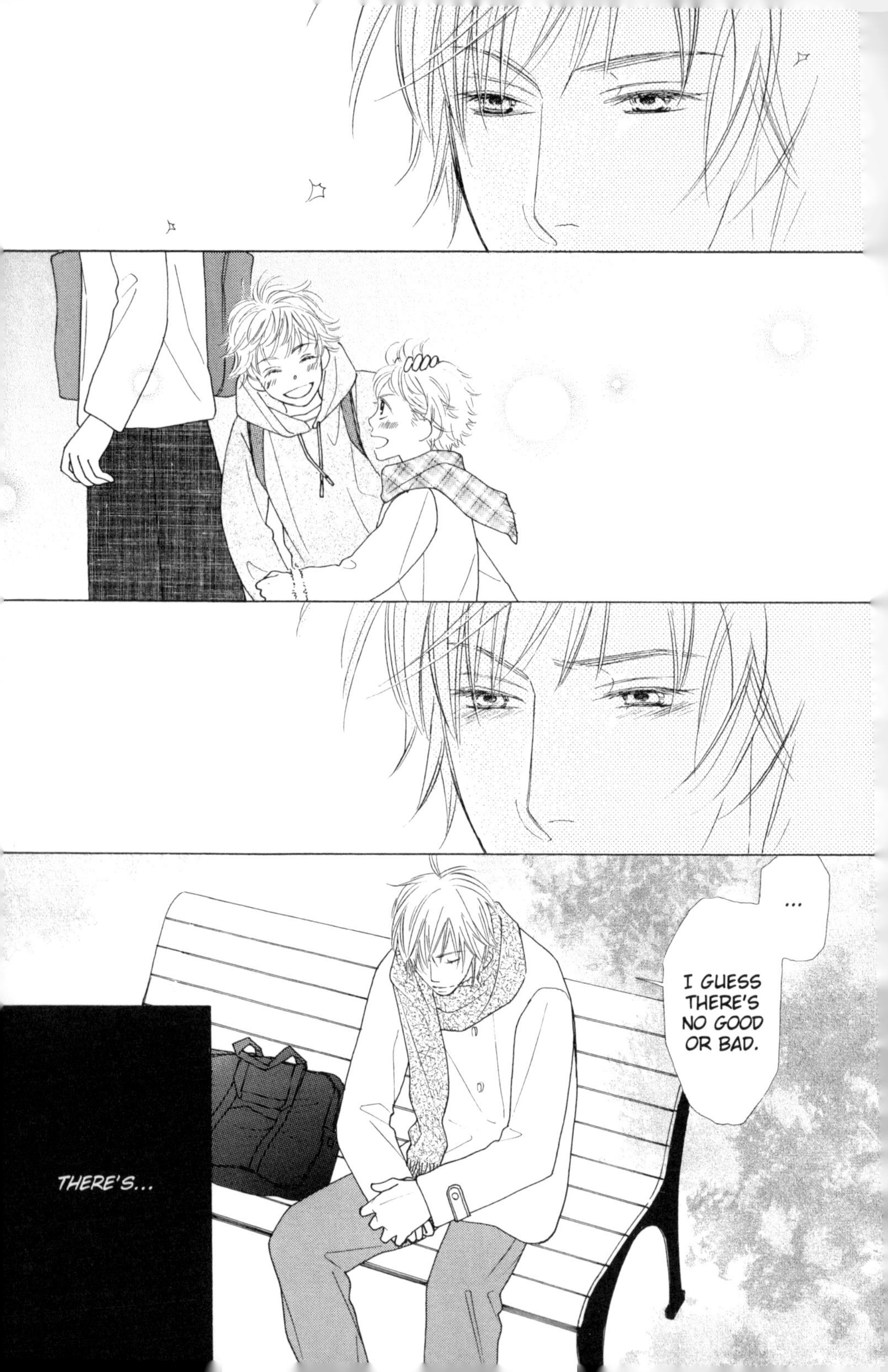
...
I GUESS THERE'S NO GOOD OR BAD.
THERE'S...

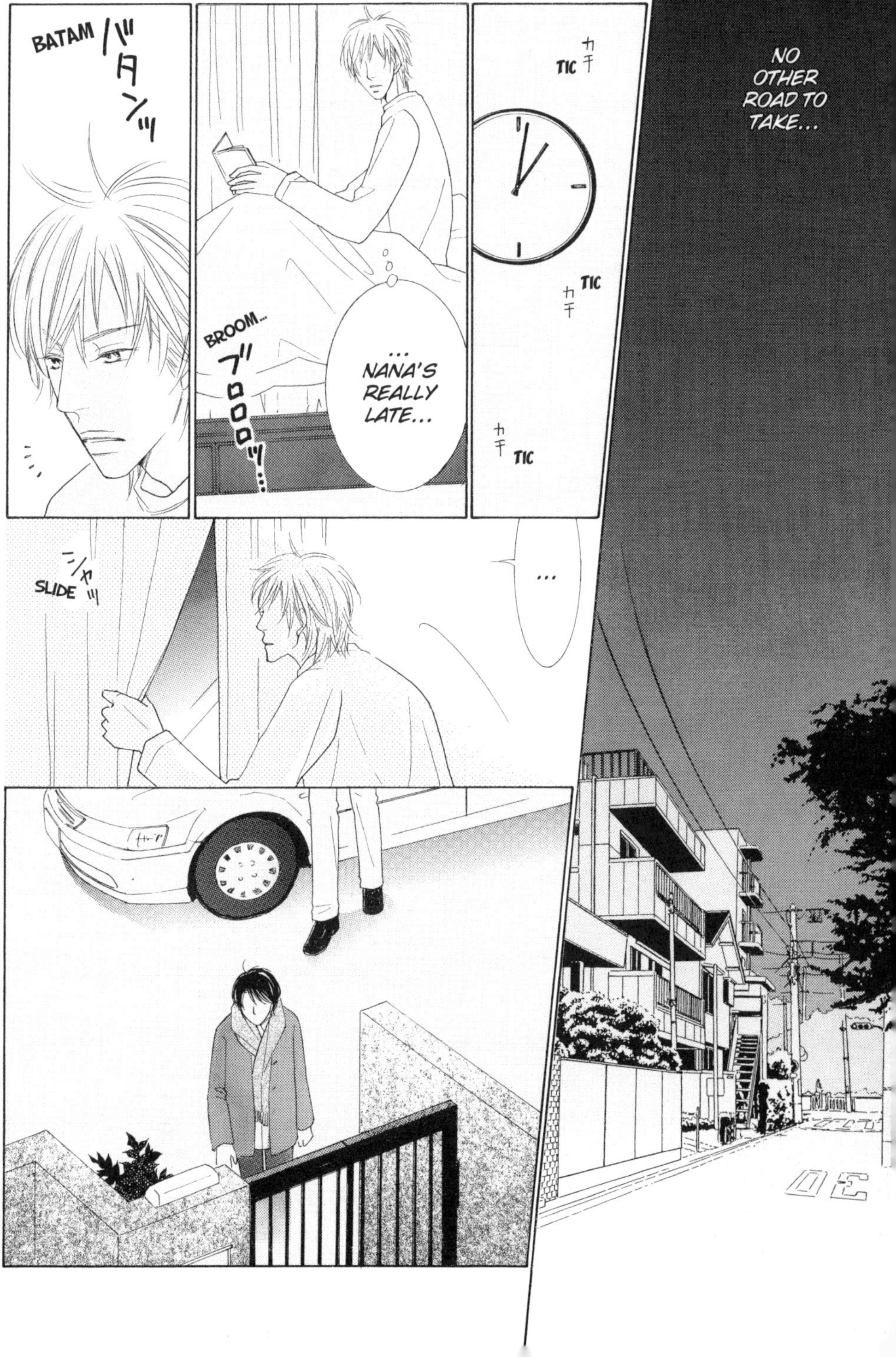
NO OTHER ROAD TO TAKE...
カチ
TIC
TIC
カチ
カチ
TIC
... NANA'S REALLY LATE...
BROOM...
ブロロロッ...
BATAM
バタンッ
...
シャッ
SLIDE

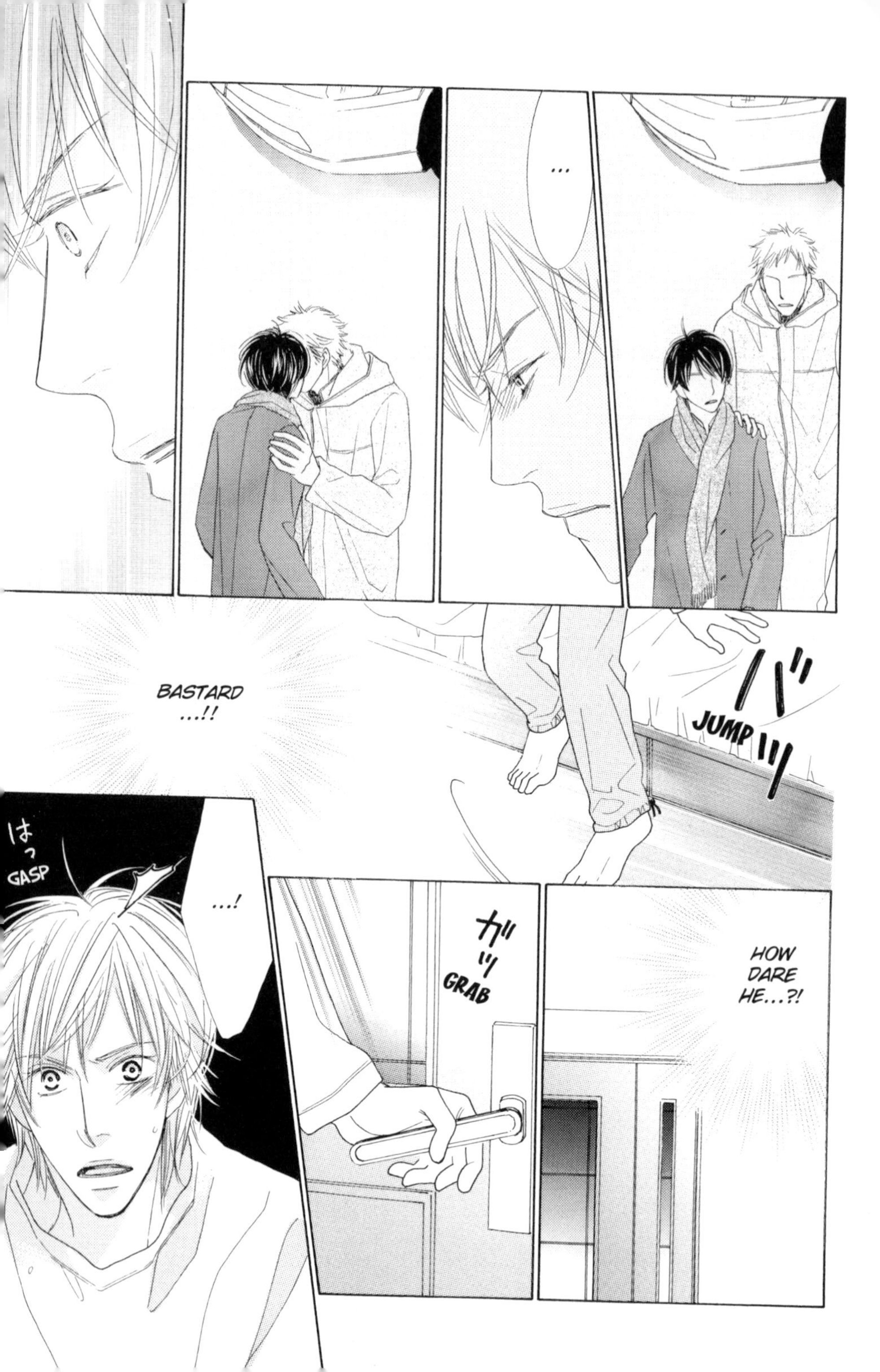
...
バッ
JUMP
BASTARD ...!!
HOW DARE HE...?!
ガッ
GRAB
...!
はっ
GASP

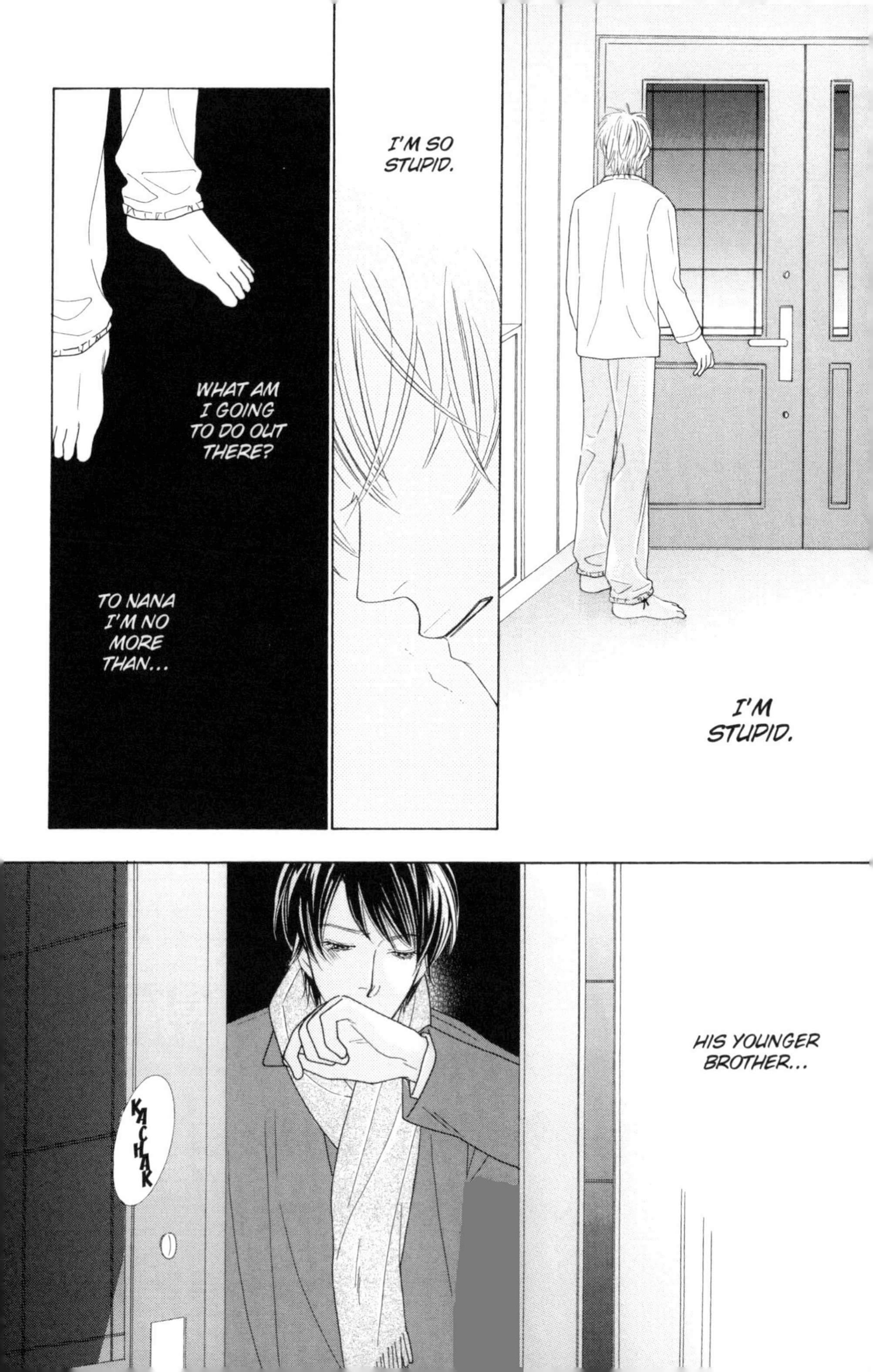
I'M STUPID.
I'M SO STUPID.
WHAT AM I GOING TO DO OUT THERE?
TO NANA I'M NO MORE THAN...
HIS YOUNGER BROTHER...
KACHAK

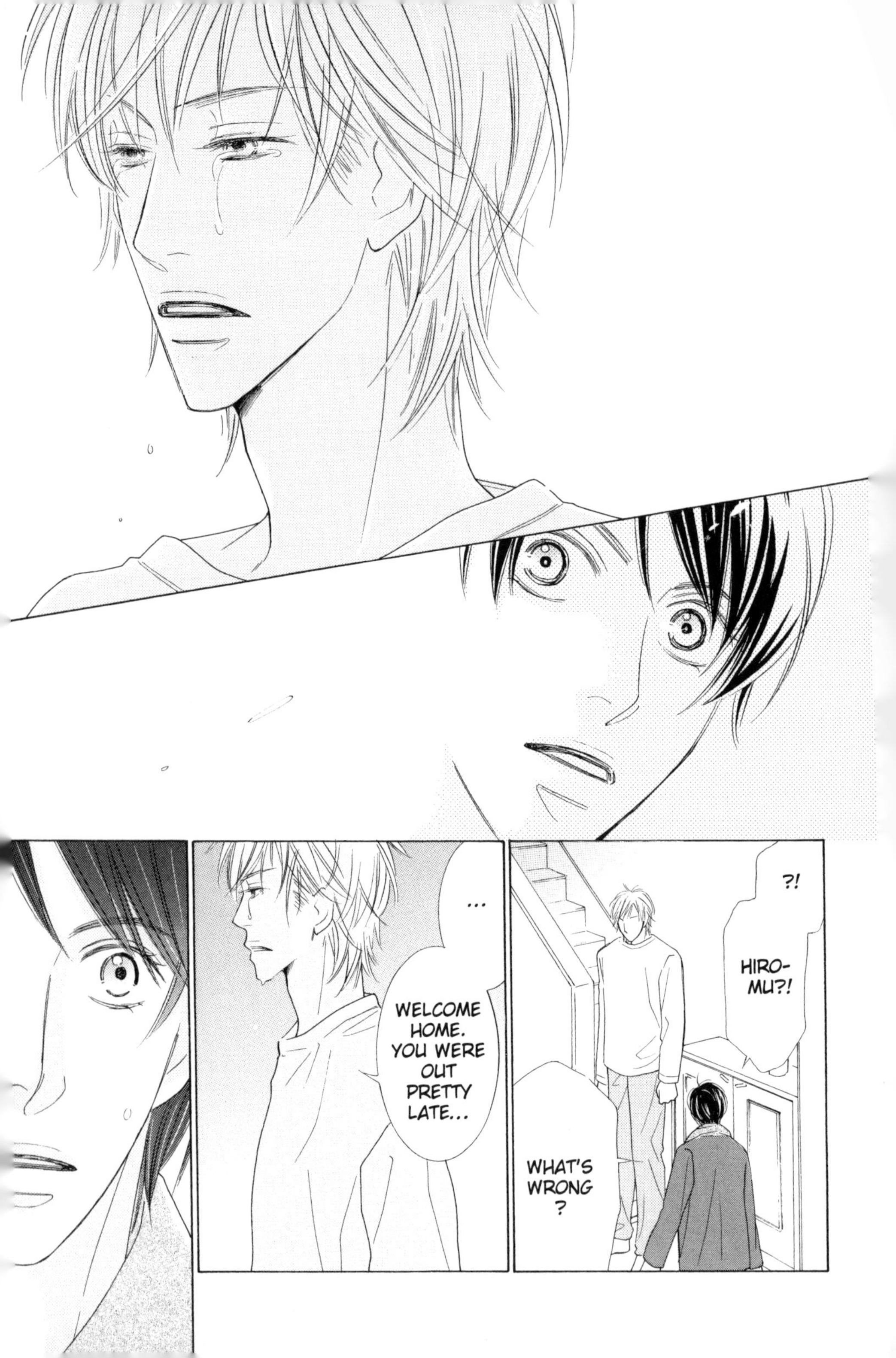
?!
HIRO-MU?!
WHAT'S WRONG ?
...
WELCOME HOME. YOU WERE OUT PRETTY LATE...

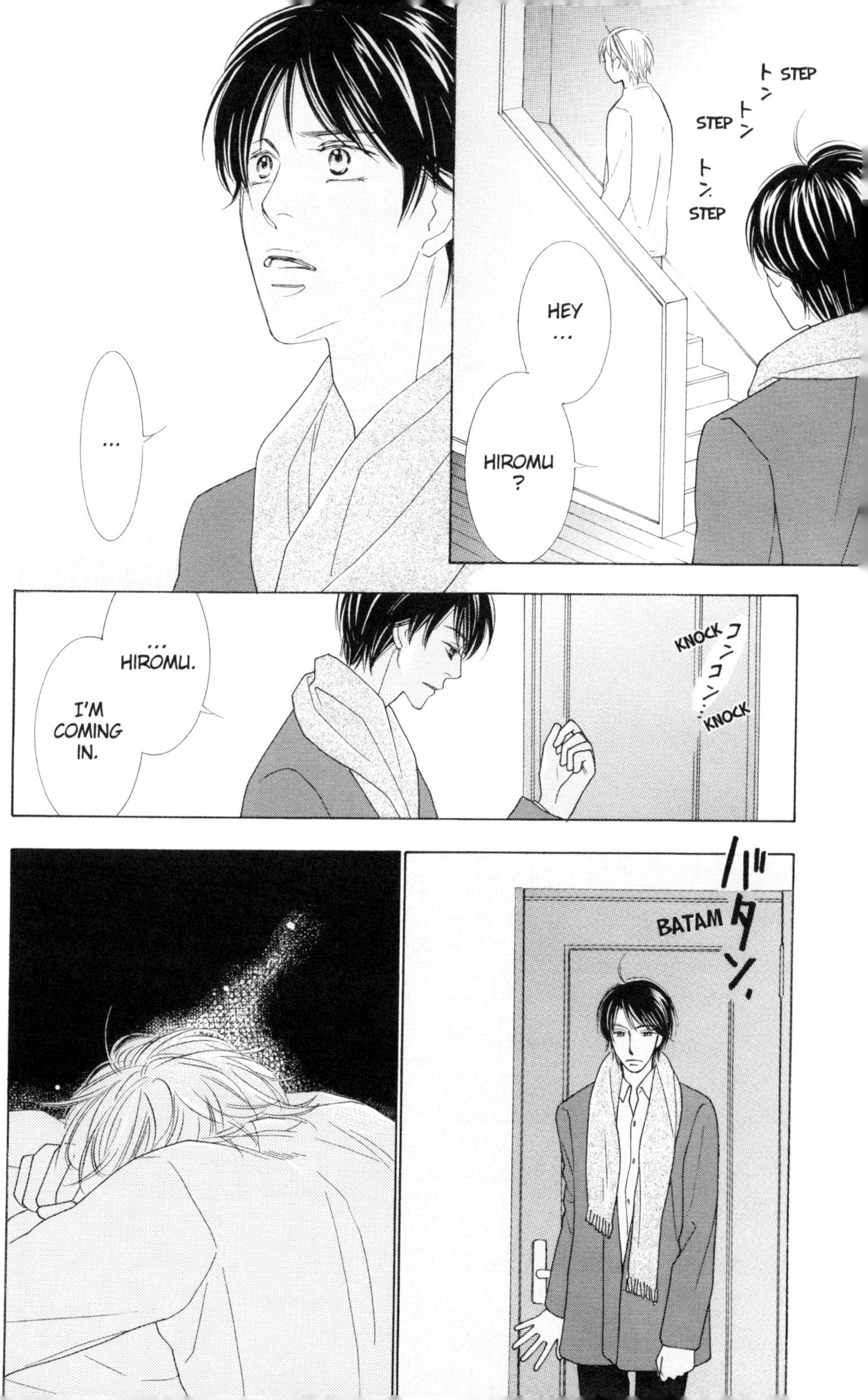

トン STEP
STEP トン
トン STEP
HEY ...
HIROMU ?
...
KNOCK コンコン KNOCK
... HIROMU.
I'M COMING IN.
バタン BATAM

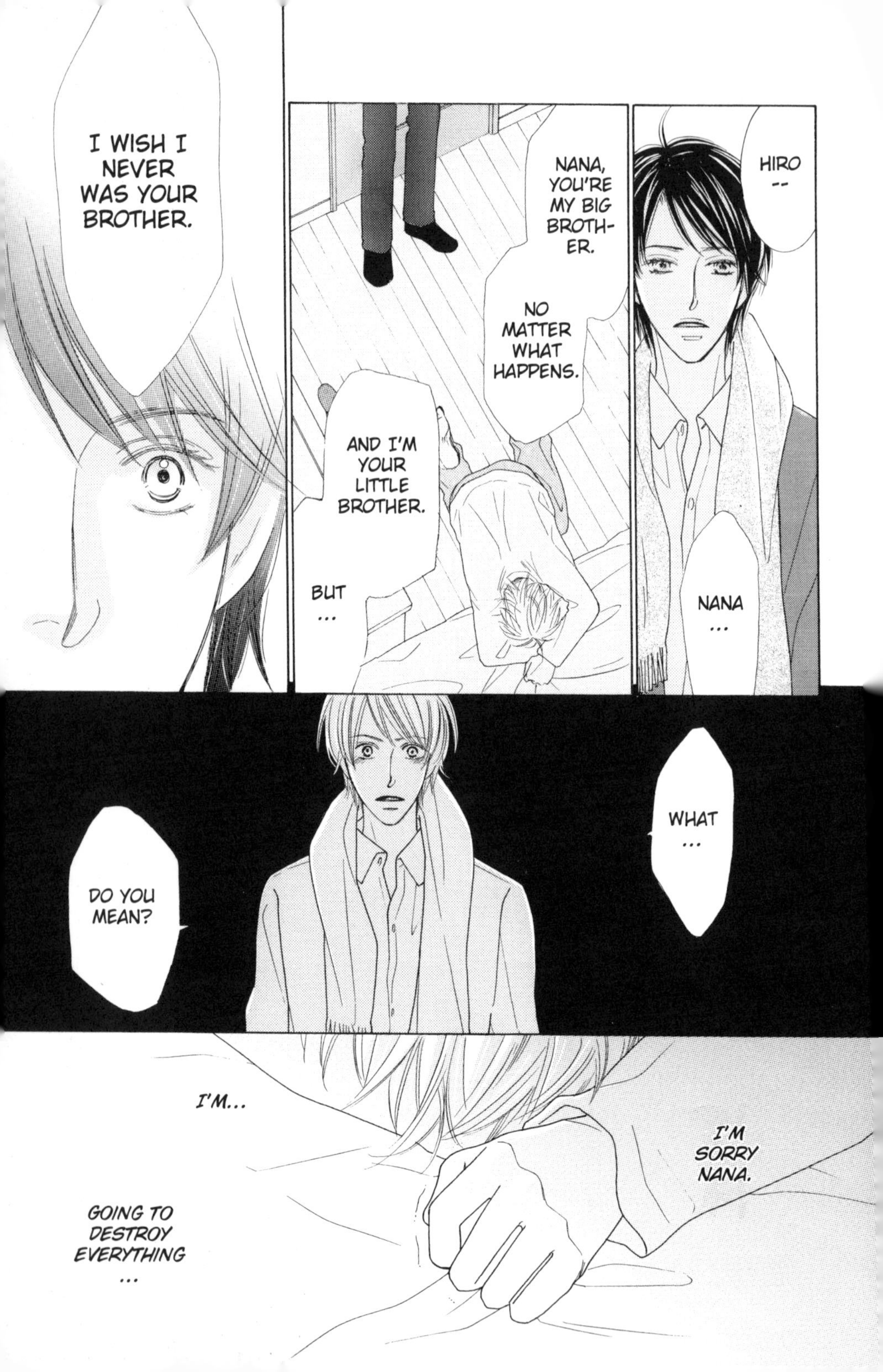
HIRO --
NANA ...
NANA, YOU'RE MY BIG BROTH- ER.
NO MATTER WHAT HAPPENS.
AND I'M YOUR LITTLE BROTHER.
BUT ...
I WISH I NEVER WAS YOUR BROTHER.
WHAT ...
DO YOU MEAN?
I'M SORRY NANA.
I'M...
GOING TO DESTROY EVERYTHING ...

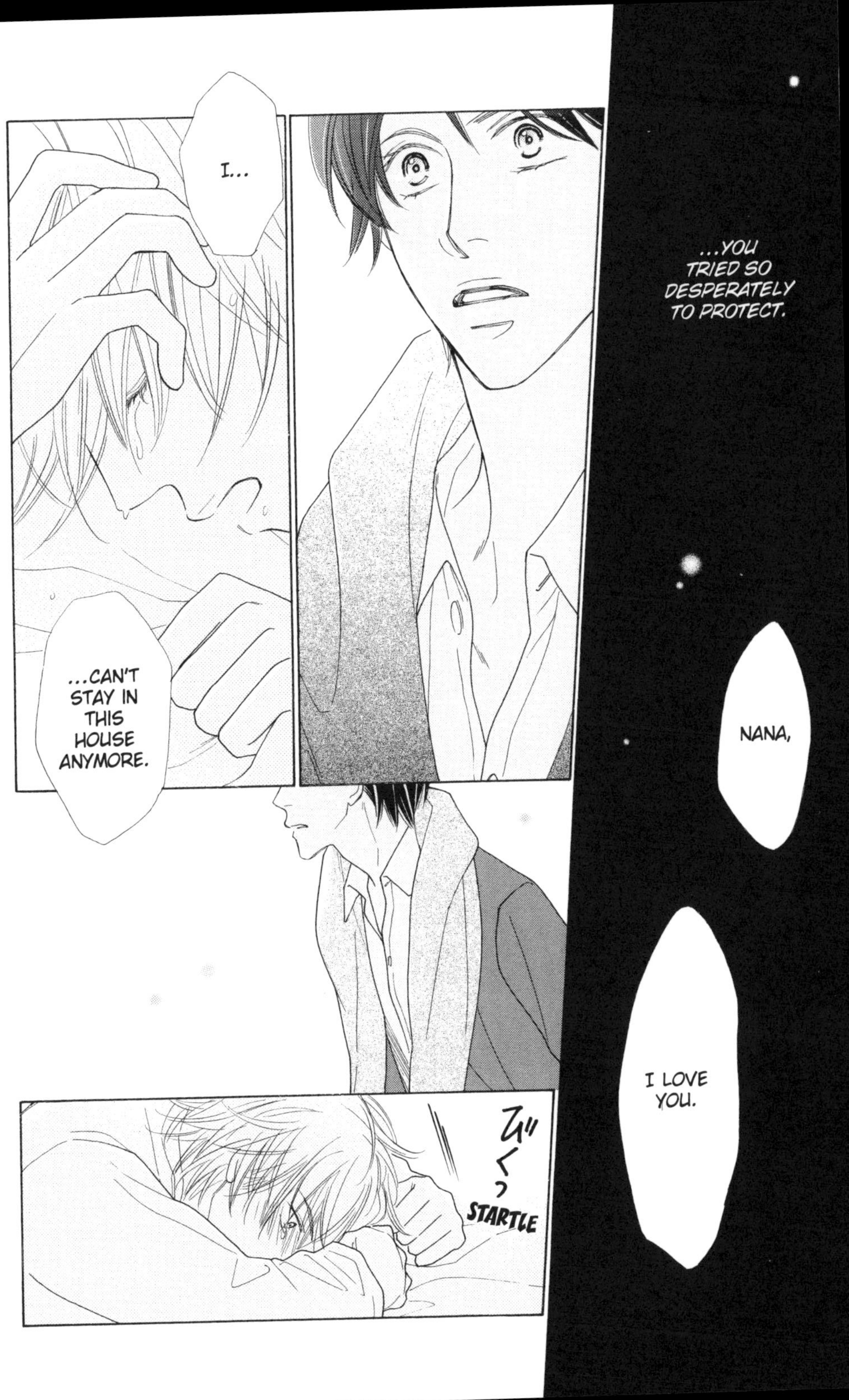
...YOU TRIED SO DESPERATELY TO PROTECT.
NANA,
I LOVE YOU.
I...
...CAN'T STAY IN THIS HOUSE ANYMORE.
びくっ
STARTLE

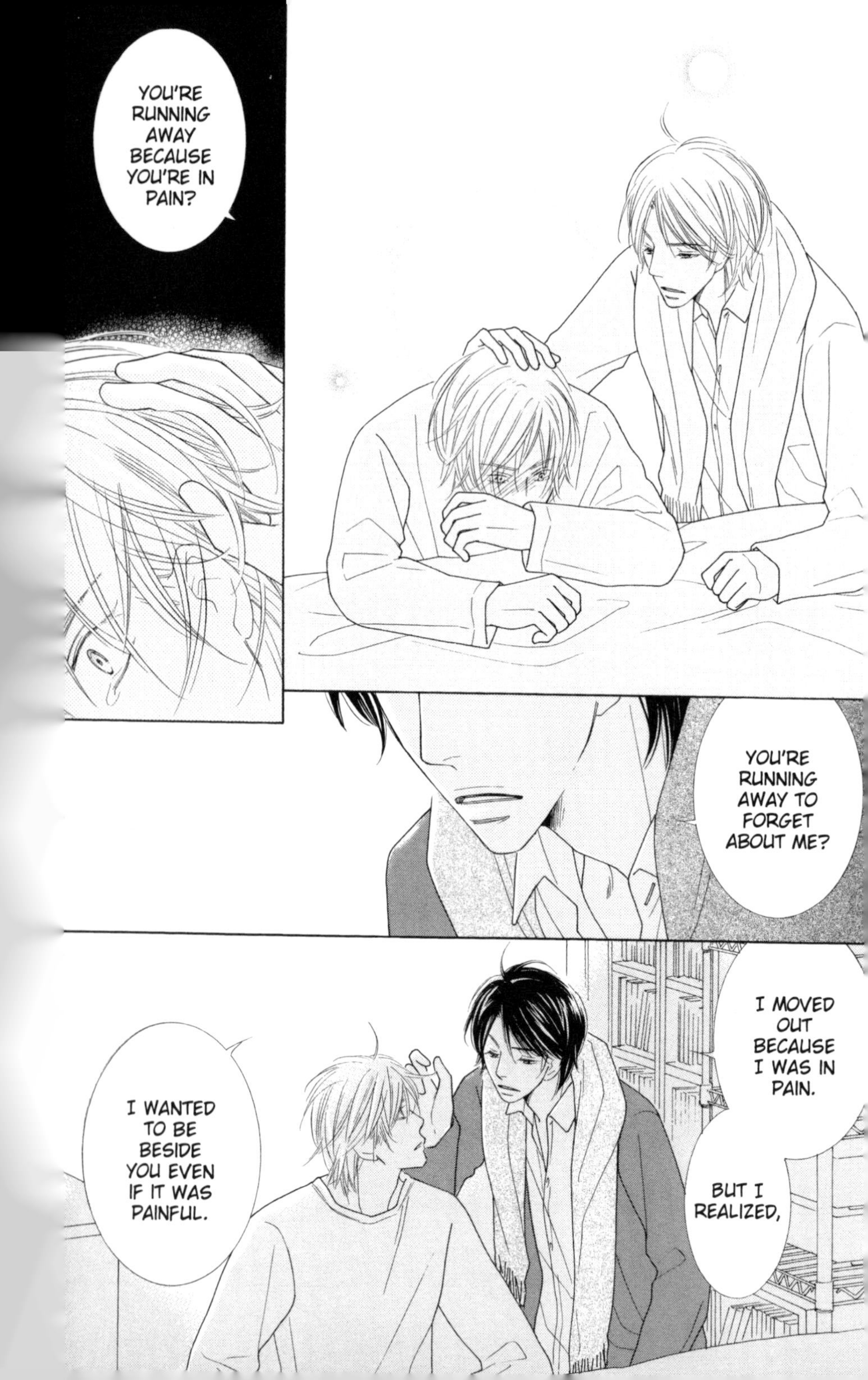
YOU'RE RUNNING AWAY BECAUSE YOU'RE IN PAIN?
YOU'RE RUNNING AWAY TO FORGET ABOUT ME?
I MOVED OUT BECAUSE I WAS IN PAIN.
BUT I REALIZED,
I WANTED TO BE BESIDE YOU EVEN IF IT WAS PAINFUL.

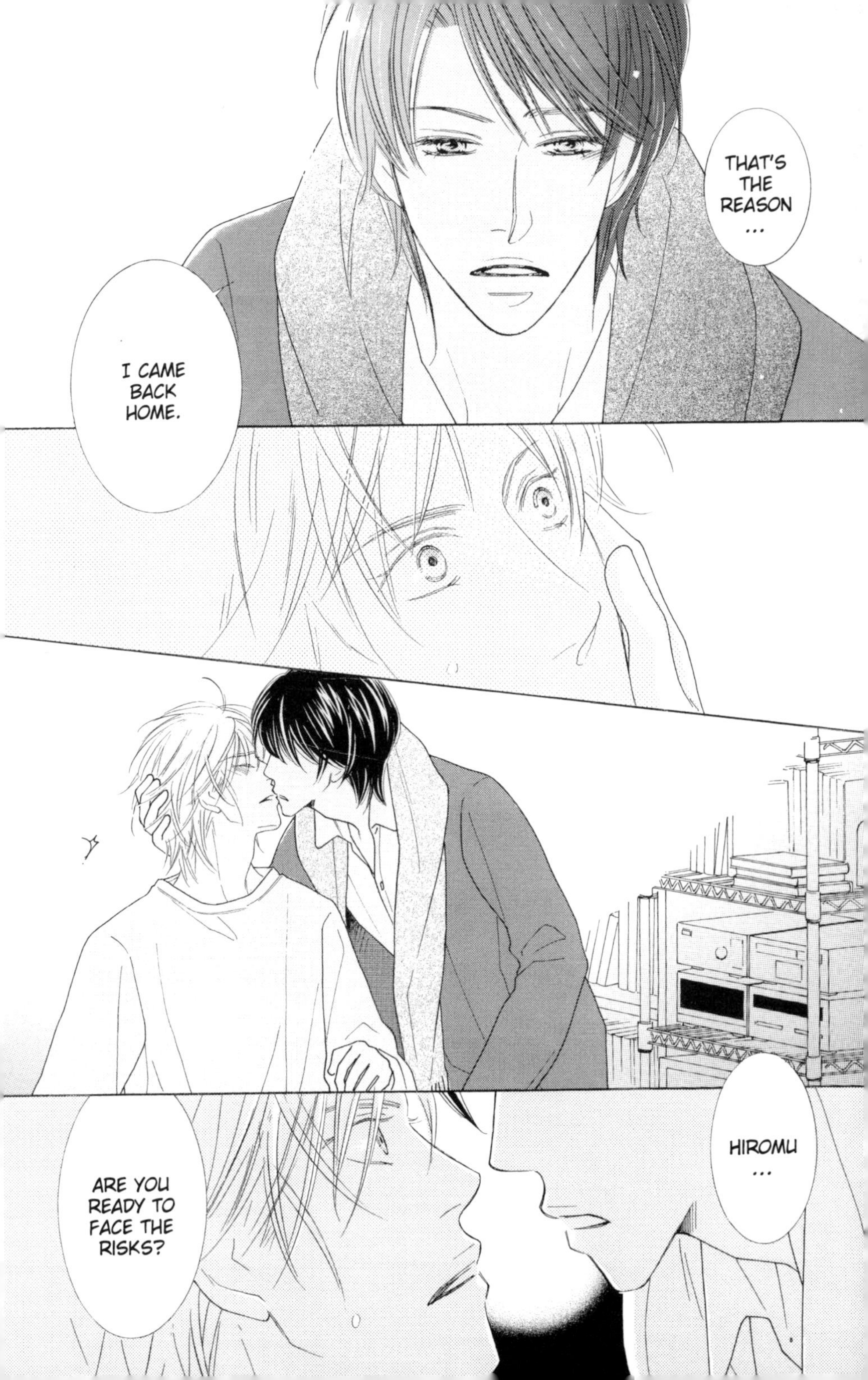
THAT'S THE REASON ...
I CAME BACK HOME.
HIROMU ...
ARE YOU READY TO FACE THE RISKS?

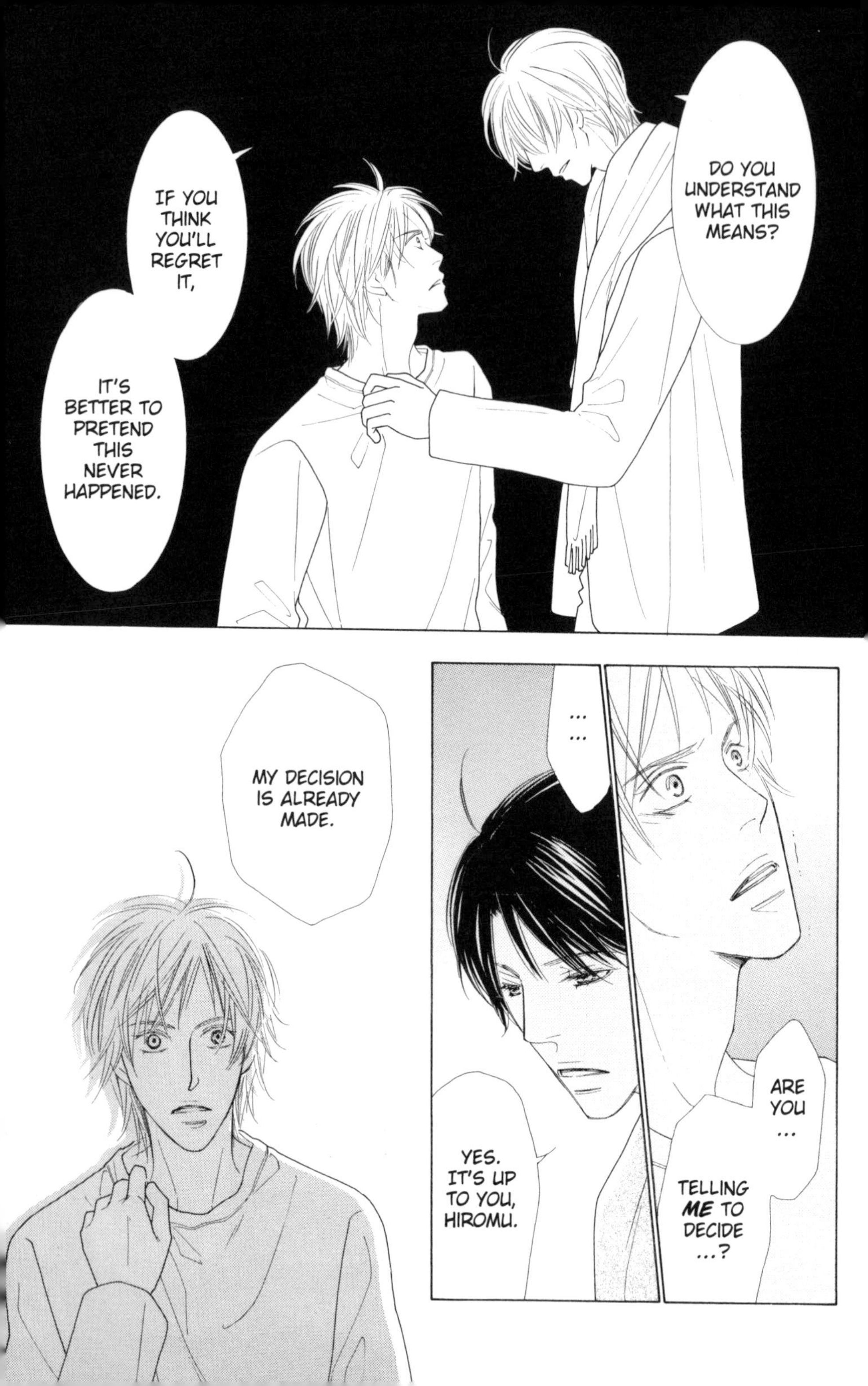
DO YOU UNDERSTAND WHAT THIS MEANS?
IF YOU THINK YOU'LL REGRET IT,
IT'S BETTER TO PRETEND THIS NEVER HAPPENED.
ARE YOU ... TELLING *ME* TO DECIDE ...?
... ...
YES. IT'S UP TO YOU, HIROMU.
MY DECISION IS ALREADY MADE.

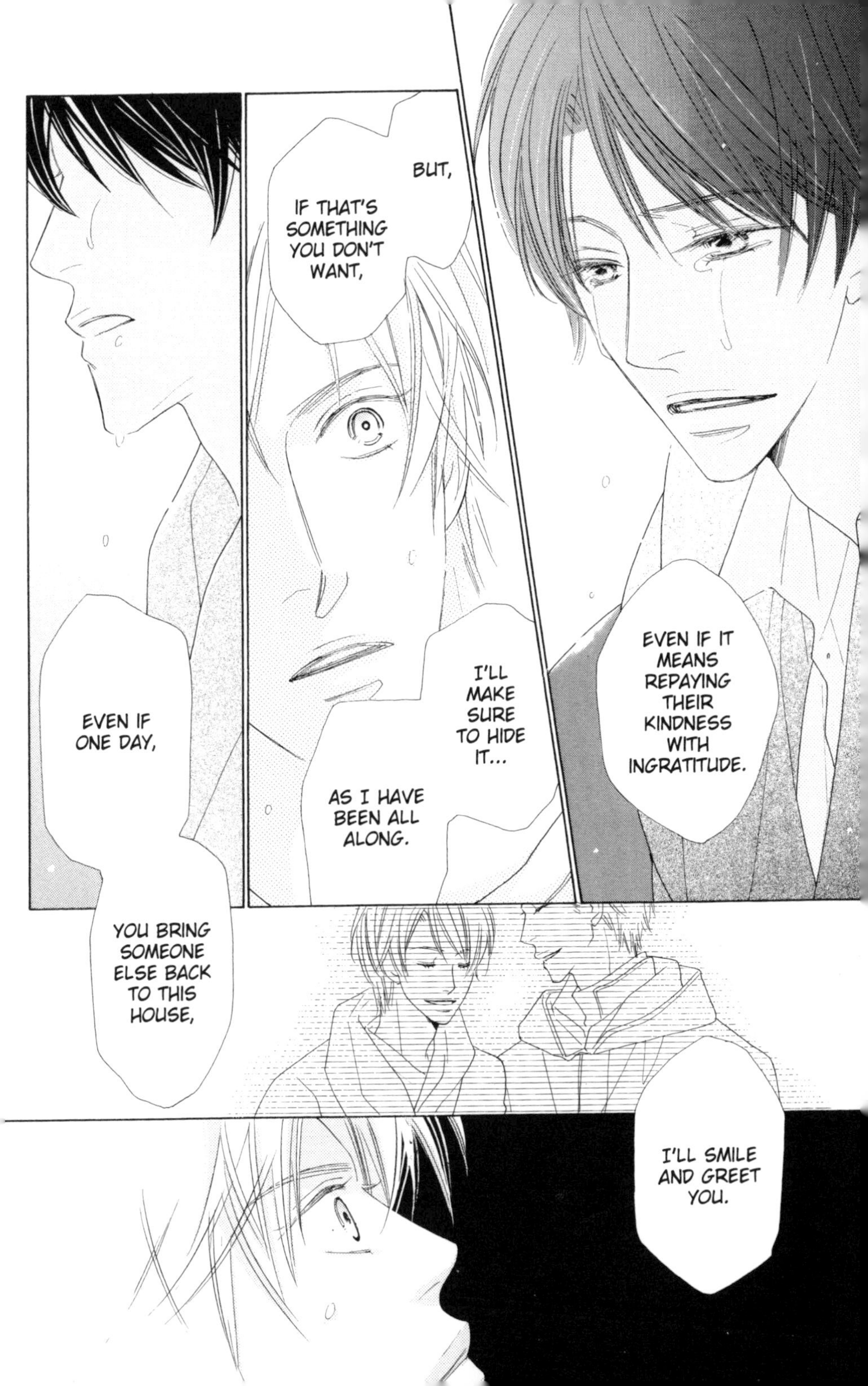
EVEN IF IT MEANS REPAYING THEIR KINDNESS WITH INGRATITUDE.
BUT,
IF THAT'S SOMETHING YOU DON'T WANT,
I'LL MAKE SURE TO HIDE IT...
AS I HAVE BEEN ALL ALONG.
EVEN IF ONE DAY,
YOU BRING SOMEONE ELSE BACK TO THIS HOUSE,
I'LL SMILE AND GREET YOU.

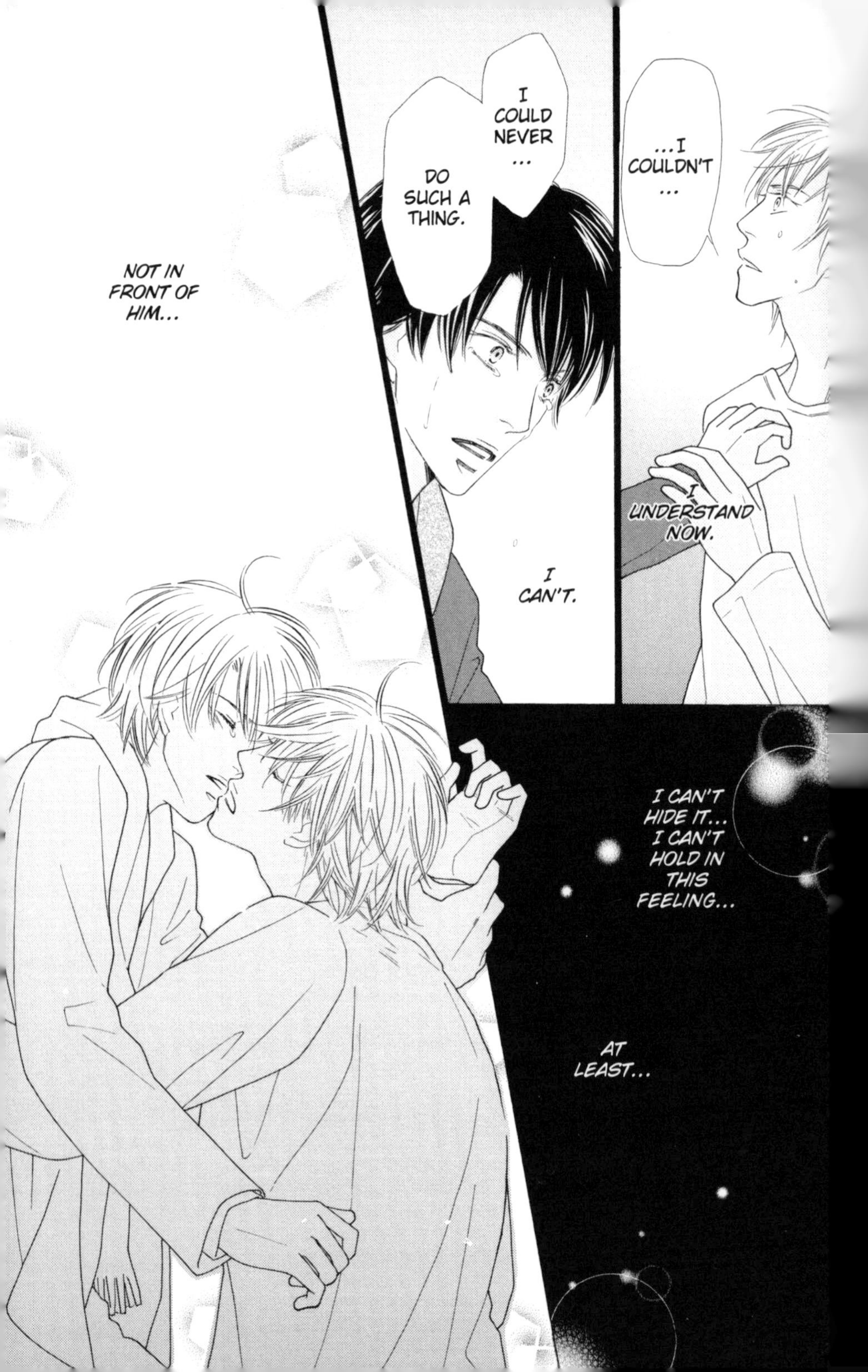
...I COULDN'T ...
I UNDERSTAND NOW.
I COULD NEVER ...
DO SUCH A THING.
I CAN'T.
I CAN'T HIDE IT... I CAN'T HOLD IN THIS FEELING...
AT LEAST...
NOT IN FRONT OF HIM...

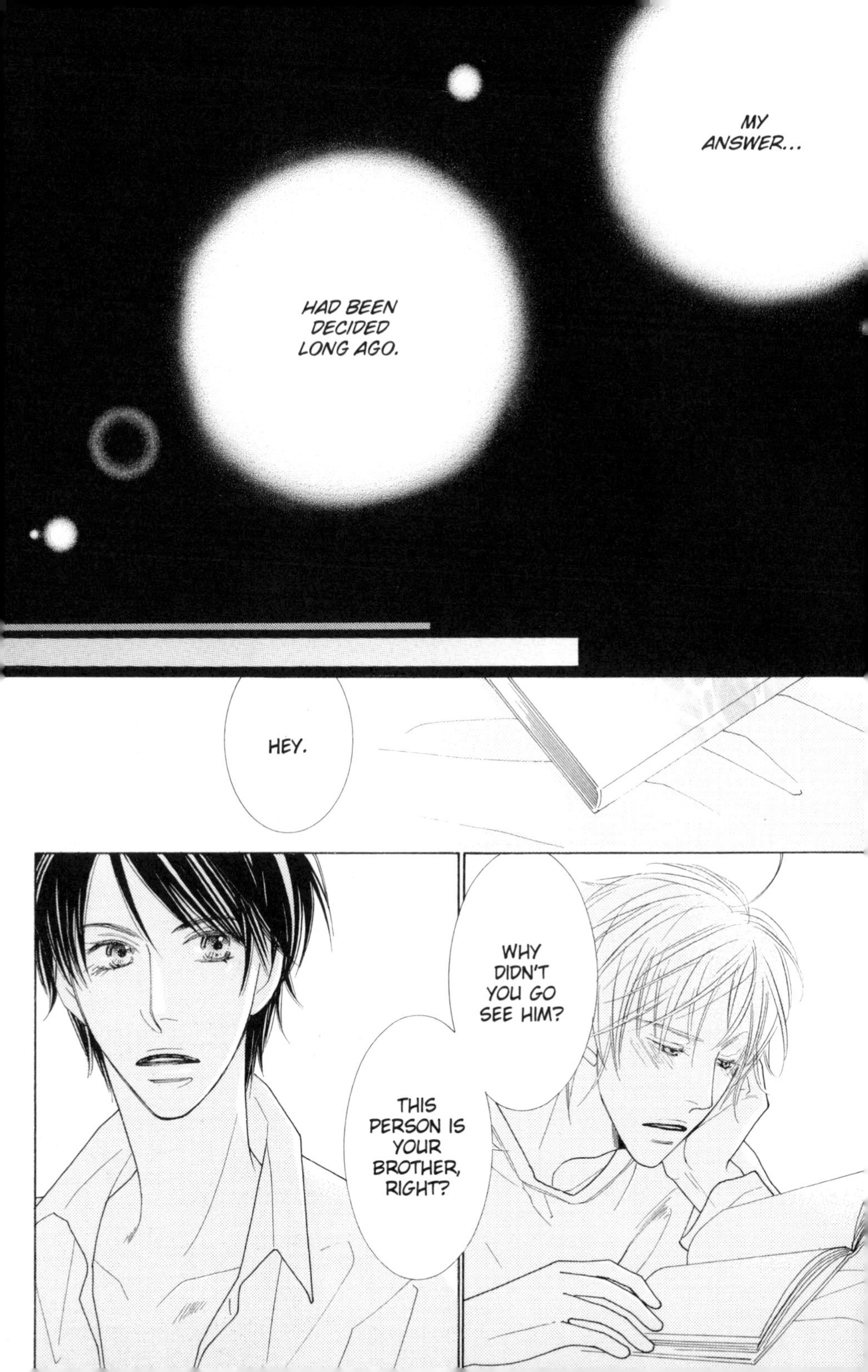
MY ANSWER...
HAD BEEN DECIDED LONG AGO.
HEY.
WHY DIDN'T YOU GO SEE HIM?
THIS PERSON IS YOUR BROTHER, RIGHT?

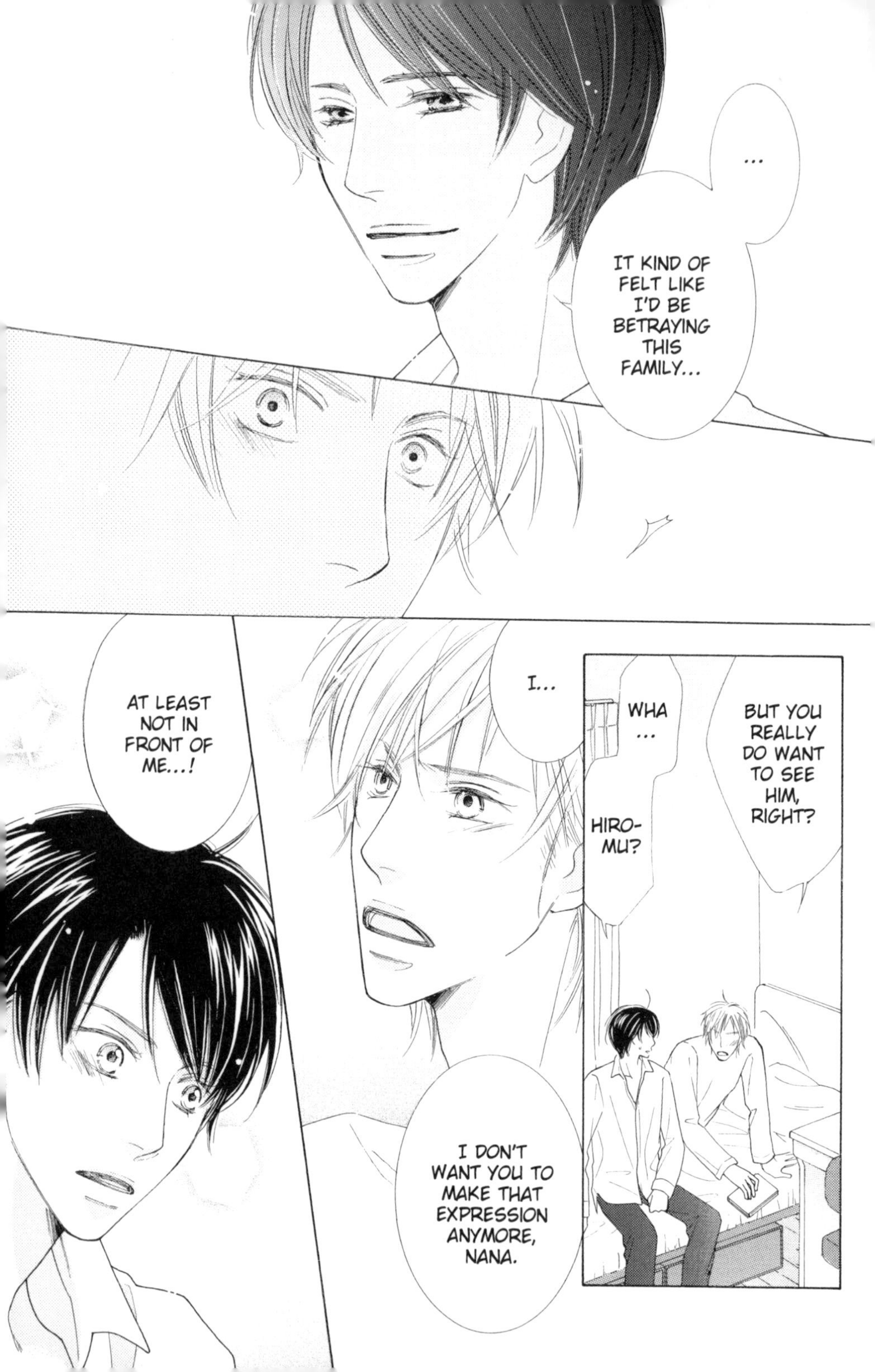
...
IT KIND OF FELT LIKE I'D BE BETRAYING THIS FAMILY...
BUT YOU REALLY DO WANT TO SEE HIM, RIGHT?
WHA ...
HIRO-MU?
I...
I DON'T WANT YOU TO MAKE THAT EXPRESSION ANYMORE, NANA.
AT LEAST NOT IN FRONT OF ME...!

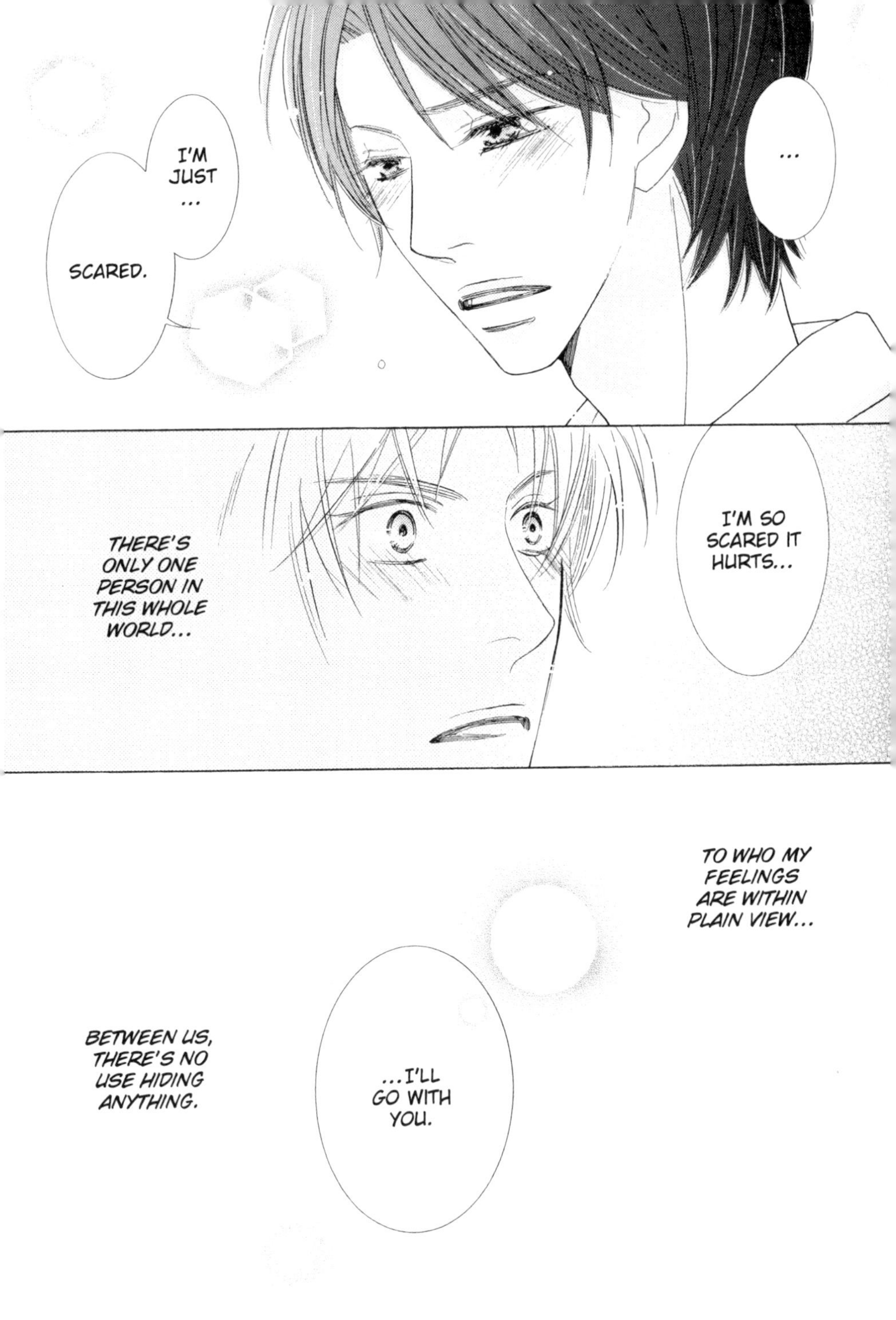
...
I'M JUST ... SCARED.
I'M SO SCARED IT HURTS...
THERE'S ONLY ONE PERSON IN THIS WHOLE WORLD...
TO WHO MY FEELINGS ARE WITHIN PLAIN VIEW...
...I'LL GO WITH YOU.
BETWEEN US, THERE'S NO USE HIDING ANYTHING.

WITHIN PLAIN VIEW / THE END

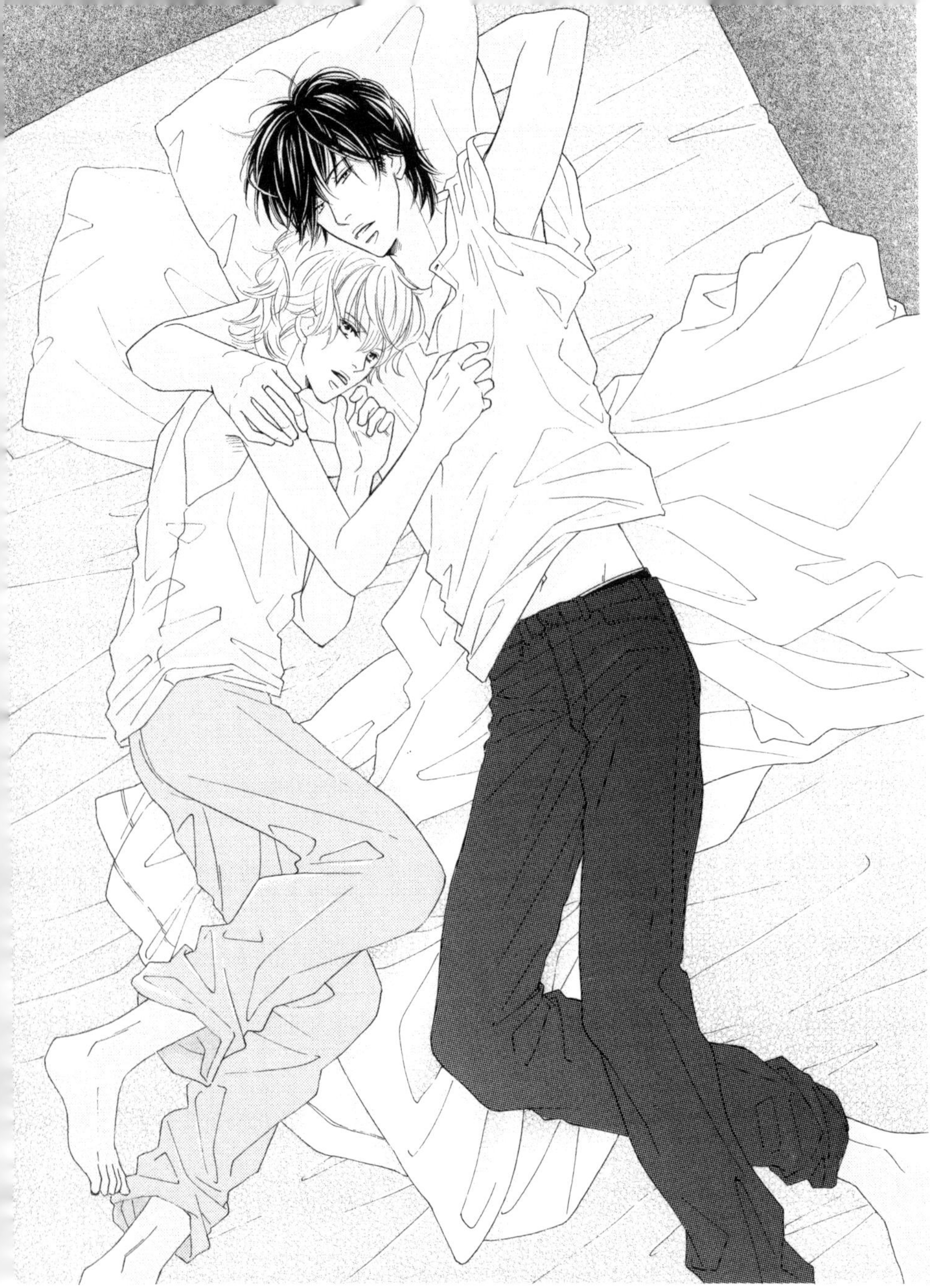

SEVEN ******* he has no name.nana. he has no luck.mitsuha.

SEVEN

PRESENTED BY MOMOKO TENZEN

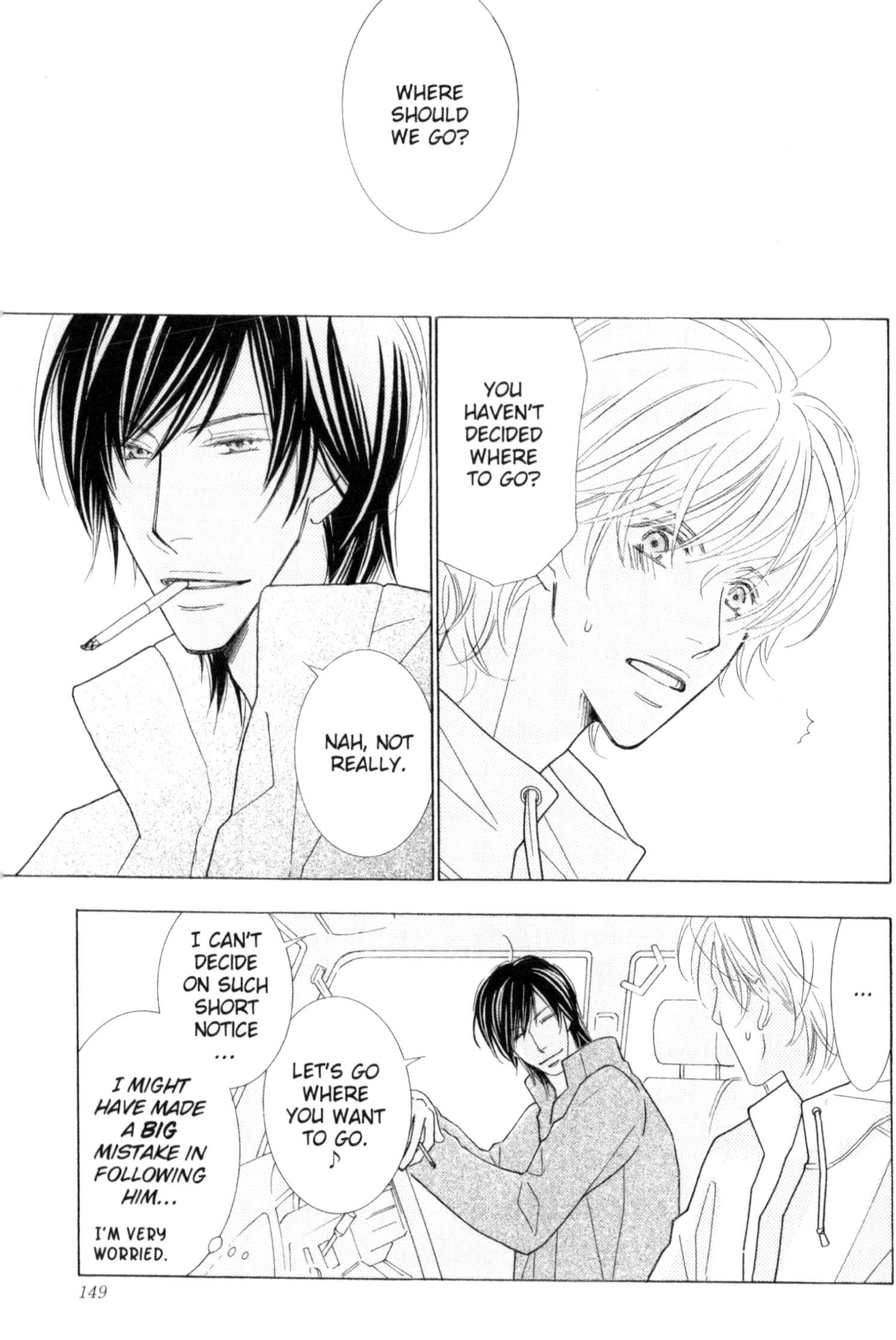
WHERE SHOULD WE GO?
YOU HAVEN'T DECIDED WHERE TO GO?
NAH, NOT REALLY.
...
I CAN'T DECIDE ON SUCH SHORT NOTICE ...
LET'S GO WHERE YOU WANT TO GO. ♪
I MIGHT HAVE MADE A BIG MISTAKE IN FOLLOWING HIM...
I'M VERY WORRIED.

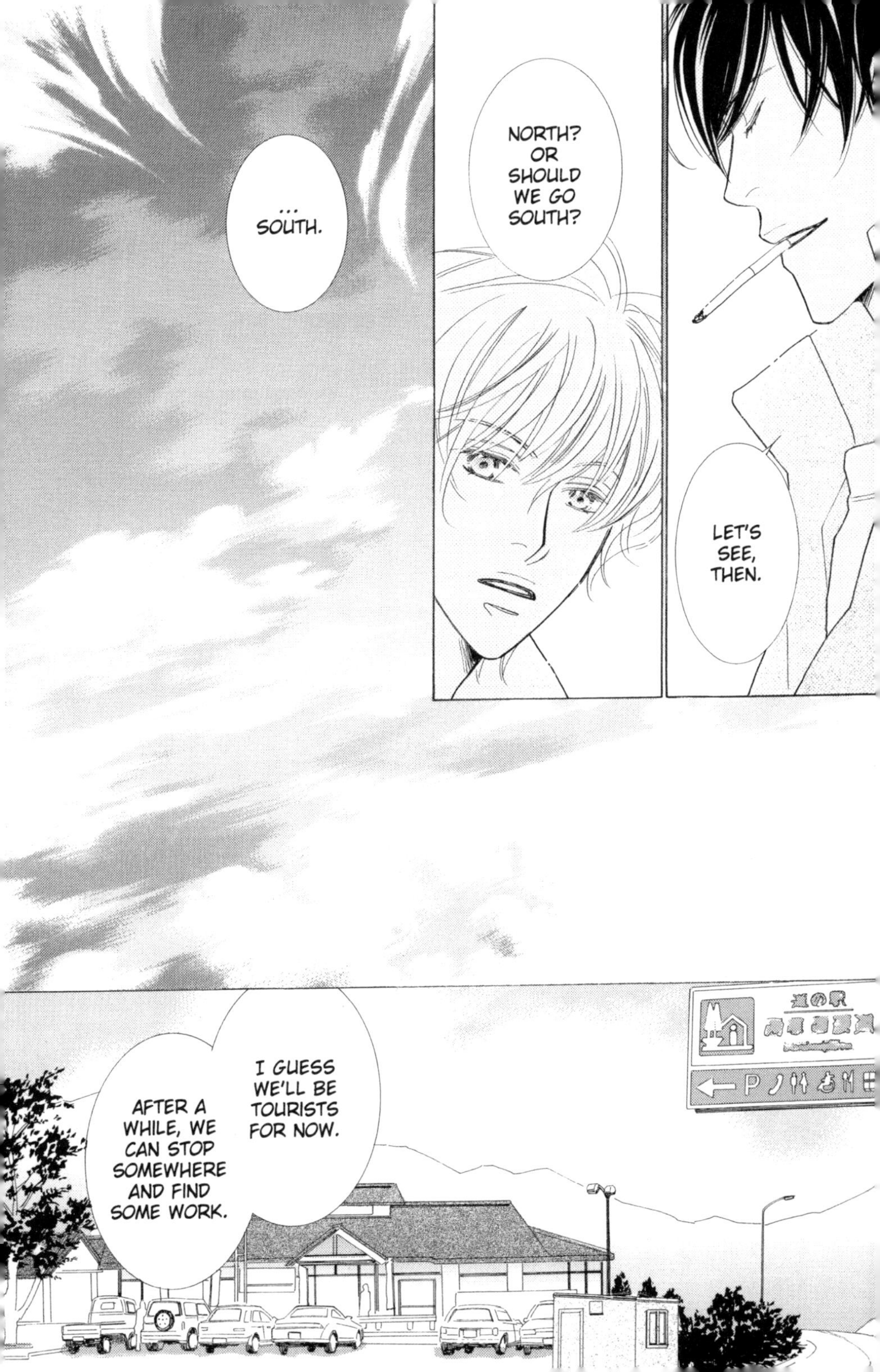
LET'S SEE, THEN.
NORTH? OR SHOULD WE GO SOUTH?
...SOUTH.
I GUESS WE'LL BE TOURISTS FOR NOW.
AFTER A WHILE, WE CAN STOP SOMEWHERE AND FIND SOME WORK.

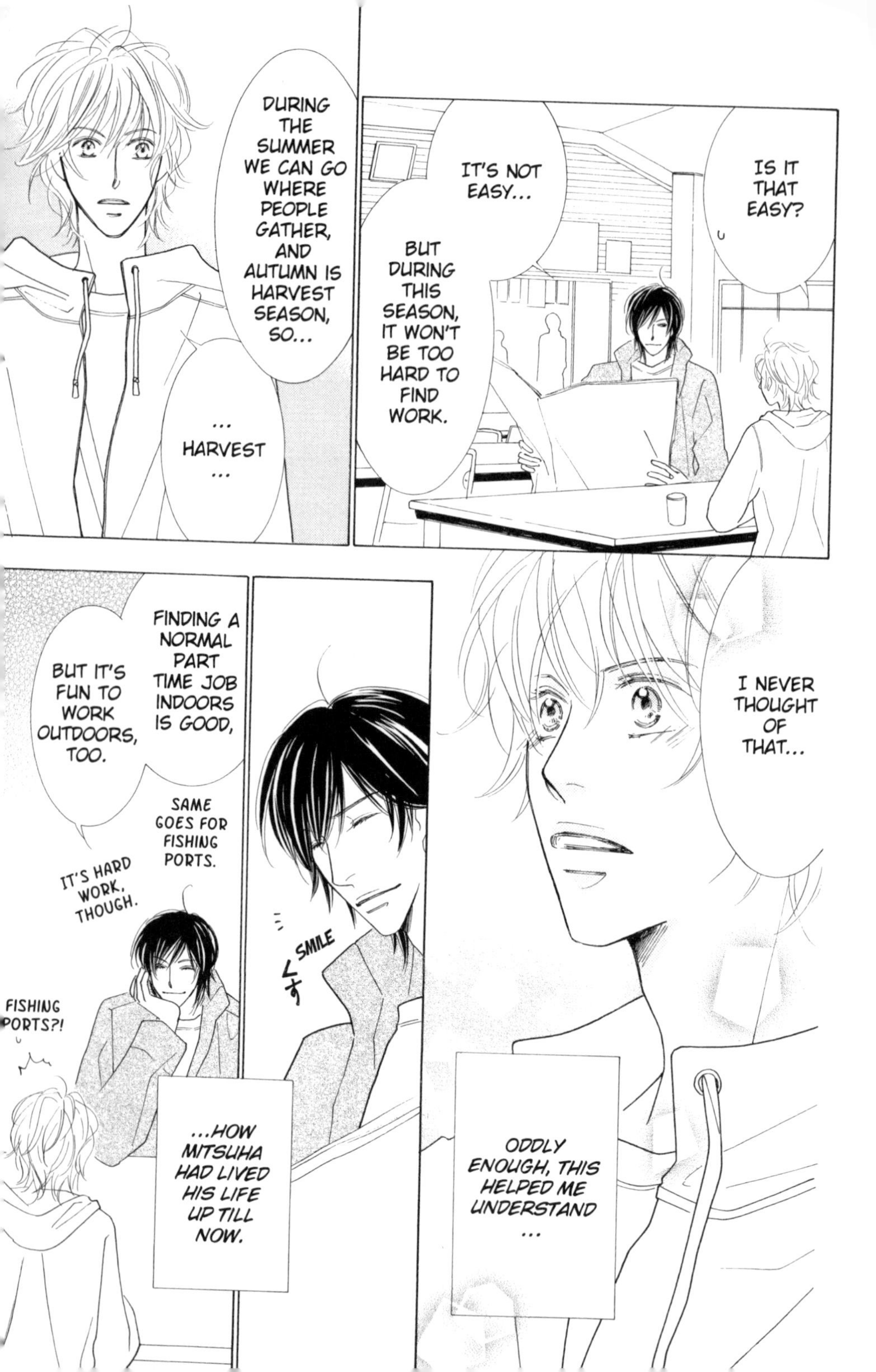
IS IT THAT EASY?
IT'S NOT EASY...
BUT DURING THIS SEASON, IT WON'T BE TOO HARD TO FIND WORK.
DURING THE SUMMER WE CAN GO WHERE PEOPLE GATHER, AND AUTUMN IS HARVEST SEASON, SO...
...HARVEST...
I NEVER THOUGHT OF THAT...
ODDLY ENOUGH, THIS HELPED ME UNDERSTAND...
SMILE
FINDING A NORMAL PART TIME JOB INDOORS IS GOOD,
BUT IT'S FUN TO WORK OUTDOORS, TOO.
SAME GOES FOR FISHING PORTS.
IT'S HARD WORK, THOUGH.
FISHING PORTS?!
...HOW MITSUHA HAD LIVED HIS LIFE UP TILL NOW.

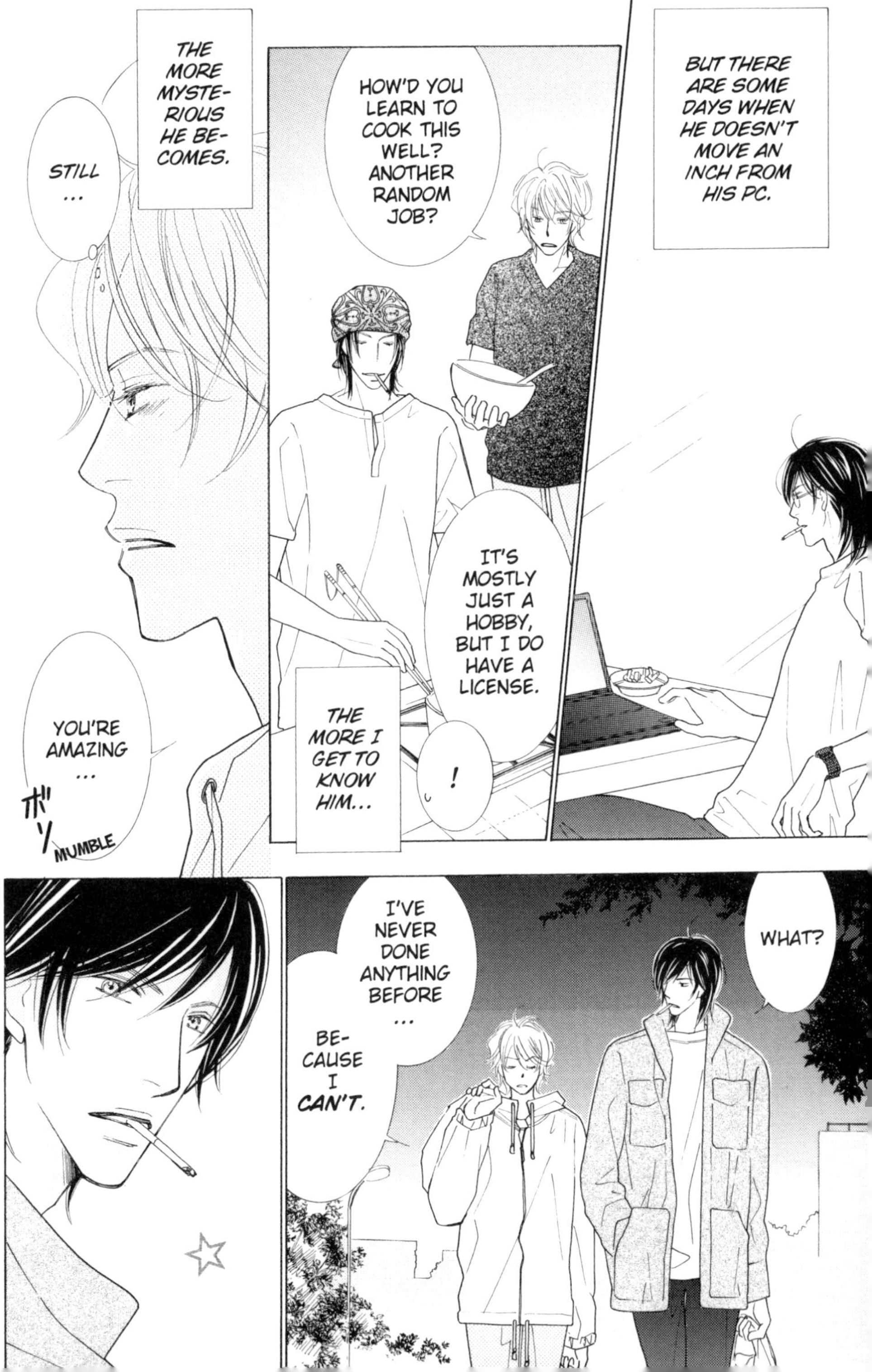
BUT THERE ARE SOME DAYS WHEN HE DOESN'T MOVE AN INCH FROM HIS PC.
HOW'D YOU LEARN TO COOK THIS WELL? ANOTHER RANDOM JOB?
IT'S MOSTLY JUST A HOBBY, BUT I DO HAVE A LICENSE.
!
THE MORE I GET TO KNOW HIM...
THE MORE MYSTE-RIOUS HE BE-COMES.
STILL...
YOU'RE AMAZING...
ボソ MUMBLE
WHAT?
I'VE NEVER DONE ANYTHING BEFORE...
BE-CAUSE I **CAN'T**.

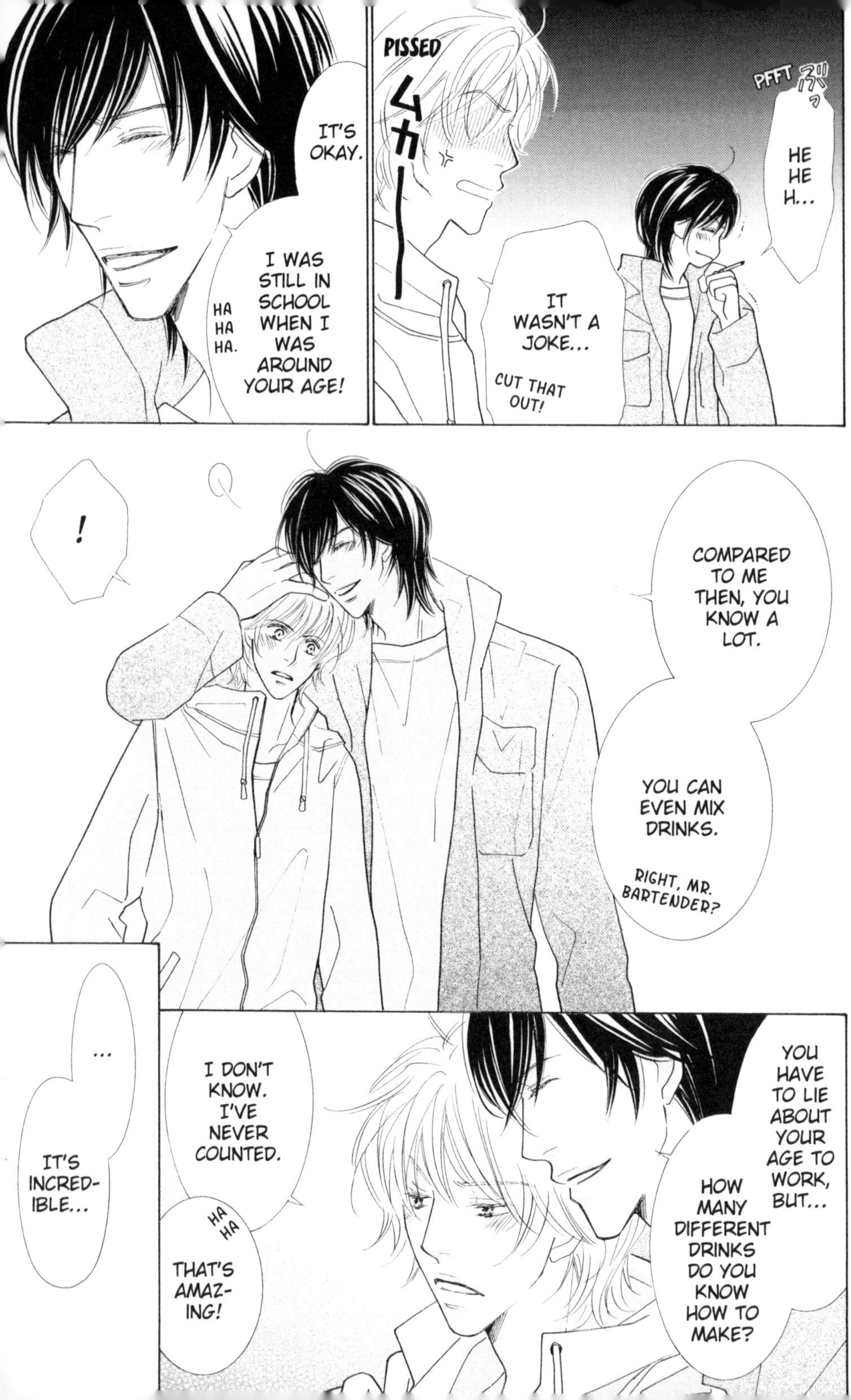
PFFT ぶっ
HE HE H...
PISSED
ムカー
IT WASN'T A JOKE...
CUT THAT OUT!
IT'S OKAY.
I WAS STILL IN SCHOOL WHEN I WAS AROUND YOUR AGE!
HA HA HA.
COMPARED TO ME THEN, YOU KNOW A LOT.
YOU CAN EVEN MIX DRINKS.
RIGHT, MR. BARTENDER?
!
YOU HAVE TO LIE ABOUT YOUR AGE TO WORK, BUT...
HOW MANY DIFFERENT DRINKS DO YOU KNOW HOW TO MAKE?
I DON'T KNOW. I'VE NEVER COUNTED.
HA HA
THAT'S AMAZ-ING!
...
IT'S INCRED-IBLE...

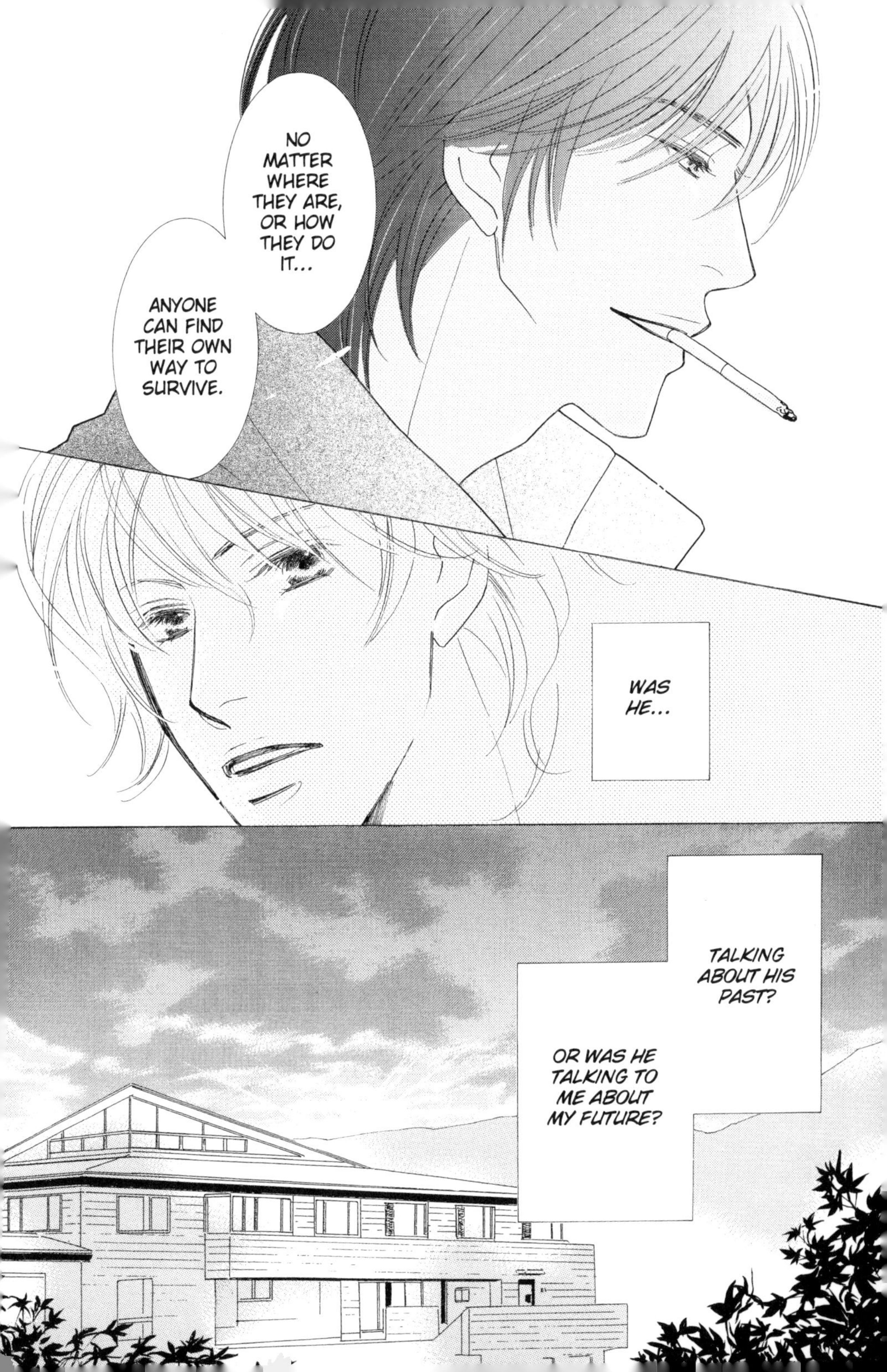
NO MATTER WHERE THEY ARE, OR HOW THEY DO IT...
ANYONE CAN FIND THEIR OWN WAY TO SURVIVE.
WAS HE...
TALKING ABOUT HIS PAST?
OR WAS HE TALKING TO ME ABOUT MY FUTURE?

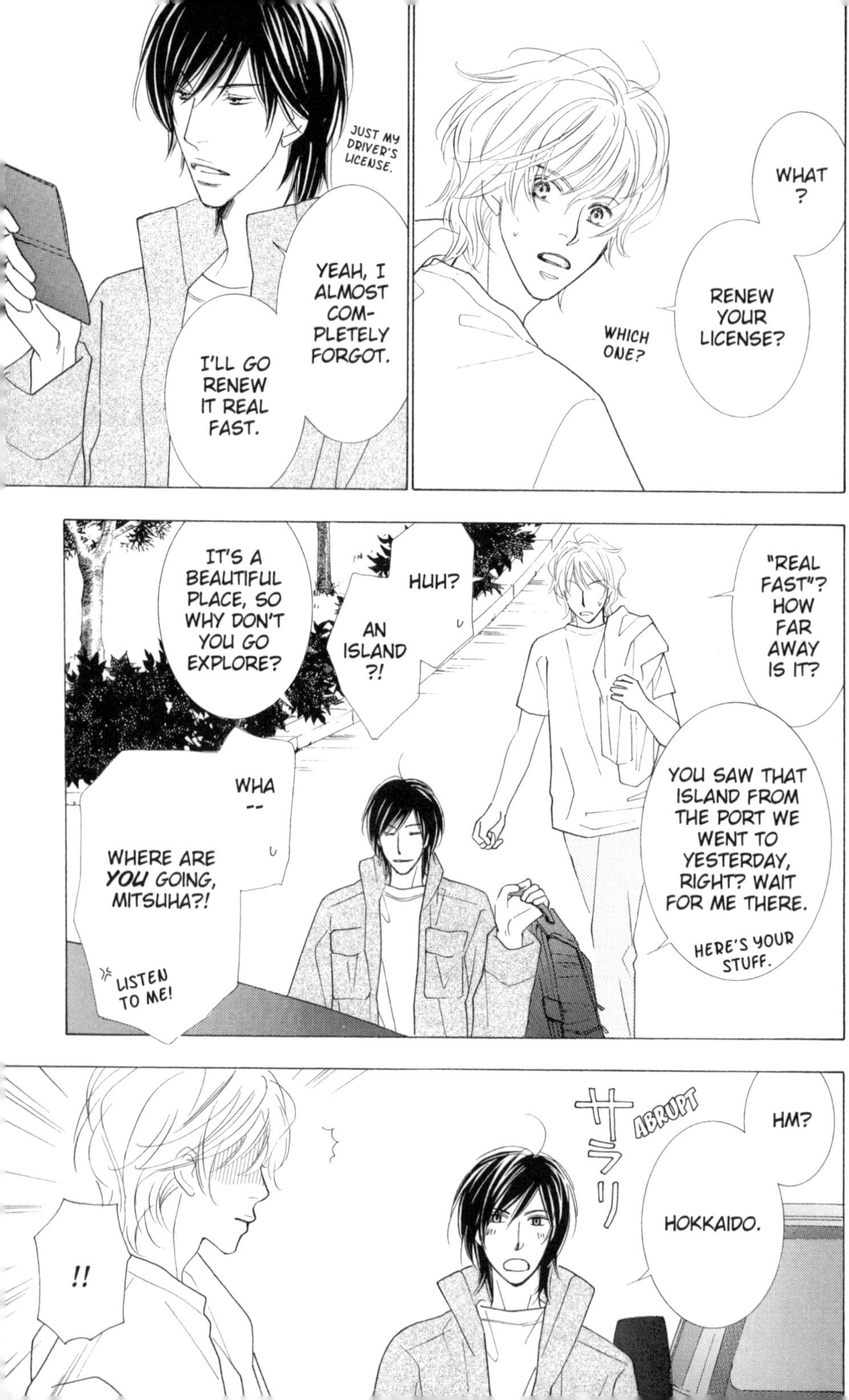
WHAT?
RENEW YOUR LICENSE?
WHICH ONE?
JUST MY DRIVER'S LICENSE.
YEAH, I ALMOST COMPLETELY FORGOT.
I'LL GO RENEW IT REAL FAST.
"REAL FAST"? HOW FAR AWAY IS IT?
YOU SAW THAT ISLAND FROM THE PORT WE WENT TO YESTERDAY, RIGHT? WAIT FOR ME THERE.
HERE'S YOUR STUFF.
HUH?
AN ISLAND?!
IT'S A BEAUTIFUL PLACE, SO WHY DON'T YOU GO EXPLORE?
WHA--
WHERE ARE YOU GOING, MITSUHA?!
LISTEN TO ME!
HM?
HOKKAIDO.
サラリ
ABRUPT
!!

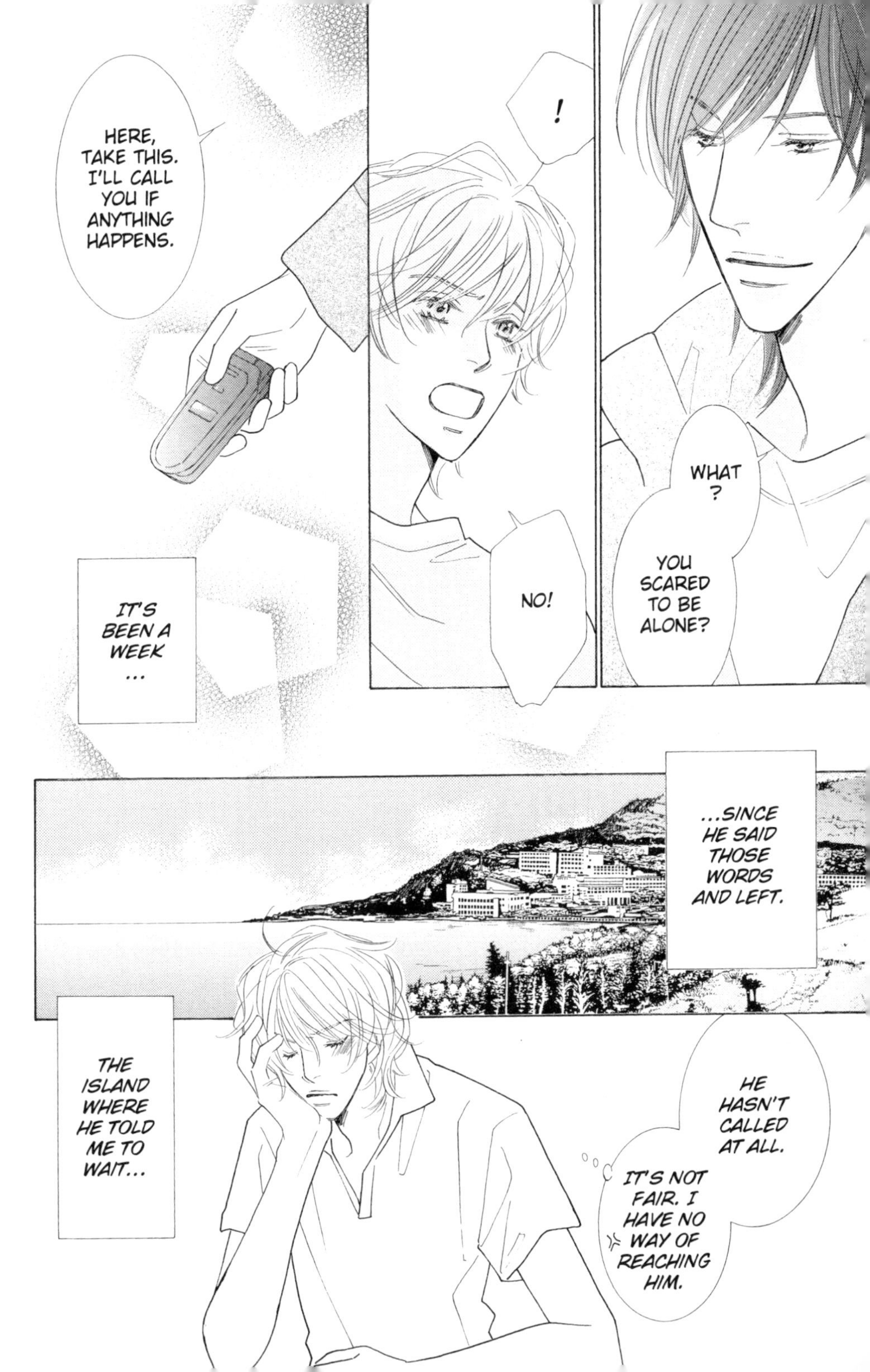
WHAT?
YOU SCARED TO BE ALONE?
!
NO!
HERE, TAKE THIS. I'LL CALL YOU IF ANYTHING HAPPENS.
IT'S BEEN A WEEK...
...SINCE HE SAID THOSE WORDS AND LEFT.
THE ISLAND WHERE HE TOLD ME TO WAIT...
HE HASN'T CALLED AT ALL.
IT'S NOT FAIR. I HAVE NO WAY OF REACHING HIM.

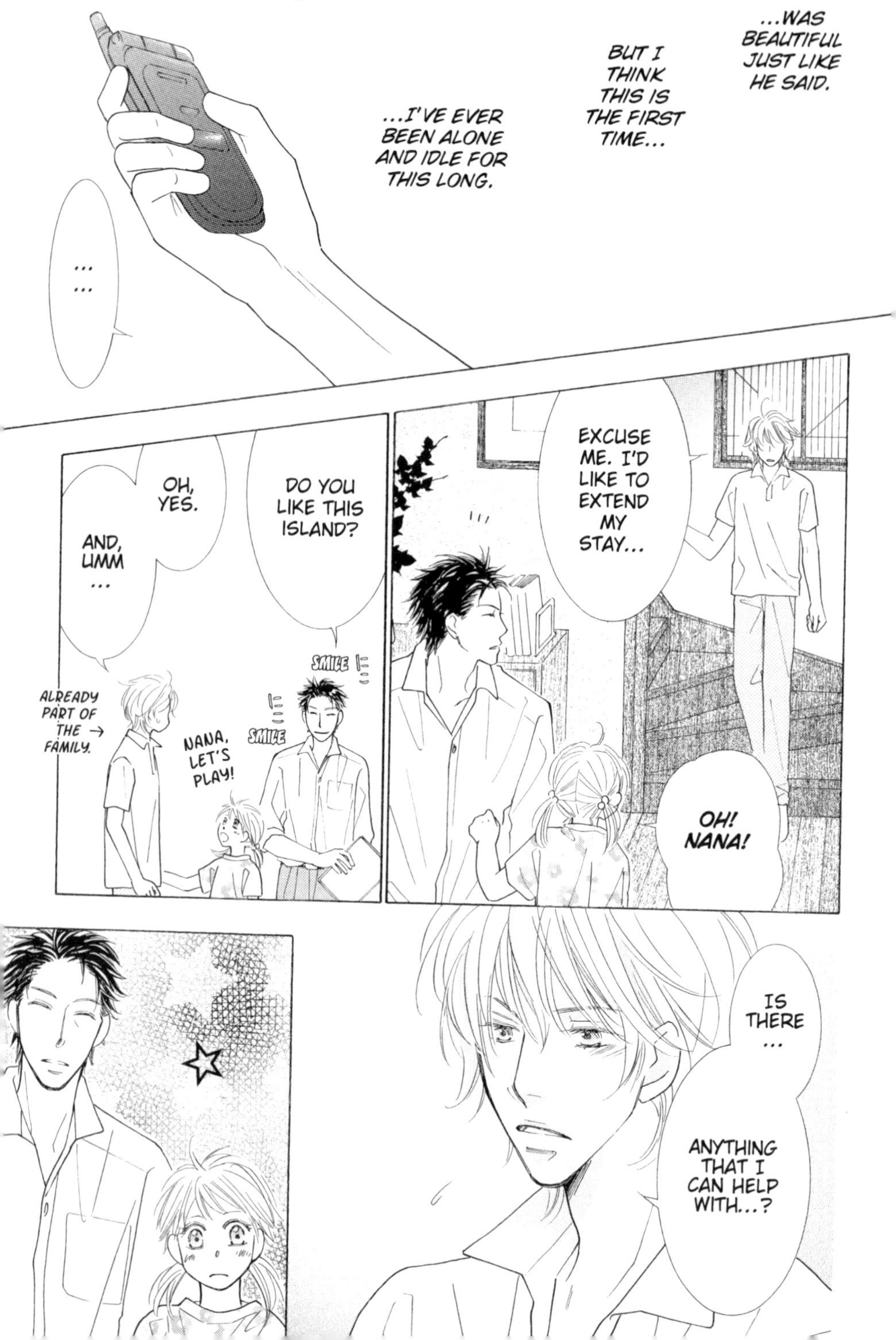
...WAS BEAUTIFUL JUST LIKE HE SAID.
BUT I THINK THIS IS THE FIRST TIME...
...I'VE EVER BEEN ALONE AND IDLE FOR THIS LONG.
......
EXCUSE ME. I'D LIKE TO EXTEND MY STAY...
OH! NANA!
DO YOU LIKE THIS ISLAND?
SMILE
OH, YES.
SMILE
AND, UMM ...
NANA, LET'S PLAY!
ALREADY PART OF THE FAMILY.
IS THERE ...
ANYTHING THAT I CAN HELP WITH...?

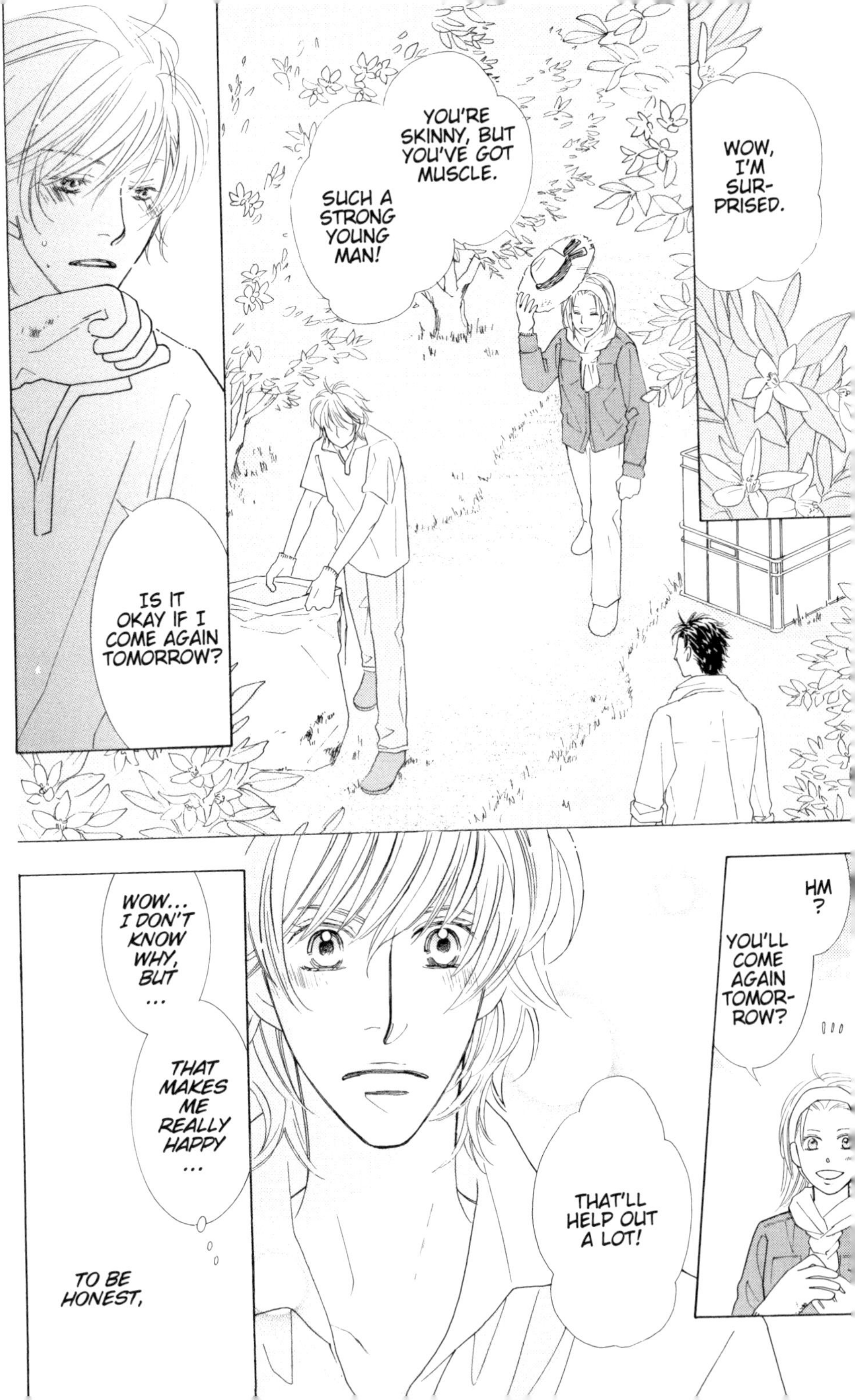
WOW, I'M SUR-PRISED.
YOU'RE SKINNY, BUT YOU'VE GOT MUSCLE.
SUCH A STRONG YOUNG MAN!
IS IT OKAY IF I COME AGAIN TOMORROW?
HM?
YOU'LL COME AGAIN TOMOR-ROW?
THAT'LL HELP OUT A LOT!
WOW... I DON'T KNOW WHY, BUT...
THAT MAKES ME REALLY HAPPY...
TO BE HONEST,

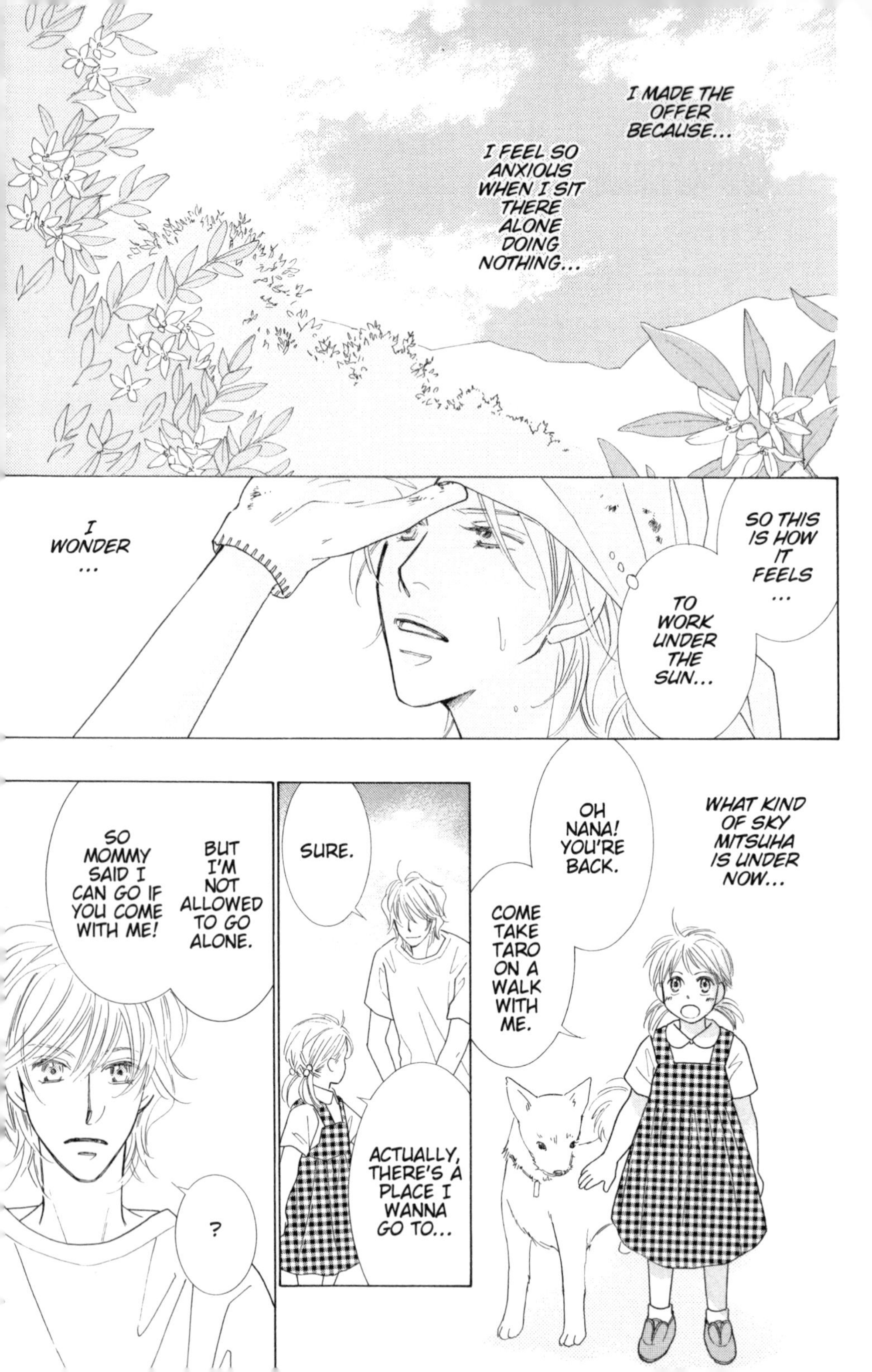
I MADE THE OFFER BECAUSE...
I FEEL SO ANXIOUS WHEN I SIT THERE ALONE DOING NOTHING...
SO THIS IS HOW IT FEELS...
TO WORK UNDER THE SUN...
I WONDER...
WHAT KIND OF SKY MITSUHA IS UNDER NOW...
OH NANA! YOU'RE BACK.
COME TAKE TARO ON A WALK WITH ME.
SURE.
ACTUALLY, THERE'S A PLACE I WANNA GO TO...
BUT I'M NOT ALLOWED TO GO ALONE.
SO MOMMY SAID I CAN GO IF YOU COME WITH ME!
?

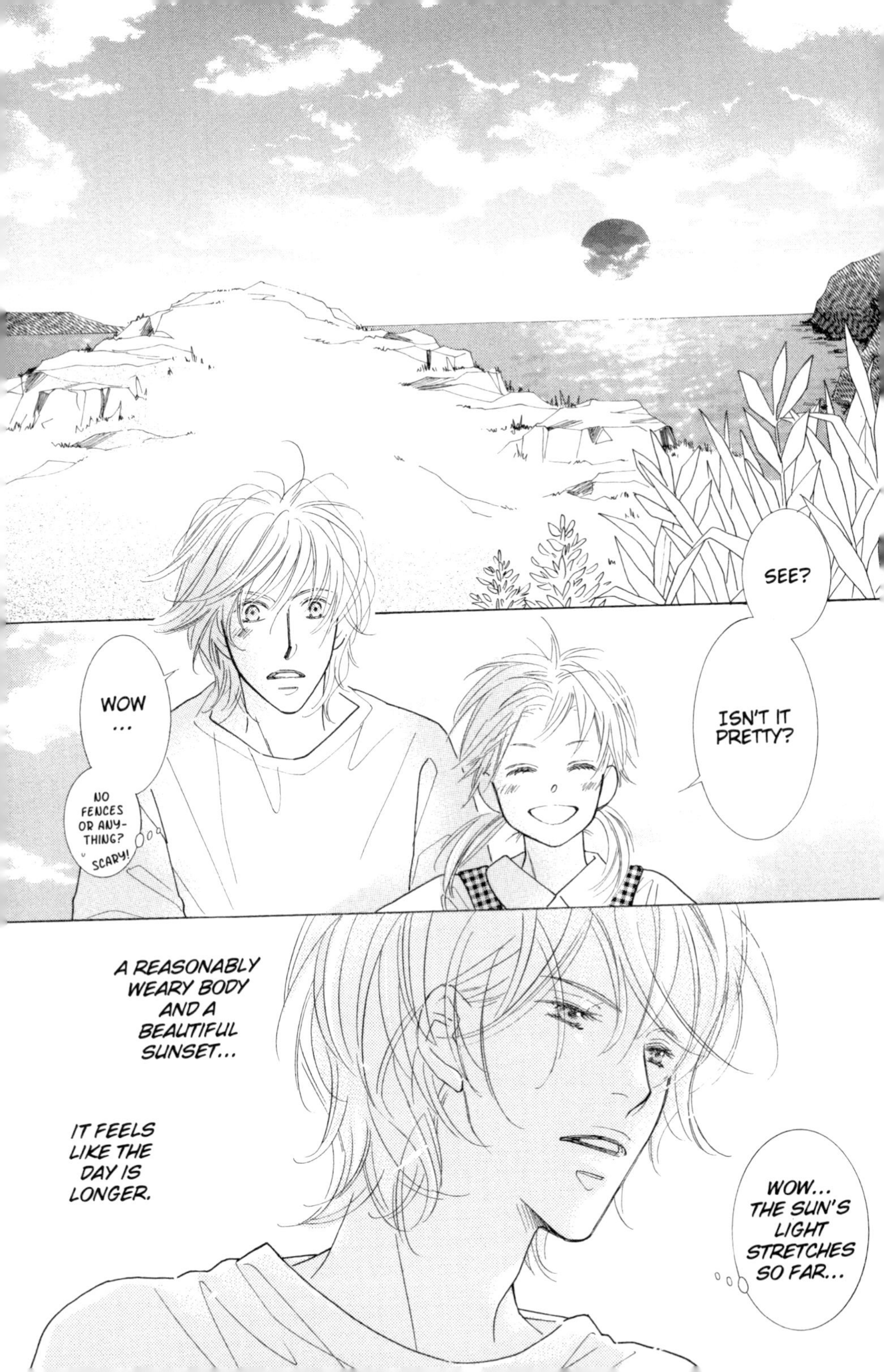
SEE?
ISN'T IT PRETTY?
WOW ...
NO FENCES OR ANY-THING? SCARY!
A REASONABLY WEARY BODY AND A BEAUTIFUL SUNSET...
IT FEELS LIKE THE DAY IS LONGER.
WOW... THE SUN'S LIGHT STRETCHES SO FAR...

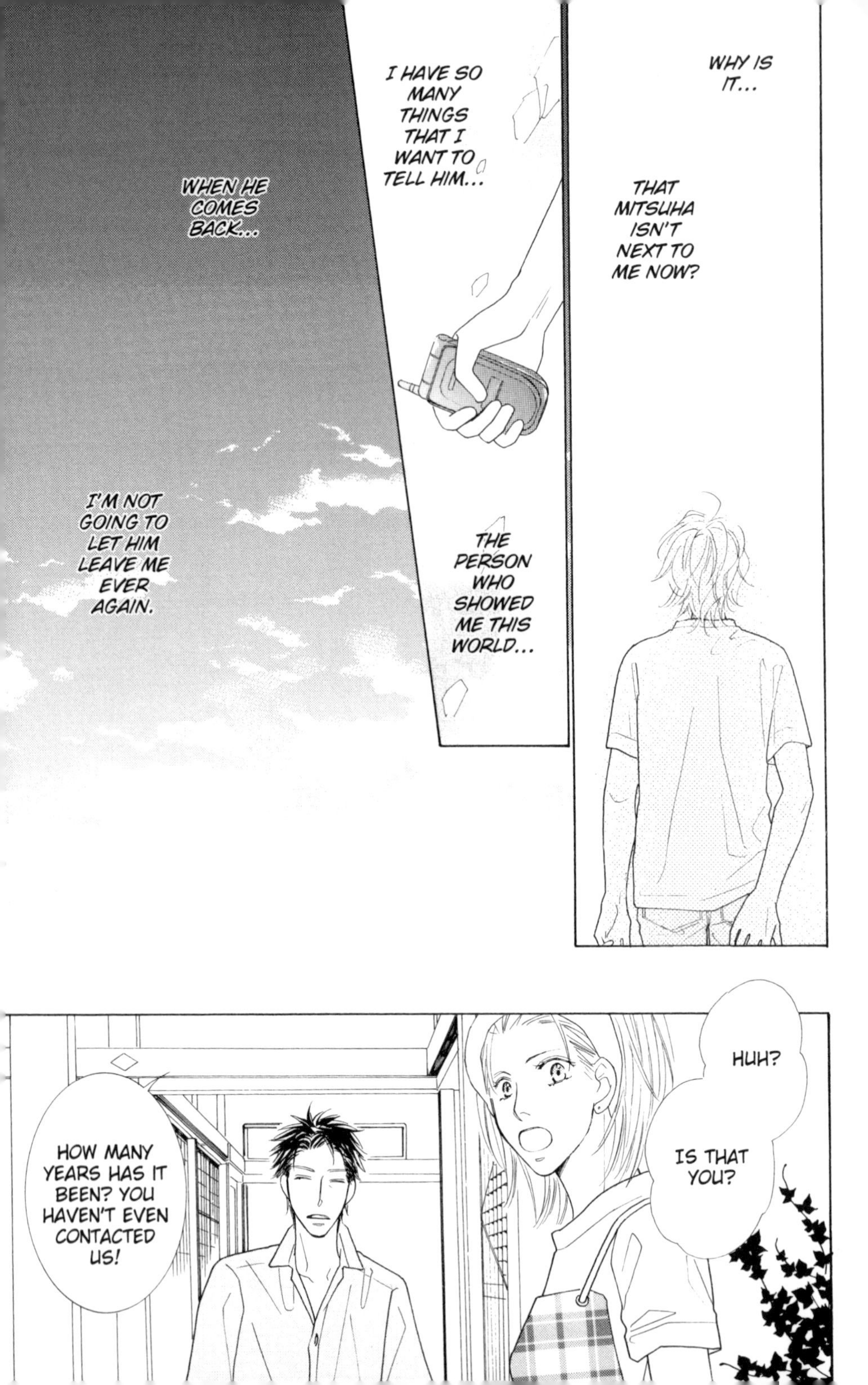
WHY IS IT...
THAT MITSUHA ISN'T NEXT TO ME NOW?
I HAVE SO MANY THINGS THAT I WANT TO TELL HIM...
THE PERSON WHO SHOWED ME THIS WORLD...
WHEN HE COMES BACK...
I'M NOT GOING TO LET HIM LEAVE ME EVER AGAIN.
HUH?
IS THAT YOU?
HOW MANY YEARS HAS IT BEEN? YOU HAVEN'T EVEN CONTACTED US!

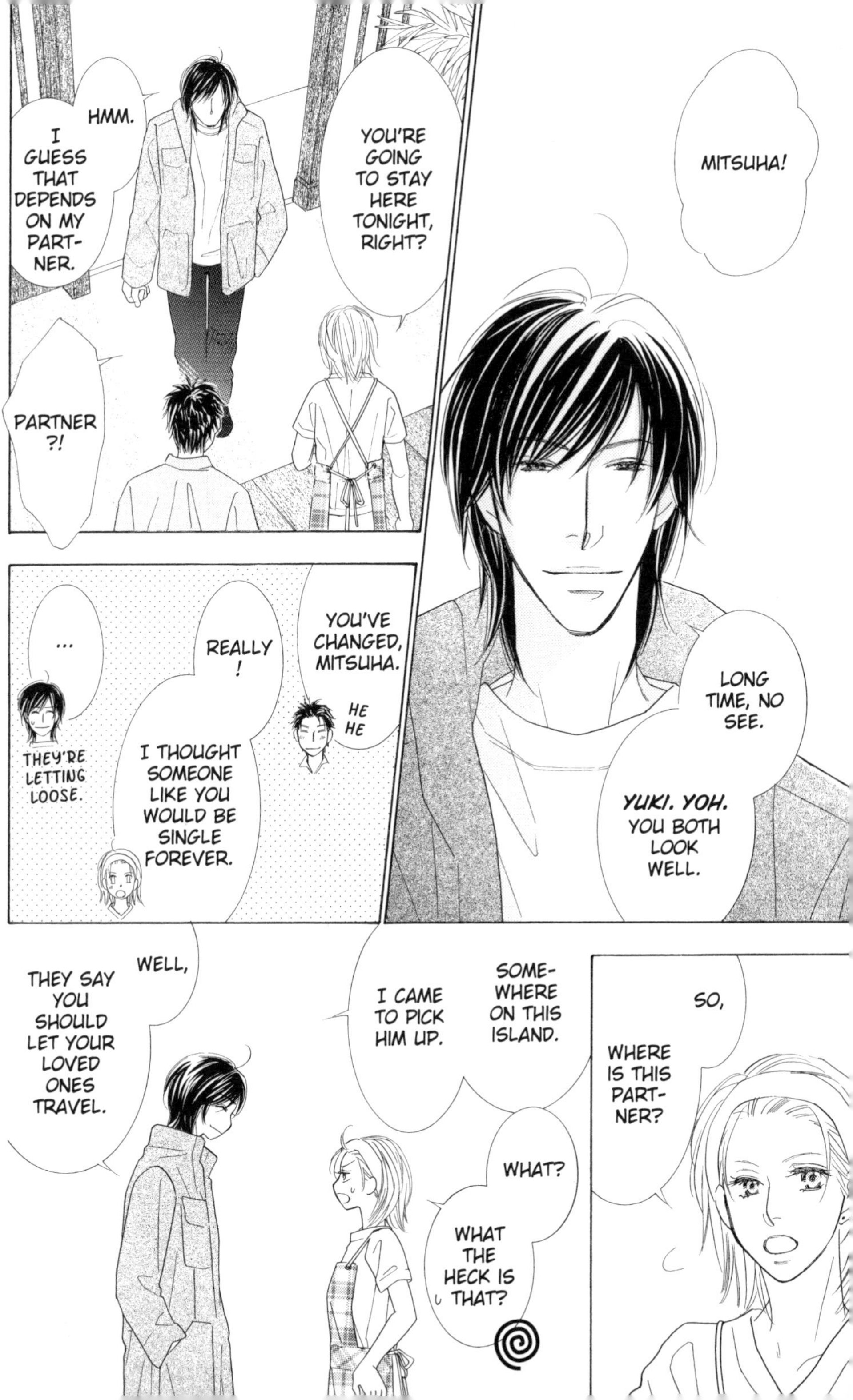
MITSUHA!
LONG TIME, NO SEE.
YUKI. YOH. YOU BOTH LOOK WELL.
YOU'RE GOING TO STAY HERE TONIGHT, RIGHT?
HMM.
I GUESS THAT DEPENDS ON MY PARTNER.
PARTNER ?!
YOU'VE CHANGED, MITSUHA.
HE HE
REALLY!
I THOUGHT SOMEONE LIKE YOU WOULD BE SINGLE FOREVER.
...
THEY'RE LETTING LOOSE.
SO,
WHERE IS THIS PARTNER?
SOMEWHERE ON THIS ISLAND.
I CAME TO PICK HIM UP.
WHAT?
WHAT THE HECK IS THAT?
WELL,
THEY SAY YOU SHOULD LET YOUR LOVED ONES TRAVEL.

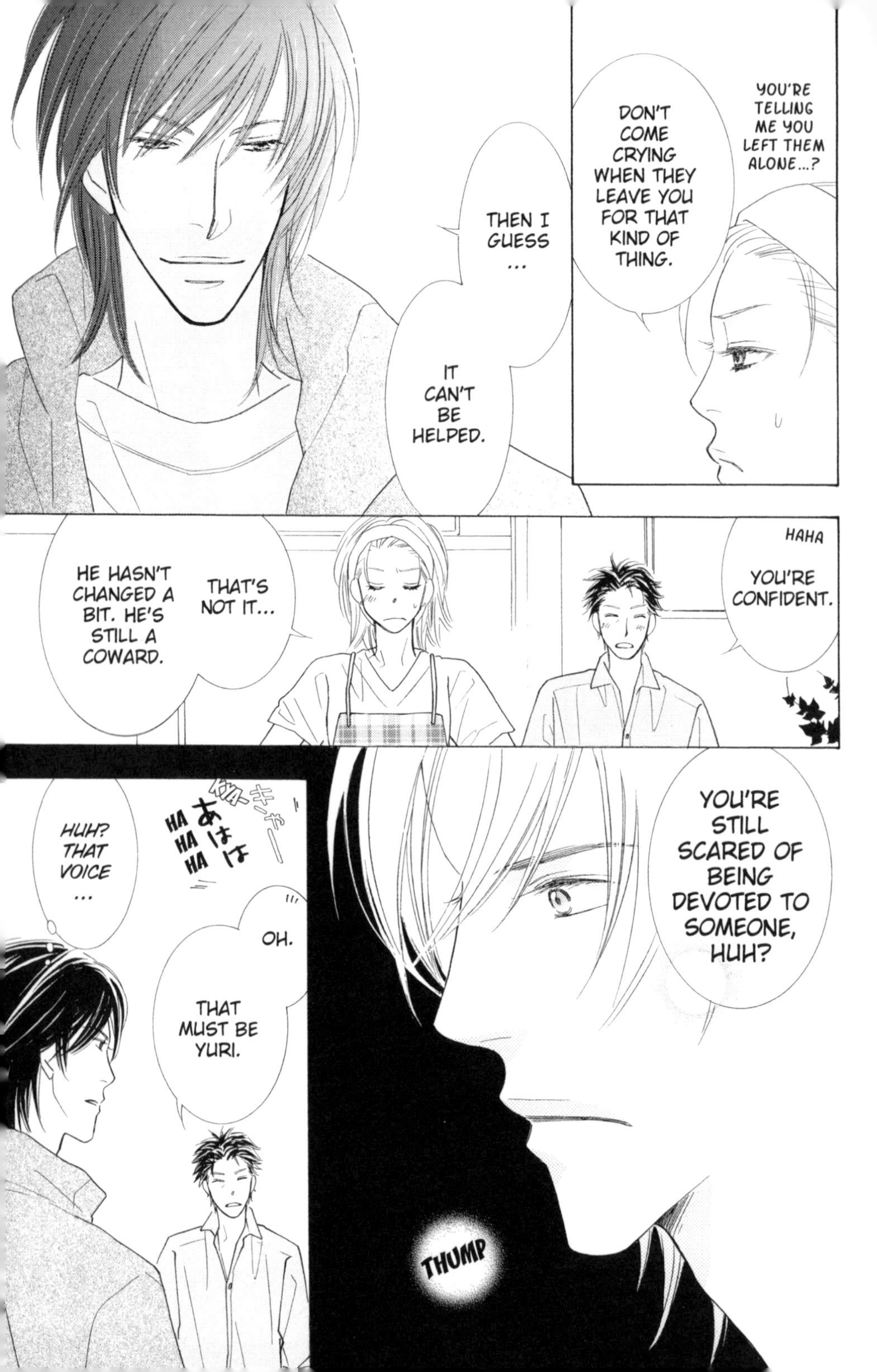
YOU'RE TELLING ME YOU LEFT THEM ALONE...?
DON'T COME CRYING WHEN THEY LEAVE YOU FOR THAT KIND OF THING.
THEN I GUESS ...
IT CAN'T BE HELPED.
HAHA
YOU'RE CONFIDENT.
THAT'S NOT IT...
HE HASN'T CHANGED A BIT. HE'S STILL A COWARD.
YOU'RE STILL SCARED OF BEING DEVOTED TO SOMEONE, HUH?
THUMP
KYA キャー
HA HA HA あはは
HUH? THAT VOICE ...
OH.
THAT MUST BE YURI.

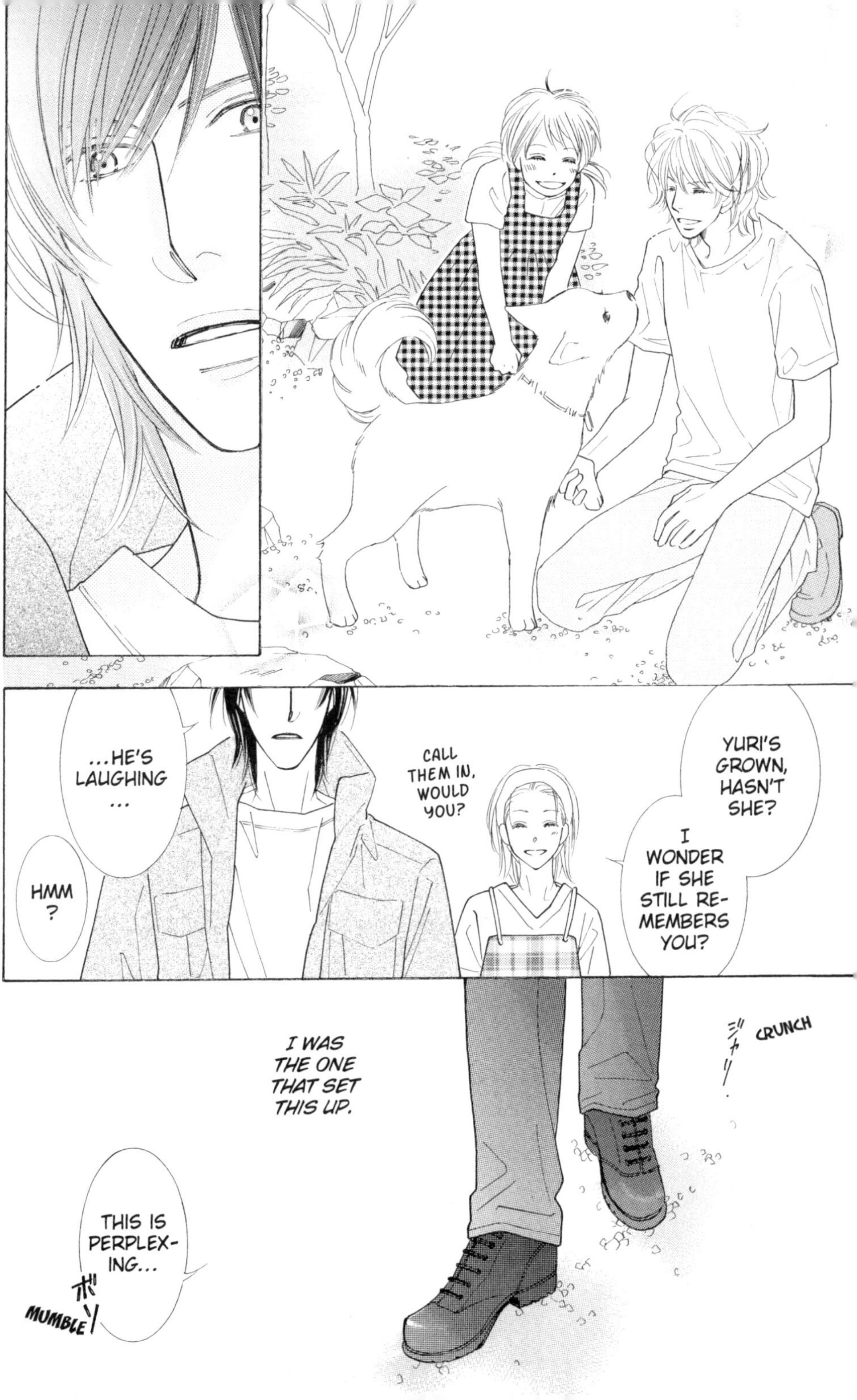
YURI'S GROWN, HASN'T SHE?
I WONDER IF SHE STILL RE-MEMBERS YOU?
CALL THEM IN, WOULD YOU?
...HE'S LAUGHING...
HMM?
ジャリ CRUNCH
I WAS THE ONE THAT SET THIS UP.
THIS IS PERPLEX-ING...
ボソ MUMBLE

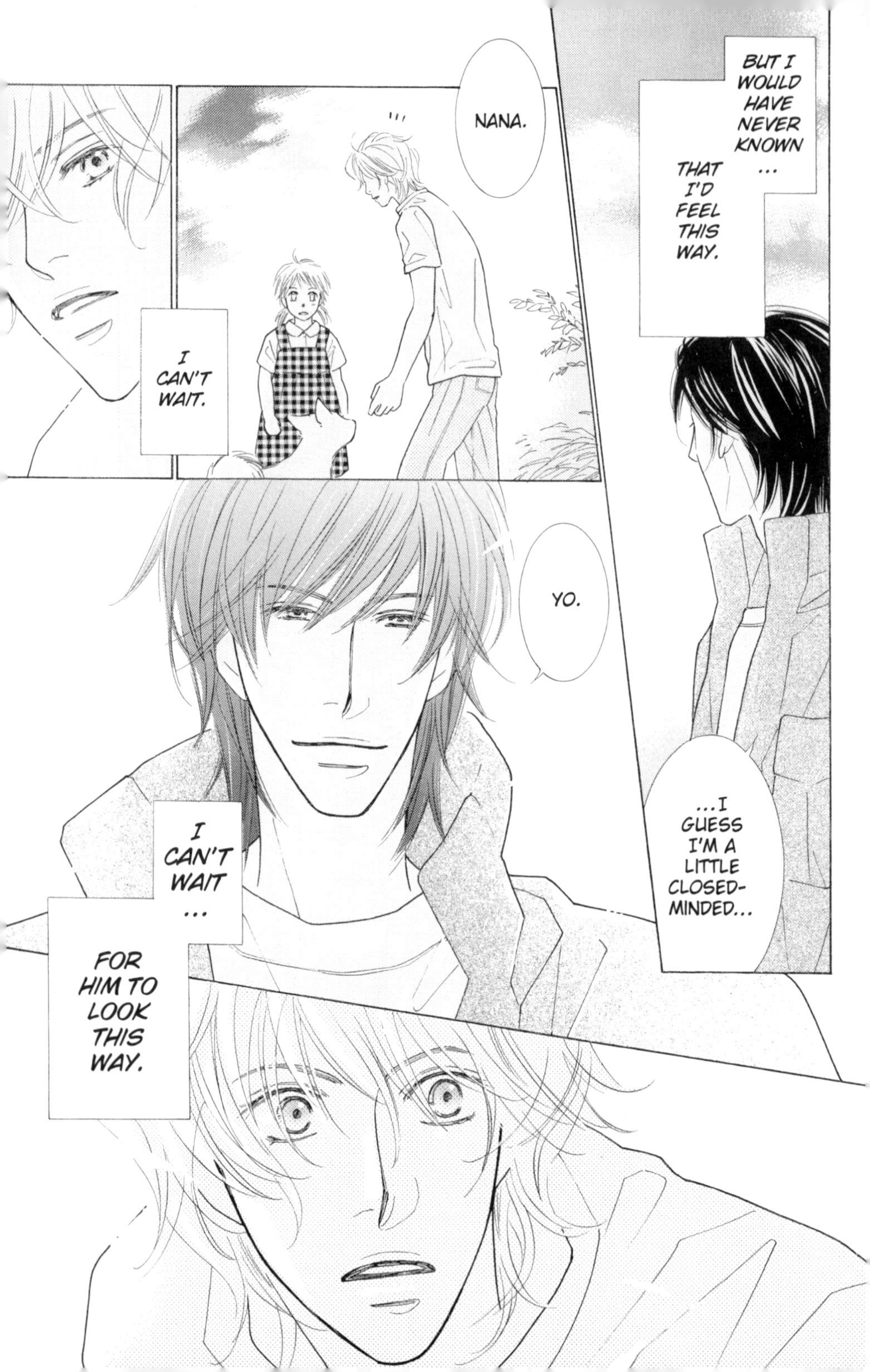
BUT I WOULD HAVE NEVER KNOWN...
THAT I'D FEEL THIS WAY.
...I GUESS I'M A LITTLE CLOSED-MINDED...
NANA.
I CAN'T WAIT.
YO.
I CAN'T WAIT...
FOR HIM TO LOOK THIS WAY.

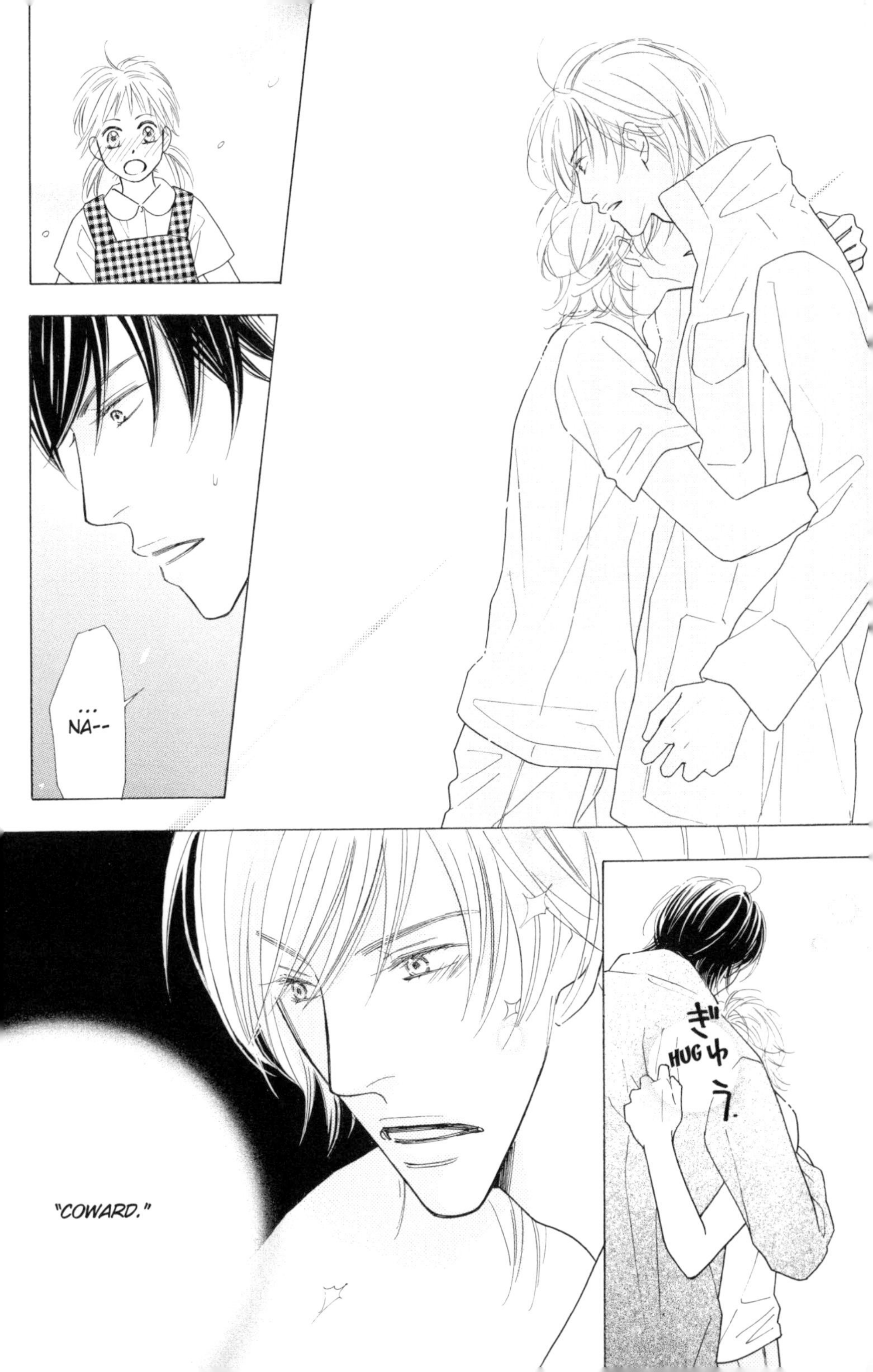
...
NA--
ぎゅう
HUG
"COWARD."

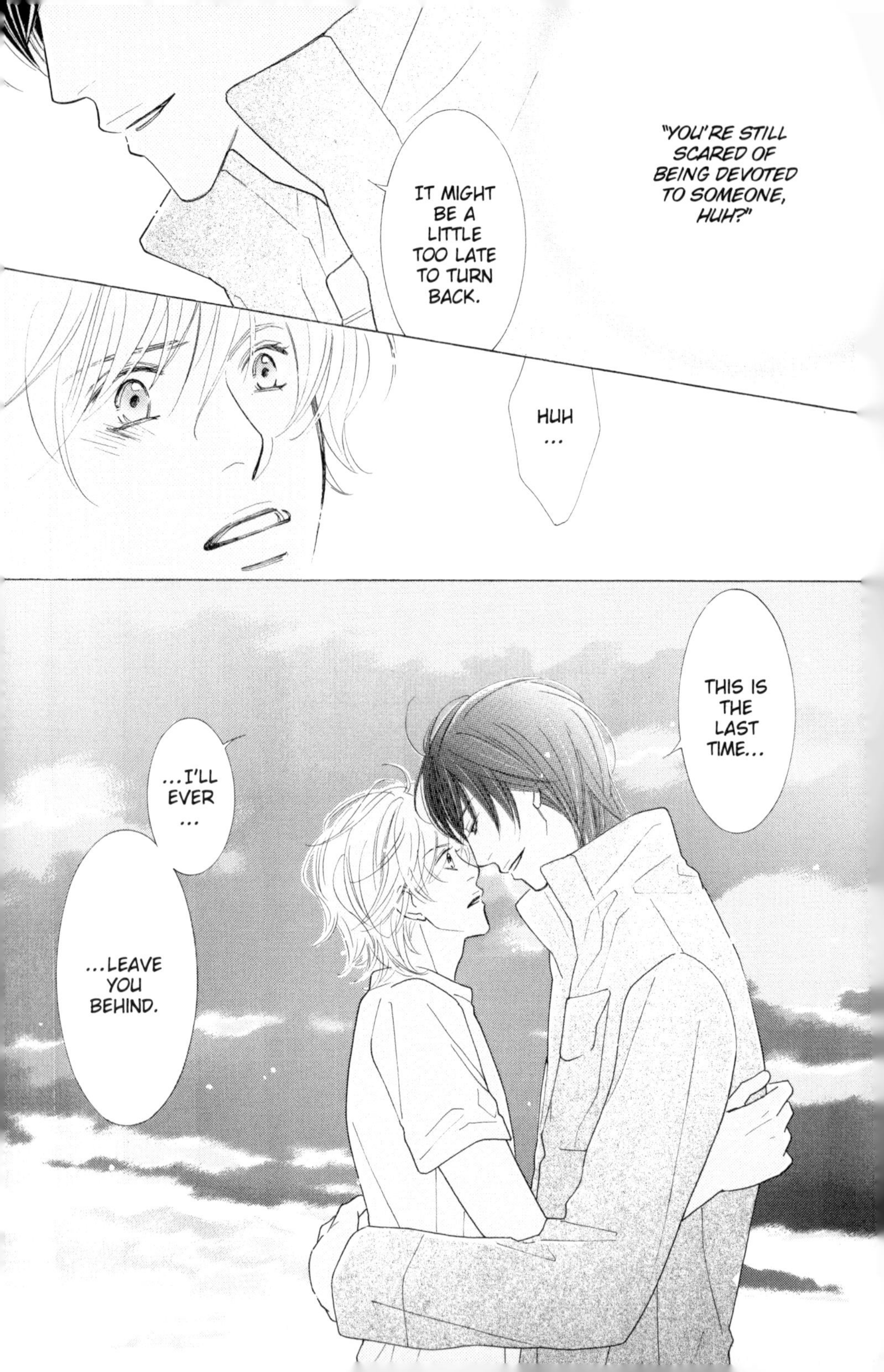
"YOU'RE STILL SCARED OF BEING DEVOTED TO SOMEONE, HUH?"
IT MIGHT BE A LITTLE TOO LATE TO TURN BACK.
HUH ...
THIS IS THE LAST TIME...
...I'LL EVER ...
...LEAVE YOU BEHIND.

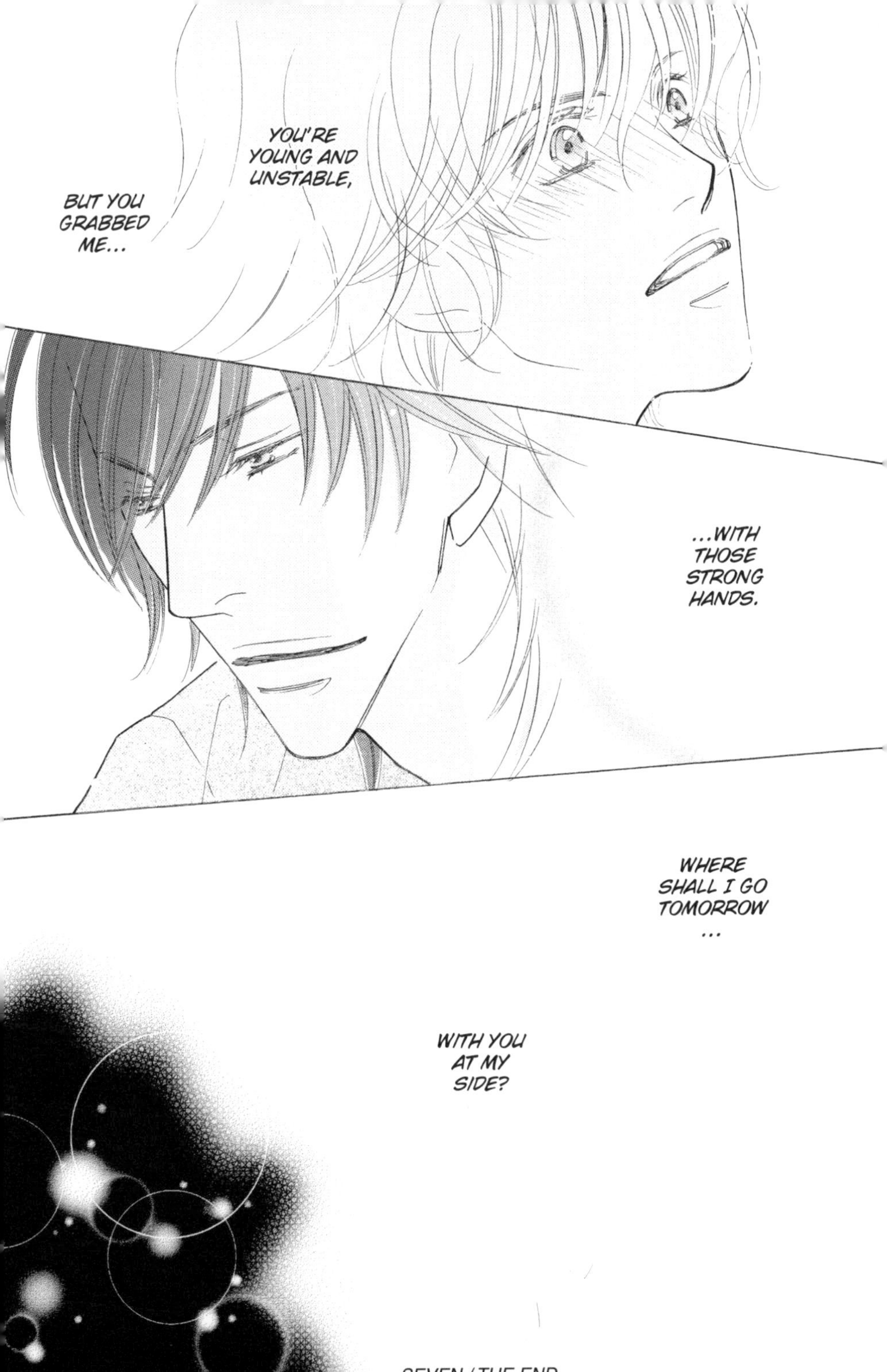
YOU'RE YOUNG AND UNSTABLE,
BUT YOU GRABBED ME...
...WITH THOSE STRONG HANDS.
WHERE SHALL I GO TOMORROW ...
WITH YOU AT MY SIDE?

SEVEN / THE END

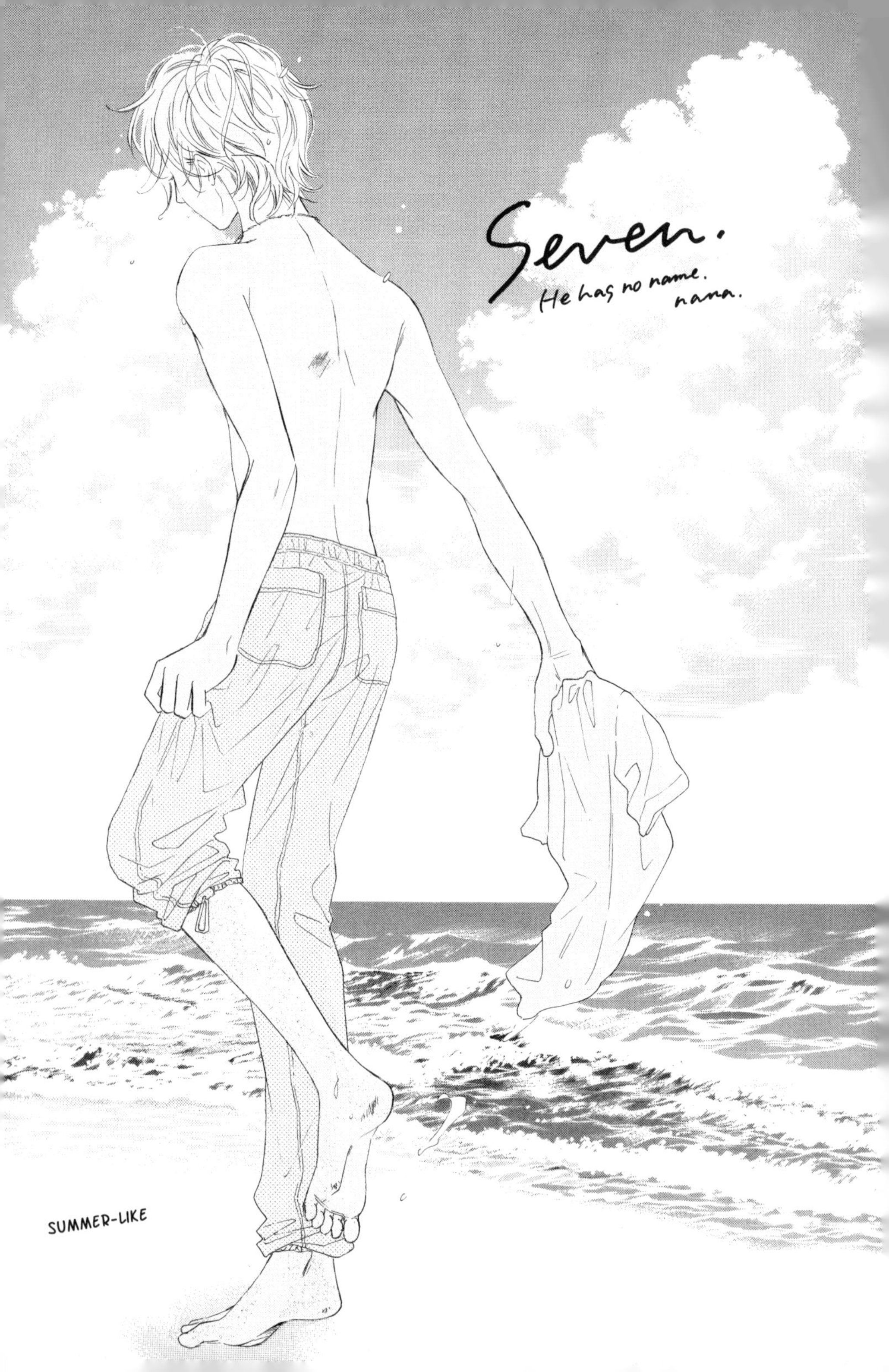
Seven.
He has no name.
nana.
SUMMER-LIKE

AFTERWORD

❀ HELLO, OR NICE TO MEET YOU. I'M MOMOKO TENZEN. THIS IS MY FOURTH BOOK... I'M SO HAPPY. I THANK YOU VERY MUCH FOR READING IT!

❀ A FEW COMMENTS ABOUT THIS WORK.

"SEVEN" NANA AND MITSUHA. THEY WERE BOTH THE TYPE OF CHARACTERS I DON'T USUALLY DRAW, SO... MAYBE BECAUSE OF THAT, THIS WORK WAS A LITTLE TOUGH FOR ME. (NOT THAT I DON'T LIKE IT.) JUST WHEN I THOUGHT "I'M STARTING TO UNDERSTAND THEM!!" THE STORY WAS OVER. *SOB* IT'S A SHAME THAT I CAN'T CONTINUE IT, BUT I NEED TO LEARN HOW TO GIVE UP SOMETIME SOON... I'M SO BAD... OH, EI WAS EASY TO DRAW FOR ME AND I LOVED HIM.

"BENEATH THE WHITE LIGHT" - IT'S A BROTHER STORY... BUT THERE'S A LOT OF THINGS I REGRET. I REGRET THAT I COULDN'T REALLY PORTRAY A LOT (ACTUALLY MOST) OF NANA'S CHARACTER. HIROMU WAS A LITTLE EASIER TO DRAW. THEY HAVE A LOT TO DEAL WITH IN THE FUTURE.

❀ Special Thanks to

♥ MY FAMILY AND FRIENDS AND LOVED ONES. IF IT WEREN'T FOR YOU GUYS, I WOULDN'T BE WHERE I AM TODAY.

♥ MY EDITOR UTSUNOMIYA. I'D LIKE TO THANK YOU OF COURSE, BUT AT THE SAME TIME, I'M SO SORRY FOR SO MANY THINGS. I'LL SHAPE UP. OR AT LEAST I'LL TRY TO.

♥ PRODUCTION STAFF FOR THIS BOOK AND ALL THE PEOPLE INVOLVED IN THE SALE OF THIS BOOK.

♥ TO ALL OF MY READERS.
I WISH YOU MUCH HAPPINESS!

❀ THE MORE I DRAW (I HAVEN'T DRAWN TOO MUCH, BUT), THE MORE I GET LOST ON HOW TO DRAW MANGA. WHY IS IT SO HARD...? WELL IT'S PRETTY OBVIOUS, BUT... I THINK ABOUT THESE OBVIOUS THINGS... GET DIZZY... AND THAT'S HOW I SPEND MY DAY. BUT IT WOULD MAKE ME HAPPY IF YOU WERE ABLE ENJOY THIS BOOK.

`TILL NEXT TIME!

May. 2004
Momoko Tenzen.

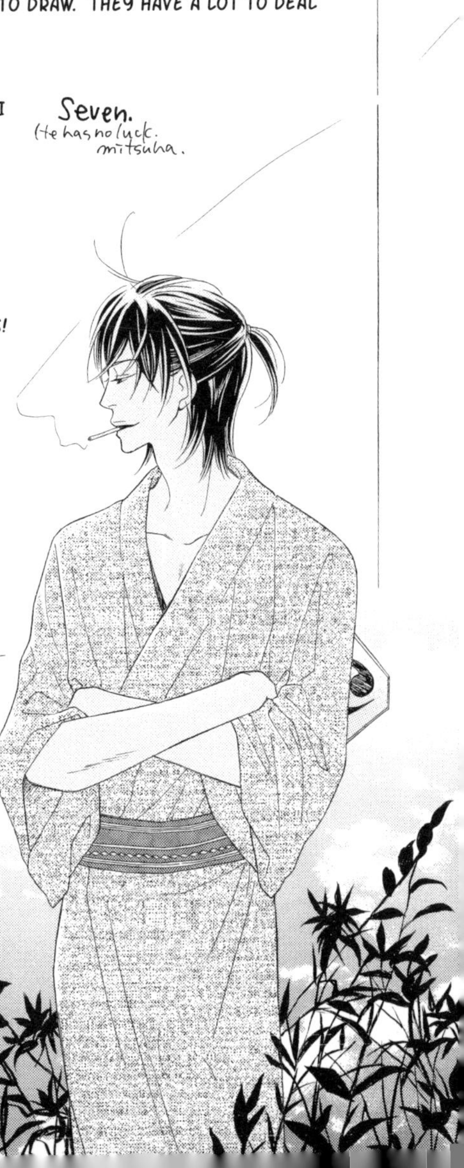
Seven.
He has no luck.
mitsuha.
SUMMER-LIKE...?
(HE'S IN A YUKATA BUT HE LOOKS LIKE HE'S DOING SOME SORT OF COSPLAY...)

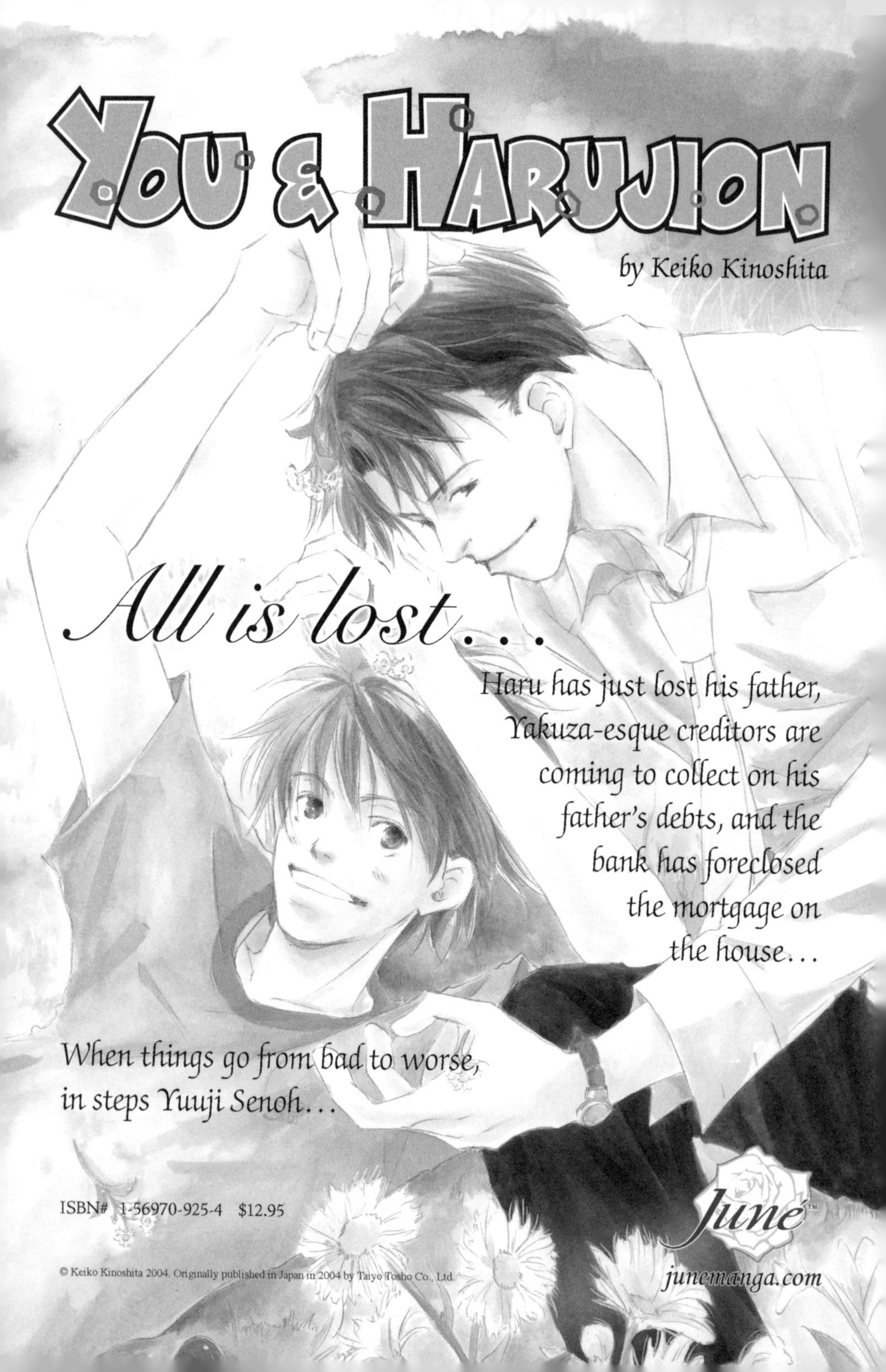

YOU & HARUJION
by Keiko Kinoshita
All is lost . . .
Haru has just lost his father, Yakuza-esque creditors are coming to collect on his father's debts, and the bank has foreclosed the mortgage on the house…
When things go from bad to worse, in steps Yuuji Senoh…
ISBN# 1-56970-925-4 $12.95
© Keiko Kinoshita 2004. Originally published in Japan in 2004 by Taiyo Tosho Co., Ltd.
Juné™
junemanga.com

When the music stops...
love begins.

Il gatto sul G

*Kind-hearted Atsushi finds Riya injured
on his doorstep and offers him a safe haven
from the demons pursuing him.*

By Tooko Miyagi

Vol. 1 ISBN# 1-56970-923-8 $12.95
Vol. 2 ISBN# 1-56970-893-2 $12.95

june™

junemanga.com